No Stress Tech Guide To
Contact And Customer Relationship Management (CRM) Using ACT! 2010

By Indera Murphy

Tolana Publishing
Teaneck, New Jersey

No Stress Tech Guide To Contact And Customer Relationship Management (CRM) Using ACT! 2010

Published By:
Tolana Publishing
PO Box 719
Teaneck, NJ 07666 USA

Find us online at www.tolanapublishing.com
Inquiries may be sent to the publisher: tolanapub@yahoo.com

Our books are available online at www.amazon.com, www.barnesandnoble.com and www.alibris.com.
They can also be ordered from Ingram.

ISBN-13: 978-1-935208-09-9
ISBN-10: 1-935208-09-8

Library of Congress Control Number:

Printed and bound in the United States Of America

Notice of Liability
Every effort has been made to ensure that this book contains accurate and current information.
However, the publisher and author shall not be liable to any person or entity with respect to any
loss or damage caused or alleged to be caused directly or indirectly, as a result of any information
contained herein or by the computer software and hardware products described in it.

Trademarks
All companies and product names are trademarks or registered trademarks of their respective
companies. They are used in this book in an editorial fashion only. No use of any trademark is
intended to convey endorsement or other affiliation with this book.

Cover by Mary Kramer, Milkweed Graphics, www.milkweedgraphics.com

Quantity Discounts

Quantity discounts are available for corporations, non-profit organizations and educational
institutions for educational purposes, fundraising or resale. www.tolana.com/wholesale.html

v1.0b

Who The Book Is For

This book is for everyone that wants to learn ACT! 2010. People that are upgrading from a previous version of the software will have a refresher of the basics and then learn about the features and options that are new in this version of ACT!.

About The No Stress Tech Guide Series

The No Stress Tech Guide To Contact And Customer Relationship Management (CRM) Using ACT! 2010, is part of the growing series of computer software training books that are designed to be used in a classroom setting, an online class or as a self-paced learning tool. The books contain an abundance of screen shots to help reduce the "stress" often associated with learning new software.

Tolana Publishing believes that the following principals are important when it comes to computer software training books:

⇒   The print should be large enough so that the reader does not have to squint.
⇒   The step-by-step instructions should really work and not leave something out.
⇒   Features or options that do not work as intended should be pointed out, not to bash the software company, but so that you do not think that you are crazy <smile>.
⇒   That there should be a realistic mix of theory, real world examples and hands-on exercises. It is important to know the past, because it helps you transition into the future with ease and dignity.

Other Titles In The No Stress Tech Guide Series

	ISBN-13
Microsoft Works 7	978-0-9773912-2-6
Microsoft Works 8 & 8.5	978-0-9773912-1-9
Windows XP	978-0-9773912-0-2
Crystal Reports XI For Beginners (2nd Edition)	978-1-935208-00-6
OpenOffice.org Writer 2	978-0-9773912-4-0
ACT! 2007	978-0-9773912-5-7
Microsoft Works 9	978-0-9773912-7-1
Crystal Reports For Visual Studio 2005	978-0-9773912-6-4
Crystal Reports Basic For Visual Studio 2008	978-0-9773912-8-8
Crystal Reports 2008 For Beginners	978-0-9773912-9-5
What's New In Crystal Reports 2008	978-1-935208-01-3
ACT! 2009	978-1-935208-07-5
Crystal Xcelsius 4.5	978-1-935208-02-0
Xcelsius 2008	978-1-935208-05-1
OpenOffice.org 3 Writer	978-1-935208-09-9

Forthcoming Titles

OpenOffice.org 3 Calc
Crystal Reports For Visual Studio 2010

About The Author

Dr. Indera E. Murphy is an author, educator and IT professional that has over 20 years of experience in the Information Technology field. She has held a variety of positions including technical writer, programmer, consultant, web designer, course developer and project leader. Indera has designed and developed software applications and web sites, as well as, manage technology driven projects in several industries. In addition to being an Executive Director and consultant, Indera is also an online adjunct professor. She teaches courses in a variety of areas including project management, technical writing, information processing, Access, HTML, Windows, Excel, Dreamweaver and critical thinking.

Why A Book On ACT! 2010

After reading the brief Users Guide that comes with ACT!, I felt that users, especially new users, would prefer to have more assistance in learning how to get the most out of ACT!. The Users Guide provides a starting point of reference, but often the Users Guide refers you to the Help system to get more information. As a professor and author, I do not feel that flipping between a book and the Help system is the most ideal way to learn how to use a software package.

I know that many books claim to have "step-by-step instructions". If you have tried to follow books that make this claim and you got lost or could not complete a task as instructed, it may not have been your fault. When I decided to write computer books, I vowed to really have step-by-step instructions that actually included every step. This includes steps like which file to open, which menu option to select, when to save a file and more. In my opinion, it is this level of detail that makes a computer book easy to follow.

CONTENTS

GETTING STARTED WITH ACT! 2010

Overview

The fastest and easiest way to overcome an obstacle is to have someone that has been there, to be by your side every step of the way. That is the goal of this book, to be by your side, while you learn ACT! 2010.

This book is a visual guide that shows you how to create and modify contact, company, group and opportunity records. There are over 800 illustrations in this book that practically eliminate the guess work and let you know that you are doing the steps correctly. Real world examples are provided to help give you an idea of when to use certain features. There is more to ACT! than knowing how to enter contact information. ACT! is robust and has a lot of features.

Learning new tips and shortcuts will allow you to work faster and smarter. The more that you know about ACT!, the easier your day to day contact and customer relationship management experiences will be.

From time to time, I will point out functionality that may not work as expected. When I do this, I am not complaining, merely pointing out things that you should be aware of.

By the time that you complete all of the exercises in this book, you will know more than the basics of ACT!. While you can jump from one section of the book to another, mainly because you paid for the book and can do as you please, I hope that you complete all of the exercises in the order that they are presented, because that will help you gain a better understanding of the features and functionality that ACT! offers. You will also gain more insight into how the features work together.

So sit back and lets get started.

Thank you for purchasing this book!

LESSON 1

What Is ACT! And What Can It Do For Me?

ACT! is a very popular Contact and Customer Relationship Management (CRM) database software package that is used by individuals and companies. In the beginning, ACT! was primarily used by sales people, but over the years the user base and types of companies that use ACT! has expanded. There are more than 2.8 million ACT! users. CRM software provides a way to keep your contacts, which can be business associates, customers, friends, family, vendors, potential customers and any type of contacts that you have, organized. More importantly to many users, ACT! has the ability to create an audit trail or history for each contact. This makes it easier to remember your relationship with each contact.

ACT! is used to store information like addresses, contact type, to-do lists, meeting and sales information, as well as, other information that will help you maintain existing contacts and develop new contacts. ACT! also has built in applications that allow you to do word processing, send faxes, create and send email. One feature that you may find very useful is the variety of ways that you can look up contact information. Additionally, you can put contacts into groups like friends, sales reps and territory. You can also design and run reports. One of the best features of ACT! is that you can customize it to better meet your needs.

There are several editions of ACT!: ACT! 2010, which can support up to 10 simultaneous users per database, ACT! 2010 Premium and ACT! 2010 Corporate edition. The biggest difference between the last two editions is that the latter allows you to access your data online.

The list of features that ACT! has for managing contacts is extensive. There are over 40 fields that can be used to store general contact information like name, company, email and address. Not only can you keep your contact information organized, you can attach documents that you create in other software packages to the contacts and activities in the database. That is just the beginning of what ACT! offers. The list below provides some of the functionality that ACT! has.

- ☑ Over 50 pre-built reports that present the data in an easy to understand format.
- ☑ The ability to customize existing reports and create your own reports.
- ☑ Automate the creation of a series of tasks that you have to complete for contacts on a regular basis.
- ☑ Put a copy of the database on your laptop to work remotely. When you return to the office, you can sync your copy with the live copy of the database that is on a server.
- ☑ Create activities and reminders for tasks that you need to complete, on a contact by contact basis.
- ☑ Use dashboards, graphs and pipelines to help make business decisions.

ACT! is relatively easy to learn. One reason that ACT! is easy to learn is because it has many of the same options that are in other software packages that you may have already used. This includes options on menus and keyboard shortcuts. When you first start using ACT!, you may think that there are not a lot of features, but there are more features then meets the eye. The majority of people that use ACT!, use it to manage contacts, but there is nothing stopping you from using it to keep track of your book, movie or music collection. If you already know that you need a custom contact management database, you may find it helpful to take notes on the features that you will need to create a database that meets your needs.

If you have read any reviews of ACT!, you have probably read that using the software will make you more efficient and will save you time when it comes to managing your contacts. That is true. What the reviews do not point out or make obvious is that to get the most out of ACT! or any software package for that matter, one has to know more than the basics of the software.

What's New In ACT! 2010

What's new in ACT! depends on the version of ACT! that you are upgrading from. The older the version of ACT! that you are upgrading from, the more new features you will notice. The list below contains some of the new or modified features in ACT! 2010.

☑ The workspace has been modified. The new Welcome page provides faster access to features that you may use the most.
☑ Crystal Reports™ can now easily connect to ACT! databases. This allows you to create new reports outside of ACT!. You can also connect ACT! databases to other report writers.
☑ Two new dashboards - Administrative and Contacts have been added and over 10 new dashboard chart components have been added.
☑ The Opportunity (sales tracking) layout has been modified to allow opportunities to function more like contacts, companies and groups. The opportunity screens look more like the Contacts layout. You can add new fields and tabs, set security and manage activities, notes and more, that are related to the opportunity. Over 10 new opportunity reports have been created.
☑ Social media functionality for Facebook™, Google™, LinkedIn™, Yahoo™ and more has been added.
☑ The Administration feature now allows you to create up to 50 remote databases at the same time.

Overall Objectives

This book is written to accommodate classroom and online training, as well as, to be used as a self-paced training course. While there are no prerequisites to successfully complete the exercises in this book, having a general knowledge of any of the following would be helpful.

☑ Prior version of ACT!
☑ Windows environment
☑ Database structures
☑ Report design

Step-by-step instructions are included throughout this book. This book takes a hands-on, performance based approach to teaching you how to use ACT! and provides the skills required to use the software efficiently. After completing this book you will be able to perform the following tasks and more:

☑ Customize ACT!
☑ Create, edit and duplicate contact, company, group and opportunity records
☑ Use the Lookup command
☑ Sort contact records
☑ Link company and contact records

☑ Run and customize reports
☑ Schedule activities and create opportunities
☑ Modify report templates and menus
☑ Import and export data
☑ Perform database maintenance tasks

Lesson 1 Objectives

In this lesson you will learn about the following:

☑ What ACT! can do for you
☑ The Help system
☑ Software support options
☑ Creating and copying databases

Conventions Used In This Book

I designed the following conventions to make it easier for you to follow the instructions in this book.

☑ The Courier font is used to indicate what you should type.
☑ **Drag** means to press and hold down the left mouse button while moving the mouse.
☑ **Click** means to press the left mouse button once, then release it immediately.
☑ **Double-click** means to quickly press the left mouse button twice, then release the mouse button.
☑ **Right-click** means to press the right mouse button once, which will open a shortcut menu.
☑ Click **OK** means to click the OK button on the dialog box.
☑ Press **Enter** means to press the Enter key on your keyboard.
☑ Press **Tab** means to press the Tab key on your keyboard.
☑ Click **Save** means to click the Save button in the software.
☑ Click **Finish** means to click the Finish button on the dialog box.
☑ SMALL CAPS are used to indicate an option to click on or to bring something to your attention.
☑ This icon indicates a tip or additional information about the topic that is being discussed.
☑ This icon indicates a shortcut or another way to complete the task that is being discussed.
☑ This icon indicates a warning, like a feature that has been removed or information that you need to be aware of.
☑ This icon represents a question that I posted in the ACT! forum, but either did not receive an answer to, by the time this book went to print or the answer that I received did not resolve the problem or question that I had.
☑ **NEW** This icon represents a new or modified feature in ACT! 2010.
☑ The blinking cursor is the marker that is in a field or document and appears to the right of where you are typing. This is also known as the INSERTION POINT or KEYBOARD CURSOR. This is different then the pointer that is controlled by the mouse. The MOUSE POINTER usually looks like an I-beam when not in use.

☑ When you see "**YOUR SCREEN SHOULD HAVE THE OPTIONS SHOWN IN FIGURE X-X**", or something similar in the exercises, check to make sure that your screen does look like the figure. If it does, continue with the next set of instructions. If your screen does not look like the figure, redo the steps that you just completed so that your screen does match the figure. Not doing so may cause you problems when trying to complete exercises later in the book.

☑ The section heading **EXERCISE X.Y:** (where X equals the lesson number and Y equals the exercise number) represents exercises that have step-by-step instructions that you should complete. You will also see sections that have step-by-step instructions that are not an exercise. Completing them as you go through the book is optional, but recommended.

☑ [See Lesson 2, Contact Fields] refers to a section in a lesson that you can use as a reference for the topic that is being discussed.

☑ [See Lesson 2, Figure 2-8] refers to an illustration (screen shot) that you can use as a reference for the topic that is being discussed.

☑ "Clear the (name of option)" means to remove the check mark from the option specified in the instruction.

☑ "Save the Contact file as" means to open the Contact file and save it with the new name that is specified in the instruction. Doing this allows you keep the original file unchanged.

☑ "Save the My practice document as" means to open the My practice document and save it with the new file name specified in the instruction. Doing this lets you keep the original document.

☑ I use Winzp to extract files from a zip file. If you do not own this utility, you can use the one that comes with Windows. If you have another software package that extracts files, you can use it to extract the files for this book.

☑ **VIEW** ⇒ **CALENDAR** ⇒ **DAILY**, means to open the **VIEW** menu, select **CALENDAR**, then select **DAILY**, as shown in Figure 1-1.

Figure 1-1 Menu navigation technique

Assumptions

Yes, I know one should never assume anything, but the following assumptions have been made. It is assumed that . . . .

☑ You know that the operating system used to write this book is Vista Home Professional. If you are using a different version of Windows, some of the illustrations may have a slightly different look.

☑ You are familiar with the Windows environment, including Windows Explorer and are comfortable using a mouse.

☑ You understand that this book is based on ACT! 2010.

☑ You know that this button will minimize the open window and place an icon for the open window on the Windows taskbar. When you want to view the window again, click the button on the taskbar and the window will reappear.

☑ You know that this button will open the current window to the full size of your computer screen.

☑ You know that this button will close the window that is open.

☑ You understand that references to folders are folders on your computers hard drive and not a server. If your ACT! database is on a server, that is where the default ACT! folders should be located.

☑ You will have the My_ACTDemo database open at the beginning of each lesson, starting with Lesson 2, unless instructed otherwise. You will create this database later in this lesson.

☑ You have access to the Internet to download any updates that may be available for ACT! and to download the practice files needed to complete some of the exercises in this book.

☑ When you see <smile>, that signifies my attempt of adding humor to the learning process.

☑ Optional: That you have access to a printer, if you want to print any of the reports that you run or create.

☑ Optional: You have Microsoft Word and Excel, version 2003 or higher installed, if you want to complete the exercises that use these packages.

Interactive Message Symbols

Like many other software packages, ACT! will display interactive messages that require a response from you to confirm an action. Table 1-1 explains the three types of interactive message symbols and what they mean.

Symbol	Name	This interactive message type . . . . .
	Information	Provides information about an action that you just performed.
	Warning	Usually requires you to make a decision.
	Critical	Requires you to make a decision before moving on to the next step.

Table 1-1 Interactive message symbols explained

What's Not Covered

Rarely does any one book cover all of the features that a software package has. I cannot speak for every author, but I did not omit features or topics to cheat or mislead you. The size of this book should be proof of that <smile>. It is often a question of time and importance of the topic in relation to what the most used features are of the software. The reason that the following features are not covered in this book is two-fold: They will not prevent you from using over 95% of the features in ACT! and some of the features listed require additional software, hardware or both. Another reason they are not covered is because there are as many different set-ups for the additional software and hardware, as there are people using it.

For example, I may use Brand X PDA and you use Brand Y PDA. What works for me may not work for you. If I wrote instructions that you could not follow, you would think that there is something really wrong with me and even worse, you may think that I did not know what I was doing.

☑ Options only found in the Premium or Corporate editions of ACT!, which aren't many.
☑ Sending broadcast faxes.
☑ Using ACT! with your PDA.
☑ Using ACT! with Microsoft Outlook.

What Is A Database?

A **DATABASE** is a repository used to store a collection of related information. An ACT! database is used to store contacts and all of the information for each contact that you have. It seems to be human nature to want to enter as little data as possible, often to save time. ACT!, is more useful in the long run if it has more data. A database has records and fields.

A **FIELD** holds one piece of information, like the contact name or title.

A **RECORD** is a collection of fields about one entity like a contact, company or group.

NEW Welcome Window

When you first open ACT!, you will see the window shown in Figure 1-2. This window provides quick access to many of the features that you may use the most.

 On my laptop with Vista, I only saw this layout of the Welcome window once. I could view this layout on my XP laptop at any time.

Figure 1-2 Welcome window

Figure 1-3 shows the Welcome window when a database is open. The options in the Related Tasks section are explained below.

Figure 1-3 Welcome window with database open

NEW Welcome Window Related Tasks

WHAT'S NEW IN ACT! Opens the New and Improved Features topic page in the online help file.

ACCESS FEATURES TOURS Opens the Feature Tours topic page in the online help file.

VIEW HELP TOPICS Opens the How Do I Start Using ACT! page in the online help file.

MODIFY PREFERENCES AND SETTINGS Opens the Preferences dialog box.
[See Lesson 2, Preferences Overview]

CHANGE COLOR SCHEME OF ACT! Opens the Colors & Fonts tab on the Preferences dialog box.
[See Lesson 2, Colors & Fonts Tab Preferences]

CHANGE DEFAULT VIEW Opens the Startup tab on the Preferences dialog box.
[See Lesson 2, Startup Tab Preferences]

EXPLORE DEMO DATABASE Opens the demo database that comes with ACT!.

Demo Database

ACT!, like many other software packages, comes with a fully functional demo database that you can use to learn how to use the software. This is the database that you will use to complete the exercises in this book. If you have made changes to the data in the demo database prior to using this book, you should copy the original database to your hard drive (or server if the demo database is on a network). That way, your data and results will match the exercises in this book.

First Time Opening An ACT! Database

1. Click the Explore Demo Database link in the Welcome window Related Tasks list shown above in Figure 1-3.

If this is the first time that you are opening the demo database, it will take a few seconds to open.

Getting Help In ACT!

There are several ways to get help for a problem that you may have when using the software. All of the help options approved by Sage Software (the makers of ACT!) are on the Help menu. The exception is the community forums, which are discussed later in this lesson. The more popular options are discussed below.

NEW The Help System

The Help system in ACT! has been modified. In ACT! 2009 and earlier, the Help system opened in a dialog box. When you open the Help system, it opens in a browser window instead of opening on the right side of the ACT! workspace. To open the Help system, follow the instructions below.

1. Help ⇒ Help Topics. You will see the window shown in Figure 1-4. There are six buttons on the toolbar at the top of the help window, as shown in Figure 1-5. The buttons are explained in Table 1-2.

Figure 1-4 Help window

Figure 1-5 Help system toolbar buttons

Button	Description
1	The **HIDE NAVIGATION** button will display and hide the navigation frame on the left side of the Help window, as shown in Figure 1-6. Compare this to the window shown earlier in Figure 1-4. To close the left side of the window, click this button again.
2	The **BACK** button displays the previous topic that you viewed. This option is only available after you have viewed at least two help topics.
3	The **FORWARD** button works similar to the Back button. The Forward button also displays topics that you have already viewed.
4	The **PRINT TOPIC** button will print the help topic that is currently displayed.
5	The **EXPAND ALL** button displays all of the topic pages in the navigation section of the Help window.
6	The **COLLAPSE ALL** button hides all of the topic pages in the navigation section of the Help window.

Table 1-2 Help System toolbar buttons explained

 To make the left pane of the window wider, place the mouse pointer in the position illustrated above in Figure 1-4, then drag the mouse to the right.

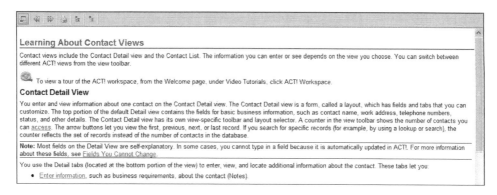

Figure 1-6 Navigation of the help window hidden

If you leave the Help window open while using ACT!, the contents on the right side of the window will automatically change and display an overview page based on the view that is displayed in the ACT! window. For example, if you switch to the Group List view, the Help page for the Group List view will be displayed.

Table Of Contents Tab

2. Click on the **TABLE OF CONTENTS** tab, if it is not already selected, then click on the New and Improved Features topic.

The Table of Contents tab is the online manual. This tab is like a table of contents in a book. Click on the subject that you want to see more topics for, then double-click on a topic to view. The page shown in Figure 1-7 has links to information about the new features in this version of ACT!, as well as, the new features in previous versions.

Figure 1-7 New and Improved Features

Index Tab

You have probably seen this style of help in other software applications. Each of the tabs (Table of Contents, Index and Search) provide help in a slightly different way. Figure 1-8 shows the options on the **INDEX** tab. The Index tab is like the index in a book. It provides a list of most features and options in ACT!.

Figure 1-8 Index tab

Type in the name of the feature that you are looking for at the top of the navigation section or scroll down the list on the Index tab, which is in alphabetical order. You can also enter a keyword and then click on the topic to view more information about it.

Search Tab

3. Click on the **SEARCH** tab.

If you type in a keyword on the Search tab, then click the Search button, shown in Figure 1-9, you will see a list of topics that relate to the keyword that you typed in. Select the topic that is closest to what you are looking for, then double-click on the topic in the list.

The advantage that the Search tab has over the Index tab is that you do not have to know the exact name or phrase of what you are looking for. You should try using both tabs and see which one gives you the best results.

If the Alarms dialog box is getting on your nerves, you can minimize it or click the **CLEAR ALARM** button on the dialog box.

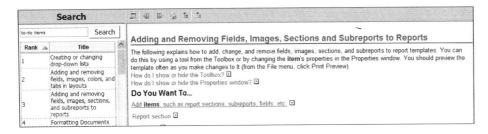

Figure 1-9 Search tab

4. Close the browser window.

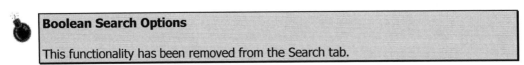

Boolean Search Options

This functionality has been removed from the Search tab.

. . . .

Feature Tours

This option is on the Help menu shown in Figure 1-10. It contains tutorials for some of the popular features in ACT!.

Your computer has to be connected to the Internet to view the tours.

Follow the steps below to run the Activities tour.

1. Help ⇒ Feature Tours ⇒ Activities.

2. The tour will start. When you are finished viewing the tour, close the browser window.

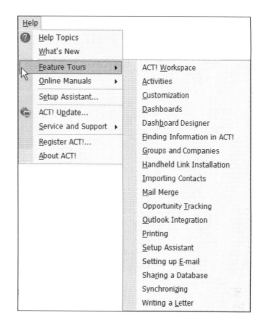

Figure 1-10 Feature Tours menu options

Online Manuals

The manuals that come with the software are installed when ACT! is installed. You can open them from the Help menu shown above in Figure 1-10. To view them, you need to have the free Adobe Acrobat Reader installed. It is probably already installed on your computer. If it is not, the Adobe Reader software can be downloaded from the link below. (You do not have to download and install any of the software that comes with the Adobe Reader, for the reader to work.) You can also use the full version of Adobe Acrobat or another software package that can open and view PDF files.

http://get.adobe.com/reader/

Community Forums

If you have a question about ACT!, you can post a message in the community forum. The link below is for the home page of the forum. If you do not already have an account for the forum, you will be prompted to create one. The account is free. Sage Software does provide staff to answer questions in the forum. The questions are also answered by other ACT! users.

http://community.act.com/sage/

Request A Feature

As you go through this book and think of a feature that you wish ACT! had, or a feature that you think needs to be improved, it is probably a good idea to send the company a message explaining the addition or change that you would like to see in future versions of the software.

They do read the messages, but sadly, it may take a few version releases before a suggestion is implemented, depending on when they receive the request. I have sent them quite a few suggestions after using prior versions of ACT!. They are listed on the "Wish List" page for ACT! on our web site. It is important to note that as far as I can tell, they do not respond to the messages unless they have a question about your suggestion. The link below is where you can submit your request. If the link below does not work, look for the "Request A Feature" link on www.act.com.

http://www.act.com/community/feature/index.cfm

Setup Assistant Wizard

 In ACT! 2008 and earlier, the Setup Assistant Wizard was called the **GETTING STARTED WIZARD**.

The Setup Assistant option on the Help menu shown above in Figure 1-10 can be used to help you with the following:

① Checking to make sure that your e-mail and word processor preferences are set up correctly.
② Creating a database to store your contact information in.
③ Converting an existing database to work with the current version of ACT!.
④ The setup process to integrate your Outlook calendar with the calendar in ACT!.

While the wizard will complete all of the tasks listed above, you can pick and choose the options that you want to set up.

Exercise 1.1: How To Check For Updates

From time to time, it is a good idea to check to see if there are updates for ACT!. Updates provide changes to the software. Sometimes they are improvements to existing functionality and sometimes they are fixes to features that are not working correctly. This type of update is sometimes called a **HOT FIX**.

Your computer needs to be connected to the Internet to check for updates. In a multi-user environment, you probably will not have to check for or install updates because this is usually handled by tech support or a Database Administrator. Before installing any update, you should back up any existing databases that you use.

1. Help ⇒ ACT! Update, as shown above in Figure 1-10, is used to check for updates.

If there are no updates available, you will see the message shown in Figure 1-11 in the lower right corner of your computer screen.

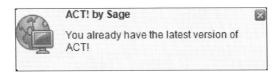

Figure 1-11 Latest version of ACT! installed message

In the lower right corner of your computer screen you may see a message that says to "Click here" for a description and download. If so, click on the option.

You will see a dialog box similar to the one shown in Figure 1-12 if there is an update available.

Figure 1-12 Available Update Details dialog box

If you want to read about the update, click on the link on the dialog box otherwise, click the **DOWNLOAD** button. When this book went to print, there were no updates for ACT! 2010. This screen shot is from a prior version of ACT!.

2. Click Yes when prompted to continue without backing up your data. You can select this option now because you have not created any databases yet.

3. When prompted, close ACT!. The update will be installed and the database will be updated if necessary.

Exercise 1.2: Create A Folder For Your Files

You will create and modify databases in this book. You will also download files and databases. It would be a good idea to store all of the files and databases for this book in the same folder on your hard drive so that you can find them easily. You will create a folder at the root of the C drive. If you want to create the folder in another location or under an existing folder, navigate to that location prior to starting step 2 below. The steps below explain how to obtain and download the practice files that are used in this book.

1. All of the files that are used in this book are in a zip file named act_2010.zip. To have the link for the files sent to you, send an email to act2010@tolanapublishing.com. If you do not receive an email in a few minutes with the subject line ACT! 2010 Files, check the spam folder in your email software.

2. Once you receive the email with the link to the files, open Windows Explorer and click on the Local Disk (C) drive.

3. File ⇒ New ⇒ Folder.

4. Type ACT Book as the folder name, then press Enter. Leave Windows Explorer open.

 Unless stated otherwise, all of the databases and files that you create in this book should be saved in the folder that you just created. I will refer to this folder as "your folder" throughout the book.

5. Go to the web page listed in the email that you received and download the zip file into the folder that you just created.

6. In Windows Explorer, click on the folder that you created.

    You should see the zip file on the right side of the window.

    Right-click on the zip file and select **EXTRACT TO HERE**, as illustrated in Figure 1-13. The files will be copied to your folder.

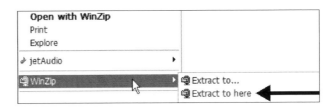

Figure 1-13 How to extract the files

What Is The "My Record"?

The My Record is the contact record that is displayed when you first open a database in ACT!. This record contains information about you and is used when you create documents like letters that require information about you, like your name and address. This saves you a lot of time because you do not have to enter this information for every document that you create.

If the database that you use is also used by other people, your My Record may have already been created for you by the administrator of the database. The first time that you use a database you should make sure that the information on your contact record is accurate and as complete as possible. Having the information filled in on your My Record is really important if you plan to use the templates that come with ACT!. If the information is not filled in on the My Record, a lot of your information that would automatically be filled in, in a mail merge document or template will be missing or inaccurate. Each person that uses the database has a My Record.

The My Record information is also used to track who created a record, who last modified a record and who deleted a record. This is how different users are designated as the owner (which ACT! calls the Record Manager) of a (contact, company, group or opportunity) record in the database. If the database will be used by more than one person, each person should create a My Record, otherwise they will have to log on as someone else. Logging on as someone else is not the best solution, in my opinion, because the other persons name will automatically be filled in when information is added, changed or deleted.

If by chance when the database opens and you do not see your contact record, something may be wrong. The things that come to mind are the following:

① The database could be corrupt.
② You did not log on as yourself.
③ Your contact information has been changed by someone else.

Look at the data on the contact record closely to see if your name has been changed and all of the other information is correct. If you are sure that the record is not yours, you should review the maintenance options covered in Lesson 21, to see if any of them will resolve the issue. If not, call the help desk at your company or post a message in the forum.

Database Naming Conventions

At some point, you may have the need to create a database. Like many other things in life, there are rules that you have to follow. Below are the rules for database names.

① The name cannot be more than 32 characters.
② The name cannot contain spaces or any of the following characters:
~ ! @ # $ % ^ & * ( ) + { } | : " < > ? ` - = [ ] \ ; ' , . /
③ The name can have a combination of letters, numbers and the under score.
The underscore is often used in place of a space in the database name.

Exercise 1.3: Create A New Database

During the process of creating a database you will create a My Record. The person that creates a database is automatically given administrator security rights to the database. In this exercise you will learn how to create a database from scratch, opposed to using the Setup Assistant Wizard to create the database.

1. Open ACT!, if it is not already open, then click the **NEW DATABASE** button or File ⇒ New Database.

2. Type `My_ACT_Database` in the **DATABASE NAME** field on the New Database dialog box.

3. Click the **BROWSE** button, then navigate to your folder.

   Click on the folder illustrated in Figure 1-14.

   (**Hint**: If necessary, click on the plus sign in front of the My Computer option to see the C drive.)

Figure 1-14 Browse For Folder dialog box

4. Click OK. This is the folder that the database will be saved in.

5. If the Currency field is not set to US Dollars, select it from the drop-down list.

6. Check the **SHARE THIS DATABASE WITH OTHER USERS** option.

 Anyone that you plan to share the database with must be using the same version of ACT! that the database was created with. If you (the creator of the database) are using the Standard version of ACT! 2010, other people that want to use your database have to use this version also. For example, they cannot use an older version of ACT! with a database that is in ACT! 2010 format.

7. Type your first and last name in the **USER NAME** field.

   Other then your name, you should have the same options filled in that are shown in Figure 1-15.

   If you wanted the database to be password protected, you would enter the password in the last two fields on the dialog box.

   It is not a requirement for ACT! databases to have a password.

Figure 1-15 Information for a new database

 User names are not case sensitive, but passwords are.

8. Click OK. The database will now be created. When it is finished, there will be one contact record in the database, which is the My Record that is automatically created for the user name on the New Database dialog box, shown above in Figure 1-15. You would add your information to the contact record when you see it on the screen.

9. When you see the message shown in Figure 1-16, click No.

Figure 1-16 Startup view message

Password Protected Databases

If the database is used by more than one person, you will see the dialog box shown in Figure 1-17 when you open the database.

You would have to enter your user name and password exactly as it was entered on the dialog box shown above in Figure 1-15 or how it was set up by the Database Administrator (by default, that is the person that created the database).

Figure 1-17 Log on dialog box

ACT! Folders

When ACT! is installed, several folders are automatically created. When you create a database, you can use these folders to store files in or you can create your own folders.

Viewing A Database

Earlier you created a database. You may find it helpful to view the structure and folders of databases in ACT!, so that you will know where files are located.

1. Open Windows Explorer.

2. Navigate to and click on your folder. You should see the files and folders shown in Figure 1-18. You will also see the files that you downloaded, even though they are not shown in the figure.

Figure 1-18 Contents of the ACT Book folder

3. Close Windows Explorer.

Database Tips
Below are some tips that you should know about ACT! databases.

① The folders shown on the left side of Figure 1-18 above, are automatically created when a new database is created. They are used to store files that are created or used by ACT!.
② When a database is created, approximately 20 MB of hard drive space is allocated for it.
③ The **.ADF** file is the database file.
④ The **.ALF** file is the log file for the database. This file should be backed up. If this file becomes corrupt and you do not have a copy of it, you will need to contact Sage in order to be able to use the database again.
⑤ The **.PAD** file is used to open the database. It is a shortcut that points to the database. If you want to share a database that is on a shared server with other people, give them a copy of this file. .PAD stands for Pointer to ACT! database.
⑥ ACT! databases store three types of files, as discussed in Table 1-3.

File Type	Description
Database	This is the database file that contains the contact records, notes, activities and all of the data that you see when you use ACT!.
Database Supplemental	These files are automatically created when ACT! is installed. Reports and templates are supplemental files. (1)
Personal Supplemental	These are files that you create and save, like letters or spreadsheets. (1)

Table 1-3 ACT! file types

(1) You will learn more about supplemental files in Lesson 10.

Exercise 1.4: How To Copy A Database

The exercises that you will complete in this book will modify the demo database that comes with ACT!. Therefore, it is a good idea to make a copy of the demo database and use the copy to complete the exercises.

1. File ⇒ Open Database. Navigate to the following location on your hard drive:

   Windows XP
   C:\Documents and Settings\YourUserName\My Documents\ACT\ACT For Windows 12\ Databases

   Vista C:\Users\YourUserName\ACT\ACT for Windows 12\Databases

   You should see the ACT2010Demo.PAD file shown above in Figure 1-18.

2. Double-click on the **.PAD** file. If you see a message stating that the database needs to be updated, click Yes to create a back up.

3. Click OK on the Back Up Database dialog box. The update process could take a few minutes.

4. When the database opens, File ⇒ Save Copy As, then type My_ACTDemo in the **DATABASE NAME** field.

5. Click the Browse button, then double-click on your folder.

6. Check the option **SHARE THIS DATABASE WITH OTHER USERS**. You should have the options shown in Figure 1-19.

Figure 1-19 Save Copy As dialog box

7. Click OK. It will take what seems like a long time (a few minutes) to save a copy of the database.

8. Click OK when you see the "Save As was successful" message.

ACT! WORKSPACE

Overview

In this lesson you will learn about the ACT! workspace. You will also learn the following:

☑ Setting default preferences
☑ Changing layouts
☑ The views in ACT!
☑ Detail view tabs

LESSON 2

NEW Workspace Overview

When you open a database you will see the new Welcome startup view unless the **STARTUP VIEW** preference option has been changed. As you will see, the workspace has been modified. The goal of this lesson is to help you learn the new interface.

1. Click the Contacts button on the left. You will see the Contacts Detail view shown in Figure 2-1.

Table 2-1 explains the sections of the workspace. Parts of the workspace will change based on the view that is selected.

Figure 2-1 ACT! workspace

	Name	Description
①	Title bar	Displays the name of the database that is open. The icon in the left corner of this section opens the Control menu shown in Figure 2-2. The options on this menu are used to close, restore, move, size, minimize or maximize the ACT! window.
②	Menu bar	Contains the default menus and commands for the current view. The menu options are explained in Table 2-2. (1)
③	Global toolbar	Contains a button for each of the options that you will probably use the most. The buttons are shortcuts to items on the menu bar. The Global toolbar buttons are explained in Table 2-3.

Table 2-1 Sections of the ACT! workspace explained

	Name	Description
④	Detail or List View toolbar	The options on this toolbar change, depending on the type of records that are displayed.
⑤	Detail	Contains basic information for the contact, company or group. Many of these fields are used in templates and reports, which means that the information should be as accurate as possible.
⑥	Tabs	The fields on each tab contain information about the contact, company or group. The information that you see on the tabs depends on the access rights and security that you have. This means that different people that use the database will see different information. The data on the tabs are related to the contact, company or group record that is displayed in the top half of the window. You can create additional tabs, which you will learn how to do in Lesson 19. (1)
⑦	Navigation Pane	The buttons in this section are used to display a different view, lookup records and access tasks related to the view. (1)
⑧	Layout button	The options on this button are used to customize the Navigation Pane.
⑨	Status bar	This section is primarily used to provide additional information about the contact, company or group record that is currently displayed. On the Opportunity List view, totals are displayed in this section.

Table 2-1 Sections of the ACT! workspace explained (Continued)

(1)   This option can be customized.

Figure 2-2 Control menu

Menu Bar

The options on the menu are the same for each view. The options are explained in Table 2-2.

Menu	Description
File	The options on this menu are used to open, close, save, import, export, backup and print data.
Edit	The options are used to modify data in the view. The options on this menu change, based on the view that is selected.
View	Is used to select a different view, display the mini calendar, select a tab or refresh data.

Table 2-2 Menu bar options explained

Menu	Description
Lookup	Is used to select the field to use to search for records in the database and create queries.
Contacts	The name of this menu option changes based on the view that is selected. It has options for the type of data that is displayed. For example, if the Opportunity view is displayed, this menu option changes to Opportunities.
Schedule	The options are used to create an activity or activity series, as well as, granting calendar access.
Write	The options are used to create emails, letters and other types of documents.
Reports	The options are used to select a report to run.
Tools	This menu contains options for creating new fields, creating and modifying layouts, database maintenance, converting old databases, synchronizing databases, customizing menus and toolbars and selecting preferences.
Help	The options on this menu were explained in Lesson 1. [See Lesson 1, Help System]

Table 2-2 Menu bar options explained (Continued)

NEW Global Toolbar

Figure 2-3 shows the Global toolbar. The buttons are explained in Table 2-3. In ACT! 2009 and earlier, these buttons were on the Detail or List view toolbar.

Figure 2-3 Global toolbar

Button	Description
1	Is used to select the type of new record that you want to create, as shown in Figure 2-4.
2	Schedules a telephone call activity. (2)
3	Schedules a meeting activity. (2)
4	Schedules a To-Do activity. (2)
5	Is used to create a note.
6	Is used to create a history record.
7	Is used to search for records.
8	Is used to look for data in records using a keyword search.
9	Is used to compose and send an email.
10	Opens the ACT! email application.
11	Opens the Help system.

Table 2-3 Global toolbar options explained

(2) This option is for the current record on the detail view. It can be used with multiple records on the list view, if the records are selected or tagged.

Figure 2-4 New button (Global toolbar) options

NEW Navigation Pane

The Navigation Pane has been modified. Table 2-4 explains the buttons on the Navigation Pane. Figures 2-5 to 2-11 show the views.

Button	Description
Welcome	Displays the **WELCOME** view shown in Lesson 1.
Contacts	Displays the **CONTACT DETAIL** view shown earlier in Figure 2-1.
Groups	Displays the **GROUP DETAIL** view shown in Figure 2-5.
Companies	Displays the **COMPANY DETAIL** view shown in Figure 2-6.
Calendar	Displays the **CALENDAR** view shown in Figure 2-7.
Task List	Displays the **TASK LIST** view shown in Figure 2-8.
Opportunities	Displays the **OPPORTUNITY LIST** view shown in Figure 2-9.

Table 2-4 Navigation Pane buttons explained

Button	Description
Reports	Displays the **REPORTS** view shown in Figure 2-10.
Dashboard	Displays the **DASHBOARD** view shown in Figure 2-11.

Table 2-4 Navigation Pane buttons explained (Continued)

Figure 2-5 Group Detail view

Figure 2-6 Company Detail view

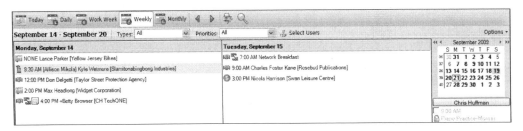

Figure 2-7 Calendar (weekly) view

Figure 2-8 Task List view

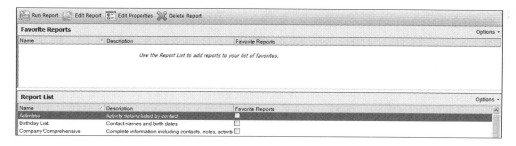

Figure 2-9 Opportunity List view

Figure 2-10 Reports view

Figure 2-11 Dashboard view

Minimize And Restore The Navigation Pane

If you need more space in the workspace, you can minimize the Navigation Pane by clicking on the arrow shown in Figure 2-12. When you click this button, the Navigation Pane is reduced, as shown in Figure 2-13.

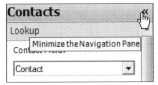

Figure 2-12 Minimize Navigation Pane button

If you click on any of the buttons shown on the left side of Figure 2-13, that view will be displayed. If you click in the Contacts section, the **LOOKUP** and **RELATED TASKS SECTIONS** of the Navigation Pane will be restored, as shown in Figure 2-14.

Click on the arrow button at the top of the Navigation Pane to restore it.

Figure 2-14 Lookup section of the Navigation Pane restored

Figure 2-13 Navigation Pane minimized

NEW Lookup Section

This section of the Navigation Pane is used to find records. This drop-down list field (Contact Field in Figure 2-14 above) contains all of the fields that can be searched. The options in the drop-down list change, depending on the view that is currently displayed.

NEW Related Tasks

The links in this section of the Navigation Pane are shortcuts to tasks that are on menus. The options change depending on the view that is currently displayed. The Related Tasks options are explained at the end of the lesson that the view is covered in.

Resizing The Top And Bottom Sections Of Detail Views

The **DETAIL** views have two sections which are sometimes referred to as primary and secondary sections. These sections can be resized as needed. The primary section is at the top of the view and contains basic information like the name and address for the contact, company or group. The top section of a detail view contains fields that you will probably enter a lot of information in because they are the fields that are used for most contacts when they are added to the database. The secondary section is at the bottom of the window and displays the tabs.

The information on each tab is for the contact, company or group displayed at the top of the window. As you scroll through the records, the data in both sections will change. This is known as **RELATIONAL DATA** because the data on the tabs is related to the contact, company or group displayed at the top of the window. You may need to make the bottom half (the Tabs section) longer or shorter. If this is the case, follow the steps below.

1. Place the mouse pointer on the bar illustrated in Figure 2-15.

Figure 2-15 Mouse pointer in position to resize a section of the detail view

2. Press and hold down the left mouse button, then drag the bar up or down as needed.

Detail View Tabs

As shown earlier in Figure 2-1, there are 14 tabs on the Contact Detail view: Activities, Opportunities, History, Notes, Documents, Groups/Companies, Secondary Contacts, Relationships, Web Info, Personal Info, Contact Access, Latest Activities (only on the 800x600 layout), User Fields and Marketing Results.

The fields on each of these tabs is used to enter more information for each contact. Click on each of these tabs now to become familiar with the types of data that can be entered for a contact. The company and group detail views have some of the same tabs as the contact view, plus tabs that the contact detail view does not have. Table 2-5 illustrates which detail view has which tabs.

Table 2-6 explains the type of information on each tab that comes with ACT!.

Tab	Contacts	Company	Group
Activities	X	X	X
Opportunities	X	X	X
History	X	X	X
Notes	X	X	X
Documents	X	X	X
Groups/Companies	X		
Secondary Contacts	X		
Relationships	X		
Web Info	X	X	
Personal Info	X		
Contact Access	X		
Latest Activities	X		
User Fields	X		
Marketing Results	X		
Billing and Shipping		X	
Company Profile		X	
Company Access		X	
Divisions		X	
Contacts		X	X
Group Address (3)			X
Group Access (4)			X
Subgroups			X

Table 2-5 Detail view tabs

(3)   This tab is named **ADDRESS** on the ACT Demo layout.
(4)   This tab is named **GROUP INFO** on the ACT Demo layout.

Tab	Type Of Information
Activities	Scheduled activities. [Lesson 7] (5)
Billing and Shipping	Billing and shipping addresses for the company. [Lesson 5]
Company Access	Contains information about the person that created and last edited the company record. [Lesson 5]
Company Profile	Tracks the region, industry, revenue, SIC Code and more for each company. [Lesson 5]
Contact Access	Contains information about the person that created and last edited the contact record. [Lesson 3] (6)
Contacts	List of contacts in the company or group. [Lesson 3]
Divisions	Lists the divisions that are associated to the company. [Lesson 5]
Documents	Lists files that have been attached to the record currently displayed. [Lesson 10] (5)
Group Access	Contains information about the person that created and edited the group record. [Lesson 6] (6)

Table 2-6 Information stored on tabs explained

Tab	Type Of Information
Group Address	Address for the group. [Lesson 6]
Groups/Companies	Groups that the contact belongs to. This tab is only available in the Contact Detail view. [Lesson 5]
History	Displays completed and deleted activities, as well as, changes to other types of records. [Lesson 10] (5)
Latest Activities	ACT! automatically tracks the date that the last email, call, meeting and letter sent took place for each contact. The last date that the contact record was edited and by who is also tracked. [Lesson 3]
Marketing Results	Displays the email, survey and drip marketing E-Marketing tools. [Lesson 10]
Notes	Notes that have been created for a contact. [Lesson 10] (6)
Opportunities	Open and closed sales. [Lesson 8] (5)
Personal Info	Home address information and alternate phone numbers for the contact. [Lesson 3]
Relationships	Displays the relationships the Contact has with other contacts in the database. [Lesson 3]
Secondary Contacts	Names of people associated with the contact. [Lesson 10]
Subgroups	Shows a list of the subgroups for the group. [Lesson 6]
User Fields	You can customize all of the fields on this tab, so that you can enter any information that does not fit in any other field in the database. [Lesson 3]
Web Info	Displays social networking web sites for the contact. [Lesson 10]

Table 2-6 Information stored on tabs explained (Continued)

(5) Depending on the view, the data displayed on this tab is for a contact, company, group or activity. In some instances, the data on this tab displays data from multiple detail views.
(6) Stores the Public/Private status of the contact, company or group. **PUBLIC** status means that anyone that opens the database can view the record. This is the default status. **PRIVATE** status means that only the person that created the record can view it.

Preferences Overview

Preferences are used to change ACT! to work the way that you want or need it to. Some of the preferences require administrator rights. As you go through the preferences, try to think about how you will use ACT! in terms of how the preferences can be modified to work best for you. It may be a good idea to write down the options that you want to change and what you want to change them to. That way, after you have completed this book, you can make the changes.

For example, if you plan to keep most of the databases that you use in one folder, you could set that folder as the one that ACT! looks in first. The default folder for databases is the My Documents folder in Windows. I have watched many people lose work that was stored in the My Documents folder because they were not aware of the pitfalls of storing work in a folder that Windows creates. ACT! allows you to change the default location for databases, documents, reports, queries and any other type of file that you can create or use in ACT!.

Exercise 2.1: View And Modify The Preferences

In this exercise you will learn about the preferences in ACT!. You will also modify some of the preferences for the My_ACTDemo database.

1. Open the My_ACTDemo database.

2. When prompted that the database will be verified, click OK. The update process takes a minute or so. When it is complete, click OK.

3. Tools ⇒ Preferences.

General Tab Preferences

The options shown in Figure 2-16 are used to select preferences for the database.

Figure 2-16 General tab preferences

 Administrator or manager rights are needed to change the **DUPLICATE CHECKING** and **ALLOW HISTORY EDITING** options.

The options in the **FILE TYPE** drop-down list shown in Figure 2-17 contain the types of files that you can set a folder location for. This means that you can store the databases in one location (folder) and the documents that you create in a different location. If you want to save different file types in the same folder, you have to select the same folder for each file type.

Figure 2-17 File type options

 The **BACKUP LOCATION** file type shown above in Figure 2-17 is new.

The **FILE TYPE** and **LOCATION** options are something that you will want to change after you complete the exercises in this book because these options should reflect the location of the database that you use the most.

1. Click the **BROWSE** button shown earlier in Figure 2-16, then navigate to and click on your folder.

2. Click OK to close the Browse For Folder dialog box. The **LOCATION** field should have changed to the folder that you selected in step 1.

3. Select your folder as the location for the Documents file type. You should have the options shown in Figure 2-18.

Figure 2-18 Modified Personal Files Locations options

4. Click the **SALUTATION PREFERENCES** button. Select the option, **USE CONTACT'S FIRST NAME**, then click OK.

5. Click the **DUPLICATE CHECKING** button, then open the **RECORD TYPE** drop-down list and select Company.

6. Change the first **THEN ON** field to <None>, as shown in Figure 2-19.

Figure 2-19 Duplicate checking options for company records

7. Click OK, then click the Apply button.

Colors & Fonts Tab Preferences

The options on this tab are used to change the default font, style, text and background colors that are displayed.

The options on the right side of the tab shown in Figure 2-20 are used to customize all of the views (lists), tabs, calendar and compositions (the dialog box that you enter notes on) in the **VIEWS** list.

Click on the object that you want to modify in the Views list, then change the options on the right side of the dialog box as needed.

Figure 2-20 Colors & Fonts tab preferences

 If you want to make the same change to more than one of the options in the Views list, click on the first option that you want to change. Press and hold the CTRL key down, then click on the other options that you want to modify, as shown in Figure 2-21.

Once you have selected all of the views and windows that you want to customize, select the font settings, style, appearance and background color options that you want. There is no global change option available, so this is the work around that I came up with. This will provide a consistent look when you go from one part of ACT! to another. This means that you will not have the top half of the Contact Detail view with a green background and the background color of the tabs on the Contact Detail view purple, unless that is what you want.

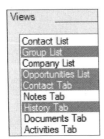

Figure 2-21 Multiple options selected to be customized at the same time

If available and checked, the **SHOW GRID LINES** option on the Colors & Fonts tab will change the layout of data on a tab to look like a spreadsheet, as shown in Figure 2-22.

Date	Time	Regarding			Record Manager	Share With
8/13/2009	3:51 PM	The **TechONE System** is perfect for their organization. • 100% ROI in less than 6 months • Eco Friendly. Would give them an advantage in the efforts to be "green" company wide.			Chris Huffman	Yellow Jersey Bikes [CMP]
5/15/2007	3:59 PM	Met Lance at one of the the Tour de France fund raisi parties held for our country's team.			Chris Huffman	Yellow Jersey Bikes [CMP]

Figure 2-22 Show grid lines option turned on

You may want to change the colors and fonts or add grid lines to the Notes and History tabs because they will contain more data than the other tabs and having color or gridlines may make the entries easier to read.

ⁿᵉʷ Themes

As shown in Figure 2-23, there are two color scheme themes that you can select. The default is Sage Green. Themes are used to make global color changes to the workspace.

Figure 2-23 Theme Color Scheme options

Calendar & Scheduling Tab Preferences

Each of the buttons shown in Figure 2-24 are used to open a dialog box that has options for a specific preference.

The **CALENDAR PREFERENCES** options are used to set the work days and time period increments for the calendars.

The **SCHEDULING PREFERENCES** options are used to set the default values for all of the activity types.

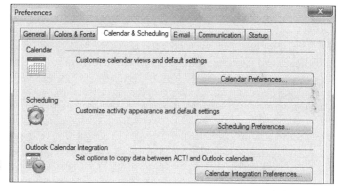

Figure 2-24 Calendar & Scheduling tab preferences

The **CALENDAR INTEGRATION PREFERENCES** options are used to configure how data will be copied between ACT! and Outlook calendars.

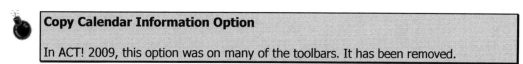

Copy Calendar Information Option

In ACT! 2009, this option was on many of the toolbars. It has been removed.

E-mail Tab Preferences

The options shown in Figure 2-25 are the settings for the e-mail software that you will use with ACT!.

It is not a requirement to configure email software because you can use the Email Editor that comes with ACT!. These settings do not change the options that you currently have set in your e-mail software.

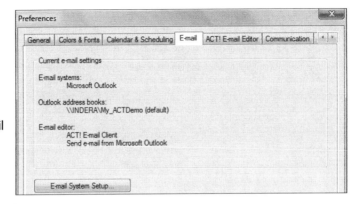

Figure 2-25 E-mail tab preferences

If you do not see any settings on this tab, it means that you have not set up an email package to use with ACT!. The **E-MAIL SYSTEM SETUP** button shown above in Figure 2-25 opens the **E-MAIL SETUP WIZARD,** which is used to configure Internet Mail, Outlook or Outlook Express as the email software that you want ACT! to recognize. The email choices that you see may be different because the choices depend on the email software that ACT! finds and recognizes on your computers hard drive.

ACT! E-mail Editor Tab Preferences

The options shown in Figure 2-26 are used to configure the ACT! Email Editor. You will only see this tab when there is at least one email software package configured.

The options on this tab are used to select the incoming and outgoing e-mail settings.

You can even set an option to notify you when you receive e-mail.

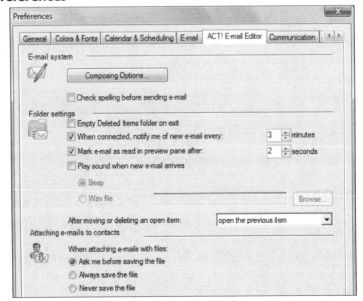

Figure 2-26 ACT! Email Editor tab preferences

If the **CHECK SPELLING BEFORE SENDING E-MAIL** option is selected, emails that you compose will be spell checked automatically before they are sent.

The **COMPOSING OPTIONS** button on the ACT! Email Editor tab opens the dialog box shown in Figure 2-27.

This dialog box contains additional e-mail options that can be selected.

Figure 2-27 Composing Options dialog box

Communication Tab Preferences

The options shown in Figure 2-28 are used to select the default word processor, spell check, fax software and print options that you will use.

The **DIALER PREFERENCES** option requires your computer to be connected to a phone line, similar to using dial-up Internet service. These options allow ACT! to dial phone numbers for you.

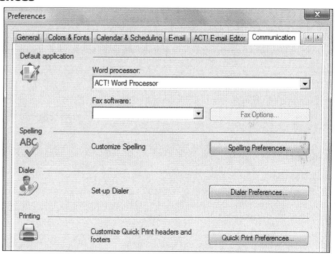

Figure 2-28 Communication tab preferences

The **QUICK PRINT PREFERENCES** button on the Communication tab opens the dialog box shown in Figure 2-29.

These options are used to select the header and footer options for printing the lists that you saw earlier in Figure 2-20.

The **FOOTER OPTIONS** button opens the dialog box shown in Figure 2-30.

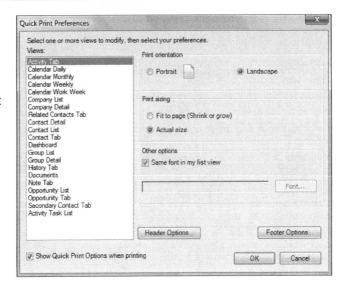

Figure 2-29 Header and Footer print options

Header And Footer Options Buttons

When I click either or these buttons on the dialog box shown above in Figure 2-29, I get the following error message: "Input string was not in a correct format". This error has been reported, but so far it has not been fixed.

Figure 2-30 Footer Options dialog box

1. If the ACT! Word Processor option is not selected, as shown earlier in Figure 2-28, select it now, then click the **SPELLING PREFERENCES** button.

The options in the **UPON SAVING, CHECK SPELLING** section shown in Figure 2-31, are used to select which tabs on the detail views will have spell checking enabled automatically.

If you have a custom dictionary from another application that you want to use in ACT!, you can select it by clicking the Browse button in the **SELECT USER DICTIONARY** section.

Figure 2-31 Spelling Preferences dialog box

User Dictionaries

User dictionaries are used to save words that are not in the main dictionary. This is helpful because once you save a word in this dictionary, it will not be considered a misspelled word in ACT!. If you use Microsoft Office and have created a custom dictionary, you can use it in ACT!.

You can create several user dictionaries. For example, if you are in the legal field you could create a legal dictionary and store the legal words that you need in it. If you need to add or delete words that are in the **USER** dictionary, click the **MODIFY** button shown above in Figure 2-31.

The options on the dialog box shown in Figure 2-32 are used to add and delete the words in the user dictionary.

Figure 2-32 Modify Dictionary File dialog box

2. On the Spelling Preferences dialog box, click on the **ACTIVITIES** option in the list, then press and hold down the Shift key.

   Scroll to the end of the list and click on the last option. All of the options should be highlighted, as shown in Figure 2-33.

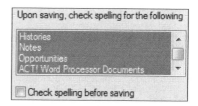

Figure 2-33 ACT! tabs selected

3. Clear the **CHECK SPELLING BEFORE SAVING** option if you do not want to have the spell checker run automatically each time you create an entry on one of the tabs that you just highlighted. You can run the spell checker manually as needed.

4. Click OK, then click the Apply button on the Communication tab.

Startup Tab Preferences

The options shown in Figure 2-34 determine what will happen each time ACT! is opened and what happens when records are added to the database.

If you primarily use the same ACT! database, you can click the **STARTUP DATABASE** button and select the database that you want to have open automatically when ACT! is opened.

Figure 2-34 Startup tab preferences

If you do not want the database to open with the Welcome view, select the view that you want from the **STARTUP VIEW** drop-down list. You can also select the Dashboard option.

If checked, the **AUTOMATICALLY CHECK FOR UPDATES EVERY** option is used to let ACT! know how frequently you want to check for software updates. If your database is on a server, you should not select this option because the administrator needs to update the copy of ACT! and the database that is on the server before the desktop copies of ACT! (the copy that is installed on your computer) are updated.

I disable automatic update options in all software because I prefer to create an image of my hard drive before installing updates, just in case the update doesn't want to play nice with the other software that I have installed, if you know what I mean. The other reason that I disable this option is because ACT! will open faster because it will not have to check for updates before the software opens.

The **CHECK FOR UPDATES** option should be disabled on remote databases because remote databases should only be updated after the main database has been updated. In Lesson 20 you will learn about remote databases.

The **RECORD CREATION** options are covered in detail in Lesson 10.

The **COMPANY PREFERENCES** options are covered in detail in Lesson 5.

Exercise 2.2: Select A Database And View To Automatically Open With ACT!

Earlier you learned that a database could be selected to open automatically when ACT! is opened. You will select the copy of the database that you just created to open automatically when you open ACT!. This will be the database that you use to complete the majority of exercises in this book.

1. Tools ⇒ Preferences ⇒ Startup tab.

2. Click the **STARTUP DATABASE** button.

3. Select the **NAMED DATABASE** option, then click the button at the end of the drop-down list field.

4. Double-click on the My_ACTDemo.pad file in your folder.

    You should have the options selected that are shown in Figure 2-35.

    Click OK.

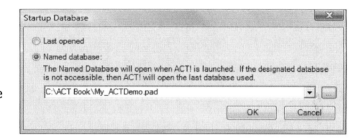

Figure 2-35 Startup Database dialog box options

5. On the Startup tab, open the Startup View drop-down list and select **CONTACTS**.

6. Click Apply, then click OK. The next time that you open ACT!, this is the database that will automatically open.

7. File ⇒ Exit, to close ACT!, then reopen it.

The database may need to be verified. This is only done the first time that a database is opened. Look in the upper left corner of the ACT! workspace. You should see the name of the database in the Title bar.

If you know that you will use more than one database and have set one database as the default (the one that opens automatically), make sure that you have the one that you need open, before you start adding records. Otherwise, you may find that you have entered data in the wrong database. If you find that this is the case, you can use the Import tool that is covered in Lesson 20 to copy the records to the correct database, then delete the records from the database that they were added to by mistake.

Exercise 2.3: Viewing Layouts

ACT! comes with the two basic layout styles that are shown in Figure 2-36 for the Contact, Group, Company and Opportunity Detail views. The demo database has an additional layout (ACT! Demo) as shown.

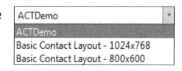

Figure 2-36 Basic layouts

Layouts are the background, fields and tabs on the ACT! window. They can be modified to better meet your needs or you can create your own layout. Fields and tabs can be added, re-arranged or hidden as needed.

The options in this drop-down list contain layouts for the type of view (contact, company, group or opportunity) that is currently displayed. Each layout for each view can contain different fields. For example, the Basic Contact Layout 1024x768 displays more fields than the Basic Contact Layout 800x600.

1. Open the **LAYOUT** drop-down list on the Detail View toolbar and select **BASIC CONTACT LAYOUT - 800x600**, if it is not already selected.

2. File ⇒ Save, to save the changes.

It is possible that a database will require more than one layout. Different people or groups of people that are using the database may need to see different fields or may need to have the fields appear in a different order. Images and text can also be added to a layout. You can switch layouts at any time. You will learn how to modify layouts in Lesson 19.

The Views In ACT!

There are several views in ACT! (Contacts, Groups, Companies, Opportunities, Reports, Calendar, Task List, and Dashboard) that you can view records and reports in.

The icons on the left side of the workspace on the Navigation Pane are used to switch to a different view.

The view can also be changed from the **VIEW** menu, as shown in Figure 2-37.

Figure 2-37 View menu options

 Like other software, the items on a menu like the one shown above in Figure 2-37 that have an icon in the left column means that the option is on at least one toolbar in the software.

CREATING AND EDITING CONTACT RECORDS

Overview

In this lesson you will learn about contact records, including the following:

- ☑ Adding and deleting contact records
- ☑ Enter information on the Notes, Documents and Personal Info tabs
- ☑ Editing contact information
- ☑ Using the Date field calendar
- ☑ Attaching files on the Documents tab
- ☑ Creating relationships
- ☑ Duplicating contact information
- ☑ Using the Undo command

LESSON 3

What Is A Contact?

A contact in ACT! is any person or group of people that you need to have up to date information on, at your finger tips. When many people hear the word CONTACT, they immediately think of a business associate contact. It is true that many people use ACT! strictly for managing business contacts, but you can have friends, family members, prospects and vendors, as well as, business contacts in the same database. As you will see, ACT! handles much more than names and addresses.

If you are brand new to ACT!, this lesson and the next one are probably the most important ones for you to fully understand because creating, editing and looking up contacts are the tasks that you will spend most of your time doing. The key thing to remember when entering data is to be consistent. This will make finding contacts in the database easier.

Contact Detail View Toolbar

Figure 3-1 show the Contact Detail view toolbar. Table 3-1 explains the buttons on the toolbar. The buttons provide quick access to some of the most used options for contacts. Each view (contact, company, group etc) has its own toolbar. For example, the Contact List and Contact Detail views have a similar toolbar. You will see that not all buttons are enabled for both views.

Figure 3-1 Contact Detail view toolbar

Button	Description
1	Displays the Contact Detail view.
2	Displays the Contact List view.
3	Displays the first record. (1)
4	Displays the previous record. (1)
5	The **RECORD COUNTER** displays the record number (By default, contacts are displayed in alphabetical order) of the contact that is currently displayed and how many records there are in total. **41 OF 199** means that you are currently viewing record 41 and that there are 199 records. (1)
6	Displays the next record. (1)
7	Displays the last record. (1)
8	Saves the record. (2)
9	Opens the Quick Print Options dialog box.
10	Duplicates the current contact record.
11	Opens the word processor.
12	Call the contact on the phone through the Dialer application.
13	Is used to attach a file to the contact record.

Table 3-1 Contact Detail view toolbar buttons explained

Button	Description
14	Opens Internet Explorer to Google Maps web site and displays a map based on the address of the contact record that is currently displayed.
15	Is used to select a layout for the view. (2)
16	Displays the ACT! E-marketing options, which requires a paid subscription.

Table 3-1 Contact toolbar buttons explained (Continued)

(1)   This option is either for the entire database or current lookup, which is a subset of records in the database. You will learn about lookups in Lesson 4.
(2)   This option is only available from the Contact Detail view.

Contact List View Toolbar

In addition to the buttons shown above in Figure 3-1, the buttons shown in Figure 3-2 are only available on the Contact List view. Table 3-2 explains the buttons on the toolbar.

Figure 3-2 Contact List view toolbar buttons

Button	Description
1	Is used to customize the columns in the view.
2	Exports the data to an excel spreadsheet.

Table 3-2 Contact List view toolbar buttons explained

 List View Buttons

The buttons shown above in Figure 3-2 are also available on the Company, Group and Opportunity List views.

 If you cannot remember the name of a button on the toolbar, hold the mouse pointer over the button. You will see the name of the button, as illustrated in Figure 3-3. This is known as a **TOOL TIP**.

Figure 3-3 Tool tip illustrated

Difference Between The Enter And Tab Keys

You can use both of these keys to move from field to field when adding or editing data. The **TAB** key is used to move from field to field on the layout. The Tab key stops at every field by default.

The **ENTER** key is used to move from field to field also. The difference is that the Enter key does not stop at every field. It stops at the most used fields. The order that these keys move in can be changed.

 In Lesson 1 you made a copy of the demo database to use with this book. A copy of the database does not make your My Record the default My Record. This means that when you open the My_ACTDemo database, the default My Record will be the creator of the original database, which is Chris Huffman. Do not change the owner to yourself. The exercises in this book are based on Chris Huffman being the default My Record owner.

Exercise 3.1: Creating A New Contact Record

You do not have to enter information in all of the fields, but you should enter enough information to make the contact record meaningful. You will learn how to enter data on several of the tabs on the Contact Detail view in this exercise.

The **ACTIVITIES TAB** is covered in Lesson 7. The **OPPORTUNITIES TAB** is covered in Lesson 8.

1. Click the **NEW** button on the Global toolbar. You will see a blank record. Notice that the record counter has been incremented by one. There should now be 200 records in the database.

 You can also press the **INSERT** key to add a new contact or select Contacts ⇒ New Contact.

2. Type Sarah Baker in the Contact field, then press Enter.

Notice that the contacts first name has automatically been filled in the Salutation field. That is because you selected the option on the Preferences dialog box, to automatically fill in the salutation field with the contacts first name.

3. Type Capri Book Company in the Company field.

    The button at the end of the Contact field on the Contact Detail view opens the dialog box shown in Figure 3-4.

    This button is called an **ELLIPSIS** button in ACT!. In other software, this is called the Browse button, which provides the same functionality.

Figure 3-4 Contact Name dialog box

By default, ACT! automatically splits a contact name into three fields. Initially, the options on this dialog box display what ACT! thinks the first, middle and last name are, based on the preferences selected on the Contact Name dialog box.

If a name has not been separated correctly, open the drop-down list for the name that is not correct and select the correct one. This may happen when someone's first or last name is two names like Johnnie Mae Westbrook. In this example, the contacts first name is Johnnie Mae. By default, ACT! will interpret it as shown in Figure 3-5. These separation options are what enables contacts to be sorted or used in a lookup by first or last name, even though the first and last name are in the same field.

By default, ACT! has been set up to not use Mr., Mrs., Ms., Esq., MD, PhD and Dr. as part of the first, middle or last name. I entered my name with "Dr" in front of it, then opened the Contact Name dialog box and saw that ACT! separated my name correctly, as shown in Figure 3-6. You can change these options as needed. You will learn how to change them in Lesson 16.

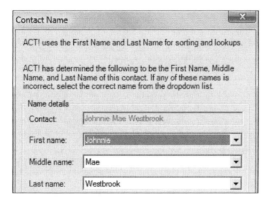

Figure 3-5 Contact with two first names   **Figure 3-6** Contact name separated correctly

4. Open the Title field drop-down list.

   Scroll down the list and select the Sales Manager title, as illustrated in Figure 3-7.

   The **EDIT LIST VALUES** option is used to add, edit or delete the values in the drop-down list.

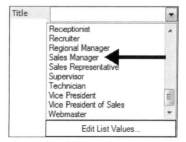

Figure 3-7 Title drop-down list values

5. Switch to the Basic Contact Layout - 1024x768.

6. Type `pur` in the Department field, then press Enter. Notice that the "Purchasing" department has been filled in automatically. (The Department field was on the 800x600 layout in ACT! 2009 and earlier.)

7. Type 765 417 5330 in the Phone field. (Do not put spaces between the numbers. I typed it that way to make it easier for you to read.) Notice that the phone number was automatically formatted.

Phone Number Formatting

Like the salutation field, the phone number fields also have default formatting. The **ELLIPSIS** button at the end of the Phone and Mobile fields will open the dialog box shown in Figure 3-8. The options shown are used to change how the phone number will be formatted. The default phone number format is for the US. If you enter a phone number for a different country and do not know the correct format for the country, open the Country field drop-down list shown in Figure 3-8 and select the country. After you click OK on the Enter Phone Number dialog box, the phone number will be formatted for the country that you selected.

The **EDIT FORMATS** button on the Enter Phone Number dialog box opens the dialog box shown in Figure 3-9. You can create your own phone number format or select one of the other formats shown in Figure 3-9 to be the new default format.

Figure 3-8 Enter Phone Number dialog box

Figure 3-9 Edit Phone Formats dialog box

Using Country Codes

The **COUNTRY CODE** is the prefix that you have to enter before you dial the area code. The Country Code for the United States is 1, as shown above in Figure 3-8 in brackets. Being able to look up the country code in the Country drop-down list is helpful if you have contacts in other countries and do not know the country code.

8. Enter the information in Table 3-3 in the appropriate fields on the Contact Detail view.

    The top portion of your contact record should look like the one shown in Figure 3-10.

    This is the contact record that you will use to enter data on various tabs in the remainder of this exercise.

Field	Type This
Address 1	123 Main St
City	Los Angeles
State	CA
Zip	90277
Country	USA
ID/Status	Supplier

Table 3-3 Contact information

Figure 3-10 Information for a new contact

As shown above in Figure 3-10, there are two address fields. ACT! actually has three address fields. This view only displays two of them. All three fields are for one address, not three different addresses. Often, the physical street address goes in the Address 1 field and the other two address fields are used to enter the floor, suite or room number, for example.

Some company addresses also include a building name. These are examples of the type of address information that could be entered in the second and third address fields. If a contact has more than one company address, like a street address and a PO Box, you could use fields on the User Fields tab as long as the layout for that tab is modified to reflect what the fields are being used for.

The Notes Tab

The data on this tab is a log of each note that you or another user of the database created about the contact, company or group. The entries on this tab are created automatically each time a note is created. An unlimited number of notes can be created for each contact, company or group. Table 3-4 explains the buttons on the Insert Note dialog box toolbar shown in Figure 3-11.

Figure 3-11 Insert Note dialog box toolbar

Button	Description
1	Prints the note.
2	Previews the note to show how it will look when it is printed.
3	Spell checks the note.
4	Changes the font for the body of the note.
5	Changes the font size for the body of the note.
6	Changes the font color for the body of the note.
7	Makes the selected text in the note bold.
8	Makes the selected text in the note italic.

Table 3-4 Insert Note dialog box toolbar buttons explained

Button	Description
9	Underlines the selected in the note text.
10	Draws a line through the selected text. This is usually done to indicate text that you want to delete.
11	Left aligns the text in the body of the note. This is the default alignment for text.
12	Centers the text in the body of the note.
13	Right aligns the text in the body of the note.
14	Creates a bulleted list in the body of the note.

Table 3-4 Insert Note dialog box toolbar buttons explained (Continued)

1. On the **NOTES** tab, click the **INSERT NEW NOTE** button illustrated in Figure 3-12. Notice that the Date and Time fields are filled in automatically on the Insert Note dialog box. If you had created a My Record in this database, your name would be in the **RECORD MANAGER** field.

Figure 3-12 Insert New Note button illustrated

2. In the field at the bottom of the dialog box type `This is my first note. It has an attachment and is associated to 3 contacts at Liberty.`

The **CONTACT** button on the Insert Note dialog box opens the dialog box shown in Figure 3-13.

If you need to attach the same note to other contacts, select the other contacts on this dialog box.

Figure 3-13 Select Contacts dialog box

Sorting Contact Records On The Select Contacts Dialog Box

If you click on the Name or Company columns in the **CONTACTS TO SELECT FROM** list or the **SELECTED CONTACTS** list, you can sort the contacts in ascending or descending order.

New Contact Dialog Box

Clicking the **NEW CONTACT** button shown above in Figure 3-13, opens the dialog box shown in Figure 3-14. This dialog box is used to create a new contact record.

Figure 3-14 New Contact dialog box

Add/Remove Dialog Box

The ellipsis button at the end of the **SHARE WITH** field on the Insert Note dialog box will open the dialog box shown in Figure 3-15.

Figure 3-15 Add/Remove dialog box

The options on this dialog box are used to share the note with everyone in a group, company or opportunity. By default when you click the button at the end of the Share with field, you will see a message about showing public notes. You will learn about companies in Lesson 5 and groups in Lesson 6.

The Add/Remove dialog box replaces the Select Group/Company dialog box in ACT! 2009 and earlier.

3. Click the Contact button on the Insert Note dialog box.

4. Select the three contacts at Liberty Savings & Loan, as shown in Figure 3-16, by clicking on the first contact at the company, then press and hold down the Shift key and click on the last contact at Liberty.

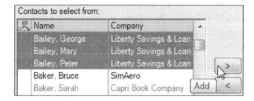

Figure 3-16 Contacts selected to add the note to

5. Click the **ADD** button shown above in Figure 3-16.

   There should be four names in the **SELECTED CONTACTS** list on the Select Contacts dialog box, as shown in Figure 3-17.

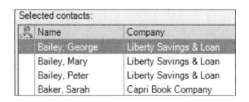

Figure 3-17 Contacts that will have the note attached

6. Click OK to close the dialog box.

How To Attach A File To A Contact Record

The **ATTACH** button on the Insert Note dialog box provides two options to attach a file to a note, as shown in Figure 3-18. The options are explained below.

Figure 3-18 Attach button options

① Selecting the **FILE** option stores a copy of the file with the note. Changes can be made to the copy of the file that is attached to the record. These changes will not be made in the original file. The opposite is also true. Changes made to the original file will not be available in the copy of the document that is attached to a record in an ACT! database. Select this option if you know for sure that you will not need to see any changes that may be made to the original document, when the document is opened from inside of ACT!. This option also increases the size of the database.

② The **SHORTCUT** option creates a link to a file. The link is not dynamic, which means that if the file is moved to another folder, renamed or deleted, the shortcut will no longer work.

If the attached file needs to be opened by other users of the database and the shortcut attachment option is selected, the file needs to be in a location (a folder) that other users have access to. I don't know how the computers in your office are networked, but I doubt that the person down the hall from you has access to the hard drive on your computer. If you find out that they do, you need to call your IT department immediately and have them change the status of your hard drive to not be shared <smile>.

1. Click the **ATTACH** button on the Insert Note dialog box, then select the File option.

2. Double-click on the **L2 ATTACH** file in your folder.

   The Insert Note dialog box should look like the one shown in Figure 3-19. You will have a different date and time.

   Checking the **PRIVATE** option will prevent other people that use the database from viewing the note.

   You would be the only person that can see this note.

Figure 3-19 Insert Note dialog box

3. Click OK to close the Insert Note dialog box.

4. Click OK on the **SPELL CHECK STATUS** dialog box if you enabled the automatic spell checker. If you wanted to spell check the note manually, click the **SPELL CHECK** button on the Insert Note dialog box toolbar. The entry on the Notes tab should look like the one shown in Figure 3-20.

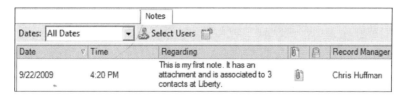

Figure 3-20 Information added to the Notes tab

A file that is attached to a note does not appear on the Documents tab.

Tips For Viewing And Deleting Attachments On The Notes Tab

① Notes are displayed with the most recent one at the top of the list.
② To view an attachment, double-click on the note that has the attachment, then click on the **ATTACHMENT** link on the Edit Note a dialog box.
③ To delete an attachment from a note, double-click on the note. Click the Attach button, then select **FILE**. You will see the message shown in Figure 3-21. Click Yes and the attachment will be deleted.

Figure 3-21 Remove Attachment message

Attaching Files On The Documents Tab

Earlier you attached a document to a note. The Documents tab displays the documents that are associated with the current contact. The documents on this tab cannot be linked to another contact from this tab. There is an option on the Documents tab that is also used to attach a document to the current contact.

1. On the **DOCUMENTS** tab, click the **ADD DOCUMENT** button, then select the File option.

2. Double-click on the **L2 DOCUMENTS TAB** file in your folder. You will see a reference to the document, as shown in Figure 3-22.

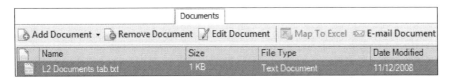

Figure 3-22 File added to the Documents tab

Tips For Viewing And Deleting Attachments On The Documents Tab

① To view an attachment on the Documents tab, double-click on the attachment.
② To delete an attachment from the Documents tab, right-click on it and select **REMOVE DOCUMENT**.

Attached Documents

When you attach a file in ACT!, a copy of the file is placed in the Attachments folder of the database. The original copy of the file is still where is was before you attached it. If you make changes to the original file (the one outside of ACT!), you will not see the changes when you open the attachment in ACT!. You can edit the attached documents, as well as, view, email and print them. In Lesson 10 you will learn how to edit attached documents. You have the three options discussed below to manage attachments:

① You can reattach the original file to the note if the original file was changed and you need the changes attached to the note.
② You can copy the original file that you changed, to the Attachments folder, as long as the original file still has the same file name. This will overwrite the file in the Attachments folder.
③ You can make the changes to the copy in the Attachments folder.

NEW Relationships

This tab is used to create and display contact relationships. The Relate Contact dialog box looks similar to the Insert Note dialog box.

1. On the **RELATIONSHIPS** tab, click the **RELATE CONTACT** button. At the top of the dialog box, you should see the name Sarah Baker.

If you want to relate the contact to one other contact, open the first drop-down list and select the contact.

If you want to relate the contact to more than one contact at the same time, like all contacts in a company or group and all of them have the same relationship, follow the steps below.

2. Click the Contacts button, then select **SELECT CONTACTS**. You will see the Select Contacts dialog box, shown earlier in Figure 3-13.

3. Open the Select from drop-down list and select Companies.

4. Open the drop-down list to the right of the Select from drop-down list and select Verge Records.

5. Add all of the contacts from the company to the Selected Contacts list, then click OK.

6. Open the drop-down list for Sarah Baker and select Business Partner.

7. Open the last drop-down list and select Vendor.

8. In the field at the bottom, type This relationship is for the record company to write a jingle for a commercial.

9. Your dialog box should look like the one shown in Figure 3-23.

    Click OK.

    You will see a separate entry for each contact at the record company on the Relationships tab, as shown in Figure 3-24.

Figure 3-23 Relate Contact dialog box

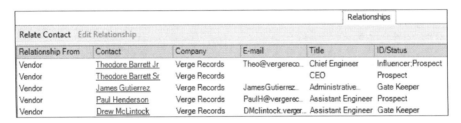

Figure 3-24 Contacts added to the Relationships tab

Entering Information On The Personal Info Tab

 In ACT! 2008 and earlier, this was called the **HOME ADDRESS** tab.

In addition to the fields for the contacts home address, the following fields are also available on this tab:

① The **PERSONAL E-MAIL** field should not be used for the business e-mail address, especially if you plan to use the Mail Merge wizard to create an email mail merge. The wizard does not use this field. (3)

② The **MESSENGER ID** field is used to store the contacts Instant Messenger ID or screen name.

③ The **WEB SITE** field is used to store the contacts personal web site. (3)

(3) The location of this field varies, depending on the layout. On the 800x600 layout, this field is on the Personal Info tab. On the 1024x768 layout, this field is on the top portion of the window.

Editing The Web Site And Personal E-mail Fields

These fields among others, can be edited differently then most of the contact fields. You can delete the contents of the field and re-type it or you can right-click in the field and select **EDIT WEB SITE**, as shown in Figure 3-25 or **EDIT PERSONAL E-MAIL**. If selected, these options select (highlight) the information in the field so that you do not have to delete it before you start typing in the field.

Figure 3-25 Edit Web Site field shortcut menu

1. Select the 800x600 layout.

2. On the **PERSONAL INFO** tab, type 1899 Payton Place Village Drive in the Address 1 field.

3. Add the information in Table 3-5 to the appropriate fields.

Field	Type This
City	Sacramento
State	CA
Zip	99990
Home Phone	7817661308

Table 3-5 Home Address information

Using The Date Field Calendar

Date fields, like the Birthday field, will have a calendar like the one shown in Figure 3-26. You can use the calendar to select the date or you can type the date in the field.

Find the month and year in the calendar, then click on the day that you need by using the options that are explained below.

The **TODAY** button will add the current date to the field.

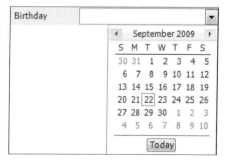

Figure 3-26 Date Field Calendar

Clicking the **LEFT ARROW** button at the top of the calendar will display previous months.

Clicking the **RIGHT ARROW** button will display future months.

What I like about date fields is that you do not have to type a four digit year or type a zero as the first digit of a month or day. You can type 6/2/09 and ACT! will convert it to the date shown in Figure 3-27.

Figure 3-27 Date field converted

The **BIRTHDAY** field does not require you to enter the year the contact was born. Entering the day and month is sufficient. The current year will be filled in automatically if you do not enter it. In Lesson 4 you will learn about this and other **ANNUAL EVENT** fields and how to use them as a lookup field.

4. Click on the arrow at the end of the Birthday field, then select your next birthday on the calendar. The information on the Personal Info tab should look similar to the information shown in Figure 3-28.

   Notice that the phone number was not automatically formatted. That is because the Home Phone field is a Free Form format field.

Figure 3-28 Personal Info tab fields

Contact Access Tab

 In ACT! 2008 and earlier, this was called the **CONTACT INFO** tab.

The fields shown in Figure 3-29 are filled in and updated by ACT! automatically. The values cannot be changed.

The **RECORD MANAGER** field lists the current owner of the contact record.

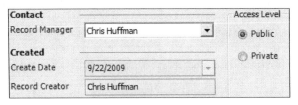

Figure 3-29 Contact Access tab fields

The **CREATE DATE** field stores the date that the record was created. I do not know why this field has a drop-down list because this field is filled in automatically when the record is created.

The **RECORD CREATOR** field stores the name of the user that created the contact record.

The **ACCESS LEVEL** options are used to make the contact record **PUBLIC** (anyone with rights to the database can view it) or **PRIVATE** (only the Record Manager can view it).

Latest Activities Tab

The fields shown in Figure 3-30 store the last time that a user of the database was in touch with the contact.

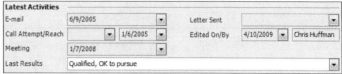

Figure 3-30 Latest Activities tab fields

User Fields Tab

The fields on the User Fields tab shown in Figure 3-31 are free form. They are used to enter data that does not fit into any of the fields that currently exist in the database.

Figure 3-31 User Fields tab fields

Later in the book you will learn how to change the labels of these fields to something meaningful for the data that you enter on this tab.

While the fields on the User Fields tab seem like a good idea to use, they can be dangerous if more than one person is using the database. That is because by default, any user that has rights to modify the layout, add, edit or delete information, can do just that.

For example, one user may decide to use the User 2 field to store an alternate email address for the contact. Another user may use the User 2 field to store the date that they mailed the contact a sample product. If this happens, one of these types of data will have to be moved to a different field. This may have to be done manually, record by record, which is probably not something that you want to do.

Saving Data

If any of the fields on the view that you are using have the **GENERATE HISTORY** option enabled, a history record will be created and will appear on the History tab when the record is saved. There are two ways to save the data that you enter, as discussed below.

   ①   Move to another record.
   ②   Click the Save Changes button on the toolbar.

Exercise 3.2: Duplicating Contact Information

In Exercise 3.1 you created a new contact record for a company that was not already in the database. In this exercise you will create a new contact record based on information from an existing contact record. This is known as duplicating a contact. This will save you time because you do not have to retype the company information. Duplicating a contact record that has the company information that you need, duplicates data in some of the fields in the top half of the Contact Detail view. There are two ways that you can duplicate records, as discussed below:

① You can duplicate the primary fields, which are the company, phone, fax, address, city, state, zip code, country and web site fields. These are the primary fields that ACT! sets up as the default. You can make other fields primary fields as needed.

② All of the fields. If this option is selected, the only fields not duplicated are the contact name and e-mail address fields.

Opportunity fields cannot be used as primary contact fields.

Creating A New Contact Based On The Primary Fields

1. Switch to the 1024x768 layout.

2. Display the contact Jonathan Jenkins.

   (**Hint**: You can type the name in the **CONTAINS** field shown in Figure 3-32.)

Figure 3-32 Contact Lookup options

3. Click the **DUPLICATE CONTACT** button on the Contact toolbar.

   You should see the dialog box shown in Figure 3-33.

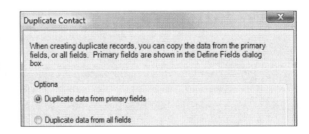

Figure 3-33 Duplicate Contact dialog box

4. Select the option **DUPLICATE DATA FROM PRIMARY FIELDS**, if it is not already selected, then click OK. You should see a new record with the primary fields filled in.

5. Delete the email address.

6. Add the information in Table 3-6 to the new contact record. The top half of the contact record should look like the one shown in Figure 3-34. Keep the record visible to complete the next exercise.

Field	Type This
Contact	Dan Day
Title	Analyst
Department	Engineering

Table 3-6 Duplicate contact information

Figure 3-34 Contact information

 Other Ways To Open The Duplicate Contact Dialog Box

① Right-click on a blank space on the Contact Detail view and select **DUPLICATE CONTACT**.
② Contacts ⇒ Duplicate Contact.

Exercise 3.3: Using The Undo Command

This command can be useful when you need to reverse your last entry in a field. The command will only work if the cursor has not been moved out of the field that you need to edit. The record for Dan Day should still be on the screen.

1. Change the Zip Code to 10040. Do not press the Enter or Tab key.

2. Edit ⇒ Undo. The Zip Code 75214 should have been restored.

3. Change the Zip Code to 10053, then press Enter.

4. Open the Edit menu.

   Notice that the **UNDO** option is not available, as illustrated in Figure 3-35.

Figure 3-35 Edit menu Undo option

The two reasons that this option is not available is because after another record is displayed or another option is selected, the record is automatically saved.

5.   Press the **ESC** key to close the menu.

 The **UNDO CHANGES TO CONTACT** option shown above in Figure 3-35 will delete the record created by the Duplicate Contact command.

NEW Contact Detail View Related Tasks

The options shown in Figure 3-36 are primarily found on detail views. Some options are also on list views. The options are explained below.

Figure 3-36 Contact Detail view related tasks

VIEW ALL CONTACTS Is the same as selecting Lookup ⇒ All Contacts. This option is helpful when you have already created a lookup and now want to display all of the records. It is quicker to use this link, then opening the Lookup menu and selecting the option. It may just be my laptop, but the View All Contacts link takes longer to display all of the records then the option on the Lookup menu does.

WRITE LETTER Opens the ACT! Word Processor and displays a letter template, as shown in Figure 3-37.

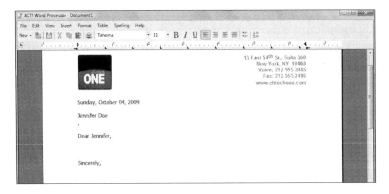

Figure 3-37 Letter template

ATTACH FILE Opens the Templates folder so that you can select a file to attach to the current contact. The file is added to the History tab. I was expecting to see the file on the Documents tab. I don't understand why the default folder is the Templates folder. There should be an option for this on the Preferences dialog box to select the default folder location.

PRINT CURRENT SCREEN Opens the Quick Print Options dialog box so that you can select options for how the screen will be printed.

PRINT MAILING LABELS & ENVELOPES Opens the Print dialog box that has options for printing labels and envelopes.

MODIFY LAYOUT Opens the current contact detail view layout in the Layout Designer, so that the layout can be changed.

ADD CONTACT TO GROUP Opens the Add/Remove dialog box to select groups and companies to add the contact to.

RELATE TO ANOTHER CONTACT Opens the Relate Contact dialog box. [See Relationships, earlier in this lesson]

SCHEDULE SERIES OF ACTIVITIES [See Lesson 7, Activity Series]

𝖭𝖤𝖶 Contact List View Related Tasks

The options shown in Figure 3-38 are for the Contact List view. The options that are only on the list view are explained below.

Figure 3-38 Contact List view related tasks

EXPORT TO EXCEL Exports the contacts that are displayed on the list view to Excel.

IMPORT CONTACTS Opens the Import Wizard. [See Lesson 20, Exercise 20.2]

CHANGE COLUMNS Opens the Customize Columns dialog box.

WRITE E-MAIL USING TEMPLATE Opens the Template folder (for the database) so that you can select a template to use for the email that you want to create. Once you select the template, a new email window will open with the template that you selected.

MAIL MERGE CONTACTS Opens the Mail Merge Wizard. [See Lesson 15, Exercise 15.2]

SORT LIST Opens the Sort dialog box to sort the contacts displayed in the view.

CREATE GROUP OF CONTACTS Displays the Group Detail view. All of the contacts displayed in the view will be added to the group that you create.

FINDING CONTACTS IN A DATABASE

Overview

In this lesson you will learn how to use the following search techniques:

- ☑ Lookup options on the Navigation Pane
- ☑ Lookup command
- ☑ Keyword Search lookups
- ☑ Multiple field lookups
- ☑ Narrow lookup option
- ☑ Add to lookup option
- ☑ Annual Events lookup

You will also learn the following:

- ☑ How to modify more than one record at the same time
- ☑ How to sort records
- ☑ How to delete records

LESSON 4

Finding Records

Having a database with hundreds or thousands of contacts is great. Being able to find the contacts that you need to access quickly, is a core reason of putting contact information into a database. ACT! comes with several lookup options to find contacts. Depending on the contacts that you need to find, one lookup option is probably a better solution then the other lookup options. Many of the lookup options are covered in this lesson. Some are specifically for contacts and others can be used to look up other types of records.

NEW Lookup Options On The Navigation Pane

At the top of the Navigation Pane is a lookup section, as shown in Figure 4-1.

Each of the other views on the Navigation Pane has a lookup section.

The options in this section provide quick access to some of the lookup options in ACT!.

Figure 4-1 Contacts Navigation Pane lookup options

The drop-down list is used to select the field that you want to search on. The fields on the tabs of the detail views are also included in this list.

The **MORE OPTIONS** link opens the Lookup dialog box.

The steps below demonstrate how to use the lookup options.

1. Open the drop-down list and select the field that you want to search on.

2. Type in the value that the field that you selected must have.

3. Click the Go button.

Exercise 4.1: Using The Lookup Options In The Navigation Pane

1. Click the View All Contacts link in the Navigation Pane.

2. Open the Contact field drop-down list and select Company.

3. Type Circle in the Contains field, then click the Go button. You will see all of the contact records in the Contact List view that have Circle in the Company field.

The Lookup Command

The Lookup command is used to find a record or records based on criteria that you select. Other software packages use the term **QUERY** when discussing finding specific records. You can find all contacts in one state or all contacts that have the same title. You can use the Lookup command to find contacts by Company, First Name, Last Name, Phone Number, City, State,

Zip Code or ID/Status. Later you will learn how to find contacts using other fields. The biggest limitation to lookups is that the criteria cannot be saved. After you complete the lookup exercises, you will better understand why it is so important to enter data correctly and to enter as much data as possible for each record that you create.

Lookup Contacts Dialog Box Options

This dialog box provides several options to help you find the records that you need. The options are explained below.

The options shown in Figure 4-2 are used to select how to find the records. These options are used to include or exclude records.

Figure 4-2 Search criteria options

The options shown in Figure 4-3 are used to select the type of records to search, to find the contacts that you are looking for.

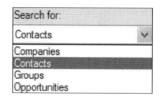

Figure 4-3 Record type search options

Current Lookup Options

The options shown in Figure 4-4 are used to determine the type of lookup that you want to create. The options are explained in Table 4-1.

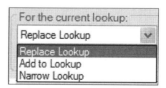

Figure 4-4 Lookup options

Option	Description
Replace Lookup	This is the default option. It creates a new lookup.
Add to Lookup	This option will add the contacts from the lookup that you are creating now, to the previous lookup that you created.
Narrow Lookup	This option searches the records from the previous lookup to exclude (remove) records from it, based on the criteria that you select in the current lookup.

Table 4-1 For the current lookup drop-down list field options explained

Exercise 4.2: Using The Lookup Command

1. Lookup ⇒ State.

2. Open the drop-down list to the far right and select NY or type NY in the field.

3. Click on the button before the words **SHOW MORE OPTIONS** on the dialog box. You should have the options shown in Figure 4-5.

    Click OK.

    You should see that record 1 of 25 is displayed.

Figure 4-5 Lookup Contacts dialog box

Notice the field in Figure 4-5 with the tool tip. I will refer to that field as the Search field.
If checked, the **INCLUDE PRIVATE** option is used to search your private records.
If checked, the **INCLUDE USERS** option is used to retrieve other database users "My Records",
if they meet the search criteria.

The result of a lookup will only display records that match the criteria that you select.
Notice that the view changed to the Contact List view. If you click the Detail View button on the toolbar, you will be able to see more information for each of the contacts that were retrieved by the lookup.

Notice that the information on the Status bar in the lower left corner of the window displays
LOOKUP: STATE. This lets you know what field was selected for the current lookup.

4. Lookup ⇒ All Contacts, or click the View All Contacts link in the Related Tasks section of the Navigation Pane. All of the contacts will be displayed.

5. Click the Detail View button on the Contacts toolbar.

 Contact Detail View Lookup Shortcut

Using the lookup options on the menu or clicking the **MORE OPTIONS** link in the Lookup section of the Navigation Pane is probably how most people create a lookup, but there is another way. Right-click in the field that you want to use as the lookup field and select **LOOKUP [FIELD NAME]**, as illustrated in Figure 4-6. The Lookup Contacts dialog box shown above in Figure 4-5 will open.

Figure 4-6 Contact field shortcut menu

Exercise 4.3: Using Keyword Search Lookups

Keyword search lookups are used to find records based on information in any field. You can perform a keyword search for a word or phrase in any field, including fields on the tabs. This is different from the lookup that you created in the previous exercise. The lookup that you created in the previous exercise searched for records that **START WITH** the value that you typed in or selected. Keyword searches are different. They retrieve records that have the value any place in a field.

This is very helpful when you remember a word or phrase, but do not remember what field it is in. Depending on how many tables you select to search in, the keyword search could take a while because all of the fields are searched, including fields on the System tabs, which each have their own table in the database. [See Lesson 19, Tabs Overview]

1. Lookup ⇒ Keyword Search, or click the **SEARCH** button on the Global toolbar. You should see the Keyword Search dialog box.

2. Type Sales in the **SEARCH FOR** field.

3. Select the **CONTACTS** Record type option, if it is not already selected, then clear the **OPPORTUNITIES** option.

   You should have the options selected that are shown in Figure 4-7.

Figure 4-7 Keyword Search criteria

These options will search for the word "Sales" in all contact, activity, history, notes and relationships fields.

The **FIELDS** option in the Look in section includes all fields for the record type that is selected.

4. Click the **FIND NOW** button. The records shown at the bottom of the dialog box match the criteria that you selected.

You should see that the keyword search criteria "Sales" was found 829 times. Currently, there are not 829 records in the database. This is not the number of records that have the search criteria. It is the number of fields that have the word "Sales" in it. This means several records have the word "Sales" in more than one field.

Viewing The Keyword Search Results

When you view records retrieved from the search, the Keyword Search dialog box stays open. This allows you to go back to it to select other records to view in detail. You can also change the search options and perform another search. There are several options that you can select from, to view the results in the Contact Detail view, as discussed below.

① You can scroll through the list of records at the bottom of the Keyword Search dialog box. You may recognize the record(s) that you are looking for.
② If you right-click on a single record at the bottom of the dialog box and select **GO TO RECORD**, as illustrated in Figure 4-8, the detail record will be displayed.
③ You can select more than one record to view by clicking on one record, then pressing and holding down the **CTRL** key and clicking on the other records that you want to view, as shown in Figure 4-9. Once the records are selected, right-click and select **LOOKUP SELECTED RECORDS**.
④ Click the **CREATE LOOKUP** button at the top of the Keyword Search dialog box. This option will create a lookup to display every record with the Record Type that you selected on the Keyword Search dialog box.

Figure 4-8 Keyword Search shortcut menu options

Figure 4-9 Records selected to view

5. Select the first 10 records on the Keyword Search dialog box, then right-click on any of the highlighted records and select **LOOKUP SELECTED RECORDS**.

Notice that the Keyword Search dialog box is minimized in the lower left corner of the screen. The reason that there are only three contact records is because some of these contact records have more than one field that has the word "Sales" in it.

6. Close the Keyword Search dialog box. Lookup ⇒ All Contacts, when you are finished viewing the contact records.

> **Keyword Search Viewing Tips**
>
> ① Selecting the **LOOKUP ALL** option on the shortcut menu shown earlier in Figure 4-8 is the same as clicking the Create Lookup button.
> ② Double-clicking on a record in the bottom half of the Keyword Search dialog box is the same as right-clicking on a record and selecting Go To Record.
> ③ To select adjacent records, click on the first one, then press and hold down the **SHIFT** key and click on the last record that you want to view.

Exercise 4.4: How To Create A Lookup Using Multiple Fields

In Exercise 4.2 you learned how to perform a lookup using one field. In this exercise you will learn how to look up records using more than one field. If you wanted to email managers that are in Boise, you would have to search two fields. You would have to search the City field for "Boise" and you would have to search the Title field for "Manager".

If you open the Lookup menu you will see the City field. You will not see the Title field. It appears that you cannot search the Title field. The **OTHER FIELDS** option on the Lookup menu contains the fields that are not listed on the Lookup menu. You can also right-click in the Title field on the view and select the lookup option from the shortcut menu, as shown earlier in Figure 4-6.

1. Lookup ⇒ City.

2. Type Boise in the Search field, then press Enter. There are three contacts in Boise. Notice that only two contacts have the Manager title.

Using The Narrow Lookup Option

Until now, when you performed a lookup the Replace Lookup option was used. The Replace option tells ACT! to remove the records from the previous lookup and start over.

The **NARROW LOOKUP** option is used to reduce the number of contacts that are the result of the previous lookup. In this exercise, the previous lookup selected all contacts in Boise. Now you want to find the managers in Boise. If you selected the Replace lookup option you would get all managers, no matter what city they are in. This is not what you want in this exercise. The Narrow Lookup option will only search the records that were retrieved from the previous lookup.

1. Lookup ⇒ Other Fields. Open the Field drop-down list and select Title.

The **OTHER FIELDS** option does not provide any additional fields to search on, that are not already in the Field drop-down list. If the field that you want to search on, is not on the Lookup menu, you can select any field to open the Lookup Contacts dialog box and select the field that you need from the **FIELD** drop-down list.

2. Open the Search drop-down list and select Manager.

3. Select the **NARROW LOOKUP** option.

    The Lookup Contacts dialog box should have the options shown in Figure 4-10.

Figure 4-10 Options to search for a specific job title

4. Click OK. You should now have two records in the lookup. This means that one of the three original contact records retrieved does not have "Manager" in the Title field.

This may seem like a lot of work to remove one record. If the database retrieved thousands of records that met your initial lookup criteria, being able to perform another lookup to remove 1,000 records from the search automatically, makes this a good feature to use.

Exercise 4.5: Using The Add To Lookup Option

If you wanted to find contacts with a Texas address or were sales reps, using the Replace lookup or Narrow lookup options would not give you the results that you are looking for. The **ADD TO LOOKUP** option is used to combine the results from different lookups. The records from the various lookups do not have to be related. This is the type of lookup that you will learn how to create in this exercise.

1. Lookup ⇒ State. Type TX in the Search field.

2. Make sure that the **REPLACE LOOKUP** option is selected. Click OK. 14 records should have been retrieved.

3. Lookup ⇒ Other Fields. Select Title from the Field drop-down list.

4. Select Sales Representative from the Search drop-down list.

When performing lookups, you should select an item from the Search drop-down list as much as possible, even though the Search field will allow you to type in an entry. If you type in an entry and the entry that you type in is not used on any record, you will not retrieve the records that you expect.

5. Select the **ADD TO LOOKUP** option. Click OK. There should be 20 records displayed. All of the records in the lookup either have "TX" in the State field or "Sales Representative" in the Title field. If someone typed Texas in the State field on contact records, those records would not be retrieved in this search.

Finding Contact Records That Are Missing Information

In Exercise 4.4, the goal was to find contacts that meet specific criteria to send an email to. In order to send the contacts an email, they need to have an email address. You can use the Lookup command to find contacts that do or do not have an email address. Searching for records that do not have data in certain fields is a good way to keep contacts from having data missing.

Exercise 4.6: Find Contacts Without An Email Address

In this exercise you will find all contacts that do not have an email address.

1. Lookup ⇒ E-mail Address. Select the **DOES NOT CONTAIN DATA** option, illustrated in Figure 4-11.

Figure 4-11 Options to find all contacts without an email address

2. Click OK. 97 contacts should be in the Contact List view. To verify that the records do not have an email address, click the Detail View button. View a few records and look at the E-mail field. You will see that the field is empty.

The reason that I had you view the records on the Contact Detail view is because the E-mail field is not displayed by default on the Contact List view. You will learn how to modify a layout to display the fields that you need.

Exercise 4.7: Finding Contacts That You Added To The Database

One way to help keep data accurate and consistent is to review it. Everyone that uses the database should do this periodically. The frequency that data is checked and verified depends on how many records are added and how often data is modified.

In this exercise you will create a lookup that finds all contacts that you added to the database in the last month. The fields that you need for this search are the Record Creator and Create Date fields on the Contact Access tab. In Lesson 17 you will create a report to print this data.

1. Lookup ⇒ Other Fields.

   Select the options shown in Figure 4-12.

   You have to type in the Record Creators name. Click OK.

Figure 4-12 Record Creator field lookup criteria

2. Lookup ⇒ Other Fields.

   Select the options shown in Figure 4-13.

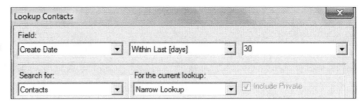

Figure 4-13 Create Date field lookup criteria

3. Click OK. You should see the two records shown in Figure 4-14. These records should look familiar because you created them earlier.

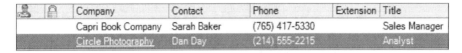

		Company	Contact	Phone	Extension	Title
		Capri Book Company	Sarah Baker	(765) 417-5330		Sales Manager
		Circle Photography	Dan Day	(214) 555-2215		Analyst

Figure 4-14 Contacts that you added to the database in the last 30 days

Annual Events Lookup

Annual events is another type of lookup. Examples of annual events are anniversaries, birthdays and yearly salary reviews. By default, annual events do not appear on calendars, but they can be added to a calendar. Creating a lookup is one way to be able to view annual events.

 Annual event fields only search the month and day portion of the date field, because they are tracked from year to year.

Exercise 4.8: Lookup Annual Events

In this exercise you will create a lookup to find all contacts with a birthday between January 1, 2008 and March 31, 2008.

1. Lookup ⇒ Annual Events.

   The options in the **SEARCH FOR** drop-down list shown in Figure 4-15 display all of the types of annual events that are currently being used in the database.

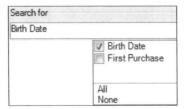

Figure 4-15 Annual event types

2. Accept the Birth Date search option, then select the **DATE RANGE** option.

3. Open the first date drop-down list field and select January 1, 2008, as shown in Figure 4-16. Open the second date drop-down list field and select March 31, 2008. You should have the options selected that are shown in Figure 4-17.

Figure 4-17 Birth Date annual event search options

Figure 4-16 Date field calendar

4. Click the **FIND NOW** button. You will see the contacts that have a birthday in the date range that you selected.

5. Close the Annual Events Search dialog box and display all of the contacts.

If you click the **SCHEDULE TO-DO** button, you can create an activity for the contact that is selected at the bottom of the Annual Events Search dialog box. The contacts name will appear on the Schedule Activities dialog box. This option will not recognize more than one selected contact.

 Annual Events Search Viewing Tips

The records shown at the bottom of the Annual Events Search dialog box match the criteria. The options discussed below are how you can view the results.

① You can search for more than one annual event at the same time. As shown earlier in Figure 4-15, you can check more than one annual event type or you can select the **ALL** option to lookup all of the annual event types that are in the database.
② If you right-click on a single record at the bottom of the Annual Events Search dialog box and select **GO TO CONTACT**, the record will be displayed.
③ Click the **CREATE LOOKUP** button. This button will create a lookup to display every record that is displayed at the bottom of the Annual Events Search dialog box.
④ Double-clicking on a record is the same as right-clicking and selecting **GO TO CONTACT.**

ACT! Annual Events Report

The **PRINT LIST** button on the Annual Events Search dialog box prints the report shown in Figure 4-18.

Contact	Company	Phone	Birth Date
Emily Dunn	Boomer's Artworx	(602) 555-4874	3/11/1959
Allison Mikola	CH TechONE	(212) 555-2485	1/13/1968
Melissa Pearce	CH TechONE	(212) 555-2485	3/15/1965
Jonathan Sommer	CH TechONE	(212) 555-2485	2/5/1973
Morty Manicotti	Corleone's Pasta Company	(480) 555-4512	3/17/1967
Todd Hornsby	Harbor Lights Restaurant	(757) 555-1221	3/15/1970
Alexander O'Brien	Manxsys Financial	(206) 555-4247	1/7/2003
Gracie Anderson	Searchlight Casting	(480) 555-3764	1/4/1968
Brandon Sloan	Sierra's Cafe	(562) 555-2142	1/7/1968
William Rosemann	Williams Consulting	(03) 680 4 445	1/21/1982

Figure 4-18 ACT! Annual Events report

Contact Activity Lookup

This type of lookup is used to find contacts whose records were or were not updated since a certain date. The lookup searches on any or all of the following tabs: Notes, History, Activities, Opportunities and Contact Access. This lookup is useful if you have a lot of contacts that you need to keep up with on a regular basis. It is also a good way to make sure that the data is accurate and that none of your contacts are being neglected or have fallen off of your radar, as they say.

Exercise 4.9: Find Contacts That Have Not Been Updated

In this exercise you will search for contacts that have not had the notes, opportunities or activities updated since February 1, 2008.

1. Lookup ⇒ Contact Activity.

2. Change the **SINCE DATE** to 2/1/2008.

 I am not sure why, but the value in the **SINCE DATE** field is saved in ACT!. This means that the next time that you open this dialog box, the date that you selected the last time that you used the dialog box will automatically be in this field.

3. Clear the following options: Contact fields and Histories. You should have the options selected that are shown in Figure 4-19.

 The Histories and Activities options are used to select specific categories to search for, as shown in Figure 4-20.

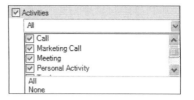

Figure 4-20 Activity options

Figure 4-19 Contact Activity dialog box options

4. Click OK. There should be 29 records on the Contact List view. This would be the list that you would work from, because the contact records have not been updated in a long time.

 Contact Activity Lookup Tips

① Lookups are not case sensitive. Typing "Marketing" or "marketing" will return the same results.

② **LOOKUP** ⇒ **PREVIOUS** displays the last nine searches that you ran, as shown in Figure 4-21. You can select the search that you want to run again. When you reopen ACT!, these searches will not be available because they are not saved.

③ Right-click in a field in the top half of the Contact Detail view and select Lookup (Field Name) to open the Lookup dialog box.

④ When only one record meets the lookup criteria, it is displayed in the Contact Detail view. You do not have to display all contacts before creating a lookup.

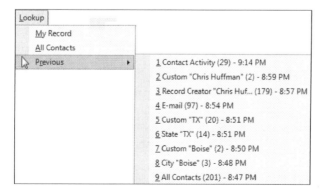

Figure 4-21 Previous searches

Modifying Several Records At The Same Time

You may have the need to change the data in the same field(s) on several records. You could make the changes one record at a time or you could create a lookup to retrieve all of the records that you need to change and change all of them at the same time.

> If you do not create a lookup first, the changes will be made to every record in the database.

If you have several company contacts at the same address and the company moves, you could look up the company address that you need to change and change all of the records at the same time, if the address fields are not linked. You can also change data on the User Fields, Personal Info and Secondary Contacts tabs this way.

The **REPLACE FIELD** command is used to change the data in a field for multiple records at the same time.

Exercise 4.10: How To Modify Several Records At The Same Time

In this exercise you will change the value in the Last Results field and add a note to a user defined field for all contacts in NY. The tasks that you will learn in this exercise are helpful for updating several records at the same time, as well as, keeping the data consistent and accurate.

> It is a good idea to make a back up copy of the database before modifying several records at the same time. This is known as a **GLOBAL** change. This type of change cannot be undone. You do not have to create a back up copy now because this is a practice database.

Change The Last Results Field

1. Create a lookup to find all records in the State of NY. The lookup should find 25 records.

2. Edit ⇒ Replace Field. You will see the Replace Data dialog box.

3. Open the Replace Contents of drop-down list and select the **LAST RESULTS** field.

4. Open the Value drop-down list and select **DISCUSSED OPPORTUNITIES**, as shown in Figure 4-22.

Figure 4-22 Replace data options for the Last Results field

5. Click OK. When you see the Replace/Swap/Copy message that lets you know that all records in the current lookup will be modified, click Yes to modify the records.

Change The Value In A User Defined Field

In this part of the exercise you will use the Replace Field command to change the value in a user defined field. User defined fields are free form fields that are used to enter data that there is no existing field for.

1. Switch to the 800x600 layout.

2. Edit ⇒ Replace Field.

3. Select the User 10 field from the first drop-down list, then type Should this record be private? in the **VALUE** field, as shown in Figure 4-23.

Figure 4-23 Replace data options for the User 10 field

4. Click OK, then click Yes to modify the records.

Observe the following information about the 25 records in the lookup, by clicking the Detail View button.

① The **LAST RESULTS** field on the Latest Activities tab has been set to Discussed opportunities. (1)
② The **EDIT ON** field on the Latest Activities tab has today's date. (1)
③ The **USER 10** field on the User Fields tab has the text that you typed in the Value field shown above in Figure 4-23.

(1) On the 1024x768 layout, the Latest Activities fields are on the top portion of the view, instead of on a tab.

Exercise 4.11: How To Delete Data From Several Records At The Same Time

Just like you can add or change data in a field for multiple records, you can also delete data from a field for multiple records at the same time. You will learn how in this exercise.

1. With the 25 NY records still in the lookup, Edit ⇒ Replace Field.

2. Select the User 10 field from the first drop-down list and leave the Value field empty. Leaving the Value field empty will overwrite the data in the field with blanks, which produces the same effect as deleting data in the field.

3. Click OK, then click Yes. You can view the information on the User Fields tab. You will see that the User 10 field for the 25 records is now blank.

4. Lookup ⇒ All Contacts.

Using The Contact List View

Until now, you have been using the Contact Detail view to look at records. This view only displays one record at a time. The Contact List view resembles a spreadsheet and displays all of the contacts that you have the right to see. Options not covered on the Contact List view in this lesson are covered in Lesson 10. [See Lesson 10, Tagging Contacts]

The first two columns on the Contact List view shown in Figure 4-24, are used to visually bring things to your attention.

The first column will have a key icon in it if the contact record is a user of the database.

The second column will display a lock icon if the record was marked private by the current user (you).

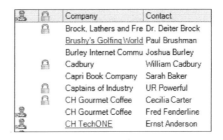

Figure 4-24 Contact List view

Sorting By Columns In The Contact List View

You can sort the records in the Contact List view by clicking on the column heading that you want to sort on. The default sort order is based on the Company field.

1. On the Contact List view, click on the Contact column heading.

Notice that the records are now sorted by the contacts last name, even though the first and last names are in the same column. The Last name field is the field that the Contact column actually sorts on.

You should see a triangle in the Contact column heading. If the triangle points up like this ▲, the records are sorted in ascending (A to Z or 1 to 10) order. If the triangle points down like this ▼, the records are sorted in descending order (Z to A or 10 to 1).

 If your database has hundreds or thousands of records, you may not want to scroll down the list even though the records are currently sorted to find the contact that you need. If that is the case, the steps below will show you how to find to a specific record in the list without scrolling.

2. Open the Options drop-down list shown in Figure 4-25 at the far right and select Show Look For.

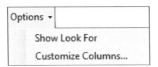

Figure 4-25 Options drop-down list

3. Click on the column heading, not the arrow on the column heading, of the field that has the value that you want to look for. In this exercise, click on the Contact column.

4. Type the first few letters of what you are looking for. In this example, type York, because that is a contacts last name.

You will see the first contact in the list that matches what you typed in, is highlighted. Also notice that the letters that you typed in are in the **LOOK FOR** field even though you did not click in this field before you typed in the information.

The more letters that you type, the closer ACT! will be able to find the record that you are looking for. This works for all columns, as long as the list is sorted on that column before you start typing in the search criteria.

View Detail Information From The Contact List View

If you want to view all of the data for a contact from the Contact List view, double-click on the contact that you want to view. If you click on a field that is hyperlinked (blue), like the company or web site fields, you will open the Company Detail record or the web site.

How To Select And View Specific Records

If you have a database with thousands of records, you will probably not want to see all of the records in the Contact List view. You can select (highlight) any of the records and only view the records that you select.

1. Click the List View button. Click on the Company column heading. The records should be in alphabetical order by company. If not, click on the Company column heading again.

2. Click on the first record with the company name A1 Services. Press and hold down the Shift key, then click on the last record with the same company name.

3. Press and hold down the CTRL key, then select all of the Beautiful Friendship company records.

    The Contact List view should look like the one shown in Figure 4-26.

Figure 4-26 Contact List view with records selected

4. Right-click in the Contact List view on a highlighted record and select the option, **LOOK UP SELECTED CONTACTS** on the shortcut menu, as illustrated in Figure 4-27.

    In the Contact List view you should now only see the eight records that you selected.

Figure 4-27 Contact List view shortcut menu

Exercise 4.12: Sorting Records

Earlier, you learned how to sort records in the Contact List view by clicking on a column heading. That is how to sort on a single column. If you want to sort on more than one column or sort on a column that is not displayed on the Contact List view, you have to use the Sort dialog box. Follow the steps below to sort records in the Contact views.

1. Lookup ⇒ All Contacts.

2. Edit ⇒ Sort. You should see the Sort dialog box.

3. Open the **SORT BY** drop-down list. You will see all of the fields on the current layout. Select the State field, then select the **ASCENDING** sort order option.

4. Open the **AND THEN BY** drop-down list and select the Referred By field, which is not displayed on the Contact List view, then select the Descending sort order option.

5. You should have the options selected that are shown in Figure 4-28.

   Click OK.

   The records are now sorted by the State and Referred By fields.

Figure 4-28 Sort dialog box options

Exercise 4.13: How To Delete Contacts From The Database

If you no longer need to keep information on a particular contact or secondary contact, you can delete the record. Once you delete a record, it is gone forever unless you restore it from a back up copy of the database. The contact record is deleted from all companies that it is associated or linked to. The contact is also deleted from any group that it is a member of. When deleting a contact you have the following options:

① Delete the current contact.
② Delete all of the contacts in the current lookup.

When you delete a contact, the Notes and History records for the contact are also deleted. The programmer in me knows that just deleting records from a database is usually not the best solution. A better solution would be to export the records that you do not need to another database. You can name this database anything that you like. This second database is sometimes referred to as a **HISTORY** or **ARCHIVE DATABASE**, meaning that it does not contain any current or active records. Once you export the records from the live database to the second database, you can delete them from the live database.

How To Delete One Record

1. Right-click on the record for William Cadbury that does not have a company name and select **DELETE CONTACT**.

2. Click the Delete Contact button shown in Figure 4-29, then click Yes to confirm that you want to delete the record.

Figure 4-29 Delete contact confirmation dialog box

How To Delete Multiple Records At The Same Time

If you need to delete several records, create a lookup to find the records that you want to delete.

1. Lookup ⇒ Company. Type A1 in the Search field.

2. Press Enter or click OK. Five records should be displayed.

3. Contacts ⇒ Delete Contact.

4. Click the **DELETE LOOKUP** button shown above in Figure 4-29.

5. Click Yes to confirm that you want to delete the records.

6. In a few seconds, you will see a message that tells you that no more records match the lookup criteria. Click OK.

View The My Record

Now that you have edited and deleted records, you can check the History tab to see the entries for the changes that you made to the database.

1. Lookup ⇒ My Record.

2. On the History tab, the first seven entries should be for the records that you deleted or changed, as shown in Figure 4-30.

   The **REGARDING & DETAILS** column is used to let you know what the change to the record is.

Figure 4-30 History log of deleted and changed records

3. Lookup ⇒ All Contacts.

CREATING COMPANY AND DIVISION RECORDS

Overview

In this lesson you will learn about the following company and division record options:

- ☑ Using the Companies tree
- ☑ Creating company and division records
- ☑ Associating and linking contacts to companies
- ☑ Duplicating company and division records
- ☑ Using the Company Lookup command

LESSON 5

Company And Division Records Overview

Company records allow contacts associated with a company to be managed easier. If a company has a lot of contacts, it may be easier to manage the contacts if divisions were created for the company. Brick and mortar companies have divisions, departments and business units. Companies in ACT! can have them also. You can create companies and divisions that best meet your needs. It is also possible that you may not need any companies or divisions. Figure 5-1 shows the Company Detail view.

Figure 5-1 Company Detail view

The **COMPANY** record type is used to keep track of contacts in the same company. In a way, a company record is similar to a group. This may be why the groups and companies are on the same tab on the Contact Detail view. You can see all of the companies and groups except dynamic groups that a contact is a member of. It would be nice if there was a way to know if the entries on this tab are a company or group. Contacts can be associated with more than one company.

An example of when you would associate a contact to more than one company would be if one consultant (a contact) did work for multiple companies that are in your database. You can create activities, notes and opportunities, as well as, attach documents to a company record. In ACT!, any of the following are acceptable ways to categorize contacts in a company. These categories would be divisions that you create. I am sure that you can come up with several others.

① By department.
② By title.
③ By contacts home state.

Keep in mind that company records in ACT! do not have the same limitations as brick and mortar companies. Company records in ACT! function more like folders, meaning that the contact records associated to a company, do not have to have anything related. While the company records displayed in the Companies tree have the name of a company, you can create a company record with any name that you want. You could create a company record that has your first name as the company name.

In addition to being able to create 15 levels of divisions per company record, you can also create **SUBDIVISIONS**. Subdivisions are used to further divide the contacts into categories per company, which makes it easier to manage hundreds or thousands of records associated with the company.

An example of when it would be appropriate to create subdivisions would be for a company that has 1,000 sales reps. I would create a division called "Sales Reps". I would then create subdivisions for each of the product lines the company has like telephones, digital cameras, camcorders and televisions. I would add the sales reps to the appropriate subdivision(s) based on the product line(s) that the sales rep sells. As you can see, divisions and subdivisions can be used to organize contacts in the way that works best for you. A contact that is in a division does not have to also be part of the company. This means that you can add a contact to a division without being required to associate it to the company. Divisions are independent of the company that they are created under.

Differences Between Companies And Groups

In this lesson you will learn how to create company records. In the next lesson you will learn how to create group records. On the surface, company and group records may appear to be the same and have the same functionality, but there are some differences.

Company records have more functionality than group records. For example, company records have more fields that can be used to automatically fill in fields on a contact record. The opposite is also true. Fields on a contact record can be used to fill in fields on a company record.

Creating a group is like saving a lookup because the records do not have to have the same data in a specific field. When you view contacts from the Company Detail view you can see the notes, activities and opportunities for all of the contacts in the company on the same tab. The same is true if contact records are viewed from the Group Detail view.

Company Detail View Toolbar

Many of the buttons on the Company Detail view toolbar are the same as the contact and group toolbars. Figure 5-2 shows the Company Detail view toolbar. Table 5-1 explains the buttons on the toolbar.

Figure 5-2 Company Detail view toolbar

Button	Description
1	Displays the Company Detail view.
2	Displays the Company List view.
3	Saves the record. (1) (2)
4	Opens the Quick Print Options dialog box.
5	Adds or removes a contact from a company. (2)
6	Updates the linked contacts for the selected company.
7	Attach a file. (2)
8	Creates a lookup of the selected company.
9	Is used to select a different layout. (1)
10	Displays the ACT! E-marketing options, which requires a paid subscription.

Table 5-1 Company Detail view toolbar buttons explained

(1) This option is only available from the Company Detail view.
(2) This option applies to companies and divisions.

Companies Tree

The Companies tree is on the left side of the Company Detail view. At the top of the Companies tree, the number of companies and divisions in the database are displayed. This tree displays all of the companies, divisions and subdivisions in the database, as illustrated in Figure 5-3.

A plus sign in front of an entry in the tree means that there is at least one company or division below it.

Figure 5-3 Companies tree

If you click on an entry in the tree, you will see the detail information for it on the right side of the window. The companies and divisions at this level are recognized as divisions.

Company records in the Companies tree may or may not contain the same companies that you see in the Contacts view. For example, in the Contact List view you will see the following companies, Cadbury, County Tennis Supplies and Liberty. If you look in the Companies tree, you will not see an entry for these companies. It is not a requirement that every company have a company record.

You can use the tree to complete several tasks including moving, creating and deleting a company. Any task that you can do for a company, you can also do for a division or subdivision. Like other features in ACT!, the Companies tree has a shortcut menu, as shown in Figure 5-4.

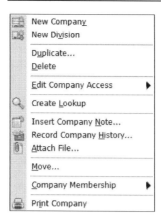

	New Company
	New Division
	Duplicate...
	Delete
	Edit Company Access ▶
	Create Lookup
	Insert Company Note...
	Record Company History...
	Attach File...
	Move...
	Company Membership ▶
	Print Company

Figure 5-4 Companies tree shortcut menu

Exercise 5.1: Create New Contact Records

To complete some of the company exercises, you need to add more contact records to the database.

1. Create contact records for the following names. You only have to enter the name in each record. John Doe, Jennifer Doe, Charles Smith, Mary Wood and Bill Grant.

2. Create contact records for the following names: Laura Smith and Tom Wood.
   Type Lookup in the Company field for these two records. They will be used later in this lesson to lookup contacts and link them to a company.

Exercise 5.2: Create A Company Record

1. Click the **COMPANIES** button on the Navigation Pane.

2. Click the **NEW** button on the Global toolbar, then create records for the two companies in Table 5-2.

   The first record should look like the one shown in Figure 5-5.

Field	Company #1	Company #2
Company	My Company	My Other Company
Address 1	123 Main St	456 South St
City	Hitsville	Hollywood
State	CA	CA

Table 5-2 Company record data

Business Card

Company	My Company	Address 1	123 Main St
Phone		Address 2	
Fax		City	Hitsville
Toll-Free		State/ZIP	CA
Web Site		Country	

Status

ID/Status	Referred By

Figure 5-5 New company record

ACT! tries to prevent you from creating duplicate records. If you enter a company name that already exists as a company record in the database, you will see the warning message shown in Figure 5-6 when you try to go to another company record.

Figure 5-6 Duplicate company warning message

If you recall, in Lesson 2 you changed how ACT! checks for duplicate companies.
If you click Yes, the company record that you just created will be added to the database.
If you click No, you will have to change the company name to save the record.

Exercise 5.3: Create Divisions For A Company

Creating a division uses the same screen as the one for creating a company record.

1. Display the company (or division) record that you want to create a division for. For this exercise click on the company, My Company in the Companies tree.

2. Right-click on the Company Name in the tree and select **NEW DIVISION**.

3. Type the division name in the Company field. For this exercise type Finance in the Company field.

4. If you click on the company in the Company tree you will see the division. You will also see the **HIERARCHY** of the company and its divisions on the Divisions tab, as illustrated at the bottom of Figure 5-7.

Figure 5-7 Division associated to a company

5. Create the divisions in Table 5-3 under the correct company.

Division	Company
Technology Division	My Company
Marketing	My Other Company
Sales Division	My Other Company

Table 5-3 Divisions to create

Associating Contacts To Companies And Divisions

Contacts can exist in an ACT! database without being linked or associated to a company. Companies can be in the database without having contacts linked to them. There is no requirement that contacts and companies be linked or associated, so do not be alarmed if you have contact records that are not linked to company records or vice versa. Although, I am not sure why someone would create a company and not associate any contacts to it, it is acceptable in ACT!. There are two ways to associate contacts to companies as discussed below.

① **Manually** This method entails creating the link between a contact and a company. ACT! refers to this type of link as a **STATIC** link. That is because the link will remain intact until you manually change it.

② **Automatically** This method entails creating a query that selects the contact records that will be linked to a company. ACT! refers to this type of a link as a **DYNAMIC** link. This is because the contacts associated to a company will change automatically, depending on whether or not the data in the contact record meets the criteria in the query. A contact record can meet the criteria in the query this week and not meet the criteria next week, if the data in any of the contact record fields that the query uses, changes. You will learn how to create queries in Lesson 11.

Exercise 5.4: Associate A Contact To A Company Record

There are several ways to associate contacts to a company record. In this exercise you will learn different ways to accomplish this task. Contact records can be associated to companies from the contact record. The opposite is also true. Contact records can be associated to companies from the company record.

1. Open the company record for My Other Company in the Company Detail view. On the Divisions tab, you should see the two divisions that you created for the company.

2. Click the Add/Remove Contacts to Company button on the Company toolbar.

3. Click the **CONTACTS** button on the dialog box, then type Doe in the Look for field.

4. Select the contact record for John Doe, then click the Add button.

5. Click OK.

   The contact should be in the **STATIC MEMBERS** section of the dialog box, as shown in Figure 5-8.

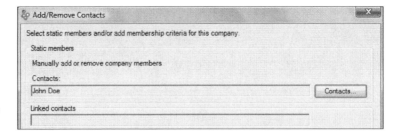

Figure 5-8 Add/Remove Contacts dialog box

6. Click OK. You will see the contact on the Contacts tab on the Company Detail record.

More Ways To Open The Add/Remove Contacts Dialog Box From A Company View

① Companies ⇒ Add/Remove Contacts.
② Right-click on the company name in the Companies tree or Company column (in the Company List view) and select Company Membership ⇒ Add/Remove Contacts
③ On the Contacts tab, click the Add/Remove Contacts button.
④ On the Contacts tab, on a blank space in the Contact List section, right-click and select Company Membership ⇒ Add/Remove Contacts, on the shortcut menu.

How To Open The Add/Remove Dialog Box From A Contact View

The options on this dialog box can also be used to add contacts to companies.

① Contacts ⇒ Add Selected to Company. You will see the dialog box shown in Figure 5-9.
② On the Contact List view, right-click and select Add Contacts to Company from the shortcut menu. You will see the dialog box shown in Figure 5-9.
③ On the Groups/Companies tab, select Companies and Divisions from the **SHOW FOR** drop-down list field, then click the Add/Remove Companies button, illustrated in Figure 5-10.

The entries in the list on the right are companies, divisions, subdivisions and groups that the contact is a member of.

I find this dialog box helpful because you can add and remove companies and divisions for the contact at the same time.

Figure 5-9 Add/Remove dialog box

Figure 5-10 Company options on the Groups/Companies tab on the Contact Detail view

Exercise 5.5: Create A Company Record From A Contact Record

Earlier you created a company record from scratch. Creating a company record from a contact record that has the address information for the company will keep you from having to type the same information in again. You can create a company record from a contact record by following the steps below.

Create Company From Contact Option

In ACT! 2010, selecting this option generates the error message shown in Figure 5-11. Currently, the way to fix this error is to open the Define Fields dialog box, select the Customer ID field and change the Permission to Full Access, as shown in Figure 5-12. When you learn how to use the Define Fields dialog box, you can come back and complete this exercise.

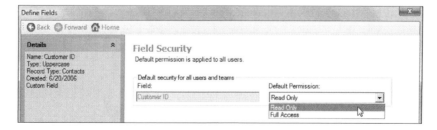

Figure 5-11 Read only error message

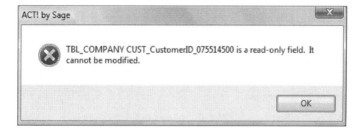

Figure 5-12 Field security options

1. Select the contact that has the information for the company record that you want to create. In this exercise select the contact Jane Bellamy of Boomers Artworx.

2. Contacts ⇒ Create Company from Contact.

The Company Detail view will open and the company name and address fields will automatically be filled in. If you needed to make any changes to the information for the new company record, you could. Notice in the Companies tree that the company name is similar to another company. The difference is the apostrophe in the other company name.

Exercise 5.6: Create A Contact Record From A Company Record

Creating a contact record from a company record that has the address information will keep you from having to type in the same information again. You can create a contact record from a company record by following the steps below.

1. Select the company in the Companies tree that has the information for the contact record that you want to create. In this exercise select the company Circle Photography.

2. Companies ⇒ Create Contact from Company. The Contact Detail view will open and the company name and address fields will automatically be filled in.

3. Type Test Record in the Contact field, then display another record.

Refreshing Linked Data In Contact Records

It is possible that you may not be viewing the most current data in the database. This happens when there are several people adding and editing records in the database. To make sure that you are viewing the most current data, refresh the data of the contact record that is displayed in the Contact Detail view.

Contacts ⇒ Update Linked Contact, will refresh the data. If this option is not available on the menu, it means that the contact is not linked to a company record.

Linking Company And Contact Records

If you scroll through the contact records you will see that some company names are blue and underlined and others are not. The company names that are blue and underlined are hyperlinked. You can click on this link to open the company, division or subdivision record.

Fields on the contact record that are linked will automatically be updated when the corresponding field in the company record is updated. This means that if the company name field on the company record changes from DEF Company to HIJ Company, any contact records that are linked to the DEF company on the company name field will automatically be updated if the **AUTOMATICALLY LINK NEW CONTACTS TO THEIR COMPANY RECORD** option is checked, as shown in Figure 5-13.

Tools ⇒ Preferences ⇒ Startup tab ⇒ Company Preferences button, will open the Company Preferences dialog box shown in Figure 5-13.

Figure 5-13 Company Preferences dialog box

The ellipsis button at the end of the Company field on a contact record that is not already linked, opens the dialog box shown in Figure 5-14.

If the contacts company name already exists in the database, you can link the contact to the company by selecting the company name on the dialog box.

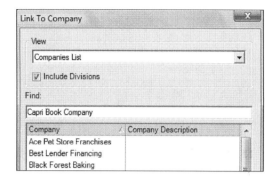

Figure 5-14 Link To Company dialog box

Associate vs Linking

On the surface, these terms sound like they have the same functionality. Understanding the difference is important if you have the need to make some contacts private. In ACT!, associating and linking have different functionality as discussed below. I find it somewhat deceiving how the "Private" option works.

In "My world", when you mark a contact as private, whether or not the contact is "linked" to a company, any information that you enter on any of the tabs for the contact is also marked as private by default. The exception would be if you manually override the private option for a specific piece of information. If a history record is created, the history record would also be automatically marked as private. Well, I started this paragraph off by saying in "My world".

The scenario that I just described is **NOT** how the private option works in ACT! if the contact record is marked as private and "linked" to a company record. When a note or history record is created for a contact that is linked to a company record, they are visible (available for other users to see) from the company record by default. If this is not what you want to happen, mark the note as private on the Insert Note dialog box.

Depending on a users rights, they may not be able to see all of the contact information that is displayed under the company record. Users that have rights to the contact record will be able to view the activity and opportunity records that are displayed under the company record.

Linking Issues

Overall, linking contacts to companies is a good feature to have and use. Depending on how sensitive some of the contact data is, you may not want it to be shared. Some contact data is automatically shared. I think that it is important that you understand how linking works.

By default, contact notes, history, activity and opportunity records are displayed under the company record(s) that they are linked to. I thought that if the link between a contact and company was removed, that the contacts history, activity and opportunity records would also be removed from the company record, but that is not the case.

I can understand why they are not automatically removed because the primary purpose of company records is to build a profile of the company, which includes the interactions with all of the contacts associated or linked with the company. I just wanted to let you know that the contacts linked data is not automatically removed from the company record when the contact record is unlinked.

Solutions
Fortunately, there are ways to prevent notes and history records that you want to remain private, from being displayed under the company record.

① As you already learned, when you create a note you can mark it as **PRIVATE**.
② If you know that you do not want any contact note and history records to be displayed under company records, clear the **SHARE NEW NOTES AND HISTORIES ON LINKED CONTACTS. . .** option shown earlier in Figure 5-13. With this option cleared (not checked), you can share a specific note if you have the need to do so.

Contacts can be associated to multiple companies and divisions, but can only be linked to one company.

Associating Companies And Groups

You can associate companies and groups to the following types of records: Activity, history, notes and opportunity with relative ease, as you will learn throughout this book. Each of the dialog boxes listed below have an **ASSOCIATE WITH** or **SHARE WITH** field. Click the ellipsis button at the end of either of these fields and select the companies and groups that you want to associate to the record.

    ①   Schedule Activities [See Lesson 7, Figure 7-1]
    ②   Record History [See Lesson 10, Figure 10-19]
    ③   Edit History [See Lesson 10, Figure 10-24]
    ④   Insert Note [See Lesson 3, Figure 3-19]

Exercise 5.7: Creating Manual Links Between Contacts And Companies

In this exercise you will learn several ways to link contact and company records.

Manually Link A New Contact With A Company

In this part of the exercise you will create the contact record and then link it to a company.

1. Open a new contact record and enter the name Jane Doe.

2. Click the ellipsis button next to the Company field, then select the company, My Company and click OK. You will see that the company name is a link on the Contact Detail view.

3. Click the Save Changes button. If you click on the company link, you will see the company record on the Company Detail view.

Manually Link An Existing Contact With A Company

In this part of the exercise you will learn how to link an existing contact to a company.

1. Right-click in the Contact field in the Contact Detail view and select **LOOKUP CONTACT**.

2. Type Charles Smith in the Contact field, then press Enter.

3. Click the ellipsis button next to the Company field. Select the company, My Company, then click OK.

> **Link Or Associate Contacts To Divisions Or Subdivisions**
>
> You can link or associate a contact to a division or subdivision the same way that you link a contact to a company. In both parts of Exercise 5.7, instead of selecting the company, select the division or subdivision.

Exercise 5.8: Link Multiple Contact Records To A Company Record

This type of linking is another example of the static link option that you learned about earlier. This is one way that you can change the company that several contacts are linked to, at the same time.

1. Create a lookup that retrieves records that have **LOOKUP** in the Company field.

2. Select (highlight) both records in the Contact List view, then Contacts ⇒ Link to Company.

3. Select the company, My Other Company, then click OK.

4. Click OK when prompted that no more records match the search criteria.

If you look at the My Other Company record on the Company Detail view, you will see that both contacts (Laura Smith and Tom Wood) have the new company name. Their old company name was "Lookup".

Exercise 5.9: Understanding The Power Of Linking

In the previous exercise you linked two contact records to a company record. Figure 5-15 shows the company and contacts associated with it. Notice that the Company field for John Doe is blank. This is how you can visually tell which contacts are linked to a company and which ones are associated to a company. In this exercise you will rename the company and observe the changes.

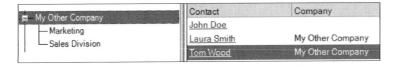

Figure 5-15 Contacts linked and associated to the same company

1. Open the My Other Company record in the Company Detail view.

2. Change the Company name to My New Company.

3. View ⇒ Refresh. This will update the company name throughout the database.

Linking And Unlinking Contact And Company Fields

You have learned that you can link the company name field on the contact record to the company name field in the company record. This is also true for other fields on the contact record.

An important concept to remember about linking fields is that the fields that you want to link should be the same data type or a compatible data type. Otherwise, you will have trouble linking the fields. For example, you should not try to link a date field to an email field.

 If you created a linked company record field it is applied to all company records, not just a particular record. The same is true if you unlink a company record field.

Viewing Linked Fields

Companies ⇒ View Linked Fields, will display how company fields are linked to contact fields, as shown in Figure 5-16.

The **DEFINE FIELDS** button opens a dialog box that is used to create, edit or delete fields. You will learn more about this option in the next exercise.

Figure 5-16 View Linked Fields dialog box

Exercise 5.10: Create A Linked Billing Address Field

In this exercise you will modify the Billing Address 1 field in the company record so that it is linked to the contact User 5 field. This is not a link that you would create in a live database because it really does not make a lot of sense. The fields that are normally linked between contact and company records are already linked in this database, as shown above in Figure 5-16. Therefore, I had to select fields that were not already linked, to demonstrate how to use the linking feature.

1. Tools ⇒ Define Fields.

   Notice that the database is locked, as illustrated in Figure 5-17.

Figure 5-17 Locked database notification illustrated

2. Open the **VIEW FIELDS FOR** drop-down list on the Define Fields dialog box and select Companies, if it is not already selected.

3. Click on the Billing Address 1 field.

   Click the **EDIT FIELD** link, illustrated in Figure 5-18, then click Next.

Figure 5-18 Edit Field link illustrated

4. On the Customize field behavior screen, check the **LINK TO CONTACT FIELD** option, then open the drop-down list. Notice that some fields are not enabled in the drop-down list. You cannot select these fields to link to, because they have already been linked to a field.

5. Scroll down the list and select the User 5 field, then click Finish.

   In Figure 5-19, you will see that the Billing Address 1 field is linked to the User 5 contact field.

Figure 5-19 Billing Address 1 field linked to the User 5 contact field

6. Click Close.

Billing And Shipping Tab

> In ACT! 2008 and earlier, this was called the **ADDRESSES** tab.

The fields shown in Figure 5-20 are used to store the billing and shipping address of the company, division or subdivision.

Figure 5-20 Billing and Shipping tab fields

Updating Contact Address Fields From The Linked Company Record

If a company moves, you would update the address fields on the company record. The next step is to update the contact records that are linked to the company record so that they display the updated address information. Before changing the company record, it is a good idea to view the linked contacts to make sure that they have the address that you are about to change.

Companies can have several locations which means that there would be different addresses for the same company. You could create divisions under the company or create a different company record for each location. The steps below will show you how to change the address on the company record and update the linked contact records. For now you can read the steps. In the next exercise you will be able to practice this technique.

1. Open the company record and change the information in the linked field, then save the changes.

2. Click the **UPDATES LINKED CONTACTS FOR THE CURRENT COMPANY** button on the Companies toolbar.

3. Click **YES** when you see the message shown in Figure 5-21.

Figure 5-21 Update linked contacts message

Test The Linked Field That You Created

To test the linked field, you will enter data in the Company Billing Address 1 field and observe how the linked contact records are updated.

1. Select the company My New Company, then click on the Billing and Shipping tab.

2. Type `Test field link` in the Address 1 Billing field.

3. Click the Updates linked contacts for the current company button on the Companies toolbar. Click Yes when you see the message shown above in Figure 5-21. The contact records will now be updated.

 If you click the Save Changes button after making this type of change, you will also see the dialog box shown above in Figure 5-21.

4. On the Contacts tab on the Company Detail view, click on one of the records that has the company name, My New Company.

5. On the User Fields tab of the contact record, you should see the text that you entered in the Billing Address 1 field in the User 5 field, as shown in Figure 5-22.

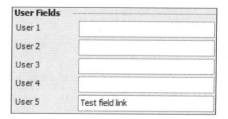

Figure 5-22 User 5 field updated

User Fields Tab

In the exercise that you just completed, you added data to a user field. If this were a live database you would rename the user field and update the layout. If you do not do this, other people that use the database will not know what type of data should be entered in the field.

Company Profile Tab

The fields shown in
Figure 5-23 track the
region, industry, revenue,
SIC Code and more for
each company, division
and subdivision.

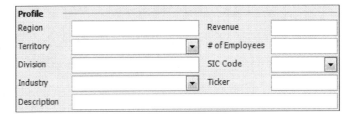

Figure 5-23 Company Profile tab fields

Company Access Tab

  In ACT! 2008 and earlier, this was called the **COMPANY INFO** tab.

The fields shown in Figure 5-24, except for
the Access Level options are updated by
ACT! automatically. These fields store
when the company record was created,
by who and when it was last changed.

Figure 5-24 Company Access tab fields

The **RECORD MANAGER** field can be manually changed to another user by the record owner.
The **EDITED ON/BY** field contains when and who last updated the record.

Unlink A Company Record Field

If you have a company record field that is linked, but no longer need it to be linked, follow the
steps below. You do not have to complete these steps now.

1. Tools ⇒ Define Fields.

2. Select the field that you want to unlink, then click the **EDIT FIELD** link.

3. Click Next, then clear the
   LINK TO CONTACT FIELD option
   shown in Figure 5-25.

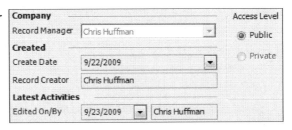

Figure 5-25 Customize field behavior options

4. Click Finish, then click Close.

Previously linked contact record fields that have data will keep the data even though the field is no longer linked to a company record field. Keep in mind that contact records can link to company records, which would update the company record when a contact record is changed.

Adding Contacts To Divisions

There are several ways to add contacts as discussed below. It would be easier if we could use drop and drag to add or move a contact record from one company or division to another one.

① Right-click on the division in the Companies tree and select
COMPANY MEMBERSHIP ⇒ **ADD/REMOVE CONTACTS**. You will see the Add/Remove Contacts dialog box.

② Right-click on the contact on the Company Detail view and select
COMPANY MEMBERSHIP ⇒ **ADD/REMOVE CONTACTS**. You will see the Add/Remove Contacts dialog box.

③ Right-click on the contact on the Company Detail view and select
COMPANY MEMBERSHIP ⇒ **ADD SELECTED TO COMPANY**. You will see the Add/Remove dialog box.

Exercise 5.11: Using The Companies Tree To Move A Division

You can drag divisions from one company to another. You can also drag a company to another company and make it a division.

1. In the Companies tree, expand the two companies that you created earlier in this lesson by clicking on the plus sign in front of them.

2. Drag the Finance division from the first company to the second company.

   Click Yes when prompted if you are sure that you want to move the company, in this case a division, to a new location.

   The Companies tree should look like the one shown in Figure 5-26.

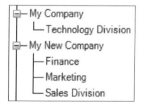

Figure 5-26 Division moved from one company to another

3. Use the Companies tree to move the contacts in Table 5-4 to the appropriate division.

Contact	Move From	Move To
Tom Wood	My New Company	Marketing
Laura Smith	My New Company	Sales Division
Jane Doe	My Company	Finance
Charles Smith	My Company	Sales Division

Table 5-4 Contacts to move

Exercise 5.12: Duplicating Company And Division Records

You can duplicate a company that has divisions, but the divisions are not duplicated.
This is known as **DUPLICATING** a company. The process is similar to duplicating contacts.

1. In the Company Detail view, right-click on the company, My New Company and select Duplicate.

2. On the dialog box shown in Figure 5-27, select the option **DUPLICATE DATA FROM ALL FIELDS**, then click OK.

Figure 5-27 Duplicate Company dialog box

3. Click the Save Changes button. Click Yes when prompted to continue.

4. You will see a company record that looks like the one that you duplicated. Type My Duplicate Company in the Company field.

5. View ⇒ Refresh. Click on the new company in the tree.

Notice that there are no divisions and that the contact John Doe is a member. That is because this contact is not linked to the company, My New Company. If you click on the company record, My New Company, you will see the two other contacts shown earlier in Figure 5-15 because they are linked to the company.

Looking Up Companies

Looking up companies is similar to looking up contacts. Lookup ⇒ Companies, will display the Lookup Companies dialog box, which is similar to the dialog box that you use to look up contacts. The differences are discussed below.

① The Title bar on the dialog box has "Lookup Companies" instead of "Lookup Contacts".
② The fields in the first drop-down list are company related fields.

Exercise 5.13: Finding Companies

It is really important to make sure that the company data is as accurate as possible. Often, when adding a new company, you may not know or have all of the information that you want to enter for the company. From time to time it is a good idea to either look up records that do not have data in certain fields or create reports that show records that are missing data. If your company does a variety of promotional campaigns, it may be important to track how each contact was obtained. You could use the Referred By field to store this information. In this exercise you will find companies where the Referred By field is empty.

1. Lookup ⇒ Other Fields.

2. Open the Field drop-down list and select Referred By.

3. Open the second drop-down list and select the option **DOES NOT CONTAIN DATA**, then click OK.

The companies and divisions that you see in the Company List view do not have the Referred By field filled in. Someone should try to fill in this information.

Create A Company Note And Attachment

Creating a note for a company is the same process as creating a note for a contact. Creating a note for a company uses the same Insert Note dialog box that is used for creating notes for contacts. Creating a note with an attachment is also the same process as attaching a file to a contact record. Right-click on the company that you want to create a note for and select **INSERT COMPANY NOTE**. The company name will automatically be filled in the Group/Company field on the Insert Note dialog box.

Viewing Company Notes

Over time, the number of notes for companies can grow. If contacts are associated with a company, the Notes tab on the Company Detail view will have even more notes for you to sift through.

As shown in Figure 5-28, the Notes tab on the Company Detail view has the **SHOW FOR** drop-down list filter.

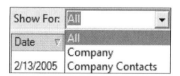

Figure 5-28 Notes tab on the Company Detail view

ALL will display both company and company contact notes.
COMPANY only displays notes that are created from a company record.
COMPANY CONTACTS only displays notes that were created for a contact in the company.

The difference between the Company and Company Contacts options are the level that the notes are created at.

Moving Companies And Divisions

Earlier in this lesson you learned that in the Companies tree you can drag companies and divisions to new locations. If you do not like to drag them, you can use the **MOVE** option on the shortcut menu shown earlier in Figure 5-4. You can complete this task from either company view. The steps below explain the process.

1. Right-click on the company or division that you want to move and select **MOVE**.

2. Select one of the options discussed below.

   ① On the dialog box shown in Figure 5-29, select the **PROMOTE DIVISION TO COMPANY** option to make the division that you selected a company.

   ② Select the **CHANGE TO BE DIVISION OF** option if you want the company or division that you selected to be a division of another company.

Figure 5-29 Move Division dialog box

3. Select the company that you want to move it to on the Move Division dialog box, then click OK.

Deleting A Company Record

If you need to delete a company record, any division records under it will be promoted to a company record, unless you delete the division record(s) first. You will not receive a warning that the company record that you are deleting has division record(s).

Removing Links Between Contact And Company Records

If a contact record is linked on the Company (name) field, it cannot be changed until you remove the link. You already learned that contact notes and history records that appear under the company record are not automatically removed. Removing the link between the contact and company is how the contact notes and history records remain under the company record. When you have the need to remove links, you can follow the steps below.

1. Open the contact record (in the Contact Detail view) that you want to remove the company link from.

2. Click the ellipsis button at the end of the Company field. You will see the message shown in Figure 5-30.

   The **UNLINK FROM COMPANY** option will remove the link between the contact and company records.

Figure 5-30 Unlink from Company dialog box

The **LINK TO A DIFFERENT COMPANY** option shown above in Figure 5-30, is used to link the contact to a different company. This would be helpful if the contact needs to be moved to a different company.

Selecting this option, then clicking OK opens the dialog box shown in Figure 5-31, which is used to select the company.

Figure 5-31 Link To Company dialog box

The company or division that you want to move the contact to, must already have a record in the database.

3. Click OK on the Unlink from Company dialog box. The link will be removed from the Company name field.

Using The Company List View

While the Company Detail view is probably the company view that you will use most often, the Company List view provides the same functionality. The Company List view shown in Figure 5-32 has the same shortcut menu options as the Companies tree shown earlier in Figure 5-3. Actually, the shortcut menu in the Company List view has more options. Like the Contact List view, you can sort on the column headings in the Company List view. If there are a lot of companies in the list you may have a need to filter them.

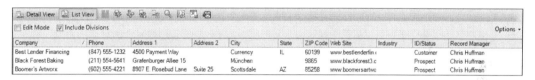

Figure 5-32 Company List view

The **EDIT MODE** option is used to modify records in the Contact List view.

The **INCLUDE DIVISIONS** option will display all of the divisions and subdivisions in the database. The problem is that the default options on the Company List view do not provide a visual way to know which record is a company, division or subdivision or which company a division or subdivision record belongs to.

If you customize the view and add the **HAS DIVISIONS**, **DIVISION** and **HIERARCHY LEVEL** fields to the view, you will be able to tell a division from a company, but not which company a division belongs to, as shown in Figure 5-33.

Hierarchy Level 0 is a company record.

Hierarchy Level 1 is a company or division record.

Hierarchy Level 2 is a division record.

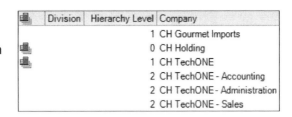

Figure 5-33 Company List view with division fields

Create A New Division

To create a new division from the Company List view, right-click on the company that you want to create the division for and select **NEW DIVISION**.

NEW Company Detail View Related Tasks

The related tasks options shown in Figure 5-34 are primarily on the detail view. Some options are also on the list view. The options are explained below.

Figure 5-34 Company Detail view related tasks

CREATE NEW CONTACT FROM COMPANY Opens a new contact record with the company fields filled in, that are filled in on the company record that was selected before clicking on the link.

For example, Figure 5-35 shows a company record in detail view (in the 1024x768 layout). Figure 5-36 shows the contact record created from this company record. Notice that the Referred By field was not automatically filled in.

Figure 5-35 Company record in detail view

Figure 5-36 Contact record created, based on a company record

ATTACH FILE Opens the template folder so that you can select a file to attach to the current company. The file is added to the History tab.

LOOKUP COMPANY CONTACTS Displays the contacts that are on the Company Contacts tab on the Contact List view.

VIEW FIELDS LINKED TO CONTACTS Opens the View Linked Fields dialog box shown earlier in Figure 5-16.

UPDATE FIELDS LINKED TO CONTACTS Is used to update the linked field data for contacts linked to the company that is selected.

WRITE E-MAIL USING TEMPLATE Opens the Template folder (for the database) so that you can select a template to use for the email that you want to create. Once you select the template, a new email window will open with the template that you selected. If you selected multiple contacts on the Contacts tab, a mail merge document will be created for each contact.

SCHEDULE SERIES OF ACTIVITIES [See Lesson 7, Activity Series]

MODIFY LAYOUT Opens the current company detail view layout in the Layout Designer, so that the layout can be changed.

NEW Company List View Related Tasks

The options shown in Figure 5-37 are for the Company List view. The options that are only on the list view are explained below.

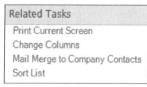

Figure 5-37 Company List view related tasks

PRINT CURRENT SCREEN Opens the Quick Print Options dialog box so that you can select options for how the screen will be printed.

CHANGE COLUMNS Opens the Customize Columns dialog box.

MAIL MERGE TO COMPANY CONTACTS Opens the Mail Merge Wizard. [See Lesson 15, Exercise 15.2]

SORT LIST Opens the Sort dialog box to sort the companies displayed in the view.

GROUPING CONTACTS

In this lesson you will learn about the following group and subgroup record options:

- ☑ Using the Groups tree
- ☑ Creating groups
- ☑ Adding contacts to a group or subgroup
- ☑ Managing group notes and attachments
- ☑ Saving the result of a lookup as a group or company
- ☑ Creating subgroups
- ☑ Converting a group to a company
- ☑ Using the Convert Groups to Companies Wizard

LESSON 6

Groups Overview

Grouping records is another way for you to be able to categorize and find contacts. You have learned how to use the lookup command to find contacts. The limitation to using the lookup command is that all of the contact records that you want to find have to have the same information in the same field. You could think of the group option as a free form way to classify or categorize contacts, because the contacts that you add to a group do not have to have any data in common. Like company records, group records can have 15 levels. You can create as many groups as you need.

If you wanted to group certain contacts together because they are all involved in the same project, you could create a group. You can add a contact to as many groups as needed. Grouping contacts helps you find and organize them quickly. The main benefit to creating groups over creating lookups, is that the group information is saved. Figure 6-1 shows the Group Detail view.

Figure 6-1 Group Detail view

The top right section of the Group Detail view displays the group name and description of the group that is selected in the tree. The bottom right section displays different information depending on which tab is selected. For example, the Group Access tab shows information about when the group was created, whether or not the group is private and who created it. The names on the Contacts tab are the contacts or companies that are in the group.

Group Detail View Toolbar

Figure 6-2 shows the Group Detail view toolbar. Table 6-1 explains the buttons on the toolbar.

Figure 6-2 Group Detail view toolbar

Button	Description
1	Displays the Group Detail view.
2	Displays the Group List view.
3	Saves the record. (1)
4	Opens the Quick Print Options dialog box.
5	Adds or removes a contact from a group. (2)
6	Attach a file. (2)
7	Creates a lookup of the group that is selected.
8	Is used to select a layout. (1)
9	Displays the ACT! E-marketing options, which requires a paid subscription.

Table 6-1 Group Detail view toolbar buttons explained

(1) This option is only available on the Group Detail view.
(2) This option applies to groups and subgroups.

Good Groups And Not So Good Groups

These are the types of groups that you can create. An example of a not so good group would be a group that contains contacts in the same state. This is not a good use of a group because you can create a lookup by state to accomplish this.

An example of a good group would be a group that contains contacts that attended an insurance seminar that you were a guest speaker at. This is a good group because there is no existing field that you could create a lookup on to find these contacts. You could create an activity for the contacts in the group. It would appear on the Activities tab for the group.

Groups Tree

The Groups tree is on the left side of the Group Detail view. At the top of the Groups tree, the number of groups and subgroups in the database are displayed at the top of the Groups tree, as shown earlier in Figure 6-1. If you click on a group in the tree, you will see the subgroups on the Subgroups tab.

A plus sign in front of a group means that there is at least one subgroup below it. The Employees group shown in Figure 6-3 has two subgroups; International Employees and USA Employees. The International Employees group has two subgroups; AsiaPac Employees and European Employees.

Figure 6-3 Groups and Subgroups on the Subgroups tab

 The **UP** button illustrated above in Figure 6-3 is enabled if the group or subgroup that is selected is part of a larger group. Clicking this button will move up the hierarchy, one level at a time. This button is also on the Company Detail view. If you double-click on any subgroup shown, the detail record for the subgroup will be displayed.

 View Groups/Companies Button And Dialog Box

The View Groups/Companies button was on the Contacts, Groups and Company Detail views in ACT! 2009 and earlier. It opened a dialog box with the same name. The dialog box was used to view companies and group. This button has been removed.

Exercise 6.1: How To Create A Group

1. Click the **GROUPS** button in the Navigation Pane.

2. Click the **NEW** button on the Global toolbar. You should see a new group record at the top on the right of the window.

 You can also right-click on a blank space in the Groups tree and select **NEW GROUP**.

3. Type `Potential Customer` in the Group Name field.

4. Press the Tab key, then type `This group contains contacts that are interested in the next version of the book` in the Description field.

 The Description field can have up to 128 characters.

5. Click the Save Changes button.

   The group record should look like the one shown in Figure 6-4.

Figure 6-4 New group record created

Notice that the **HIERARCHY** field was filled in automatically and that the group appears on the left side of the window.

Adding Contacts To A Group

There are several ways that you can add contacts to a group (or subgroup), as discussed below:

① You can scroll through the entire list of contacts in the Contact List view and select the contacts that you want, one by one and add them to a group. This is known as a **STATIC** group. The contacts stay in the group until you remove them.

② If possible, you can use the lookup command to find at least some of the contact records that you want to add to a group.

③ Select an existing group and add contacts from the existing group to the new group.

④ Contacts can automatically be added to a group if they meet the criteria of the query. This is known as a **DYNAMIC** group because contacts are added and removed based on whether or not they meet the criteria. There is no intervention on your part after creating the query. This type of group is updated each time the Groups/Companies tab on the Contact Detail or Group Detail view is displayed.

An example is a group for contacts that have the Sales Rep title. Contacts added to the database that have this title would automatically be added to the group. Any contact in the group whose title changes from Sales Rep would automatically be removed from the group. You will learn how to create this type of group in Lesson 11.

The benefit of using the last three options discussed above to add contacts to a group is that you do not have to scroll through all of the records in the database to select contacts to add to a group.

When you add a contact that has a note to a group, the contacts notes are displayed on the Groups Notes tab, unless the note is marked private. The owner of the private note will see the note on the Groups Notes tab, but other database users will not.

Exercise 6.2: How To Add Contacts One By One To A Group

The contacts that you will add to the group in this exercise are static.

1. Select the group that you want to add contacts to. In this exercise select the Potential Customer group.

2. Click the **ADD/REMOVE CONTACTS TO GROUP** button on the toolbar or click the **ADD/REMOVE CONTACTS** button on the Contacts tab. You will see the Add/Remove Contacts dialog box.

3. Click the Contacts button.

4. Click on the contact Ashley Allan, then press and hold down the **CTRL** key and click on the following names: Bruce Baker, Sarah Baker and Kirby York.

5. Click the **ADD** button.

   The four contacts that you selected should be visible in the **SELECTED CONTACTS** list, as shown in Figure 6-5.

Figure 6-5 Contacts selected to be added to the group

The options in the **SELECT FROM** drop-down list and the (Group names) drop-down list to the right of it, are used to narrow or widen the number of names that appear in the **CONTACTS TO SELECT FROM** list. If you select the **GROUPS** option from the first drop-down list and the Hot Opportunities group from the second drop-down list you will see the contacts shown on the left of Figure 6-6.

If the database has a lot of names and you do not want to scroll through the list, you can type the name that you want to add to the group in the **LOOK FOR** field.

Figure 6-6 Contacts from an existing group

 If you scroll through the list of names on the left, you will see that the names that you have already selected for the group are grayed out. This lets you know that the contact is already a member of the current group or has been selected to be a member of the current group.

6. Click OK. You should see the contacts in the **STATIC MEMBERS** section of the Add/Remove Contacts dialog box.

7. Click OK. The contacts will now be added to the Potential Customer group. You will see the contacts at the bottom of the Contacts tab, as shown in Figure 6-7.

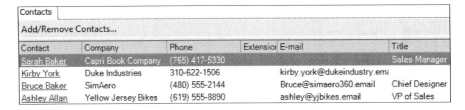

Figure 6-7 Contacts added to the group

To add a contact to a group, you can right-click on a contact record on either contact view and select **ADD CONTACT TO GROUP.**

Looking Up Groups

Looking up groups is similar to looking up companies. Lookup ⇒ Groups ⇒ Select an option, will display the same dialog box that you used in Lesson 4 to look up contacts. The differences on the Lookup dialog box are the same as the differences between contacts and companies. [See Lesson 5, Looking Up Companies]

Exercise 6.3: Finding Group Records

You have already learned how to find (look up) all of the contacts that were associated with a company. Looking up contacts that are in the same group is basically the same process. In this exercise you will create a look up for groups that do not have data in the Address 1 field.

1. Lookup ⇒ Other Fields.

2. Open the Field drop-down list and select the Address 1 field.

3. Open the next drop-down list and select the **DOES NOT CONTAIN DATA** option, then click OK.

You will see the groups that do not have any information in the Address 1 field. If you double-click on any group in the Group List view and then click on the Group Address tab, you will see that the Address 1 field is empty.

Exercise 6.4: How To Rename A Group

The steps below will show you how to rename a group. To rename a subgroup, select the subgroup in step 1 instead of a group.

1. Click on the group that you want to rename in the Groups tree. In this exercise click on the Potential Customer group.

2. Type in the new group name. Type the word Book after the word **POTENTIAL** in the Group Name field on the right.

3. Click the Save Changes button. The group will be renamed and the new name is displayed on the Groups tree.

 The reason that I click the Save Changes button is because it refreshes the view. If you clicked on another group or subgroup in the tree and then come back to the group that you changed, you would see that the group was renamed.

Exercise 6.5: Add Contacts To An Existing Group

In this exercise you will find contacts in Arizona and add them to the Potential Book Customer group. To add contacts to a subgroup, select the subgroup in step 3 below instead of a group.

Create The Lookup And Add The Contacts To The Group

1. Create a lookup to find all contacts in Arizona. There should be 19 records in the Contact List view.

2. Select (highlight) all of the records, then right-click on the highlighted records and select **ADD CONTACTS TO GROUP**, as illustrated in Figure 6-8.

Figure 6-8 Option to add the contacts to a group illustrated

 If you do not want to right-click on the records, you can use Contacts ⇒ Add Selected to Group.

3. Click on the Potential Book Customer group shown in Figure 6-9, then click OK.

Figure 6-9 Group selected to add the contacts to

View The Contacts In The Group

1. Click the Groups button on the Navigation Pane, then click on the Potential Book Customer group in the Groups tree.

2. On the Contacts tab, you should see the contacts that you just added, plus the contacts that you added in a prior exercise. Click the Save Changes button.

Exercise 6.6: Use The Lookup Command To Add Contacts To A Group

You can use this option when you have several records that have something in common that you want to add to the same group or subgroup. In this exercise you will create a lookup to find all contacts that have the Sales Representative title. After that, you will create a group and add the contacts to a group.

1. Create a lookup that finds all contacts that have Sales Representative as the title. Five records should have been retrieved. (**Hint**: Lookup ⇒ Contacts ⇒ Other Fields)

2. Click on the arrow on the New button on the Global toolbar and select Group, as shown in Figure 6-10.

Figure 6-10 New button options

3. Type `Sales Reps` in the Group Name field, then type `This group contains all of the sales reps.` in the Description field.

4. Click the Add/Remove Contacts button on the Contacts tab, then click the Contacts button.

5. Select the **CURRENT LOOKUP** option from the first drop-down list.

    You should only see the contacts from the lookup that you created, in the list of names on the left side of the dialog box, as shown in Figure 6-11.

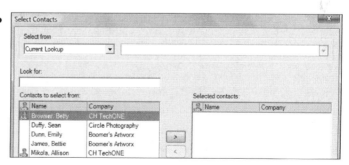

Figure 6-11 Contacts from the current look up

6. Click the **ADD ALL>>** button. All of the contacts should be in the **SELECTED CONTACTS** list on the right side of the dialog box. Click OK twice to close both dialog boxes.

7. In the Group Detail view click on the Sales Reps group in the Groups tree, if it is not already selected. On the Contacts tab you will see the five contacts that are in the group.

How To View The Groups That A Contact Is A Member Of

1. Click on the link for Emily Dunn.

2. On the Groups/Companies tab in the Contact Detail view, open the **SHOW FOR** drop-down list and select Groups and Subgroups. You will see that this contact is a member of the Sales Rep group that you just created and the Potential Book Customer group that you created earlier in this lesson.

Exercise 6.7: How To Manage Group Notes And Attachments

The Notes tab on the Group Detail view is used to view notes for the group, just like you can view notes for a contact. If you create a note for the group, you only have to type it in once and it will be associated with all contacts in the group. You can also assign a contacts note to a group. There are several ways to create a note for a group.

 All of the group management of notes and attachments discussed in this exercise also apply to creating, editing and maintaining company notes and attachments.

How To Create A Group Note And Attach A File To The Group Note

In addition to adding a note to a group, you can attach files like charts, spreadsheets or sales literature to a group. Doing this allows you to keep all of the attachments for the group in one place.

1. Click the Groups button, then click on the Potential Book Customer group.

2. On the Notes tab, click the **INSERT NEW NOTE** button. You should see the Potential Book Customer group name in the Share with field on the Insert Note dialog box.

3. Type These contacts have requested a book catalog. in the field at the bottom of the dialog box.

4. Select the text that you just typed and change the font to Comic Sans MS, then change the font size to 12.

5. Change the color to red. The color option is to the right of the Font size drop-down list. Leave the dialog box open to complete the next part of the exercise.

How To Attach A File To A Group

Attaching a file to a group record is the same process as attaching a file to a contact record.

1. Click the **ATTACH** button, then select File.

2. Double-click on the L2 Attach file in your folder. The note should look like the one shown in Figure 6-12. Click OK.

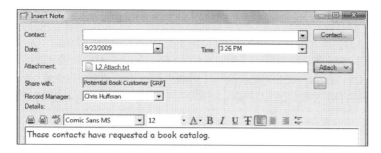

Figure 6-12 Group note

View The Group Notes And Attachments

1. On the Notes tab, open the **SHOW FOR** drop-down list and select Group. The entry should be the one for the note shown above in Figure 6-12.

2. Click on the Attachment icon for the note. The attached file will open. Close the attached file.

Exercise 6.8: Assign A Contact Note To A Group And Individual Contacts

In this exercise you will complete the following tasks:

① Create two notes for a contact that is in a group.
② Associate one of the notes to contacts in the group that the contact in the task above, is a member of.
③ Associate one of the notes to one contact that is not in the group.
④ Associate the second note to a group that the contact in the first task above is not a member of.

Add The Contact To Another Group

1. Click on the Potential Book Customer group on the Group Detail view.

2. On the Contacts tab, right-click on the contact Sarah Baker and select Group Membership ⇒ Add Selected to Group.

3. Scroll down the list of groups on the left of the dialog box and select the Prospects - Hot Opportunities group, then click the Add button.

The contact should be a member of the two groups shown on the right of Figure 6-13.

Click OK.

Figure 6-13 Add Contacts to Groups/Company dialog box

Create The Notes

In this part of the exercise you will create the notes for Sarah Baker.

1. Open the Contact Detail view for the contact Sarah Baker. (**Hint:** If you are in the Group Detail view, click on the contacts name on the Contacts tab).

2. Click on the Notes tab and create the notes in Table 6-2.

Note	Regarding Field	Formatting
1	This is the first contact note for S. Baker. It will be applied to individual contacts in 2 groups and 1 contact that is not in a group.	Change the font size to 10. Change the text color to green and bold.
2	This is the second contact note for S. Baker. It will be applied to the group via the Insert Note dialog box.	Change the color of the text to purple, bold and italic. Complete steps 3 and 4 below, before closing this note.

Table 6-2 Notes to create for Sarah Baker

3. Click the button at the end of the Share with field on the Insert Note dialog box. Click OK to share the note, as indicated in Figure 6-14.

Figure 6-14 Sharing a public note message

4. Select the Potential Book Customer group and add it to the note. You should have the options shown in Figure 6-15.

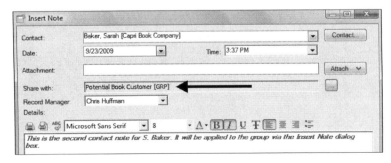

Figure 6-15 Note associated to a group

5. Click OK to close the Insert Notes dialog box.

Associate The Notes

In this part of the exercise you will associate the two notes that you just created to other contacts.

1. Locate the first note that you created in Table 6-2 above for Sarah Baker in either the Contact Detail or Group Detail view, then double-click on the note.

2. Click the **CONTACT** button on the Edit Note dialog box and add the contact George Bailey to the Selected contacts list.

3. Open the **SELECT FROM** drop-down list on the Select Contacts dialog box and select Groups, then select the Sales Reps group from the next drop-down list. You will see the contacts for the group at the bottom of the dialog box.

4. Add Bettie James to the contact list.

5. Select the Prospects group from the second drop-down list at the top of the dialog box.

6. Add the contacts Mary Bailey and Kirby York.

   You should have the contacts selected that are shown in Figure 6-16.

Figure 6-16 Group contacts selected

7. Click OK twice to close both dialog boxes.

   When you see the dialog box shown in Figure 6-17 select the first option, then click OK.

Figure 6-17 Edit shared note options

Editing A Shared Note

After creating a note, you may need to update the information in the note. When you modify a note that is shared with groups or contacts, you will see the dialog box shown above in Figure 6-17. Select the option for how you want the changes to the note to be applied.

View The Notes

1. Create a lookup by last name. Search for Bailey. You will see three contacts.

2. Switch to the Contact Detail view. George and Mary Bailey will have the first note in Table 6-2 above (in green). Peter Bailey does not. This is correct.

3. Switch to the Group Detail view. The note with green text should also be available in the Prospects group. If you do not see the note, select **GROUP CONTACTS** in the Show for drop-down list.

4. View the Potential Book Customer group notes. You will see the second note that you created in Table 6-2 above. You will also see the first note because it was created by Chris Huffman (aka you) who is a member of the Potential Book Customer group.

Show For Drop-Down List Options

The options in the **SHOW FOR** drop-down list shown in Figure 6-18 are available on the Notes, History, Activities and Opportunities tabs in the Group Detail view.

The options are used to filter the records that are displayed on the tab. [See Lesson 5, Viewing Company Notes]

Figure 6-18 Show For drop-down list options

By default, group level notes cannot be viewed on the Notes tab in the Contact Detail view. To know if there is a group note for the contact, click on the Groups/Companies tab on the Contact Detail view. Double-click on the group, then click on the Notes tab in the Group Detail view.

If the note is long, you will not see all of it on the Notes tab. If you look to the far right of the window, you should see a shaded area. This is the Preview area.

If you click on a note, you will see the entire note on the right side in the Preview area. You can resize the Preview area by placing the mouse pointer in the position illustrated in Figure 6-19, then drag the mouse pointer in the direction that you want to resize the window to.

If you do not want to have the Preview area visible, you can hide it by clicking on the Options button shown in Figure 6-19 and clearing the **SHOW PREVIEW** option, shown in Figure 6-20. You can do this on any Notes tab.

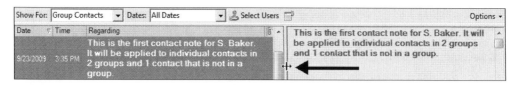

Figure 6-19 Preview area illustrated

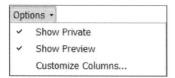

Figure 6-20 Options button drop-down list

Exercise 6.9: How To Save The Result Of A Lookup As A Group Or Company

If you create a lookup that you will need to use over and over, you can save it as a Group or Company by following the steps below. The number of records in this type of group or company can change. If the value in the field(s) that the lookup is using changes and now meets the criteria, the contact record will automatically be added to the group or company. If the value in a contact record field changes and no longer meets the lookup criteria, the record will automatically be removed from the group or company.

In this exercise you will save the results of the lookup as a group and a company. On your own, you do not have to save the same lookup results both ways. Select the option that works best for you.

1. Create an Email Address lookup for contacts that do not have an email address. 100 records should be retrieved.

2. Lookup ⇒ Groups ⇒ Save Lookup as Group.

3. Type `My Group Lookup No Email Address` as the group name, then View ⇒ Refresh, or press the F5 key.

4. Lookup ⇒ Companies ⇒ Save Lookup as Company.

5. Type `My Company Lookup No Email Address` as the company name, then View ⇒ Refresh.

If you view the records under the company and group that you just created, you will see that both have the same records. Normally, you would not save the same records to a group and company. It is done here for illustration purposes so that you can learn both methods of saving the result of a lookup.

Subgroups

A subgroup is usually a subset of the contacts in the group. In the previous exercise you created a group that contains contacts that do not have an email address. If you wanted to further categorize the contacts in the group by company, title, state, status or just about anything that you can think of, you can create a subgroup. Subgroups can be 15 levels deep, meaning subgroups can have subgroups. Subgroups are similar to divisions that companies have.

Exercise 6.10: Creating Subgroups

In this exercise you will create two subgroups for the My Group Lookup No Email Address group: One for sales reps and one for title.

1. In the Group Detail view, right-click on the My Group Lookup No Email Address group in the Groups tree and select **NEW SUBGROUP**.

2. Type `Sales Reps with no email` in the Group Name field.

3. In the Description field, type
   `This subgroup contains sales reps that do not have an email address.`

4. Click on the My Group Lookup No Email Address group in the Groups tree. You should see the subgroup.

5. Create another subgroup under the My Group Lookup No Email Address group. Use `No Title` as the subgroup name.

6. In the Description field, type
   `These contacts do not have a title.`

   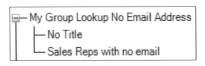

   You should have the subgroups shown in Figure 6-21.

Figure 6-21 Subgroups

Exercise 6.11: Moving (Copying) Contact Records Between Groups And Subgroups

After the subgroups are created, it is a good idea to move the appropriate records from the group to a subgroup, if applicable. In this exercise you will move contacts that have the Sales Rep title to the corresponding subgroup and contacts that do not have a title to a different subgroup. There are two ways to move contact records between groups and subgroups, as discussed below:

   ① Move the contacts manually.
   ② Use a query.

Keep in mind that the contact records are not physically removed from the group and placed in the subgroup. The contact records are copied. This means that contact records at the group level can also be in a subgroup.

There are three ways to avoid this if you think that it will drive you crazy to see the same contacts in the group and subgroup. This is one of the items on my wish list that I would like to see improved. I think it would be easier if we could move contacts between groups and subgroups.

① Do not create any subgroups. Only create groups.

② Use the Add/Remove Contacts dialog box to remove the contacts from the group after they are added to a subgroup.

③ Do not add records to a group that you really only want to see in a subgroup.

Moving Records Manually

> In ACT! 2009 and earlier, you could select multiple contacts and add them to a group. This functionality has been removed. It was on the Groups menu under the Group Membership options.

1. Click on the My Group Lookup No Email Address group, then click on the Contacts tab.

2. Sort the contacts by the Title field. The contacts that do not have a title should be at the top of the list.

3. Right-click on the first contact without a title and select Group Membership ⇒ Add Selected to Group.

> Right-clicking on several highlighted records opened the shortcut menu, but did not keep all of the records selected. This is why the records have to be moved one by one.

4. Scroll down the list and select the **NO TITLE** subgroup, illustrated in Figure 6-22, then click OK.

Figure 6-22 Subgroup illustrated

5. On the Contacts tab, select one of the contacts that have the Sales Representative title in the My Group Lookup No Email Address group and add them to Sales Reps with no email subgroup. (**Hint:** Sort the contacts on the Title field.)

6. Add two more contacts to the subgroup.

7. If you click on the Sales Reps with no email subgroup you will see the contacts that you added, as shown in Figure 6-23.

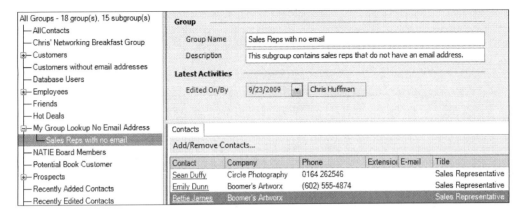

Figure 6-23 Contacts in a subgroup

Adding Contacts To A Group

In the Contact List view, you can select records that you want to add to a group, then Contacts ⇒ Add Selected to Group. You will see the dialog box shown in Figure 6-24. Select the group or subgroup that you want to add the contacts to.

This is the dialog box that use to be available from the Groups Detail view.

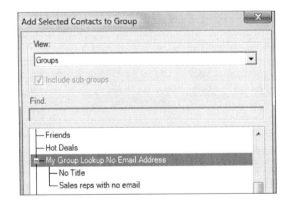

Figure 6-24 Add Selected Contacts to Group dialog box

Deleting Groups Or Subgroups

You may have a need to delete a group or a subgroup. When you delete a group or subgroup, the contacts in the group or subgroup, their notes and attachments are not deleted. The groups notes, history records and attachments are deleted.

Subgroups of the group that will be deleted are not deleted. The subgroup is automatically promoted to a group. If you need to delete a group or subgroup, you can follow the steps below. For now, you can read this section because you do not need to delete a group or subgroup.

How To Delete A Group

1. Right-click on the group in the Group Detail or Group List view and select Delete.

2. Click Yes when prompted to delete the current group.

How To Delete A Subgroup

1. Right-click on the subgroup in the Group Detail or Group List view and select Delete.

2. Click Yes when prompted to permanently delete the current subgroup.

Removing Contacts From Companies Or Groups

There may be times when you need to remove contacts from a company, division, group or subgroup. An example would be if the contact leaves the company. If this is the case, you can follow the steps below to remove contacts that are not linked to a company, division or group record. For now, you can read this section because you do not need to remove a contact from a company or group.

1. Right-click on the company, division, group or subgroup that has contacts that you want to remove in the tree, then select the appropriate option below.

    ① Company Membership ⇒ Add/Remove Contacts.
    ② Group Membership ⇒ Add/Remove Contacts.

2. Click the Contacts button on the Add/Remove Contacts dialog box.

3. Select the names that you want to remove in the **SELECTED CONTACTS** list, then click the Remove button.

4. Once you have removed the contact records, click OK twice to close both dialog boxes.

Converting A Group To A Company

Groups and subgroups can be converted to a company. If the group or subgroup that you convert has subgroups, the subgroups are not converted by default. They move up the hierarchy and quite possibly become a group. Contacts that are in the group or subgroup that is being converted, automatically become members of the company.

One reason that you may convert a group to a company is because you need to use a feature (for the contact records that are currently in a group) that only a company record has. In the next exercise you will convert the My Group Lookup No Email group to a company.

Once you convert a group to a company, it cannot be converted back.

Exercise 6.12: Using The Convert Groups To Companies Wizard

1. In the Group Detail view, right-click on the My Group Lookup No Email Address group and select **CONVERT TO COMPANY**.

2. Click Next on the first screen of the wizard. You will see the screen shown in Figure 6-25.

   The **SELECT GROUPS** screen is used to select the group(s) that will be converted to a company.

Figure 6-25 Select Groups screen

Because you selected the group before opening the wizard, the group is already selected and is in the **SELECTED GROUPS** list on the right. This means that the group is ready to be converted to a company.

If the group has subgroups that you also want to convert, check the **INCLUDE SUBGROUPS** option. If the group has more than one subgroup, the wizard does not allow you to select a specific subgroup to convert. You can convert the subgroups separately if you do not select the group first.

 Groups ⇒ Convert To Company, will also open the wizard shown above in Figure 6-25.

3. Click Next.

   The **MAP FIELDS** screen shown in Figure 6-26 is used to select the field in the company record that data from a field in the group record will be moved to.

   If you need to select a different company field, click in the company field that needs to be changed and select the field that you need from the drop-down list, as shown on the right in Figure 6-26.

Figure 6-26 Map Fields screen

If you modified the group view by adding fields to it, you will not see a corresponding field in the list of company fields. You will have to add a field to the company table first.

4. The fields are mapped correctly. Click Next on the Map Fields screen.

   The screen shown in Figure 6-27 displays the group(s) that will be converted.

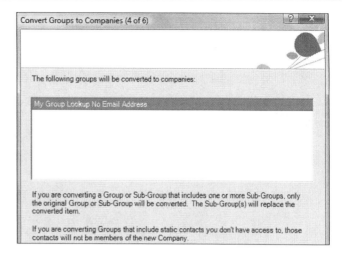

Figure 6-27 Groups to be converted screen

5. Click Next on the screen shown above in Figure 6-27. The Convert Groups to Companies screen informs you when the group has been converted.

6. Click Next after the group has been converted. Click Finish on the last screen of the wizard.

The group record has been removed. If you look in the Company Detail view you will see the My Group Lookup No Email Address company. If you need to change the company name you can.

NEW Move Group Option

This option is used to promote a subgroup to a group or make a group a subgroup of another group. The steps below demonstrate how to move a group or subgroup.

1. In either group view, click on the group or subgroup that you want to move (promote).

2. Groups ⇒ Move Group. On the dialog box shown in Figure 6-28, select one of the options explained below.

Figure 6-28 Move Group dialog box

① **PROMOTE SUBGROUP TO GROUP** This option is only available for subgroups. When selected, the subgroup is promoted to a group and the contacts are retained in the group.

② **CHANGE TO BE SUBGROUP OF** Select this option to make the group (or subgroup) a subgroup of a different group.

> The **MOVE** option is also available for companies.

Group Address Tab

The fields shown in Figure 6-29 are used to enter an address for the group.

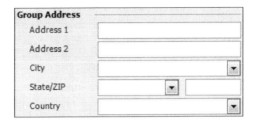

Figure 6-29 Group Address tab fields

Group Access Tab

 > In ACT! 2008 and earlier, this was called the **GROUP INFO** tab.

The fields shown in Figure 6-30 are filled in and updated by ACT! automatically.

The fields were explained in Lesson 3. [See Lesson 3, Contact Access Tab]

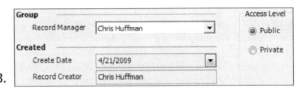

Figure 6-30 Group Access tab fields

Group List View

This view provides an easy way to see groups and subgroups, as shown in Figure 6-31.

Figure 6-31 Group List view

The icon in the first column indicates that the group has subgroups, which is a benefit over the Company List view. If you do not want to see the subgroups, clear the **INCLUDE SUBGROUPS** option.

Changing The Group Layout

If you change the group layout (for example, from the 1024x768 layout to the 800x600 layout) and get the error message "Object reference not set to an instance of an object", your preferences file could be corrupt. The steps below will show you how to delete your preferences file, so that it can automatically be rebuilt.

1. Close ACT!.
2. Start ⇒ Run, then type `actdiag` on the Run dialog box.
3. Tools ⇒ Delete Preferences.

NEW Group Detail View Related Tasks

The related tasks options shown in Figure 6-32 are primarily on the detail view. Some options are also on list view. The options are explained below.

Related Tasks

Modify Group Membership
Write Letter to Group Contacts
Attach File
View Contacts Within Group
Write E-mail Using Template
Modify Layout
Duplicate Group

Figure 6-32 Group Detail view related tasks

MODIFY GROUP MEMBERSHIP Opens the Add/Remove Contacts dialog box.

WRITE LETTER TO GROUP CONTACTS Opens the Template folder so that you can select a letter template. Once the template is selected, a mail merge of contacts in the group is created and displayed in the word processor.

ATTACH FILE Opens the Reports folder so that you can select a file to attach to the current company. The file is added to the History tab.

VIEW CONTACTS WITHIN GROUP Displays the contacts in the selected group in the Contact List view.

WRITE E-MAIL USING TEMPLATE Opens the Template folder for the database so that you can select a template to use for the email that you want to create. Once you select the template, a new email window will open with the template that you selected.

MODIFY LAYOUT Opens the current group detail view layout in the Layout Designer, so that the layout can be changed.

DUPLICATE GROUP Opens the dialog box shown in Figure 6-33, which is used to select which group fields will be duplicated on the new group record.

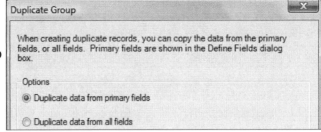

Figure 6-33 Duplicate Group dialog box

ℕ𝔼𝕎 Group List View Related Tasks

The options shown in Figure 6-34 are for the Group List view. The options that are only on the list view are explained below.

Figure 6-34 Group List view related tasks

CHANGE COLUMNS Opens the Customize Columns dialog box.

VIEW ALL GROUPS Is the same as selecting Lookup ⇒ All groups.

SORT LIST Opens the Sort dialog box to sort the groups displayed in the view.

SCHEDULING ACTIVITIES

Overview

In this lesson you will learn the following scheduling activity features:

- ☑ Timeless activities
- ☑ Scheduling a To-Do
- ☑ Scheduling the same activity for multiple contacts
- ☑ Sending email to activity contacts
- ☑ Scheduling activities for other users
- ☑ Using the alarm
- ☑ Rescheduling an activity
- ☑ Handling activity conflicts
- ☑ Group activities
- ☑ Creating and deleting recurring activities
- ☑ Scheduling random activities
- ☑ Filter and sort activities
- ☑ Creating and editing an Activity Series

Activities Overview

Activities are more formal than notes. I think of activities as a really large, well thought out and detailed to-do list for your contacts. Activities let you keep up with your contacts. While it is tempting to only enter a little information for each activity, you may not remember everything that you know now, when the time comes to complete the task that an activity is for.

There are different types of activities that you can schedule. Some activities that you will schedule with contacts are business related and others are personal. The default activity types that you can schedule with contacts are meetings, telephone calls and to-do's. Each of these activities are basically created the same way. Activities are reminders of tasks that you need to complete. You can also create your own activity types.

It is a good idea to display the contact that you want to schedule the activity with before you open the Schedule Activity dialog box. This is not a requirement because there is an option on the dialog box to select the contact(s). If you want to schedule the same activity for more than one contact, select the group or create a lookup that will display the contacts that you want to schedule the activity for. You can also create the same activity for people that are not part of the same group or lookup at the same time. In addition to being able to view activities on the Activities tab on detail views, you can also view activities on the calendar and Task List.

Figure 7-1 shows the Schedule Activity dialog box. Table 7-1 explains the options on the Schedule Activity dialog box.

Figure 7-1 To-Do Activity options

Option	Description
Create separate activity for each contact	This option is shown in the upper right corner of Figure 7-1 above. It will create an activity for each contact listed in the Schedule With field.
Activity Type	Select or change the type of activity that you are creating or editing. This field will initially be filled in based on the option that you select to open this dialog box. For example, if you click the Schedule Meeting button, "Meeting" will be the value displayed in this field when the dialog box is first opened, but you can change it.
Start Date	The date that the activity should start. The default value is today's date.
Start Time	The time that the activity should start. The default value is **TIMELESS**.
End Date/Time	This field will change automatically when the duration is selected.
Duration	Select the length of time needed to complete the activity.
Use Banner	Displays a banner on the daily calendar if the duration of the activity meets the requirement of the **SHOW FULL DAY** banner calendar preferences option. The banner is also displayed at the top of the Schedule Activity dialog box, as illustrated in Figure 7-2.
Schedule With	By default, this field contains the contact that was displayed before the dialog box was opened. Other contacts can be added.
Contacts Button	The options on this button are used to select contacts for the activity. (1)
Send invitation e-mail	If checked, this option will display a message in the banner at the top of the Schedule Activity dialog box stating that contacts will receive an email notification of the activity and users will receive a calendar email invitation. Once the activity is set up, the appropriate emails and invitations will be sent automatically.
Associate With	Select the groups, subgroups, companies and divisions that need to be included on the activity.
Regarding	Is used to provide a description of the activity. The options that will be displayed in the drop-down list depend on the activity type that is selected. (2)
Location	A free form field that is used to enter where the activity will take place.
Priority	Select how important the activity is. Setting a priority is optional.
Color	Select the color for the priority. (3)
Ring Alarm	If a time is selected from this drop-down list, your computer will beep the number of minutes selected, before the activity is scheduled to start.
Schedule For Button	Select a user in the database to assign the activity to. Activities can be scheduled for more than one user. (4)
Private	If the **PRIVATE** option shown earlier at the bottom of Figure 7-1 is selected on any tab on the Schedule Activity dialog box, other users of the database will not be able to view the activity.

Table 7-1 Schedule Activity dialog box options explained

(1) This button opens the menu shown in Figure 7-3.
The **SELECT CONTACTS** option is used to select the contact(s) that the activity is for.
The **NEW CONTACT** option is used to create a new contact, which you can add to the activity.
The **MY RECORD** option is used to add yourself to the activity. If you need to use this option, select it first, then add the other contacts. This option will remove contacts that are already in the Schedule With field, including the original contact that was there.

(2) Figure 7-4 shows the Regarding field drop-down list options for the Meeting activity type. Figure 7-5 shows the Regarding field drop-down list options for the To-Do activity type. If none of the options in the drop-down list fit your needs, you can type in a new description, which can be up to 256 characters. If you know that you will do a lot of searches or use this field as criteria for a query or report, you should customize it so that only options from the drop-down list can be selected.

(3) By default, each priority level is a different color. If you want to change the color, click the button next to the option. You will see the dialog box shown in Figure 7-6. Keep in mind that the color is associated to a priority level and not the specific activity. If you change the color, the color that you select will automatically be applied to all activities with the same priority, going forward.

(4) Click the **SCHEDULE FOR** button when you need to schedule the activity for another user of the database. In order to schedule an activity for another user, you must have rights to do so. If you have rights to schedule activities for other users and click this button, you will see the dialog box shown in Figure 7-7. Select the person that you want to schedule the activity for. The activity will display on the users calendar and Task List. Don't be surprised when the user (probably a co-worker) does not thank you for giving them more work <smile>.

You can view partial activity entries in the banner section.

Figure 7-2 Banner section illustrated

Figure 7-3
Contacts button options

Figure 7-4 Meeting options

Figure 7-5 To-Do options

Figure 7-7 Schedule For dialog box

Figure 7-6 Color dialog box

 You will only see users that you have the rights to schedule activities for in the drop-down list on the Schedule For dialog box, shown above in Figure 7-7. In Lesson 13 you will learn how to grant calendar access, which in addition to being able to view entries on another users calendar, also allows you to create activities and assign them to other users.

Activity Types

There are six default types of activities that you can create, as explained in Table 7-2.

Activity	Is Used To Schedule . . .
Call	A telephone call.
Meeting	A meeting.
To-Do	A task that needs to be completed.
Marketing Call	A telephone call. You could use this option for cold call telephone sales.
Personal Activity	A non business related task. (5)
Vacation	Vacation time. (5)

Table 7-2 Activity types explained

(5) There is no button on the toolbar for this activity type. Schedule ⇒ Other, as shown in Figure 7-8 displays the entry point for these activity types.

If you do not want to use the menu options to access these activity types, you can click on any of the schedule activity icons on the toolbar to open the Schedule Activity dialog box and then select the activity type from the drop-down list.

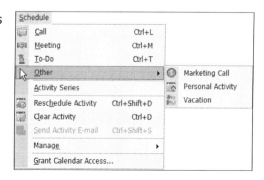

Figure 7-8 Schedule menu options

Timeless Activities

This type of activity is one that does not have a time associated with it. Many types of To-Do activities, like sending an email or fax can be timeless. When you create a To-Do activity, you will see that the default start time displayed is **TIMELESS**. You can change the start time to a specific time if you need to. You can select the timeless option as the default for any type of activity on the Preferences dialog box.

Public Or Private Activities

This option is only useful if more than one person uses the database. If the contact record is marked as private, the activities for the contact are marked as private by default. You can make activities private, even if the contact is not. The symbol illustrated in Figure 7-9 on the Activities tab, denotes that the activity is private.

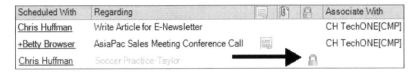

Scheduled With	Regarding				Associate With
Chris Huffman	Write Article for E-Newsletter				CH TechONE[CMP]
+Betty Browser	AsiaPac Sales Meeting Conference Call				CH TechONE[CMP]
Chris Huffman	Soccer Practice-Taylor				

Figure 7-9 Private activity illustrated

Keep the following in mind when deciding whether or not to make an activity private.

    ① Private activities will partially appear on other users calendars when your name is part of the filter that they use. The actual contents of the activity does not appear, but the word **PRIVATE** appears next to your name.

    ② When you clear a private activity, it is still marked as private when it is moved to the History tab.

    ③ Private activities are not displayed in other users Task List.

Exercise 7.1: How To Schedule A To-Do Activity

In this exercise you will create a To-Do activity.

1. Look up the contacts that have "Customer" in the **ID/STATUS** field.

2. Double-click on the record for Jim Curtis.

3. On the Activities tab of the Contact Detail view, click the **TO-DO** button on the Global toolbar. You will see the Schedule Activity dialog box.

4. Open the **REGARDING** drop-down list and select Send Quote.

5. Change the **PRIORITY** to High. Leave the dialog box open to complete the next part of this exercise.

Selecting Who To Schedule The Activity With

You cannot schedule an activity without associating it to a contact in the database. If the contact that you want to schedule the activity with is not in the database you have to add the contact to the database and then associate it to the activity.

1. The **SCHEDULE WITH** drop-down list should look like the one shown in Figure 7-10. For now, leave the current contact selected.

   If you click on the Name or Company column heading in the drop-down list, you can change the sort order.

   Clicking the **MY RECORD** button at the bottom of the drop-down list will add the My Record as the person that you want to schedule the activity with.

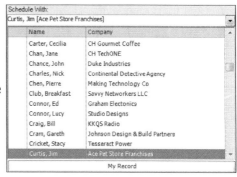

Figure 7-10 Schedule With drop-down list

How To Schedule An Activity For A New Contact

As mentioned earlier, you can schedule the activity for more than one contact. If a contact that you want to schedule the activity with is not in the database, you can create a new contact by clicking on the Contacts button on the Schedule Activity dialog box and selecting New Contact as shown earlier in Figure 7-3. Selecting this option will open the New Contact dialog box.

How To Add A New Contact To An Activity From The Schedule Activity Dialog Box

In this part of the exercise you will create a new contact for the activity.

1. Click the Contacts button on the Schedule Activity dialog box, then select New Contact. You should see the New Contact dialog box.

2. Enter the information in Table 7-3 for the new contact, then click OK.

   The address fields are on the Business Address tab.

Field	Type This
Company	Spice Plus
Contact	Jennifer Milton
Address	456 Treasury St
City	Astoria
State	PA
Zip	10210

Table 7-3 Information for the new contact

How To Select Multiple Contacts

1. Click the **CONTACTS** button on the Schedule Activity dialog box, then select the Select Contacts option. You will see the Select Contacts dialog box.

Notice that you can add a new contact from this dialog box also.

You can assign the activity to all contacts, contacts in the current lookup, a group or company. You can also assign the activity on a contact by contact basis, by selecting names from the list.

2. Open the **SELECT FROM** drop-down list and select Current Lookup. You will see the names that are from the ID/Status = Customer lookup that you created earlier in this exercise.

3. Click the **ADD ALL>>** button. You will see all of the contacts from the current lookup in the Scheduled Contacts list.

 If you wanted to assign this activity to other contacts, you could add them now. ACT! will not add names to the Selected contacts list if they have already been selected to be added to the activity.

4. Select the **GROUPS** option from the drop-down list, then open the drop-down list across from the Select From drop-down list and select the Sales Reps group.

5. Select the first three names from the Sales Reps group by holding down the **CTRL** key and clicking on each name, then click the **ADD>** button. Click OK.

6. Click the Options button in the upper right corner of the Schedule Activity dialog box and select the option, **CREATE SEPARATE ACTIVITY FOR EACH CONTACT**. This will create an entry on the Activities tab of each contact record.

7. Check the **USE BANNER** option. (**Hint**: It is below the Duration field.)

   You should have the options selected that are shown in Figure 7-11.

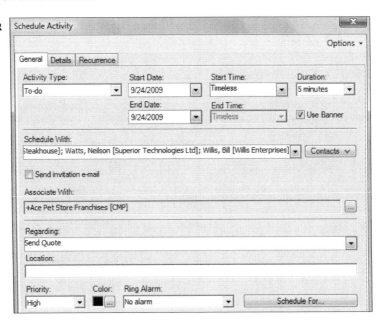

Figure 7-11 General tab activity options

Activity Linking Issue

When an activity is cleared from a contact that is linked to a company record, by default, the history record that is created for the activity can be viewed from the contact record. To prevent this from happening, clear the **ASSOCIATE WITH** field, shown above in Figure 7-11.

Details Tab Options

The options on this tab are used to add comments, as well as, add an attachment to the activity. The Details tab is used to enter more text than the Regarding field on the General tab can store.

8. On the Details tab, type This is a To-Do activity, as shown in Figure 7-12.

Figure 7-12 Details tab options

Recurrence Tab Options

The options on this tab are used to select the frequency of the activity, as well as, the start and end date for a recurring activity.

9. No options need to be selected on this tab. Click OK.

View The Activity

10. On the Activities tab, scroll through the records. You will see the To-Do activity that you created, as illustrated in Figure 7-13.

Figure 7-13 To-Do activity illustrated in the Contact Detail view

You may be asking yourself, what if I schedule an activity for a future date? How will I remember it? On the Task List view, you can view all of the activities that are scheduled in the future.

Send Invitation E-Mail Option

If you select this option on the Schedule Activity dialog box and have email software configured to work with ACT!, once you click OK on the Schedule Activity dialog box, the email will be generated.

Your email software will open and you will see an email similar to the one shown in Figure 7-14.

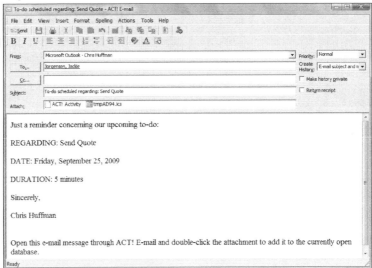

Figure 7-14 Activity e-mail that will be sent to the contacts

Viewing An Activity With Multiple Contacts

If the same activity is assigned to more than one contact, you will not see all of the contact names in the **SCHEDULED WITH** column on the Activities tab. You will see a plus sign at the beginning of the list of names, as illustrated in Figure 7-15. If you click on this link, all of the contacts associated with the activity will be displayed in the Contact List view.

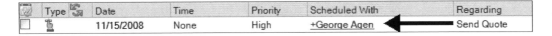

	Type	Date	Time	Priority	Scheduled With	Regarding
☐		11/15/2008	None	High	+George Agen	Send Quote

Figure 7-15 Multiple contacts for an activity illustrated

Why I Think It's Best To Schedule Phone Calls Individually

Looking at the activity illustrated above in Figure 7-15, you will not know how many people need to be called, if this was a telephone call activity. You would have to open the Schedule Activity dialog box to see the contact names, which adds an extra step to the process. If you call some of the contacts but cannot reach other contacts, it will be difficult to know which contacts you still have to call.

If you do not call all of the contacts, but mark the task as being complete, you may not remember that you still need to call other contacts that are listed on the activity because the activity will no longer appear on the Activities tab or Task List. This is the other reason why I think it is best to schedule phone calls individually. If you want to automatically have activities assigned to multiple contacts scheduled individually, select the option on the Scheduling Preferences dialog box. [See the Modifying Scheduling Preferences section later in this lesson]

Exercise 7.2: Scheduling Activities For Other Users

The **SCHEDULE FOR** button at the bottom of the General tab on the Schedule Activity dialog box is used to create an activity for another user of the database. For example, if you wanted a sales manager in your company to send a thank you note to all of your suppliers, you could schedule the activity for the sales manager. Won't the sales manager be thrilled!

How To Schedule A Call

This activity type is used to create a reminder to call a contact. In this exercise you will schedule a phone call activity for another user of the database.

1. Look up the contact George Agen.

2. Click the **CALL** button on the Global toolbar.

3. Change the Priority to Medium, then select the Regarding option, Confirm Appointment.

4. Click the **SCHEDULE FOR** button. Open the drop-down list and select Allison Mikola, then click OK.

5. You will see the banner shown in Figure 7-16 at the top of the Schedule Activity dialog box.

   Click OK.

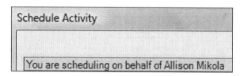

Figure 7-16 Activity banner

Exercise 7.3: Using The Alarm

This feature is designed to remind you of a scheduled activity. ACT! has to be open in order for the alarm to notify you of an activity. If ACT! is open, the Alarms dialog box will pop up. If ACT! is open, but minimized, the ACT! button on the Windows Taskbar will flash. Your computer will beep if you have the Ring Alarm option enabled. If you only select the Set Alarm option, you will only be notified at the time that activity starts, not before.

The alarm also has a snooze option, which you can use to be reminded of an activity. It works like the snooze button on an alarm clock, by notifying you in advance of the activity. You can reset the alarm to go off again at a later time. You can also clear the alarm to turn it off completely. Turning off the alarm does not clear the activity.

The snooze option is useful if you need time before the activity to prepare for it. If you want a snooze time that is not in the Ring Alarm field drop-down list, you can type it in. For example, you can enter any of the following times in the field: 46 minutes, 46 hours or 46 days.

1. Lookup the contact Jim Curtis.

2. Click the **CALL** button on the Global toolbar.

3. Open the Start Time drop-down list. Scroll down the list and click in the time slot that is to the nearest, next half hour. (If it is currently 8:20 PM, select 8:30 PM. If it is 4:35 PM, select 5 PM.)

4. Select the Regarding option, Confirm Appointment, then change the Priority to Medium.

5. Open the **RING ALARM** drop-down list and select 5 minutes. This means that you will be notified five minutes before this activity starts.

6. You should have the options selected that are shown in Figure 7-17.

   You will see a different date and time.

   Click OK.

   You should now see an entry for this activity on the contact record for Jim Curtis.

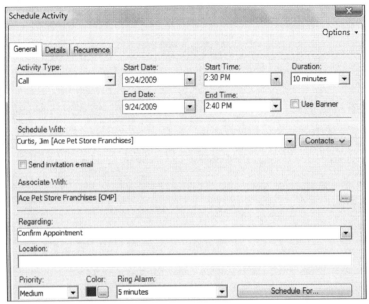

Figure 7-17 Telephone call options

If there is a conflict alert, select the closest available time in the future.

When the Alarms dialog box appears, as shown in Figure 7-18, come back to the section below: Alarm Notification Options.

For now, continue going through the book by going to Exercise 7.5: Handling Activity Conflicts.

Figure 7-18 Alarms dialog box

Alarm Notification Options

You should now see the dialog box shown above in Figure 7-18. The alarm options discussed below are available.

Select All Is used to set the same option for all of the activities that are displayed on the Alarms dialog box.

Snooze Is used to reset the snooze time on the dialog box shown in Figure 7-20.

Clear Alarm Turns the alarm off for the rest of the day. The activity will still stay on your calendar.

Clear Activity Opens the Clear Activity dialog box so that you can mark the activity as being complete.

Reschedule Opens the Schedule Activity dialog box, which is used to select a different date or time for the activity.

Go To Displays the contact record that the alarm is for.

Show Details Displays the Activity Details section, shown in Figure 7-19. It is at the bottom of the Alarms dialog box.

When the details are displayed, Show Details will change to **HIDE DETAILS**.

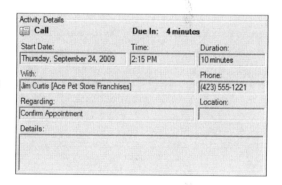

Figure 7-19 Activity details

Setting The Snooze Alarm

1. Click the Snooze button.

   You should see the dialog box shown in Figure 7-20.

Figure 7-20 Snooze Alarm dialog box

2. Select the **10 MINUTES** option, then click OK. 10 minutes from now you will be notified again of the meeting that you have scheduled.

When the alarm notifies you again, come back and complete Exercise 7.4: Rescheduling An Activity. For now, continue going through the book, where you left off or you can go get a snack <smile>.

Exercise 7.4: Rescheduling An Activity

Rescheduling allows you to change when an activity will take place.

1. On the Alarms dialog box, click on the activity for Jim Curtis.

2. Click the **RESCHEDULE** button. You will see the Schedule Activity dialog box for the activity. If you were doing this for real, you would select a new date or time on the Schedule Activity dialog box.

3. For now, click the Cancel button.

4. Click the **CLEAR ALARM** button on the Alarms dialog box, then close the dialog box. Look up the contact Jim Curtis.

5. Double-click on the activity. Change the **RING ALARM** option to **NO ALARM**, then click OK.

Exercise 7.5: Handling Activity Conflicts

ACT! will warn you of activity conflicts and to try to keep you from scheduling two activities at the same time. If this occurs, you will be notified when you are creating an activity that conflicts with an existing activity. You will have the option to reschedule the time and/or date of the new activity. In this exercise you will schedule a meeting activity for a time when an activity already exists.

1. Look up the contact Rick Blaine.

2. Click the **MEETING** button on the Global toolbar.

3. Change the Start date to 9/21/2009. You can do this by typing the date in the field or by using the calendar attached to the field. Change the Start time to 10:15 AM. (Yes, I know that this is a date in the past, but bear with me.)

4. Set the Duration to 2 hours.

5. Select the **PRESENTATION** Regarding option. You should have the options shown in Figure 7-21.

6. Click OK. You should see the message shown in Figure 7-22.

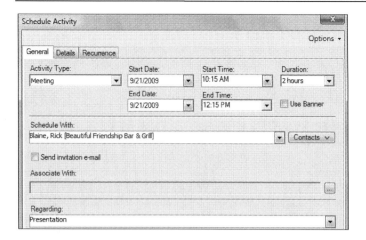

Figure 7-21 Meeting options selected

Figure 7-22 Activity warning message

Normally, you would not see this dialog box because you would not be trying to schedule an activity for a date in the past, unless you typed in a date in the past by mistake. It is being done here on purpose to demonstrate how to handle activity conflicts.

7. Click Yes to continue. You will see the dialog box shown in Figure 7-23.

This dialog box is telling you that the activity that you are trying to schedule is conflicting with an existing activity.

Figure 7-23 shows that an activity has already been scheduled with the contact on 9/21/2009 starting at 10:30 AM.

Therefore, it is probably a good idea to reschedule this activity for another date or time.

Figure 7-23 Conflict Alert dialog box

If you still want to schedule this activity, click the **ACCEPT** button. If you want to change the date or time of the activity, click the **RESCHEDULE** button.

How To Reschedule A Conflicting Activity

1. Click the **RESCHEDULE** button.

2. Change the Start date to $11/6/09$, then click OK. This date and time does not conflict with other activities.

3. Click Yes when prompted that the activity has been scheduled for a date in the past.

Exercise 7.6: Group Activities

You can schedule an activity with a group. Doing this means that each contact in the group will be associated to the group activity. The group activity will appear on the Activities tab of each contact in the group.

In this exercise you will create a group activity for the Sales Reps group. The majority of the steps to create a group activity are the same as creating an activity for one contact.

1. Open the Group Detail view, then click on the Sales Reps group.

2. Click the Meeting button on the Global toolbar.

3. Change the Start Date to tomorrow.

Notice that the group name is in the Associate With field on the Schedule Activity dialog box. You can also add individual contacts and other groups to the activity.

4. Click the Contacts button, then select the Select Contacts option.

5. Open the Select From drop-down list, then select Groups.

6. Open the next drop-down list and select the group, Sales Reps with no email. Add the contacts in the group to the list, then click OK.

7. Select the **FOLLOW-UP ON PRESENTATION** Regarding option, then click OK.

Recurring Activities

Recurring activities are activities that are repeated on a consistent frequency. The four types of recurring activities that can be created are discussed below. The recurring options look somewhat similar, but the fields perform differently. To make sure that you have selected the correct options, read the information in the banner at the top of the dialog box. It briefly explains what the options that you selected represent.

The **EVERY** field determines how many days, weeks, months or years are between each occurrence of the activity.

The **STARTS** field is the date that you want the first occurrence of the recurring activity to begin.

The **ENDS** field is the date that you want the last occurrence of the activity to happen.

There are two ways that recurring activities can be scheduled, as discussed below:

① Activities that occur on a regular basis, like monthly staff meetings.
② Activities that occur randomly, like processing payroll every other Friday.

Recurring Activity Types Explained

① **Daily** Select this option if the interval for the recurring activity is in days.

For example, the options shown in Figure 7-24 are for an activity that will happen every five days.

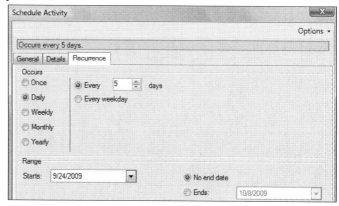

Figure 7-24 Daily recurring activity type options

② **Weekly** Select this option for activities that you want to occur weekly.

The options shown in Figure 7-25 are for a weekly meeting that will take place every Thursday and Friday, indefinitely.

Figure 7-25 Weekly recurring activity type options

③ **Monthly** Select this option for activities that you want to occur monthly.

The options shown in Figure 7-26 will create a monthly activity that takes place on the second Tuesday of every month.

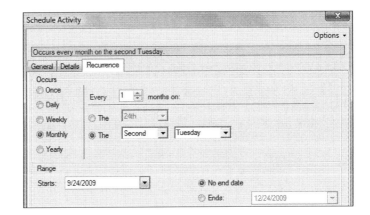

Figure 7-26 Monthly recurring activity type options

④ **Yearly** Select this option for activities that you want to occur yearly.

The options shown in Figure 7-27 will create a yearly activity that takes place on the last Tuesday in March.

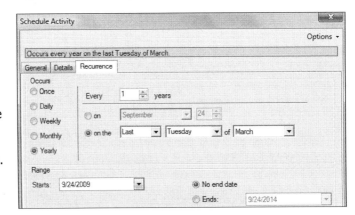

Figure 7-27 Yearly recurring activity type options

Exercise 7.7: How To Schedule Recurring Activities

If you know that you will need to have monthly meetings, you can schedule the meeting once and have ACT! automatically schedule the rest of the monthly meetings for the time period that you specify.

1. Look up the contact Rick Blaine, then click the Meeting button.

2. Select the options in Table 7-4 for the meeting activity.

Option	Change To
Start Date	The 15th of next month
Start Time	3 PM
Duration	2 hours
Regarding	Contract Negotiations

Table 7-4 Meeting activity options

3. On the **RECURRENCE** tab, select the Monthly option, then change the first **THE** option to the 15th, if it is not already.

4. Select the **ENDS** option and type in the date a year from today.

   You should have options selected that are similar to the ones shown in Figure 7-28.

   These options will schedule a meeting the 15th of each month for the next year.

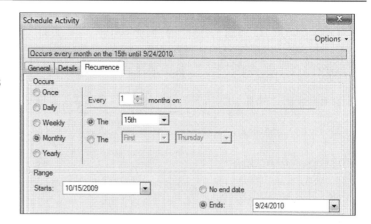

Figure 7-28 Recurrence tab options

5. Click OK. If there is a conflict, reschedule the activity and change the Start date on the Schedule Activity dialog box to the 16th.

   On the Activities tab for Rick Blaine, you will see a recurring meeting that starts on the 15th of next month, as shown in Figure 7-29.

Figure 7-29 Recurring meeting illustrated

   The recurring activity symbol is illustrated.

Only the next occurrence of recurring activities will appear on the Activities tab and Task List. All of the occurrences of a recurring activity will appear on your calendar. This means that you will see each occurrence of a weekly meeting on a calendar, but you will only see the next occurrence of the weekly meeting on the Activities tab.

Exercise 7.8: How To Schedule Random Activities

Scheduling random activities allows you to schedule a conference call on the last day of the month. If you select the 31st, ACT! will schedule the recurring activity on the last day of the month, no matter what the actual last date of the month is.

1. Look up the My Record.

2. Click the **CALL** button, then select the options in Table 7-5.

Option	Change To
Start Time	5 PM
Duration	15 minutes
Regarding	Discuss legal points
Priority	High

Table 7-5 Schedule call activity options

3. On the Recurrence tab, select the Monthly option. Open the first drop-down list and select the 31st.

    If you wanted the activity to end, you would enter a date in the **ENDS** field.

    You should have similar options to those shown in Figure 7-30.

    Click OK.

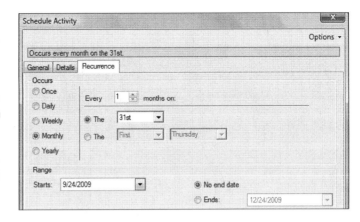

Figure 7-30 Monthly recurrence tab settings

On the Activities tab of the My Record (for Chris Huffman), you should see a phone call scheduled for the last day of the current month.

If the current month does not have 31 days, the activity will appear on the last day of the month. This may or may not be a workday.

Scheduling An Activity For The Last Workday Of The Month

In the previous exercise you created a random recurring activity that would automatically be scheduled for the last calendar day of the month.

If you need to schedule a monthly activity for the last workday of the month, select the monthly options illustrated in Figure 7-31.

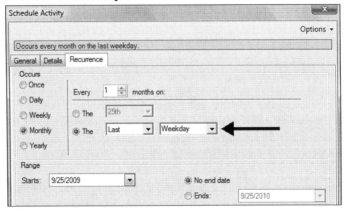

Figure 7-31 Options for a last workday of the month activity

Other Ways To Open The Schedule Activity Dialog Box

The majority of the activities that you created in this lesson used a button on the toolbar to open the Schedule Activity dialog box. There are other ways to open the Schedule Activity dialog box, as discussed below.

① Double-click on a time slot on the calendar. This is helpful because it can help prevent you from trying to schedule conflicting activities.
② Open the Schedule menu.
③ On the Activities tab of a detail view, right-click in the list of activities and select Schedule ⇒ Meeting, as shown in Figure 7-32.

Figure 7-32 Activities tab shortcut menu

Deleting Recurring Activities

If you have scheduled a recurring activity and either no longer need the remaining activities or need to clear (delete) a recurring activity for a specific date, you can.

Exercise 7.9: How To Clear All Future Recurring Activities

In this exercise you will learn how to delete all of the remaining occurrences of an activity.

1. If the My Record is not displayed, display it now.

2. On the Activities tab, right-click on the monthly Discuss Legal Points activity that you just created. Select the **ERASE ACTIVITY** option.

3. You will see the dialog box shown in Figure 7-33 letting you know that this is a recurring activity.

   Select the **DELETE ALL OCCURRENCES** option, then click OK.

Figure 7-33 Delete Recurring Activity dialog box

4. If your email software opens, close it.

Exercise 7.10: How To Clear A Single Recurring Activity

In this exercise you will learn how to clear one occurrence of the remaining occurrences of an activity.

1. Look up the contact Rick Blaine.

2. Right-click on the presentation activity on 11/6/2009 that you created earlier in this lesson and select **CLEAR ACTIVITY**.

3. Select the **ERASE** option on the Clear Activity dialog box, as illustrated in Figure 7-34, then click OK. The activity has been deleted.

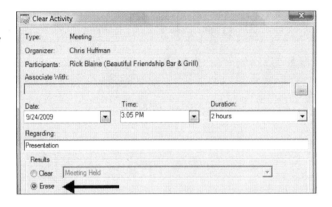

Figure 7-34 Clear Activity dialog box

Clearing Activities

It is good practice to clear activities once you complete them. When you clear an activity, a record is automatically created on the History tab of the contact that the activity belongs to. This way, if you need to know whether or not an activity was completed or ever existed, you will be able to easily tell.

Other Reasons To Clear Activities

① Some reports are based on history records that are created when an activity is cleared. Without history records, the reports will not produce the correct output.
② Allows you to schedule follow up activities.
③ You will not be reminded of the activity.
④ Fields on the Latest Activities tab are updated.

How To Clear Activities

You have already learned how to clear recurring activities from the Activities tab. Clearing other types of activities is basically the same process. You can right-click on an activity any place except the History tab, then select Clear Activity. The other ways to clear an activity are discussed below:

① On the Task List, click in the check box illustrated in Figure 7-35.
② On any Calendar view, click in the check box illustrated in Figure 7-36.

③ Select the activity on the Activities tab that you want to clear, then Schedule ⇒ Clear Activity.

Figure 7-35 Task List option to clear an activity

Figure 7-36 Calendar view option to clear an activity

Exercise 7.11: Clear An Activity For A Contact

When you clear an activity you can leave the options the way that they are or you can add or change information about the activity as needed. You should make changes that will help you remember more about the activity in the future.

1. Right-click on the Contract Negotiations activity for Rick Blaine, then select **CLEAR ACTIVITY**.

2. Click the **FOLLOW-UP** button. The follow-up option is used to schedule another activity for the contact. (Amazingly, this is called a follow up activity.) This is the equivalent of creating a paper trail.

3. Open the **REGARDING** drop-down list and select the Follow-up on Presentation option, then click OK.

4. Select the **MEETING NOT HELD** results option.

5. Check the **ADD ACTIVITY DETAILS TO HISTORY** option, if it is not already checked.

   You should have the options shown in Figure 7-37.

   Click OK.

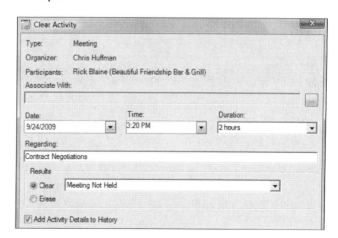

Figure 7-37 Clear Activity options

The activity for Contract Negotiations is no longer on the Activities tab. You should see a new activity with today's date that has "Follow-up on Presentation" in the Regarding field. On the History tab, you will see an entry for the meeting not held activity.

> **How To Clear More Than One Activity At The Same Time**
>
> You can clear more than one activity on the Activities tab or the Task List at the same time by selecting the activities that you want to clear, then right-click on them and select **CLEAR MULTIPLE ACTIVITIES**, as illustrated in Figure 7-38.

Figure 7-38 Task List multi select shortcut menu

Exercise 7.12: Clear An Activity For A Group

The steps below will show you how to clear a group activity. In this exercise you will clear the group activity that you created earlier in this lesson. Clearing a group activity is the same process as clearing an activity for a contact.

1. Click the Groups button, then click on the Activities tab for the Sales Rep Group.

2. You should see a Follow-up activity with tomorrows date. It may be a date in the past if you completed Exercise 7.6 before today. Right-click on the activity and select **CLEAR ACTIVITY**.

3. Click OK on the Clear Activity dialog box because none of the information for the activity needs to be changed.

Exercise 7.13: How To Filter Activities

You may only want to see certain types of activities or activities in a certain date range. Filtering is used to accomplish both of these tasks. In this exercise you will learn how to filter activities.

1. Look up the My Record. On the Activities tab, open the **TYPES** drop-down list and clear the Vacation option. If there are vacation activities, you will not see them now.

2. Right-click in the Activities tab and select Filter Activities.

3. You should see the Filter Activities dialog box. Open the Dates drop-down list and select **TODAY AND FUTURE**.

4. Open the Types drop-down list and clear the Personal Activity option. You should have the options selected that are shown in Figure 7-39. Click OK. There should be less activities displayed.

Figure 7-39 Filter Activities dialog box

 Sorting Activities

You can sort the activities on the Activities tab in ascending or descending order by clicking on the column heading of the field that you want to sort on.

Exercise 7.14: How To Delete An Activity

If you have an activity that you do not need anymore or will not complete, you can delete it. If you delete an activity, it is not automatically recorded on the History tab, but it is removed from your schedule.

1. Look up the contact Rick Blaine. Display all of the activities by changing the **DATES** option to All Dates. Change the **TYPES** option to All.

2. Click on the activity that has today's date or the most recent date if you completed the prior exercises in this lesson before today.

3. Press the Delete key.

4. Select the Erase option on the Clear Activity dialog box, then click OK.

5. Select the option to delete all occurrences if prompted, then click OK.

Modifying Scheduling Preferences

In this lesson you have created a variety of activities. ACT! has scheduling options that you can modify as needed, by following the steps below.

1. Tools ⇒ Preferences ⇒ Calendar & Scheduling tab. Click the Scheduling Preferences button.

2. Select the activity type that you want to change, then select or change the options as needed. Each activity type can have different options.

   Figure 7-40 shows the activity options that can be modified.

   The **AUTOMATICALLY ROLL OVER TO TODAY** option moves activities that have not been completed to the next day. This can be used to ensure that activities do not fall through the cracks, as they say. This option is only applied to activities that have a single user.

   If you create a lot of activities that need to be assigned to multiple contacts and want each contact to have an activity record created automatically, check the option **CREATE SEPARATE ACTIVITIES WHEN SCHEDULING WITH MULTIPLE CONTACTS.**

Figure 7-40 Scheduling Preferences dialog box

 If you want to set or remove the same option(s) for all of the activity types, select all of the activity types in the **ACTIVITY TYPE SETTINGS** list and then make the changes to all of them at the same time.

Alarm Preferences

1. Click the **CUSTOMIZE ALARMS** button on the Scheduling Preferences dialog box.

   The options shown in Figure 7-41 are used to customize the sound that the alarm will make.

Figure 7-41 Customize Alarms dialog box

2. Close all open dialog boxes.

Activity Series

ACT! comes with two activity series that you can use. You can also create your own activity series. Activity series remind me of a project plan or mini to-do list that has all of the tasks that you need to do, to complete a project. An activity series is used to schedule pre-defined activities with contacts. An activity series saves you time because you do not have to remember all of the tasks or create a series of activities manually for each contact. Like other features in ACT!, the activity series can be public or private.

The key to understanding how an activity series works is understanding the concept of the **ANCHOR DATE**. The anchor date is the date the activities in the series use as a starting point. It is the date that all activities in the series are based from. You can schedule activities, days, weeks or months before or after the anchor date. If you are trying to figure out when you would have the need to schedule an activity before the anchor date, hopefully, the following scenario will help.

If you are planning to have a product launch, a lot of activities need to be completed weeks and months before the product is actually launched. Some of the tasks that need to be completed prior to the launch include the following: Inviting the media, finding and booking a location for the launch, creating and inviting potential customers, creating and executing an advertising campaign and hiring a caterer. These activities would have a date prior to the anchor date. In this scenario, the anchor date would be the date of the product launch.

The **ACTIVITY SERIES TEMPLATE CREATION WIZARD** can be accessed from any view. It is used to create a list of activities to complete. You can create as many activity series as you need. Having a list makes it easier to remember what the next task is that needs to be completed.

Another example of an activity series would be the tasks that have to be completed when you obtain a new customer. The following items could be the activities that need to be completed for new customers.

① Verify the contact information. (Send email)
② Send the customer a welcome kit. (Send literature)
③ Call the customer five days after the welcome kit is sent out. (Confirm shipment)
④ Set up another opportunity for the customer. (Send quote)

Exercise 7.15: Create An Activity Series

In this exercise you will create an activity series that will be used as the guidelines for changing a prospect to a customer. The series will include the four activities discussed above.

1. Schedule ⇒ Manage ⇒ Activity Series Templates.

    You will see the dialog box shown in Figure 7-42.

    Select the first option, then click Next.

Figure 7-42 Activity Series Template Creation Wizard screen

Select the **EDIT AN EXISTING ACTIVITY SERIES** option, on the first wizard screen shown above in Figure 7-42, when you want to view the existing activities. You will see the screen shown in Figure 7-43. You would also select this option if you need to edit an activity series.

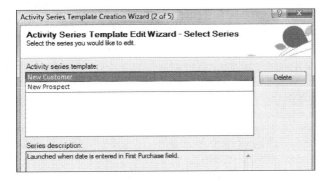

Figure 7-43 Existing activity series screen

2. Type `My Activity Series` in the Name field.

   Type `New Customers Welcome Kit` in the Description field, as shown in Figure 7-44, then click Next.

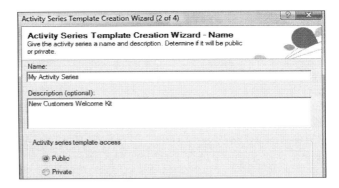

Figure 7-44 Activity Series Name screen

3. Click the Add button on the third wizard screen.

   Open the Activity Type drop-down list and select To-Do.

   Select the **SEND EMAIL** Regarding option.

   You should have the options shown in Figure 7-45.

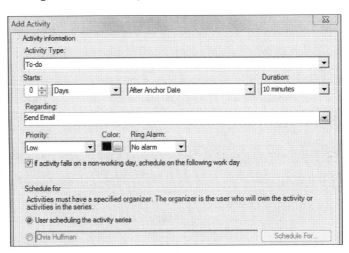

Figure 7-45 Add Activity dialog box

The **STARTS** field is how many days, weeks or month's from the Series Anchor date that you want the activity to begin.

The options in the next drop-down list are used to select the interval (days, weeks or months) that the activity needs to be completed.

The third drop-down list is used to select whether the activity should start **BEFORE** or **AFTER** the Anchor date.

4. Click OK. You should see the activity that you just created on the third wizard screen.

5. Create the activities in Table 7-6.

Field	Activity #1	Activity #2	Activity #3
Activity Type	To-Do	Call	Marketing Call
Starts	1	6	8
Regarding	Send Literature	Confirm Shipment	Follow up per email
Priority	High	Medium High	Medium

Table 7-6 Activities for the series

6. When you are finished, the Activity Series screen should look like the one shown in Figure 7-46.

   If necessary, you can resize the columns on this screen just like you can on the tabs on the Contact Detail view.

   Click Next.

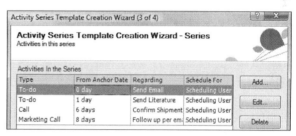

Figure 7-46 Activities in the series

7. The option **YES, SCHEDULE NOW** should be selected, as shown in Figure 7-47.

   Click Finish.

   You will see the Schedule Activity Series dialog box.

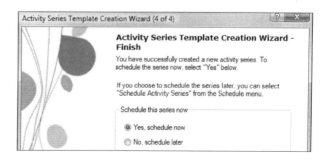

Figure 7-47 Activity Series Finish screen

Assign The Activity Series To Contacts

You can assign the activities in the series to one or more contacts as soon as you create the activity series, by following the steps below.

1. Click the Contacts button on the Schedule Activity Series dialog box and select the first option.

2. Assign the activities to all of the contacts in the Sales Reps with no email address group, then click OK.

3. Change the **SERIES ANCHOR DATE** to next Monday.

4. You should have the options shown in Figure 7-48.

   The only difference should be the anchor date.

   Click the Schedule button.

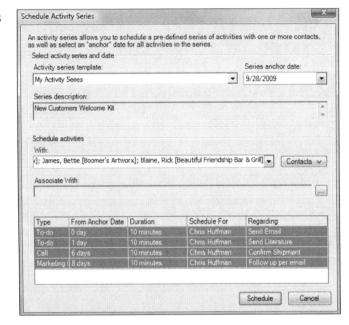

Figure 7-48 Schedule Activities Series dialog box

5. Look up the contact Emily Dunn, then click on the Activities tab.

You should see the four activities from the series, as illustrated in Figure 7-49.

Notice that they are in date order.

Type		Date	Time	Priority	Scheduled With	Regarding
		9/11/2009	None	Low	Emily Dunn	Send Quote
		9/24/2009	None	High	Emily Dunn	Send Quote
		9/24/2009	None	High	+George Agen	Send Quote
		9/28/2009	None	Low	+Rick Blaine	Send Email
		9/29/2009	None	High	+Rick Blaine	Send Literature
		10/5/2009	None	Mediu...	+Rick Blaine	Confirm Shipment
		10/6/2009	None	Medium	+Rick Blaine	Follow up per email

Figure 7-49 Activities from the series

Exercise 7.16: How To Edit An Activity Series

In this exercise you will modify the activity series that you just created. You will also assign users to tasks in the activity series.

1. Schedule ⇒ Manage ⇒ Activity Series Templates. Select the **EDIT AN EXISTING ACTIVITY SERIES** option, then click Next.

2. Select the activity series that you created, then click Next.

3. Add the following to the Description field. − (Select the anchor date to equal the date that you will send the literature), as shown in Figure 7-50, then click Next.

The reason that I include information about the anchor date in the Activity Series description is so that I will know which activity is the one driving the series. Doing this is optional.

Figure 7-50 Modified activity series description

4. Select the Send Literature activity, then click the Edit button.

5. Click the last option in the **SCHEDULE FOR** section, then click the **SCHEDULE FOR** button.

6. Open the drop-down list on the Schedule For dialog box and select Allison.

7. Click OK twice to return to the Activity Series wizard.

8. Repeat the steps above to assign a user to the activities in Table 7-7.

Activity	Assign To
Confirm Shipment	Ernst
Follow up per email	Jonathan

Table 7-7 Activities to assign to users

9. Change the Starts field of the Send Email activity to 2, then select **BEFORE ANCHOR DATE** from the drop-down list, as illustrated in Figure 7-51.

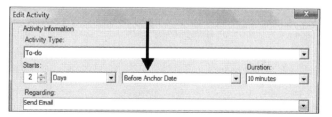

Figure 7-51 Anchor Date modified

When you are finished, the **SCHEDULE FOR** column on the wizard screen should look like the one shown in Figure 7-52.

Figure 7-52 Modified activity series

Notice that the first To-Do activity has **-2 DAYS** in the From Anchor Date column. That is because you selected the Before Anchor Date option, which means that this activity should be started two days before the anchor date.

10. Click Next. Select No, Schedule later, then click Finish.

OPPORTUNITIES

In this lesson you will learn the following tasks that will show you how to create and manage opportunities.

- ☑ Schedule a follow up activity for an opportunity
- ☑ How to edit the Product List
- ☑ How to view an opportunity
- ☑ How to associate an opportunity to a company
- ☑ Lookup opportunity options
- ☑ Export opportunities to Excel
- ☑ Creating quotes
- ☑ Change the status of an opportunity
- ☑ Opportunity reports
- ☑ Create opportunity graphs and pipelines
- ☑ Customize products and processes
- ☑ Creating process lists and stages
- ☑ Importing and exporting stages
- ☑ Importing and exporting products

LESSON 8

What Is An Opportunity?

An opportunity is a sale in progress, meaning there is some likelihood that the contact may make a purchase. Opportunities automate the sales process. You can run reports that will show what stage opportunities are in and which opportunities you have the best chance of turning into a sale. Each opportunity can only be associated to one contact, but a contact can have more than one opportunity. You can view the opportunity and check on the status. Like activities, opportunities create history records when they are created or when certain fields like the Status or Close Date is changed.

Tracking Potential Sales

ACT! provides a way to manage and track potential sales through opportunities. The tracking process is quite extensive. You can track the opportunities from the beginning, through each stage of the process. There are six stages that you can monitor in the CHT1 Sales process that comes with ACT!. You can track opportunities by dollar amount, sales rep, status and more. You can also customize the opportunity process and products that come with ACT!. You can create your own opportunity processes and import processes that are created in another software package. Opportunities can be exported, which will allow you to analyze the data in different ways.

NEW Opportunity Detail View

The Opportunity Detail View shown in Figure 8-1 replaces the Opportunity dialog box in ACT! 2009 and earlier versions. This view is used to create and edit sales. The options are explained in detail in Exercise 8.1, as you create an opportunity.

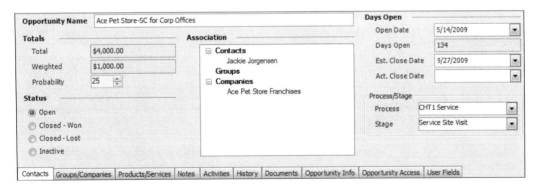

Figure 8-1 Opportunity Detail View

Four tabs on the view shown above in Figure 8-1 are specific to opportunities. The data types on these tabs are explained below.

Opportunity Detail View Tabs

① **Products/Services** This tab stores the basic information about the opportunity, as shown in Figure 8-2.

② **Opportunity Info** Figure 8-3 shows the fields on this tab. The field(s) that you may want to fill in when creating an opportunity are the Referred By and Competitor fields. Entering data on this tab is optional.

③ **Opportunity Access** The options shown in Figure 8-4 are the same as the ones on the Contact Access tab. [See Lesson 3, Contact Access Tab]

④ **User Fields** Some of the fields on this tab, as shown in Figure 8-5, are similar to fields on the User Fields tab on the Contact Detail view because they have the character field type, which is free form. You can use the fields to store data that does not fit in any of the other fields on the Opportunity view. The Opportunity Field 2 has the Date data type by default. You can rename these fields in the layout.

Name	Item #	Quantity	Cost	Price	Adjusted Price	Discount	Subtotal
TechONE System	T1SYS	2.00	$5,000.00	$12,000.00	$12,000.00	0.00%	$24,000.00
TWO Component	TWO	1.00	$1,750.00	$4,000.00	$4,000.00	0.00%	$4,000.00

Figure 8-2 Products/Services tab

Product/Services Tab Subtotal Field

I am not sure why the subtotal field is so far to the right and can't be resized like the other columns on this tab can. I had to make the workspace smaller to be able to include the subtotal field in the screen shots.

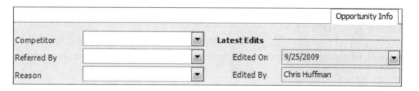

Figure 8-3 Opportunity Info tab

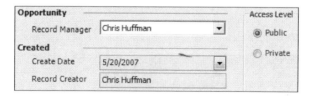

Figure 8-4 Opportunity Access tab

Figure 8-5 User Fields tab

The options in the Opportunity Field 1, shown in Figure 8-6 are different types of payments that can be accepted to pay for the order.

Figure 8-6 Opportunity Field 1 drop-down list options

The option in the Opportunity Field 2, shown in Figure 8-7 is a calendar.

This field can be used as a date field for a date that is not already captured in any of the other opportunity fields.

Figure 8-7 Opportunity Field 2 drop-down list

Opportunity Detail View Toolbar

Figure 8-8 shows the Opportunity Detail view toolbar. Table 8-1 explains the buttons on the toolbar.

Figure 8-8 Opportunity Detail view toolbar

Button	Description
1	Displays the opportunities in detail view.
2	Displays the opportunities in list view.
3	Displays the first opportunity in the view.
4	Displays the previous opportunity in the view.
5	Displays the record number currently displayed and the total number of records displayed in the view.
6	Displays the next opportunity in the view.
7	Displays the last opportunity in the view.
8	Save the changes.
9	Opens the Quick Print Options dialog box.
10	Duplicates the current opportunity.

Table 8-1 Opportunity Detail view toolbar buttons explained

Button	Description
11	Is used to add or remove contacts for the opportunity.
12	Creates a quote for the opportunity.
13	Is used to add a product to the opportunity.
14	Opens the Manage Product List dialog box.
15	Is used to select a layout.

Table 8-1 Opportunity Detail view toolbar buttons explained (Continued)

Opportunity List View

You have the option of viewing all or some of the opportunities for contacts that you have access to. You can filter opportunities. You can also print opportunities, as well as, customize the Opportunity List view, which you will learn how to do in Lesson 16.

1. Click the Opportunity List button on the Navigation Pane. If you click on a contact name you will open the Contact Detail view for the contact.

Opportunity List View Toolbar

Figure 8-9 shows the Opportunity List view toolbar. Table 8-2 explains the buttons on the toolbar, that are not on the Opportunity Detail view toolbar.

Figure 8-9 Opportunity List view toolbar

Button	Description
1	Is used to create an opportunity pipeline.
2	Is used to create an opportunity graph.
3	Opens the Manage Product List dialog box.
4	Is used to create an automatic lookup of contacts associated to the opportunities that are displayed.
5	Is used to customize the columns at the bottom of the Opportunity List view.
6	Is used to export the opportunities that are displayed to Excel.

Table 8-2 Opportunity List view toolbar buttons explained

Using The Opportunity List Filters

The filter options for the Opportunity List view are shown in Figure 8-10. They are helpful if there are a lot of opportunities displayed in the list view and you only need to see certain ones. Like other views, you can sort the data on the bottom half of the view by clicking on the column headings. The filter options are explained below.

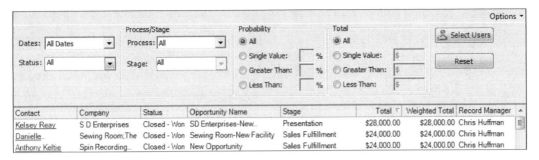

Figure 8-10 Opportunity List view

① The **DATES** drop-down list options shown in Figure 8-11 are used to select the date range that you want to see opportunities for.

② The **STATUS** drop-down list options shown in Figure 8-12 are used to select the statuses that you want to see opportunities for.

③ The **PROCESS** drop-down list options shown in Figure 8-13 are used to select the process that the opportunities must have in order to be displayed. The options shown are the processes in the demo database.

④ The **STAGE** option is only available once a process has been selected. The options in the drop-down list shown in Figure 8-14 are specific to the process that is selected. The default stage is **ALL**. The stage options show are for the CHT1 Service process.

⑤ The **PROBABILITY** options are used to select a single value and percent for opportunities that you want to see. If you only wanted to see opportunities that have a 91% or greater probability of closing (making the sale), you would select the options shown in Figure 8-15. The 90% shown in the **GREATER THAN** field will NOT return probabilities that are 90%, only probabilities that are greater. If you wanted to include 90%, you would have to enter 89% in the field.

⑥ The **TOTAL** options are used to select the total dollar amount that the opportunity must have to be displayed. If you only wanted to see opportunities that have a total amount less than $1,000, you would select the options shown in Figure 8-16.

⑦ The **SELECT USERS** button opens a dialog box that is used to select the users that you want to see opportunities for.

⑧ The **RESET** button will clear all of the filter options that you previously selected. I tend to click this button as soon as I open the Opportunity List view so that all of the opportunities are displayed before I apply any filters.

⑨ The **OPTIONS** button is used to select whether or not private opportunities should be displayed. You can also customize the columns in the Opportunities List by selecting the **CUSTOMIZE COLUMNS** option on this button.

Figure 8-13 Process options

Figure 8-11 Date options   **Figure 8-12** Status options

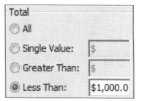

Figure 8-14 Stage options   **Figure 8-15** 90% or   **Figure 8-16** Total amount
                                  greater probability options   less than $1,000 options

 Additional Ways To Filter Contacts On The Opportunity List View

① Right-click in the list of opportunities and select **CREATE LOOKUP**.
② Click the **CREATE CONTACT LOOKUP** button on the toolbar.

 Product Name Field Not Available On Opportunity List View

In ACT! 2009 and earlier, the Product Name field was on the Opportunity List view. It has been removed. I could not find a way to add it back to the view. I don't know for sure, but I think that because the product fields are now in a different table from the opportunity fields, which may be why the Product Name field is currently not on the Opportunity List view. If so, the Product table needs to be added to the Customize Columns dialog box, so that those fields can be added to the Opportunity List view as needed.

Status Bar

Figure 8-17 shows the information that is displayed in the Status bar. You will see the total number of opportunities, the weighted and grand total dollar amounts of the opportunities that are displayed. The **WEIGHTED TOTAL** field is calculated based on the product total and the probability of closing the opportunity.

Lookup: All Opportunities   180 Opportunities, $834,585.00 Weighted Total, $1,535,400.00 Grand Total

Figure 8-17 Opportunity status bar

Opportunity List View Shortcut Menu

The Opportunity List view shortcut menu shown in Figure 8-18 has been modified from ACT! 2009.

Many of the options, like the Show Contacts, Show Products, Edit Estimated Close Date and View Summary report have been removed.

The **FILTER OPPORTUNITIES** option opens the dialog box shown in Figure 8-19. It is another way to filter the opportunities. It contains the same options that are at the top of the Opportunity List view.

The **PRINT OPPORTUNITY LIST** option creates the report shown in Figure 8-20. This report contains all of the opportunities that are displayed on the list view.

Figure 8-18 Opportunity List view shortcut menu

Figure 8-19 Filter Opportunities dialog box

Contact	Company	Status	Opportunity...	Stage	Total	Weighted Total	Record Manager
Joanne Lisle	Picture Frame...	Open	Picture Frame...	Initial...	$0.00	$0.00	Chris Huffman
Dr. Deiter Brock	Brock, Lathers...	Open	Brock, Lethers...	Needs...	$400.00	$100.00	Chris Huffman
James Finlay	Widget...	Open	Widget...	Negotiation	$500.00	$325.00	Chris Huffman
Albert Barry	Mercury...	Open	Mercury...	Initial...	$600.00	$60.00	Chris Huffman
Dan Minnick	Django...	Closed -...	Dijango...	Negotiation	$800.00	$800.00	Chris Huffman
Silvia Carlini	Hospital de la...	Closed -...	Hospital de la...	Needs...	$800.00	$800.00	Chris Huffman

Figure 8-20 Opportunity List report

Exercise 8.1: Create An Opportunity

If you have viewed the Opportunity Tracking tour in the Help system, you may think that creating an opportunity is complicated. You can view the tour or look at the examples, but the process probably won't "click" until you create a new opportunity, which is the best way to fully understand each component of an opportunity.

 Opportunities inherit the security that the contact has.

1. Open the contact record for Mary Wood in the Contact Detail view.

2. On the Opportunities tab, click the **NEW OPPORTUNITY** button, illustrated in Figure 8-21.

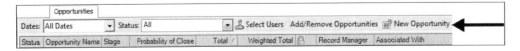

Figure 8-21 Opportunities tab options

3. Type My first opportunity in the Opportunity Name field.

 Many people use a purchase order number or the contacts company name and a sequential number as the **OPPORTUNITY NAME**.

Select The Probability

The probability is a percent. It signifies to what degree you think that the opportunity will result in a sale. Throughout the opportunity process, the probability can change.

4. Type 80 in the Probability field.

Status Options

There are four status options as discussed below.

① **Open** This is the default status for a new opportunity. This status means that there is activity for the opportunity. Often, the activity is you hearing from the contact or you contacting them.

② **Closed - Won** Select this option when the opportunity results in a sale.

③ **Closed - Lost** Select this option if the opportunity did not result in a sale and there is currently no activity for the opportunity.

④ **Inactive** Select this option if there is currently no activity for the opportunity, but there is still a chance that a sale may happen.

Association Section

This section displays the contacts, groups and companies that are associated with the opportunity.

Days Open Options

The options in this section are dates for the potential sale.

OPEN DATE Is the date that the opportunity record was created.

DAYS OPEN This field is updated automatically. It displays the number of days between the Open date and the Act. Close date.

Enter The Est. (Estimated) Close Date

This is the date that you would like to have the sale closed by. Like the Probability field, the value in this field can change during the course of the opportunity process.

5. Enter a date that is 30 days from today. The top half of the Opportunity Detail view should look like the one shown in Figure 8-22. The only difference should be the date in the Est. Close Date field.

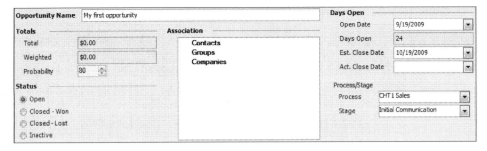

Figure 8-22 Options for a new opportunity

The **ACT. CLOSE DATE** field should be filled in when the contact buys the product or service.

> The **EST. CLOSE DATE** is the field used in date range criteria for filters, lookups and reports for open and inactive opportunities. The **ACT. CLOSE DATE** field is used in date range criteria for closed opportunities.

What Is A Process List?

A Process List contains the tasks that need to be completed for a sale. If you or your company has a set of tasks for a sale or part of a sale, you should create a process list so that everyone that creates an opportunity will complete the same set of tasks for each opportunity that is created. A process list may remind you of an activity series.

For example, you or your company may have a process for new contacts like call the contact, send the contact a brochure and go see the contact. These three tasks would be a process list that you could create. You can also incorporate an existing process list.

Select The Process

The process shown earlier in Figure 8-13 comes with ACT!. Each process has its own list of stages. Later in this lesson you will learn how to create your own process list.

Select The Stage

The stage options are based on the process that is selected. The stage indicates where the opportunity is in the sales process. This can be used to let you know which opportunities need your immediate attention.

6. Select the Needs Assessment stage.

Products And Services

The fields that you just filled in are the basic fields for an opportunity. The options on the Products/Services tab are the items for the opportunity that the contact will hopefully purchase.

It is not advised, but you can also type a new product in. It will only be available for the current opportunity. The reason that you should add the product to the list is to help keep the products consistent for all opportunities.

The **NAME** drop-down list shown in Figure 8-23 includes all of the products and services that the contact can purchase.

Figure 8-23 Name drop-down list items

Select The Products And Services For The Opportunity

1. On the Products/Services tab, click the Add button.

2. Open the Name drop-down list and select the service, ONE Component.

It is not a requirement that products or services have an item number. Item numbers should be set up when the product is added to the list. If the information is incorrect in the Product List you can change it in the opportunity that you are working on. Changing it here would only apply the change to the opportunity that you have open. It is best to change the item number in the product list.

3. Type 2 in the Quantity field.

Price Considerations

The cost and price are automatically filled in because they are stored in the product list.
If these values are not correct, you have two options to correct them, as discussed below.

① Edit the fields on the Opportunities detail view. This option only changes the values in the current opportunity.
② Edit the data in the product list. This option will change the price throughout the database.

Adjusted Price

Filling in this field is optional. It is used to give the contact a discount or price that is different then the default price for the product or service. If you change the price in this field, the discount percent is automatically recalculated.

4. You should have the options shown in Figure 8-24.

   The Display Fields button is used to add, remove and reorder the fields on the Products/Services tab.

   Click OK.

Figure 8-24 Add/Edit Product dialog box

Add A Service

In this part of the exercise you will add a service to the opportunity and learn how to set up a discount.

1. Click the Add button, then add the Service Contract service.

2. Change the discount to 20%.

3. Click OK.

   You should have the products shown in Figure 8-25.

Products/Services								
⊕ Add... ⊖ Delete								
Name	Item #	Quantity	Cost	Price	Adjusted Price	Discount	Subtotal	Discount Type
Service Contract	SC	1.00	$750.00	$2,000.00	$1,600.00	20.00%	$1,600.00	Percentage
ONE Component	ONE	2.00	$1,000.00	$2,500.00	$2,500.00	0.00%	$5,000.00	Percentage

Figure 8-25 Products and Services added to the opportunity

Giving A Discount For The Entire Order

As you just learned, you can discount each item on the opportunity. It would be nice if we could also give a discount off of the entire order. For example, "Spend $100, get $20 off". I could not find a way to create this type of discount.

The Details Tab

In ACT! 2009 and earlier, the Details tab on the Opportunity dialog box was used to enter notes. That functionality has been removed from the opportunity process. Instead, use the Notes tab.

If there is information that does not fit in any of the other fields, you can enter it in a note.

1. On the Notes tab, click the Insert New Note button.

2. Type This is my first opportunity in the field.

3. Click the Save Changes button. Leave the opportunity open.

Exercise 8.2: Schedule A Follow Up Activity For The Opportunity

The default follow up opportunity activity is a phone call. The default Regarding information is the opportunity name. If there is a stage, it is automatically included in the Regarding field, as illustrated in Figure 8-26. Scheduling an activity for an opportunity is the same as scheduling other activities. In this exercise you will schedule a phone call activity for tomorrow for the opportunity.

1. On the Contacts tab, click the **FOLLOW UP** button.

2. Change the Start Date to tomorrow, then change the Start time to 2 PM.

3. Click OK to close the Scheduled Activity dialog box.

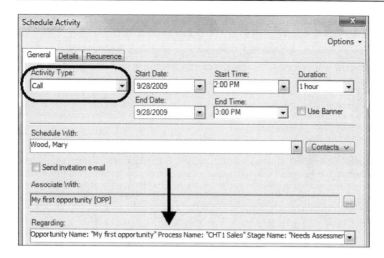

Figure 8-26 Opportunity follow up activity

Exercise 8.3: Edit The Product List

In this exercise you will learn how to add a new product to the Product drop-down list.

1. Tools ⇒ Define Fields. Click on the **MANAGE PRODUCT LIST** link.

> **Other Ways To Open The Manage Product List Dialog Box**
>
> ① Click the Manage Product List button on the Opportunity List view toolbar.
> ② Contacts ⇒ Opportunities ⇒ Manage Product List.
> ③ Click the Modify Fields for Product tab link in the Related Tasks section of the Opportunity Detail view.

2. Click the Add button, then type ACT! Book in the Name field.

3. Press the Tab key and type BK-0001 in the Item Number field, then type 10 in the Cost field.

4. Type 39.95 in the Price field.

   The item should look like the one illustrated in Figure 8-27.

Figure 8-27 New product illustrated

5. Click OK, then click Close on the Define Fields dialog box.

Exercise 8.4: How To Associate An Opportunity To A Company

In this exercise you will associate the opportunity that you created in Exercise 8.1 to a company.

1. On the Activities tab of the opportunity, double-click on the opportunity that is scheduled with Mary Wood.

2. Click the button at the end of the **ASSOCIATE WITH** field.

3. Open the View drop-down list and select Companies. Scroll down the list and select My New Company, then click the Add button.

4. Click OK. You will see the company in the Associate With field. Click OK to close the Schedule Activity dialog box.

> **Opportunity Linking Issue**
>
> As you have learned in previous lessons, linked contacts that are marked as private can still have data from various tabs displayed under the company record that it is linked to. Opportunity records of linked contacts will not be visible from the company record, but opportunity history records will be visible from a company record. If you do not want the opportunity history records of private contacts visible, you have to clear the **AUTOMATICALLY RECORD HISTORY WHEN CONTACTS ARE LINKED OR UNLINKED** option on the Company Preferences dialog box. [See Lesson 5, Linking Company And Contact Records]

Exercise 8.5: Lookup Opportunities

The Lookup Opportunity options are similar to the opportunity filter options because they are used to narrow down the opportunities that will be displayed on the screen. By default, the opportunities that are displayed from the lookup are the ones for the current user (you). If you want to view opportunities for all users or specific users, you have to select the users. In this exercise you will perform three opportunity lookups.

Figure 8-28 shows the Opportunity lookup menu options. Most of the options shown were explained earlier in this lesson in the Using The Opportunity List Filters section. The other options are explained below.

The **NAME** option uses the Opportunity Name field for the name that you want to search for.

The **PRODUCT** option uses the Name field on the Products/Services tab for the product that you want to search for.

Figure 8-28 Opportunity lookup menu options

Lookup Opportunity #1

In this lookup exercise you will find opportunities for all users that are in the Initial Communication stage of the CHT1 Sales process.

1. Click the Lookup button or Lookup ⇒ Opportunities ⇒ Other Fields, if you do not have an opportunity view displayed.

2. Select the **PROCESS** field to search on.

3. Type CHT1 Sales in the Search for field.

   You should have the options shown in Figure 8-29.

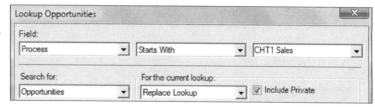

Figure 8-29 Lookup Opportunity options to find a process

4. Click OK. You will see fewer opportunities because all of the opportunities are not in the process that you selected in the lookup.

5. Click the Lookup button.

6. Select the Stage field to search on.

7. Type Initial Communication in the Search field.

8. Select the Narrow Lookup option shown in Figure 8-30.

Figure 8-30 Lookup Opportunity options to limit the search to a specific stage

9. Click OK. You will see less opportunities because all of the CHT1 Sales opportunities are not in the Initial Communication stage.

Lookup Opportunity #2

In this lookup exercise you will find opportunities that have been open for more than 30 days. This requires two lookups: one to find opportunities with the number of days greater than 30 and one to narrow down the opportunities to only those that are open. When the lookup requires searching on more than one field, the efficient rule of thumb is to select the field that will eliminate the most records first. In databases with thousands of records, this will greatly speed up the search process. Being able to see a list of these opportunities will allow you to follow up to see what you can do to close the sale.

1. Click the Lookup button, then select the **DAYS OPEN** field to search on.

2. Select the **GREATER THAN**
   option, then type 30 in the
   field next to it.

   You should have the options
   selected that are shown in
   Figure 8-31.

   Figure 8-31 Lookup Opportunity options to find
   opportunities greater than 30 days

   Click OK.

Status Field Lookup

When you need to create a lookup for the status field, you cannot type in the status
name. If you do, you will see an error message that says "The value you type is greater
than the max field length". This did not happen in ACT! 2009 and earlier versions. You
could type in the name. I suspect that the developers hooked the status field up to the
ID field, which by default is a numeric field, instead of a text field.

Until this is fixed, you have to enter a number for the status, as shown below.
0 (zero) = Open, 1 = Closed - Won, 2 = Closed - Lost, 3 = Inactive

---

3. Click the Lookup button, then select the Status field to search on.

4. Type 0 (for the Open status) in the Search field.

5. Change the Current lookup option to Narrow Lookup, then click OK. You will see the
   opportunities that have been open for more than 30 days.

NEW Table Name In Lookup

As shown in Figure 8-32, the
table name (in brackets) is visible
for fields that are not in the main
table for the lookup.

The two fields shown at the
bottom of the drop-down list are
from the Opportunity table,
which is the main table for this
lookup.

Figure 8-32 Table name in lookup

Lookup Opportunity #3

In this lookup exercise you will find opportunities that have a specific product.

1. Lookup ⇒ Product.

2. Type Two Component in the Search field, then click OK.

As shown in Figure 8-33, you cannot see the products for the opportunity. To see the products, you have to double-click on an opportunity.

Contact	Company	Status	Opportunity Name	Stage	Total	Weighted Total
Bruce Baker	SimAero	Closed - Won	SimAero-Upgrade to TWO	Presentation	$4,000.00	$4,000.00
William Cadbury	Cadbury	Open	Cadbury-Upgrade to...	Presentation	$8,000.00	$3,200.00
Milton Hershey	Hershey...	Open	Hershey Chocolate-Smelter	Needs Assessment	$4,000.00	$1,000.00
Vivian Grace	International Safari	Closed - Won	International Safari-...	Negotiation	$12,000.00	$12,000.00

Figure 8-33 Result of the lookup

How To Close An Opportunity

This is the part of the opportunity process that will probably make you happy. When a contact makes a purchase they become a customer and their opportunity needs to be closed. If a contact does not make a purchase for whatever reason, the opportunity should be closed indicating that. The steps below will show you how to close an opportunity.

1. Display the opportunity that you want to close.

2. Select the appropriate closed status. [See Status Options earlier in this lesson]

3. Select or type in a **REASON** if applicable, on the Opportunity Info tab.

4. You can also add comments on the **NOTES** tab. Once a closed status is selected and you click the Save Changes button, history records similar to the ones shown in Figure 8-34 will be created for the opportunity.

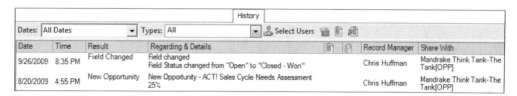

Figure 8-34 History record for a closed opportunity

Exercise 8.6: Export Opportunities To Excel

In this exercise you will export the opportunities to Excel. In Lesson 10 you will learn how to export contact data to Excel. Exporting the opportunity data will allow the data to be analyzed, as well as, create charts.

1. Lookup all of the opportunities.

2. Click the Export Current List To Excel button on the toolbar.

If you look at the bottom of the spreadsheet you will see three tabs. The first tab displays the data from the Opportunity List view.

The second tab on the spreadsheet displays a Pivot chart of the data.

The third tab displays the summary information that is displayed on the Pivot chart. If you change the options on this tab, the chart will automatically be updated to reflect the changes. You can select different options in the drop-down lists (Status, Record Manager and Data) to filter the data like you can on the Pivot chart. Doing this will cause the following to happen.

   ① The data will be recalculated on the Pivot Sheet tab.
   ② The Pivot chart will change.

The opportunity records will be exported and Excel will open automatically. The Pivot chart should look like the one shown in Figure 8-35. The Pivot Table Field List dialog box shown in Figure 8-35 displays all of the fields that were exported to Excel. You can drag any of those fields to the chart. The Pivot tab should look like the one shown in Figure 8-36.

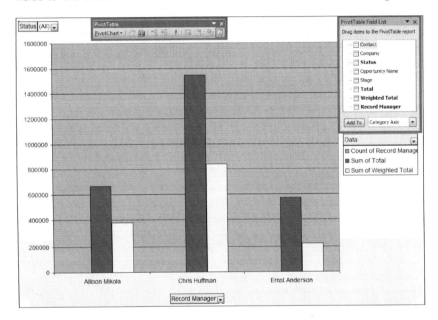

Figure 8-35 Opportunities Pivot chart

B	C	D	E
Status	(All)		
	Data		
Record Manager	Count of Record Manage	Sum of Total	Sum of Weighted Total
Allison Mikola	97	$667,600.00	$376,975.00
Chris Huffman	181	$1,547,280.00	$841,305.00
Ernst Anderson	99	$571,500.00	$224,395.00
Grand Total	377	$2,786,380.00	$1,442,675.00

Figure 8-36 Opportunities Pivot sheet tab

3. Close Excel when you are finished viewing the data. You can save the spreadsheet in your folder if you want. It is not mandatory to save it because you will not need it to complete any other exercise.

Crash Course In Pivot Table Data

This is truly a crash course in Pivot table data. Hopefully it is enough for you to understand the basic functionality if you have not used this tool in Excel before. The Pivot Chart tab displays the summary opportunity data graphically. ACT! displays the data in detail.

In the upper left corner of the chart is the **STATUS** drop-down list. If you select a different status, the data will be recalculated based on the status that you select and the chart will change. At the bottom of the chart is the **RECORD MANAGER** drop-down list. When you select a user from the list, the opportunities that the user created will appear on the chart.

Figure 8-37 shows the Pivot chart with the Status changed to **CLOSED-WON**.

The **DATA** button is used to filter the following total fields: Count of Record Manager, Grand total (Sum of Total) and the Sum of Weighted Total.

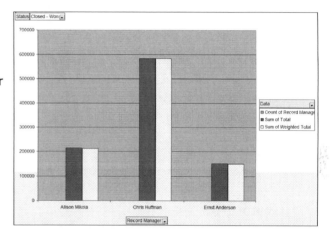

Figure 8-37 Status changed to Closed-Won

You can move the buttons around on the Opportunity Pivot tab, as shown in Figure 8-38.

Compare this to Figure 8-36 shown earlier.

B	C	D	E
Record Manager	(All)		
Status	Closed - Won		
	Data		
	Count of Record Manager	**Sum of Total**	**Sum of Weighted Total**
Total	121	$949,200.00	$946,200.00

Figure 8-38 Record Manager button moved on the Opportunities Pivot tab

If you move the Record
Manager button before
the Status button on the
Pivot tab and then view
the chart, it will look like
the one shown in
Figure 8-39.

Figure 8-39 Pivot chart after the Record Manager button is moved

Generating Quotes

Often you may need to send the opportunity that you create to a contact when they request a quote. To generate a quote you have to have Microsoft Word and Excel installed.

Quote Preferences

There are preferences for quotes that you can set.
Tools ⇒ Preferences ⇒ General Tab ⇒ Quote Preferences button, will open the Quote Preferences dialog box.

If the option **PROMPT FOR QUOTE NUMBER WHEN GENERATING** is checked, you can select a prefix for quote numbers, as shown in Figure 8-40.

Adding a quote prefix means that all quotes that you create will start with the same characters and numbers that you enter in the **QUOTE PREFIX** field. You can enter the prefix of your choice or leave it blank if you want to enter a free form quote prefix.

Figure 8-40 Quote Preferences dialog box

Exercise 8.7: Create A Quote

1. On the Opportunity List view, double-click on the quote that you created for Mary Wood.

2. Click the **CREATE QUOTE** button on the toolbar. The document shown in Figure 8-41 will open in Microsoft Word. If you want to save the quote, save it in your folder.

Notice that the shipping and handling charges have not been filled in. You have to fill this in manually.

To modify the shipping and handling field, double-click in the section that has the products. The Excel spreadsheet shown in Figure 8-42 will appear. It has the formulas for the calculations.

The tax rate that you enter should be the tax rate for your state.

If you plan to use the quote document, you may want to customize it a little by adding fields or changing the font. This quote template is really two files, as discussed below.

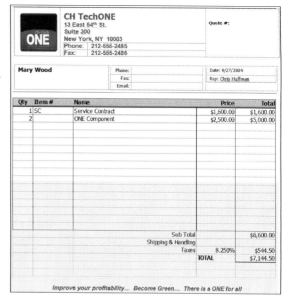

Figure 8-41 Quote

① The **QUOTE.ADT** file is the portion of the quote created as a Word template, which you can modify.
② The **QUOTE.XLT** file is the portion of the quote created in Excel, as shown in Figure 8-42. You should not modify the structure of this part of the quote template.

	A	B	C	D	E
1	Qty	Item #	Name	Price	Total
2	1	SC	Service Contract	$1,600.00	$1,600.00
3	2		ONE Component	$2,500.00	$5,000.00
4					
5					
6					
7					
27			Sub Total		$6,600.00
28			Shipping & Handling		
29			Taxes	8.250%	$544.50
30			**TOTAL**		$7,144.50
31					

Sheet1 / Sheet2 / Sheet3 /

Figure 8-42 Spreadsheet in the Word document

Exercise 8.8: How To Change The Status Of An Opportunity

Earlier in this lesson you learned that an opportunity can have one of four statuses. When you need to change a status, follow the steps below.

1. On the Opportunity List view, double-click on the opportunity that you want to change the status of. In this exercise select the opportunity for Mary Wood.

2. Select the status that you want. Select Closed-Won for this exercise.

3. On the Opportunity Info tab, type `Purchased service` in the Reason field, then click the Save Changes button.

Viewing Opportunities From The Opportunities Tab

You have created opportunities, viewed them and learned how to filter them from the
Opportunities List view. In addition to being able to view opportunities from the Opportunities
List view, you can view opportunities from the Opportunities tab on detail views. Like other tabs
that you have learned about, you can also customize the layout of the Opportunities tab.

As shown in Figure 8-43, some of the filter options that are available on the Opportunities
List view are available on the Opportunities tab. If you need more filter options, right-click in
the opportunities and select **FILTER OPPORTUNITIES**. You will see the dialog box shown in
Figure 8-44. This dialog box is a scaled down version of the one that you saw earlier in
Figure 8-19.

Figure 8-43 Opportunities tab

Figure 8-44 Filter Opportunities dialog box

Opportunity Reports

ACT! comes with reports that are specifically for opportunities. In addition to being able to
preview and print the reports, there are five other output options that you can select from.
You can save the reports and send them as an attachment in an email. You can also save them
as a PDF file. The benefit of saving the report in PDF format is that anyone with the free Adobe
Reader can view or print the report.

Report Options

 After running some of the reports on the Opportunity Reports submenu, I noticed that
the Define Filters dialog box for some opportunity reports have the options on the
General tab that are usually on the Opportunity tab. The following reports are like this:
Sales Analysis by Record Manager, Total By Status, Adjusted for Probability, Pipeline
Report and Opportunities By Record Manager.

Exercise 8.9: Sales Analysis By Record Manager Report

This report will display any or all of the available status categories, as well as, the number and percent for each category selected. It also provides a Closed/Won analysis that provides the average and total amounts for the date range and employees that you select.

1. Reports ⇒ Opportunity Reports ⇒ Sales Analysis By Record Manager.

2. Select **PAST** as the Date Range, as shown in Figure 8-45.

   The filter options for this report are used to select opportunities based on the status and date range.

Figure 8-45 Sales Analysis By Record Manager report options

3. Click OK. Your report will look similar to the one shown in Figure 8-46.

   Your report will have more records because you are running the report after I did.

Figure 8-46 Sales Analysis By Record Manager report

Exercise 8.10: Opportunities Adjusted For Probability Report

This report will allow the reader to look for trends in the opportunities that they have and are currently working on. For each status that is selected, the opportunity records will be printed. The total order amount and weighted total amount per status is calculated and printed.

1. Reports ⇒ Opportunity Reports ⇒ Adjusted For Probability.

2. Select all of the opportunity status options, then select the **PAST** Date Range.

3. Click OK. Your report should look like the one shown in Figure 8-47.

Opportunities Adjusted for Probability

Date Range: Before 9/27/2009   Weighted Total: $543,700.00

| Status | Open | Total for Status: $236,000.00 | Weighted Total for Status: $70,900.00 |

Contact	Company	Name	Stage	Est. Close	Prob.	Weighted Total	Total	Record Manager
Paul Brushman	Brushy's Golfing World	Brushy's Golfing World-New Zeeland	Presentation	8/29/2009	40%	$4,800.00	$12,000.00	Ernst Anderson
		A1 Services of UK-UK Upgrade	Initial Communication	8/30/2009	10%	$1,200.00	$12,000.00	Ernst Anderson
Bill Craig	KKQS Radio	KKQS-Chandler Power Station	Initial Communication	8/17/2009	10%	$200.00	$2,000.00	Chris Huffman
Emily Dunn	Boomer's Artworx	Boomer's Artworx-Scottsdale Gallery	Presentation	9/18/2009	40%	$4,800.00	$12,000.00	Chris Huffman
Rick Blaine	Beautiful Friendship Bar &	Beautiful Friendship-Pans	Presentation	8/30/2009	40%	$4,800.00	$12,000.00	Ernst Anderson
Stony Brooke	Duke Industries	Duke Industries-LA Operations	Commitment to Buy	8/28/2009	80%	$9,600.00	$12,000.00	Allison Mikola
Louise Harper	Stevenson & Smith	Stevenson & Smith-Home Office	Presentation	8/28/2009	40%	$4,800.00	$12,000.00	Chris Huffman

Figure 8-47 Opportunities Adjusted for Probability report

Opportunity Graphs And Pipelines

In addition to opportunity reports, ACT! has the ability to create graphs and pipelines for opportunity data. These options are accessed from the Opportunity List view. Graphs and pipelines can be printed and saved in different file formats.

Exercise 8.11: Creating Graphs

The graphs for opportunities that you can create have several options that you can use to customize the graph, like the type of graph and date range of data displayed on the graph.

Create A Bar Graph

In this part of the exercise you will create a bar graph for opportunities created in 2009.

1. On the Opportunity List view, click the **OPPORTUNITY GRAPH** button.

2. On the General tab, select the options below.

    - Display data for all users
    - Graph by month
    - Starting 1/1/2009
    - Ending 12/31/2009

    Your dialog box should have the options shown in Figure 8-48. Depending on the data that is needed to create the graph, you may need to create a lookup first.

Figure 8-48 General tab (bar) graph options

3. On the Graph tab, select the following options.

    - Allow graph to scroll
    - Show horizontal grid lines
    - 3-D Style

4. Click the button at the end of the **GRAPH** option and select a different color.

    Your dialog box should have the options shown in Figure 8-49.

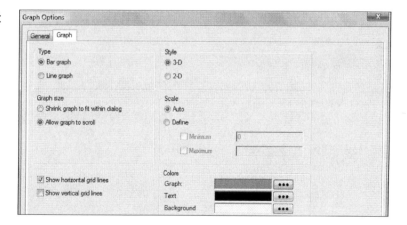

Figure 8-49 Graph tab options

5. Click the **GRAPH** button at the bottom of the dialog box.

The Graph button creates a graph based on the options that are selected.

Your graph should look like the one shown in Figure 8-50.

You may have to use the scroll bar below the graph to scroll to the right to see the charted data.

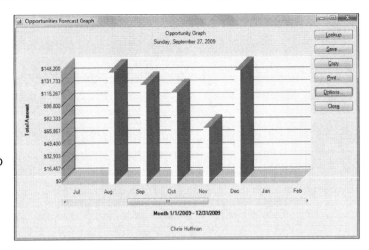

Figure 8-50 Bar graph

The **LOOKUP** button will open the Opportunity List view and display the opportunities that are depicted in the graph.

The **SAVE** button is used to save the graph in .BMP or .JPG graphic file format. Save all of the graphs and pipelines that you create in this lesson in .JPG format.

The **COPY** button sends a copy of the graph to the clipboard in Windows. This allows you to paste a copy of the graph into a document like the ACT! Word Processor or a Power Point presentation.

The **PRINT** button will print the graph.

The **OPTIONS** button opens the Graph Options dialog box shown earlier in Figure 8-48, so that you can make changes and recreate the graph.

6. Save the graph (in .jpg format), in your folder as Bar Graph, as illustrated in Figure 8-51, then close the Opportunities Forecast Graph dialog box.

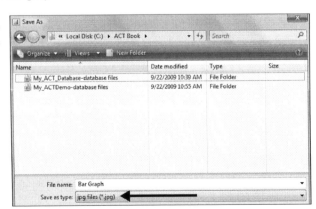

Figure 8-51 Save options for the graph

Create A Line Graph

In this part of the exercise you will create a line graph for opportunities in a specific date range.

1. On the Opportunity List view, click the Opportunity Graph button.

2. On the General tab, select the options below.

   - Display data for all users
   - Graph by week
   - Starting 11/1/2009
   - Ending 12/31/2009
   - Chart header 1 `Opportunity Line Graph`

   Your dialog box should have the options shown in Figure 8-52.

Figure 8-52 General tab (line) graph options

3. On the Graph tab, select the following options.

   - Line graph
   - Allow graph to scroll
   - Show horizontal grid lines
   - Show vertical grid lines
   - 3-D Style
   - Change the background to light yellow

   Your dialog box should have the options shown in Figure 8-53.

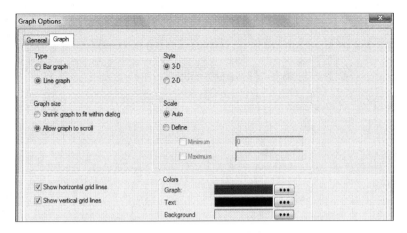

Figure 8-53 Graph tab options

4. Click the Graph button.

   Your graph should look like the one shown in Figure 8-54.

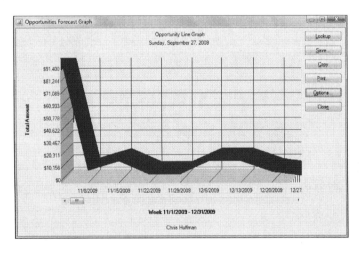

Figure 8-54 Line graph

5. Save the graph (in .jpg format), in your folder as Line Graph.

6. Close the Opportunities Forecast Graph dialog box.

Pipelines

Pipelines graphically display opportunities that have an "Open" status for a specific process at each stage. The options to create a pipeline graph are similar to the ones to create a bar or line graph.

Exercise 8.12: Create A Pipeline Graph

1. On the Opportunity List view, click the Opportunity Pipeline button.

2. Select the options below.

- All contacts
- All users
- Graph header 3
  My First Pipeline

Your dialog box should have the options shown in Figure 8-55.

Figure 8-55 Opportunity Pipeline Options dialog box

 To change a color on the pipeline graph for a stage in the process, click the ellipsis button at the end of the stage in the **COLOR** column, as illustrated above in Figure 8-55.

3. Click the Graph button.

You should see the pipeline graph shown in Figure 8-56.

Save the pipeline graph (in .jpg format), in your folder as Pipeline Graph, then close the Opportunity Pipeline dialog box.

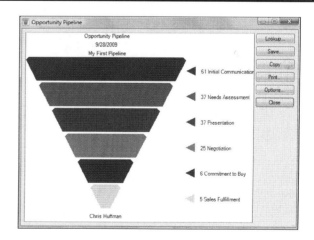

Figure 8-56 Pipeline graph

How To Create And Customize Product And Process Lists

Like the drop-down lists on the Contact Detail view, the Opportunity products and processes drop-down lists can be customized. Earlier in Exercise 8.3, you learned how to add a new product. The remaining exercises in this lesson will show you how to modify opportunity products and processes, as well as, how to import and export stages and products.

Exercise 8.13: Creating Process Lists And Stages

In this exercise you will create a process list and the stages for the process.

1. On an Opportunity view, Opportunities ⇒ Manage Process List.

2. Click on the **CREATE NEW OPPORTUNITY PROCESS** link in the Process Tasks section.

3. Type My first process in the Opportunity Process field, then type
   This process has 3 stages in the Description field, as shown in Figure 8-57.

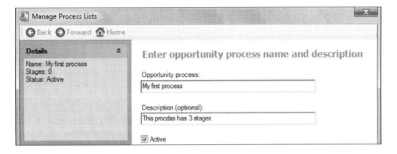

Figure 8-57 Manage Process Lists screen

4. Click Next. Click in the Name field and type First Stage.

5. Press the Tab key twice, then type 80 in the Probability field.

6. Click the Add button, then add the two other stages shown in Figure 8-58.

   The **MOVE UP** and **MOVE DOWN** buttons are used to change the order of the stages.

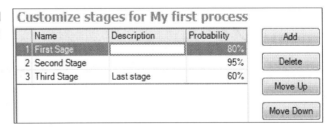

Figure 8-58 Stages for the process

7. Click Finish. You will see the process that you created. In the **PROCESS TASKS** section, notice that there are options to edit and delete processes. Leave the Manage Process Lists window open to complete the next exercise.

Exercise 8.14: Importing Stages

In the previous exercise you created an opportunity process. You also created three stages for the process. If you have a lot of stages for a process or prefer to create them in a spreadsheet, which would allow you to spell check them, you can import the spreadsheet with the stages into ACT!. In this exercise you will import three stages for the process that you created in the previous exercise. The **MANAGE PROCESS LISTS** window should already be open.

1. Select the **MY FIRST PROCESS** opportunity process, then click on the Edit Opportunity Process link.

2. Change the description to have six stages, then click Next.

3. Click the **IMPORT OPPORTUNITY STAGES** link. In your folder, double-click on the Import_Opportunity_Stages file.

   You will see the three new stages, as shown in Figure 8-59.

   If you needed to, you could rearrange the order of the stages.

	Name	Description	Probability
1	First Sage		80%
2	Second Stage		95%
3	Third Stage	Last stage	60%
4	Fourth Stage	Add to catalog mailing	90%
5	Fifth Stage	Placed Order	95%
6	Sixth Stage	Order Shipped	95%

Customize stages for My first process

Figure 8-59 Imported stages

4. Click the Finish button. Leave the Manage Process Lists window open to complete the next exercise.

Exercise 8.15: Exporting Stages

You can export the opportunity stages to a **.csv** file, which is a file format that you can open in Excel. The **MANAGE PROCESS LISTS** window should already be open.

1. Select the Opportunity Process for the stages that you want to export. In this exercise select the **CHT1 SALES** process, then click on the Edit Opportunity Process link.

2. Click Next. Click the Export Opportunity Stages link.

3. Type My Export Stages in the File name field, then press Enter.

4. If you open this file in Excel, it will look like the one shown in Figure 8-60.

   The reason column B is empty is because the stages that were exported do not have any descriptions. Close the Manage Process Lists dialog box.

	A	B	C
1	Initial Communication		10%
2	Needs Assessment		25%
3	Presentation		40%
4	Negotiation		65%
5	Commitment to Buy		80%
6	Sales Fulfillment		90%

Figure 8-60 Exported stages

5. Close the Manage Process Lists window.

Exercise 8.16: Importing Products

If you need to add a lot of products to the database or have the products in an existing file, you can import them into the database. This means that you can create the product list in Excel and save it in .csv format. In this exercise you will learn how to import data.

1. On the Opportunity List view, click the **MANAGE PRODUCT LIST** button.

2. Click the **IMPORT** button, then click the **BROWSE** button on the Import Products dialog box.

3. Double-click on the Products_To_Import file in your folder. If you cannot see it, change the Files of type option to **CSV FILES (*.CSV)**.

4. Check the Source file has column headers option shown in Figure 8-61.

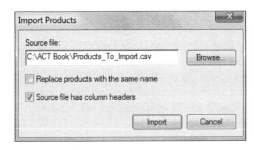

Figure 8-61 Import Products dialog box

The **SOURCE FILE HAS COLUMN HEADERS** option will not import the first row of data in the file. Check this option if the file that you are importing has column headings. If you are not sure, open the file before importing it. You can also view the products on the Manage Product List dialog box and delete the product that is really a column heading.

The **REPLACE PRODUCTS WITH THE SAME NAME** option will overwrite products that are already in the Product list with the changes in the file that you import. This is how you can update existing product information.

5. Click the Import button on the Import Products dialog box.

   Click OK when prompted that the products have been successfully imported.

   You should see the three products illustrated at the bottom of Figure 8-62.

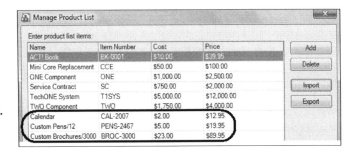

Figure 8-62 Manage Product List dialog box

6. Leave the dialog box open to complete the next exercise.

How To Create A Product List In Excel

The steps below will show you how to create a product list in Excel.

1. Create four columns: Name, Item Number, Cost and Price. Typing in the column names is optional. If you type them in, make sure that you do not import the first row of the spreadsheet.
2. Enter the information for each product.
3. Change the Save as type to **CSV (COMMA DELIMITED) (*.CSV)**, as illustrated in Figure 8-63, then save the file.

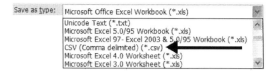

Figure 8-63 CSV file type illustrated

Exercise 8.17: Exporting Products

Exporting products can be useful if you need to change data in several records. You can export the products, make the changes in Excel for example and then import the list back into ACT!. In this exercise you will export products.

1. Open the Manage Product List dialog box if it is not already open, then click the **EXPORT** button.

2. Type My Exported Products as the file name, then press Enter.

3. You can open the exported file in Excel to view it, if you want. Close the Manage Product List dialog box.

🆕 Opportunity Detail View Related Tasks

The related tasks options shown in Figure 8-64 are primarily on the detail view. Some options are also on the list view. The options are explained below.

Figure 8-64 Opportunity Detail view related tasks

DUPLICATE OPPORTUNITY Opens the dialog box shown in Figure 8-65. It is used to select which opportunity fields will be duplicated on the new opportunity record.

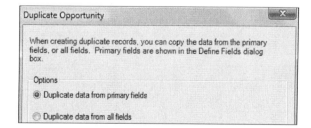

Figure 8-65 Duplicate Opportunity dialog box

CREATE QUOTE [See Exercise 8.7 earlier in this lesson]

SCHEDULE FOLLOW-UP ACTIVITY Opens the Schedule Activity dialog box. Information from the opportunity record is automatically filled in on the activity record.

MODIFY LAYOUT Opens the current opportunity detail view layout in the Layout Designer, so that the layout can be changed.

MODIFY FIELDS FOR PRODUCT TAB Opens the Define Fields dialog box so that you can modify the fields on the Products/Services tab, as well as, other tabs on the Opportunity Detail view. [See Lesson 16, Creating New Fields]

VIEW ALL OPPORTUNITIES Displays all of the opportunities in the Opportunity List view.

SCHEDULE SERIES OF ACTIVITIES [See Lesson 7, Activity Series]

NEW Opportunity List View Related Tasks

The options shown in Figure 8-66 are for the Opportunity List view.

The options that are only on the list view are explained below.

Related Tasks
Export to Excel
Print Opportunities
Change Columns
View All Opportunities
Sort List

Figure 8-66 Opportunity List view related tasks

EXPORT TO EXCEL Exports the opportunities that are displayed to Excel.

PRINT OPPORTUNITIES Opens the Quick Print Options dialog box so that you can select options for how the screen will be printed.

CHANGE COLUMNS Opens the Customize Columns dialog box.

SORT LIST Opens the Sort dialog box to sort the opportunities displayed in the view.

RUNNING REPORTS

Overview

In this lesson you will learn the following about running reports:

- ☑ Selecting report criteria
- ☑ Custom date ranges
- ☑ Printing calendars, address books, labels and envelopes
- ☑ Using the Quick Print options

Reports Overview

ACT! comes with several reports already created that you can use. They are on the Reports menu. In this lesson you will learn how to run some of the reports on the Reports menu. The reports that you run can be printed and saved. Reports are probably a key feature in ACT! because we are a report driven society. For many, reports are the only reason they enter contact information in ACT!. Once you have been using ACT! for a while you will probably see that you are running the same reports on a regular basis. Take some time once you have run reports for about a month and carefully look at the data. Are there columns on the report that do not have any data or very little data? Is the report providing the level of detail that you need? If not, you may need to modify the report and/or enter more data.

The label and envelope options are on the Print dialog box, which is accessed from the File menu. The calendars and address book print options are with the labels and envelopes. Some people think that it is strange that these options are not on the Reports menu, but if you think about it, they are not reports in the true sense of the word.

The Reports menu shown in Figure 9-1 is how you access most of the reports.

Notice the **OTHER REPORTS** options (For example, Other Contact Reports and Other Group Reports). The wording gives the impression that these options would display more reports.

As a programmer, I was not misled by this wording because these options do not have a right arrow like the Group, Company and Opportunity Reports menu options have. A programming standard when a menu option will open a submenu is to put a triangle next to the option.

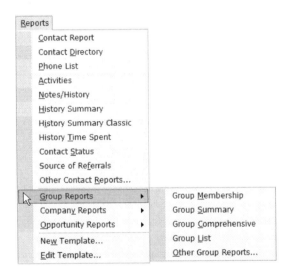

Figure 9-1 Reports menu

If you look closely, you will see that the "Other Reports" menu options have three periods (called an **ELLIPSIS**) after them. This is another programming standard. This is used to signify that selecting the option will open a dialog box.

When you select any of the "Other Reports" options, you will see the **SELECT REPORT** dialog box which has all of the reports that came with ACT!. If you modify reports or create new ones and other people will use the reports, you could save them in this folder or add them to a menu so that other people can access them. OK, the programming lesson for today is over!

Define Filters Dialog Box

The Define Filters dialog box should reduce any anxiety that you may have about selecting options to run various reports, because it is used to select the criteria for each report. Options that are not available for a report are not enabled. You have to create the lookup or run a saved query before selecting a report to run if you do not want to be limited by the options on the Define Filters dialog box. If you know that a certain report needs a lookup or query, you should create it and save it. It would be a nice feature to be able to select a saved lookup or query from the Define Filters dialog box when selecting other report criteria.

Activity, Notes, History And Opportunity Reports

The default date range option for these reports is **CURRENT MONTH**. If left unchanged, this may produce unexpected results by not displaying all of the data that you would expect to see. For example, you create a lookup or run a query that retrieves contact records that have a create date in 2008.

If you leave the default date range of the current month selected, the report will not display any activity, note, history or opportunity data for 2008. Only data for the current month will be displayed on the report. More than likely, you would be expecting to see data for these types of records from 2008.

Tips For Running Reports In This Lesson

① Unless stated otherwise, make sure that the **SEND THE REPORT OUTPUT TO** option on the General tab of the Define Filters dialog box is set to Preview for the report exercises, unless you want to print the report. The remaining report output options are explained in Table 9-1.
② Make sure that the **EXCLUDE 'MY RECORD'** option is checked on the General tab of the Define Filters dialog box. Selecting this option will keep the My Record from printing.
③ Save any report that you want to keep in your folder.
④ Close the report when you are finished viewing it.

File Type	Select This File Type If The Report . . .
Rich-Text	Needs to be edited in a word processor.
HTML	Will be posted on the Internet.
PDF	Needs to be distributed to someone that does not have ACT!. Either the full version of Adobe Acrobat or the free Adobe Reader is needed to view a PDF file.
Text	Needs to be in plain text format. Non text objects like image files are not saved in this format.
Printer	Needs to be printed on paper.
Email	Needs to be sent via email.

Table 9-1 Report output file types explained

Exercise 9.1: The Contact Report

This report will print a profile for each contact that is selected. You can filter the report to include or not include the notes, history, opportunities and activity information.

1. Reports ⇒ Contact Report.

2. On the General tab, select the **ALL CONTACTS** option.

   You should have the options selected that are shown in Figure 9-2.

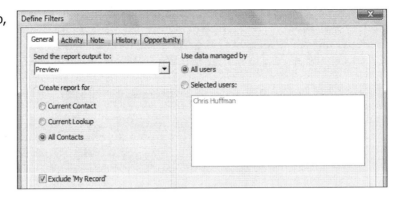

Figure 9-2 General tab options for the Contact report

 If you created a look up for the records that you want to appear on the report prior to opening the report, select the **CURRENT LOOKUP** option. If you only want the report to use the contact record that you have open, select the **CURRENT CONTACT** option.

3. On the Activity tab, clear the **MEETINGS** option. Clearing this option will keep the meeting activities from printing on the report.

4. Open the **DATE RANGE** drop-down list and select Past.

 The **PAST** date range option will only print activities that have a date in the past. The **CUSTOM** button is used to select a specific date range for the activities that you want to include on the report.

5. Clear the **INCLUDE CLEARED ACTIVITIES** option.

   You should have the options selected that are shown in Figure 9-3.

Figure 9-3 Activity options for the Contact report

6. On the Note tab, clear the Notes option.

7. On the History tab, clear the Email and Attachments options, then select the **ALL** date range option.

. . . .

8. On the Opportunity tab, clear the Closed-Won, Closed Lost and Inactive options.

9. Change the Date Range to All, then click OK. The report will open in its own window. In the lower left corner of the Print Preview window you will see the report pages being created.

Report Print Preview Toolbar

Like many other windows in ACT!, the Print Preview window has a toolbar, as shown in Figure 9-4. Table 9-2 explains the buttons on the toolbar.

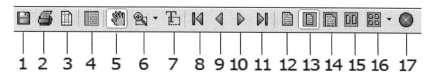

Figure 9-4 Report print preview toolbar

Button	Description
1	Saves the report.
2	Prints the report.
3	Is used to change the paper size, margins and orientation of the report.
4	The Show Navigation Bar button displays the report pages in the thumbnail view, as shown in Figure 9-5.
5	The Hand Tool button is used to move the report page around in the window.
6	The Zoom In Tool button is used to change the magnification of the report displayed on the screen.
7	The Select Text button is used to select text in the report that you want to copy to another document.
8	Displays the first page of the report.
9	Displays the previous page of the report.
10	Displays the next page of the report.
11	Displays the last page of the report.
12	The Actual Size button is used to enlarge the report on the screen.
13	The Full Page button is used to display an entire page of the report, whether or not it is readable.
14	The Page Width button is used to resize the report so that it is the size of the Print Preview window.
15	The Two Pages button is used to display two pages of the report in the window at the same time, as shown in Figure 9-6.
16	The Four Pages button is used to display four pages of the report in the window at the same time. (1)
17	Cancels the print preview process from generating the entire report.

Table 9-2 Report print preview toolbar buttons explained

Viewing Other Pages In A Report

Most reports have more than one page. If you want to move around the report quickly, the easiest way to do that is to click the **SHOW NAVIGATION BAR** button on the toolbar.

This will let you view a thumbnail of each page of the report, as shown in Figure 9-5. This option is useful if the report is large. You can scroll down the thumbnails and click on the page that you want to view.

Scrolling down the thumbnails and clicking on page 32 is faster then clicking the Next Page ▶ button 31 times if the current page is the first page of the report.

Figure 9-5 Report preview thumbnail option

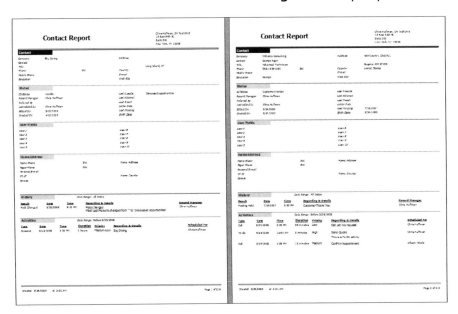

Figure 9-6 Two pages of the report visible at the same time

(1) Clicking on the arrow at the end of the **FOUR PAGES** button displays the grid shown in Figure 9-7. This is used to select how many pages to display in the window.

When you want to display a specific number of pages from the report, click in the first square in the upper left corner of the grid, then drag the mouse to the right and then down until you see the number of rows and columns that you need. In the example shown, 12 pages of the report will be displayed on the screen.

Figure 9-7 Four Pages button options

Preview The Report

1. Click the **ZOOM IN TOOL** button, then click on the report three times.

   The report will be displayed much larger, as shown in Figure 9-8.

   Compare this report to the report shown earlier in Figure 9-6.

Figure 9-8 Contact report

Save The Report

2. Click the **FILE SAVE** button on the Print Preview window toolbar. You should see the folder that you created. For now, you can accept the default file name, then click the Save button.

Exercise 9.2: The Contact Directory Report

This report is similar to the contact report in the previous exercise. The difference is that the information on the Activities, Notes, History and Opportunities tabs will not print on the Contact Directory report. This report prints the contact address information.

1. Reports ⇒ Contact Directory.

2. Select the All Contacts option, then click OK.

   The report should look like the one shown in Figure 9-9.

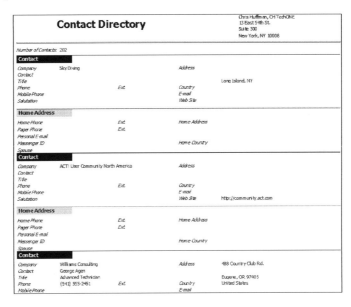

Figure 9-9 Contact Directory report

Exercise 9.3: The Phone List Report

This report will print the company, contact, phone, mobile phone and extension fields. Earlier in this lesson you learned that if you wanted to only print records based on the result of a lookup or contacts in a specific group, you have to create the lookup or select the group before you run the report. In this exercise you will create a lookup before running the report.

1. Create a lookup to find all contacts in the state of Washington. You should have six records displayed.

2. Reports ⇒ Phone List.

3. Select the Current lookup option if it is not already selected, then click OK. The report should look like the one shown in Figure 9-10.

	Chris Huffman, CH TechONE
Phone List	13 East 54th St.
	Suite 300
	New York, NY 10008

Number of contacts: 6

Company	Contact	Phone	Phone Ext
Verge Records	Theodore Barrett Jr	(206) 555-4414	
Verge Records	Theodore Barrett Sr	(206) 555-4410	
Verge Records	Paul Henderson		
Verge Records	James Gutierrez		
Verge Records	Drew McLintock		
Manxsys Financial	Alexander O'Brien	(206) 555-4247	

Figure 9-10 Phone List report

Exercise 9.4: The Activities Report

This report will print the activities that are scheduled and completed with contacts. The default option is to print the report for all users in the database.

1. Reports ⇒ Activities.

2. On the General tab, select the All Contacts option.

3. On the Activity tab, clear the To-Do's and Include cleared activities options.

How To Create A Custom Date Range

Often, you may have the need to print a report to include information for a few weeks or a few months. To do this you need to create a custom date range.

1. On the Activity tab, click the **CUSTOM** button. You will see the Select Date Range dialog box.

2. Click the **<** arrow on the **FROM** calendar until you see September 2009, then click on the 19th.

3. Type 11/20/2009 in the **TO** field, then press the Tab key.

   You should have the options shown in Figure 9-11.

   Click OK.

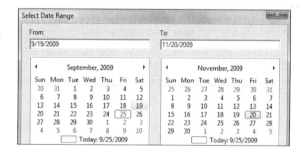

Figure 9-11 Date range options selected

4. You should have the options selected on the Activity tab that are shown in Figure 9-12.

   Click OK.

   The report should look like the one shown in Figure 9-13.

Figure 9-12 Activity tab options

			Chris Huffman, CH TechONE
Activities			13 East 54th St. Suite 300 New York, NY 10008

Date Range: 9/19/2009 - 11/20/2009

Contact				Sky Diving		
Type	**Date**	**Time**	**Duration**	**Priority**	**Regarding & Details**	**Scheduled For**
Personal Activity	9/19/2009	3:00 PM	2 hours	Medium-Low	Sky Diving	Chris Huffman

Contact		George Agen		Williams Consulting	(541) 555-2451	
Type	**Date**	**Time**	**Duration**	**Priority**	**Regarding & Details**	**Scheduled For**
Call	9/24/2009	1:55 PM	10 minutes	Medium	Confirm Appointment	Allison Mikola

Contact		Ernst Anderson		CH TechONE	(212) 555-2485	
Type	**Date**	**Time**	**Duration**	**Priority**	**Regarding & Details**	**Scheduled For**
Meeting	9/24/2009	8:30 AM	1 hour 30 minutes	Low	Breakfast Networking Group	Ernst Anderson
Meeting	9/25/2009	11:00 AM	2 hours	Low	Expense and Sales Reports	Ernst Anderson
Meeting	10/1/2009	8:30 AM	1 hour 30 minutes	Low	Breakfast Networking Group	Ernst Anderson

Figure 9-13 Activities report

Exercise 9.5: The Group Membership Report

This report will print the contacts in each group. This enables you to see which contacts are in what group. This would be a report that you may want to create a lookup or saved query for. The contacts name, company, title, phone and email fields are printed on the report.

1. Select the Sales Reps group in the Groups tree.

2. Reports ⇒ Group Reports ⇒ Group Membership.

3. Select the **CURRENT GROUP** option shown in Figure 9-14.

Figure 9-14 Group Membership report filter options

4. Click OK. The report should look like the one shown in Figure 9-15.

5. If you run the report again and select **ALL GROUPS**, the report will look like the one shown in Figure 9-16.

In ACT! 2008 and earlier, the Group Membership report would print contacts that were not in any group, at the beginning of the report, as shown in Figure 9-17. Fortunately, this has been fixed.

Group Membership

Chris Huffman, CH TechONE
13 East 54th St.
Suite 300

New York, NY 10008

Group Name	Sales Reps				
Contact	**Company**	**Title**	**Phone**	**Ext.**	**E-mail**
Betty Browser	CH TechONE	Sales Representative	(212) 555-2485		bbrowser@CHTechONE.email
Sean Duffy	Circle Photography	Sales Representative	0164 262546		
Emily Dunn	Boomer's Artworx	Sales Representative	(602) 555-4874		
Bettie James	Boomer's Artworx	Sales Representative			
Allison Mikola	CH TechONE	Sales Representative	(212) 555-2485		Allison@CHTechONE.email

Figure 9-15 Group Membership report for one group

Group Membership

Chris Huffman, CH TechONE
13 East 54th St.
Suite 300

New York, NY 10008

Group Name	International Employees				
Contact	**Company**	**Title**	**Phone**	**Ext.**	**E-mail**
Fred Fenderline	CH Gourmet Coffee	President	0208 746534		ffenderline@chgourmetgifts.email
Chris Graham	Secondary Contact	Assistant			
Group Name	Customers-TWO Component				
Contact	**Company**	**Title**	**Phone**	**Ext.**	**E-mail**
Liz Dittmeier	Brandee's Bakery	Manager	(208) 555-2445		
Sandy Ryan	Ace Pet Store Franchises	Buyer	(423) 555-1221		
Group Name	Customers-ONE Component				
Contact	**Company**	**Title**	**Phone**	**Ext.**	**E-mail**
Bruce Baker	SimAero	Chief Designer	(480) 555-2144		Bruce@simaero360.email
Julie Britton	Quality Motors	Production Manager	0124 926598		

Figure 9-16 Group Membership report for all groups

Group Membership

Chris Huffman, CH Gourmet Gifts
13 East 54th St.

New York, NY 10008

Ivan A. Stekopick	Swing Software	Vice President	(011) 465-52		IStekopick@swinfsoft27.spb.ru
Rae Stevens	Hare's Tavern Corporate	CEO	(02) 861 2		RaeStevens@harestavern.com
Tina Stewart	Wiseman Paper Products	Owner	0191 987389		
Mike Underwood	T-Bone's Steakhouse	Owner	(541) 555-2422		
Nelson Watts	Superior Technologies Ltd	Administrative Assistant	0164 222223		
Bill Willis	Willis Enterprises	Owner	(480) 555-1232		
Group Name	Customers-AsiaPac				
Contact	**Company**	**Title**	**Phone**	**Ext.**	**E-mail**
Paul Brushman	Brushy's Golfing World	Chief Golf Sales Manager	(455) 555-2221		ginger@neyfamily.net
Ed Connor	Graham Electonics	Public Relations Manager	0198 356712		
Vivian Grace	International Safari	Buyer			
Chris Mears	Mutthound Enterprises	Vice President	01789 656556		
William Rosemann	Williams Consulting	Senior Technician	(03) 680 4		WRose@williamsconsulting5.com
Rae Stevens	Hare's Tavern Corporate	CEO	(02) 861 2		RaeStevens@harestavern.com

Figure 9-17 Group Membership report in a prior version of ACT!

Exercise 9.6: The Company Comprehensive Report

This report will display the following data for a company: Contacts, notes, history, activities and opportunities. This report can be used to produce a company profile. You can select options including a date range for each type of data. For example, you can select the All date range for history records and the last year date range, for notes. The good thing is that the date range that you select for each type of data, prints at the beginning of that section of the report. The Company Summary report, which is similar, does not print contacts or notes.

1.   Create a company lookup for Ace Pet Store Franchises.

2.   Reports ⇒ Company Reports ⇒ Company Comprehensive.

3.   On the General tab, select the Current lookup option.

4.   On the Activity tab, create a date range for all of 2008.

5.   On the Note tab, select the date range All.

6.   On the History tab, select the date range 1/1/2005 to 12/31/2008.

7.   On the Opportunity tab, create a date range for 1/1/2008 to 12/31/2009, then click OK.

Figure 9-18 shows the first page of the report. Make sure that your date ranges match those shown in the figures. Figure 9-19 shows the activities and opportunities on page 4.

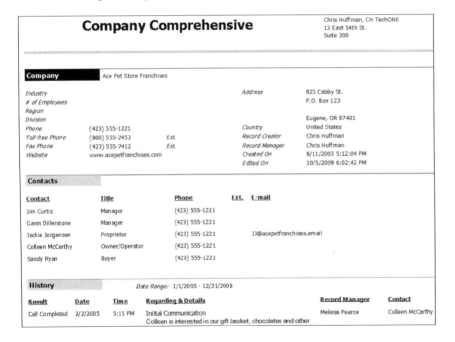

Figure 9-18 First page of the Company Comprehensive report

Activities			Date Range: 1/1/2008 - 12/31/2008				

Type	Date	Time	Priority	Scheduled With	Regarding & Details		Scheduled For
To-do	11/15/2008	10:22 AM	Low	Betty Browser	Send Quote This is a To-Do activity.		Chris Huffman

Opportunities			Date Range: 1/1/2008 - 12/31/2009				

Status	Name	Est. Close	Stage	Prob.	Total	Record Manager	Contact
Open	Ace Pet Store-Corporate Office	12/18/2009	Needs Assessment	25%	$4,500.00	Chris Huffman	Gavin Dillerstone
Open	Ace Pet Store-Corporate Offices	10/30/2009	Needs Assessment	25%	$2,000.00	Chris Huffman	Ben Barrow...

Figure 9-19 Activities and opportunities sections of the Company Comprehensive report

Other Reports

The reports that you have run so far in this lesson are just the beginning. Below are three more reports that you many find useful.

Source Of Referrals Report

This report is based on the value in the Referred By field. The report includes the total number of referrals, as illustrated in Figure 9-20.

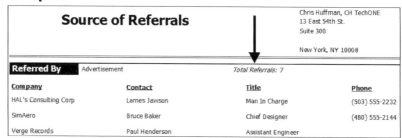

Figure 9-20 Source of Referrals report

The first section of the report will list all contacts that the Referred By field is blank, unless you do a lookup to exclude them.

History/Time Spent Report

This report provides detail information on the tasks and time that you spent with each contact, as shown in Figure 9-21.

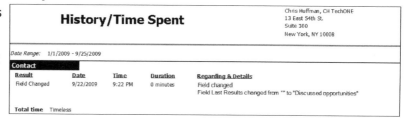

Figure 9-21 History/Time Spent report

Notes/History Report

This report prints the notes and history records for the contacts that you select, as shown in Figure 9-22.

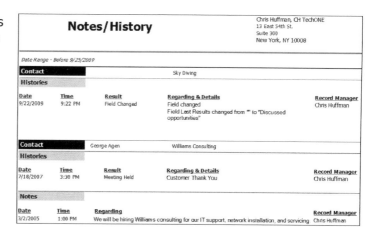

Figure 9-22 Notes/History report

NEW New Reports In ACT!

The following reports are new in ACT! 2010.

Opportunities by Estimated Closing Month
Opportunities by Process and Status
Opportunities by Record Manager and Process shown in Figure 9-23
Opportunity Summary by Record Manager and Process
Pipeline Report and Products by Sales Process and Stage
Pipeline Report by Sales Process and Stage
Won Opportunities and Days Open shown in Figure 9-24
Won Opportunities by Actual Closing Month
Won Opportunities by Sales Process
Won Opportunities by Sales Process and Competitor
Won Opportunities by Sales Process and Reason
Won Opportunities by Sales Process and Record Manger
Won Opportunity Summary by Sales Process

Opportunities By Record Manager and Process

Date Range:	All Dates		Total For Date Range: $2,427,200.00						
Record Manager	Allison Mikola		Number of Opportunities: 82	Total For Record Manager:		$616,300.00	% of Total: 25.39%		
Process	CHT1 Sales		Number of Opportunities: 73	Total For Process:		$596,300.00	% of Total: 24.57%		
Status	Open		Number of Opportunities: 46	Total For Status:		$383,500.00	% of Total: 15.80%		
Status	**Contact**	**Company**	**Name**	**Stage**	**Prob.**	**Est. Close**	**Weighted**		**Total**
Open	Nathan Cutting Brittles	Duke Industries	Duke Industries-Northern C	Initial Communication	10%	5/29/2010	$750.00		$7,500.00
Open	Mackenzie Jensen	Brandee's Bakery	Brandee's Bakery-Bakery	Initial Communication	10%	9/27/2009	$250.00		$2,500.00
Open	John Chance	Duke Industries	Duke Industries-LA Upgrad	Negotiation	65%	5/22/2010	$7,800.00		$12,000.00

Figure 9-23 Opportunities by Record Manager and Process report

Won Opportunities and Days Open

Date Range:	After 10/3/2009		Total For Date Range:		$431,400.00				
Process CHT1 Sales		Count For Process:	55	Total For Process:		$425,400.00			
Contact	**Company**	**Name**	**Open Date**	**Est. Close**	**Actual Close**	**Close Delta**	**Days Open**	**Total**	**Record Manager**
Louise Harper	Stevenson & Smith	Stevenson & SMith-Office Upgrades	5/19/2009	1/17/2010	1/17/2010	0	243	$5,000.00	Chris Huffman
Claire Haldane	E D Enterprises	ED Enterprises-New TechONE	1/4/2010	5/17/2010	5/17/2010	0	133	$12,000.00	Ernst Anderson
Vivian Grace	International Safari	International Safari-Upgrade to Warribee	11/28/2009	4/17/2010	4/17/2010	0	140	$12,000.00	Ernst Anderson

Figure 9-24 Won Opportunities and Days Open report

NEW Reports View

This view allows you to see all of the reports that you have access to. Reports that you run frequently can be added to the Favorites section of the view by checking the box in the **FAVORITE REPORTS** column shown in Figure 9-25.

Figure 9-25 Reports view

Reports View Toolbar

Figure 9-26 shows the Reports view toolbar. Table 9-3 explains the buttons on the toolbar.

Figure 9-26 Reports view toolbar

Button	Description
1	Displays the Define Filters dialog box to run the selected report.
2	Displays the report in the Report Designer, so that it can be modified.
3	Opens the dialog box shown in Figure 9-27. The report can be renamed and the description can be changed.
4	Is used to delete the report for all users. This option will delete the report from the hard drive. Use this option with caution.

Table 9-3 Reports view toolbar buttons explained

Figure 9-27 Edit Properties dialog box

The **OPTIONS** button is used to customize the columns in the Reports View. Each section of the Reports View can be customized individually. Columns can be added, renamed and reordered. At the top of Figure 9-25 shown earlier, the Last Modified column was added to the Favorite Reports section.

Reports View Related Tasks

NEW REPORT TEMPLATE Opens the Report Designer so that you can create a new report.

Printing In ACT!

So far in this lesson you have learned how to print reports that come with ACT!. Reports are not the only thing that can be printed from ACT!. The remaining exercises in this lesson show you how to print labels, envelopes, an address book and how to use the Quick Print options on the File menu.

Exercise 9.7: How To Print Labels

There are several label templates that you can select from. There is also a template that you can use to create a custom label template.

 If you do not use Avery brand labels, you may be able to find the Avery label size equivalent of the brand of labels that you use on your box of labels.

1. File ⇒ Print.

2. Select the **LABELS** Printout type, then select the Avery 5160 (label size) Paper type.

3. Click the Print button.

4. Select the appropriate **CREATE REPORT FOR** option on the Define Filters dialog box, then click OK.

   The labels should look similar to the ones shown in Figure 9-28.

Jennifer Doe	John Doe	Bill Grant
Mary Wood	Ania Dawson ABS Garages Ltd	Jim Curtis Ace Pet Store Franchises 925 Cabby St. P.O. Box 123 Eugene, OR 97401
Gavin Dillerstone Ace Pet Store Franchises 925 Cabby St. P.O. Box 123 Eugene, OR 97401	Jackie Jorgensen Ace Pet Store Franchises 925 Cabby St. P.O. Box 123 Eugene, OR 97401	Colleen McCarthy Ace Pet Store Franchises 925 Cabby St. P.O. Box 123 Eugene, OR 97401
Sandy Ryan Ace Pet Store Franchises 925 Cabby St P.O. Box 123 Eugene, OR 97401	ACT! User Community North America	Kristi Cameron American Dreams 1113 Grainey Suite A Allen, TX 75002
Hayleigh Frieda American Dreams 1113 Grainey Suite A Allen, TX 75002	Rick Blaine Beautiful Friendship Bar & Grill 13 Rue St Ferreol Marseille, 13007	Ilsa Lund Beautiful Friendship Bar & Grill 13 Rue St Ferreol Marseille, 13007

Figure 9-28 Labels

Selecting Where To Start Printing Labels

Unless you print the same number of names and addresses that the sheet of labels has, you will always have sheets of partially used labels. You can select where the labels should start to print on the sheet.

The options on the **POSITION** tab (File ⇒ Print ⇒ Select the label size, then click the Print button) on the Define Filters dialog box shown in Figure 9-29 are used to select the Row and Column that the labels should start printing on. If you need to start printing labels on the first row, third column, you would select the options shown in Figure 9-29.

It would be nice if the layout of the sheet of labels was displayed on the dialog box so that you could make sure that you selected the correct row and column before you previewed the labels. If you selected the options shown in Figure 9-29 and previewed the labels, they would look like the ones shown in Figure 9-30.

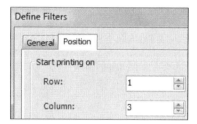

Figure 9-29 Position tab options

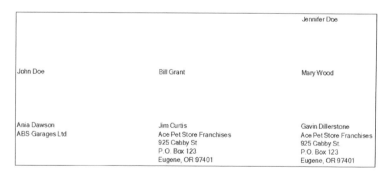

Figure 9-30 Labels with Position tab options changed

Exercise 9.8: How To Print Envelopes

In this exercise you will learn how to print envelopes using an envelope template.

1.   File ⇒ Print.

2. Select the **ENVELOPES**
    Printout type, then
    select the envelope
    size in the Paper
    type list shown in
    Figure 9-31.

    The options in the
    PAPER TYPE section
    are the envelope sizes.

Figure 9-31 Envelope options

 The **ENABLE PREVIEW** option on the Print dialog box shown above in Figure 9-31 does not work for labels, envelopes and reports. I found that this option took a while to display the address book.

3. Click the Print button.

4. Select the appropriate **CREATE REPORT FOR** option, then click OK. The envelope should look like the one shown in Figure 9-32. Notice that the return address information has been filled in. You may have a different addressee on the envelope, depending on which record was displayed before you started this exercise.

Figure 9-32 Envelope in print preview

5. Close the Print Preview window.

Exercise 9.9: How To Create And Print An Address Book

Printing an address book is useful if you need to have contact information from the database when you do not have access to a computer. You can select up to three additional fields to print in the address book. If you use a Day Timer or Day Runner, you can print the contacts in these address book formats. There are several print options that you can select from.

1. File ⇒ Print. Select the **ADDRESS BOOK** Printout type, then check the **ENABLE PREVIEW** option.

2. Select the Day-Timer Folio (2 Col) Paper type option.

   The preview should look like the one on the right side of Figure 9-33.

   The preview may take a few seconds to display.

Figure 9-33 Print dialog box

3. Click the **OPTIONS** button, then clear the Alternate Address and Secondary Contacts options, if they are checked.

4. Select the Primary Address, Phone Numbers and E-mail Address options if they are not already selected.

5. Check the **LETTER AT THE TOP OF EACH PAGE** option in the Print Settings section.

6. Open the first **ADDITIONAL FIELDS** drop-down list and select Fax Phone.

7. Change the Sort Order to **CONTACT LAST NAME**, then select the All Contacts **CREATE PRINTOUT FOR** option.

8. Change the Font size to 10. You should have the options shown in Figure 9-34.

   If you create a field it will not be listed in the **PRINT** section of the Options dialog box.

   You have to select a field that you create from one of the three **ADDITIONAL FIELDS** drop-down lists.

   Click OK.

Figure 9-34 Address Book options

9. If you want to print the address book, click the Print button on the Print dialog box.

How To View The Address Book Without Printing It

If you want to see what the address book will look like without printing it and you have the full version of Adobe Acrobat installed, select the Adobe PDF option on the Print dialog box, as illustrated in Figure 9-35.

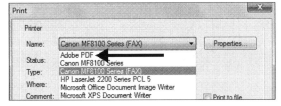

Figure 9-35 Print dialog box options

If you have another software package installed that creates PDF files, select it from the drop-down list.

Doing this will create a PDF version of the address book, as shown in Figure 9-36. You can view the PDF file on the screen or print it.

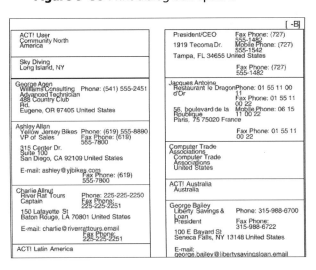

Figure 9-36 Printed address book

 If you click the Cancel button on the Print dialog box shown earlier in Figure 9-35, not only will that dialog box close, but so will the Print dialog box shown earlier in Figure 9-31. This means that all of the options that you selected to configure what you wanted to print will be lost, so you will have to select them again when you open the dialog box. This appears to be a bug because the Print dialog box shown earlier in Figure 9-31 should not close.

Exercise 9.10: Using The Quick Print Options

The **QUICK PRINT CURRENT WINDOW** and **QUICK PRINT SELECTED** options are useful if you just want to print what is on the screen. Both of these options, as well as, the Print Current Screen option in the Related Tasks section of many views, displays the dialog box shown in Figure 9-37.

The **SAME FONT IN MY LIST VIEW** option is only available when a list view is displayed. When cleared, you can select the font that you want to use to print the report by clicking the Font button. If you are going to print the data on a tab, it is probably a good idea to resize the columns on the tab so that the data is not cut off.

The Quick Print options print data exactly as it appears. It is not perfect, but it may handle your basic printing needs. The steps below show you how to print the data in the current window.

Figure 9-37 Quick Print Options dialog box

1. Look up the My Record.

2. Make sure the Contact Detail view is open, then click on the Activities tab.

3. File ⇒ Quick Print Current Window. You will see the Quick Print Options dialog box. If you click the Set Options button you can change the printing options as needed.

If you printed the data on the Activities tab that is visible, it would look similar to the data shown in Figure 9-38.

Figure 9-38 Quick print of the current tab

If you displayed the monthly calendar and used the Quick Print option to print the calendar, it would look like the one shown in Figure 9-39.

Figure 9-39 Quick print of a monthly calendar

WRAP UP OF THE BASICS

Overview

In this lesson you will learn the about following features in ACT!:

- ☑ Tagging records
- ☑ Copying data
- ☑ Swapping data
- ☑ Supplemental files
- ☑ Promoting secondary contacts
- ☑ Editing notes
- ☑ Filtering notes
- ☑ Record creation options
- ☑ Attaching web pages to a contact
- ☑ Managing links
- ☑ Marketing Results Tab
- ☑ Web Info Tab
- ☑ Export contact data to Excel
- ☑ Mapping ACT! fields to an Excel spreadsheet
- ☑ Adding graphics to ACT! notes
- ☑ Using the Timer
- ☑ Editing attached documents

LESSON 10

Wrap Up Of The Basics Of ACT!

This lesson concludes the basics of ACT!. The majority of tasks that you will use the most in ACT! are covered in the first 9 lessons of this book. The remaining lessons contain tasks that you may use a lot when first creating a database, but will use much less frequently over time. The exceptions to this are the dashboard and backing up a database, which, depending on how frequently data is modified, you may need to do daily.

The topics covered in this lesson are important to know, but in my mind were better left out of the previous lessons because they were not essential to learning and mastering the core concepts of ACT!.

Understanding The ID/Status And Referred By Fields

The majority of fields on the Contact Detail view are pretty straight forward. The fields discussed below may not be as straight forward.

The **ID/STATUS** field is most often used to categorize contacts. This means that you can enter customers, prospects, vendors and lawyers in the same database. Many people would keep each of these types of contacts in different databases or spreadsheets. Using this field allows you to maintain an unlimited number of types of contacts. This field provides an informal way to group or categorize contacts. You can add to and edit the entries that are in the drop-down lists.

When you first enter names in the database, you would select the "Prospects" ID/Status if the goal was to get the contact to purchase a product from you. If they purchase a product, you would change the value in this field to Customer.

When the value in this field is changed, an entry is automatically created on the History tab unless you change the option to not record a history record. Having this field generate a history record can be helpful if you need to know when the status of contacts change. A month after your marketing campaign, you could look up all of the contacts that are still "Prospects" for the marketing campaign and contact them by phone or email to see whether or not they received your mailing.

What may not be obvious is that the ID/Status field is what ACT! refers to as a **MULTI-SELECT** field.

This means that the field can store more than one value. Multi-select fields look like the one shown in Figure 10-1. Open the drop-down list and check the option(s) that you want to categorize the contact by.

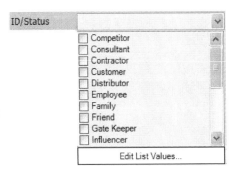

Figure 10-1 Multi-select drop-down list field

The **REFERRED BY** field shown in Figure 10-2 is used as a way to know how the contact was acquired. You could have purchased a mailing list of leads from two companies and need to track which company the lead (contact) came from.

You could also have contacts from a newsletter subscription service. How will you know how each contact was acquired if this field was left blank?

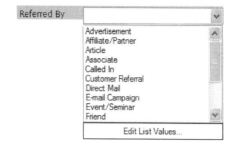

Figure 10-2 Referred By field options

Why Are Drop-Down Lists Important?

Drop-down lists provide the most used values that would be entered in a field. Drop-down lists are important because they help ensure that the data in a field is entered the same way for every record. Consistent data is especially helpful if the field will be used in queries, reports or sorting.

For example, one user types "USA" in the Country field and another user types "United States" in the Country field. When you run a query that looks for all records with "USA" in the Country field, the query will skip records that have "United States" in the field. This means that the result of the query will not contain all of the records that it should. In Lesson 3, I had you type USA in the Country field instead of selecting United States from the Country drop-down list. [See Lesson 3, Figure 3-10] If the entries in the drop-down lists do not have the types of information that you need, you can create new entries. In the next lesson you will learn how to add and delete entries in drop-down lists. [See Lesson 16, Creating and Editing Drop-Down List Fields]

ACT! has two types of drop-down lists as shown above in Figures 10-1 and 10-2. The drop-down list shown in Figure 10-1 allows more than one option to be selected. The drop-down list in Figure 10-2 only allows one option to be selected. This is the more popular type of drop-down list and the one that you are probably the most familiar with. Both types of drop-down lists can be used to select or type in the value that you want. If the value that you enter is already in the list, after typing in enough characters to make the value unique, it will automatically be filled in the field.

 Drop-down lists are used to add information to a field without typing. You can also type the first letter of the value that you are looking for. Doing this will bring you to the first entry that matches the letter that you typed in. You do not have to open the drop-down list to select an entry if you already know what you are looking for. You can type in the first few letters.

 If you enter text in a field that has a drop-down list like the City, Country, Department or Title fields, the text that you type in, may or may not be accepted. It depends on whether the **LIMIT TO LIST** option on the Define Fields dialog box is enabled for the field. This option will force the user to select an option from the list or leave the field blank. This is done to ensure accuracy in the field.

Tagging Contacts

There may be times when you need to select contacts that do not have any data in common. Tagging records is used to create a manual lookup. If you have tried to create a lookup for contacts but can't find a common denominator, you can tag the records. To tag a record, enable the tag mode, then manually click on the records. After you tag the records that you need, you can create a lookup of the tagged records. With a small database like the demo database that you are using to complete the exercises in this book, manually viewing all of the records to find the ones to tag is bearable. If the database has 5,000 records, it could take a while to find the records that you need.

Exercise 10.1: Tagging Contacts

In this exercise you will tag random contact records, add a note to the records and save them as a group. It is not a requirement to group tagged records.

1. Create a group called My Tagged Record Group.

2. Open the Contact List view. Sort the contacts by state, then check the **TAG MODE** option shown in Figure 10-3.

Figure 10-3 Tag options

The **LOOK FOR** field is used to search for a contact based on the field that the list is sorted on. If the Contact List is sorted on the Company field, you would enter the company name that you were looking for in this field.

The **EDIT MODE** option is used to modify records in the list view.

The **TAG MODE** option turns the tag functionality on and off.

The **TAG ALL** button will mark all of the contacts displayed in the list as tagged.

The **UNTAG ALL** button will remove the tag from all of the selected contacts.

The **LOOKUP SELECTED** button creates a lookup of the records that have been tagged.

The **OMIT SELECTED** button is used to remove the tagged contacts from the view. This option does not delete the records from the database.

 If you click on a record that you do not need to tag, click on the record again to remove the tag. When in tag mode, records that are tagged are highlighted, as shown in Figure 10-4.

Company	Contact	Phone	Extension	Title	Address 1	Address 2	City	State	ZIP Code
Circle Photography	Test Record				2256 Circle Lane	Suite 4	Dallas	TX	75214
Circle Photography	Dan Day	(214) 555-2215		Analyst	2256 Circle Lane	Suite 4	Dallas	TX	10053
Circle Photography	Jonathan Jenkins	(214) 555-2215		Owner	2256 Circle Lane	Suite 4	Dallas	TX	75214
Continental Detective A	John Guild	406-202-4400		Chief Investigator	26 W Granite St		Butte	MT	59701
Continental Detective A	Nick Charles	406-202-4400		Owner	26 W Granite St		Butte	MT	59701
Continental Energy	Herman Getter	(918) 555-2451		Vice President Op	54 S. Utica	Suite 220	Tulsa	OK	74137
Carleone's Pasta Comp	Morty Manicotti	(480) 555-4512		Director of Manuf	8800 Pasta Way	Suite 200	Scottsdale	AZ	85258

Figure 10-4 Tagged records

3. Tag the first record in each of the following states: AZ, CA and LA.

4. Click the **LOOKUP SELECTED** button.

At this point you could add the same note to the contact records that are tagged, create an activity that included these records, save them as a group, subgroup, company or division.

5. Click the Note button on the Global toolbar, then type
    `This contact is a tagged record that is in the Tagged Record Group.`

6. Click the **SHARE WITH** button on the Insert Note dialog box, then click OK on the Public Note message box.

7. Select the My Tagged Record Group and add it to the list on the right, then click OK.

8. The dialog box should have the options that are shown in Figure 10-5. Click OK to close the Insert Note dialog box.

Figure 10-5 Insert Note dialog box

9. Right-click on the tagged records and select Add Contacts to group. Select the My Tagged Record Group option.

10. Click OK, then clear the Tag Mode option. Now when you need to access these records you can select the group that they are in. If you view the tagged group, you will see the three contacts.

Using The Omit Selected Option

If there are records that you do not want to view, you can remove them from the list view. Removing records from a view does not delete them from the database. Using the Omit Selected option has the same effect as creating a lookup. The difference is that the Omit Selected option does it record by record, manually. To restore the records, lookup all of the contacts.

1. On the Contact List view, display all of the contacts.

2. Click on the first record in the Contact List view. The record should now be highlighted.

3. Click the **OMIT SELECTED** button on the toolbar. The record should not be visible in the window. You will see that the record count decreases by one.

Copying Data From One Field To Another

You may have a need to copy data from one field to another. Instead of doing this manually, record by record, you can create a lookup for the records that you want to copy the data to, then use the **COPY FIELD** command. Not creating a lookup first means that data will be copied to every record in the database. It is not a requirement to create a lookup first.

Exercise 10.2: How To Copy Data

In this exercise you will look up the Liberty Savings company and copy the data in the Title field to the User 6 field.

1. Create a lookup for the Liberty Company.

2. On the Contact Detail view, Edit ⇒ Copy Field.

3. Open the **COPY CONTENTS OF** drop-down list and select the Title field, then open the **TO** drop-down list and select the User 6 field.

4. You should have the options shown in Figure 10-6.

   Click OK.

Figure 10-6 Copy Data dialog box

5. Click Yes when you see the Replace/Swap/Copy message that lets you know that all of the records in the current lookup will be modified.

You will see the message shown in Figure 10-7. This message lets you know that the **TARGET** field (User 6) size is smaller than the **SOURCE** field (Title). If the target field is smaller, some of the data in the source field will not be copied to the target field.

Figure 10-7 Data Loss message

6. Click Yes on the Data Loss message window. Normally you would not want to have data loss and would click No when you see the message shown above in Figure 10-7.

View The Copied Data

1. Click the Contact Detail view button.

2. On the User Fields tab, you will see the title in the User 6 field, as shown in Figure 10-8.

Figure 10-8 User Fields tab

Swapping Data

This command is used to swap the data in one field with data from another field. Like the Copy Field command, if the target field is smaller, all of the data will not be copied to the target field.

Exercise 10.3: How To Swap Data

In this exercise you will swap the data in the Alternate Phone field with the data in the Home Phone field.

1. Create a lookup for the city of Scottsdale. You should see six records in the Contact List view.

2. Edit ⇒ Swap Field.

3. Open the **SWAP CONTENTS OF** drop-down list and select the Alternate Phone field, then open the **WITH CONTENTS OF** drop-down list and select the Home Phone field, as shown in Figure 10-9.

Figure 10-9 Swap Data dialog box

4. Click OK. Click Yes to modify records in the current lookup.

View The Swapped Data

1. Click the Contact Detail view button, then click on the Personal Info tab.

2. Scroll through the records.

You will not see a phone number in the Home Phone field because none of the records had data in the Alternate Phone field. If any of the records had data in the Alternate Phone field, it would have been swapped (moved) to the Home Phone field.

 It is recommended that you back up the database before using the **COPY FIELD** or **SWAP FIELD** command.

What Are Supplemental Files?

Supplemental files are files that ACT! uses that are not saved in the database (**.ADF**) file. The database file only stores the data that you see in the views. Examples of supplemental files include attachments, templates, reports and layouts. Many of these supplemental files are installed when you installed the software. ACT! has two supplemental file types, as discussed below.

① **Database** This file type includes the templates, reports and layout files that you see when you first open ACT!. These files are only available when ACT! is open. They are stored in folders. The default main folder name is **Name of database-database files**. Under this folder are folders for each type of file, as shown in Figure 10-10. If you copy a database, these files are also copied. If the ACT! database is stored on a server, more than likely, the database supplemental files are stored on the same server.

② **Personal** This file type includes files that are not associated to records in the database. Personal files are not backed up when a database is backed up. If you create a file that you do not want to share with other users of the database, save it in your personal supplemental folder. The other option is to create a folder outside of the default ACT! folders and save files that you do not want to share in that folder. An example of this would be the folder that you created for this book. The default folders that ACT! creates for supplemental personal files are stored in the following locations on your hard drive in Windows XP and Vista:

C:\Documents and Settings\YourUserName\My Documents\ACT\ACT for Windows 12
C:\Documents and Settings\YourUserName\Application Data\ACT\ACT for Windows 12
Vista C:\Users\YourUserName\Documents\ACT\ACT for Windows 12

After looking at the long paths above, I hope that you understand why I had you create the ACT Book folder at the root of the C drive, because it is easier to navigate to.

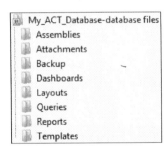

Figure 10-10 Database folders

What Are Secondary Contacts And Why Should I Use Them?

Secondary contacts are contacts that are associated to a primary contact in the database. Examples of secondary contacts include an alternate contact if the primary contact is unavailable or a primary contacts assistant. You can also create secondary contact records to store the primary contacts spouse and children.

It would be helpful if the Secondary Contacts tab would automatically change colors as soon as one secondary contact was added to a primary contact record. That would make it easier to know if there were any secondary contacts associated to the primary contact.

Exercise 10.4: Entering Information On The Secondary Contacts Tab

You can create a separate secondary contact record for the contacts children, assistant and spouse. Keep the following two things in mind when creating secondary contact records.

① Secondary contact records cannot be used in a mail merge or email campaign.
② Activity, note, opportunity and history records cannot be created or associated with secondary contact records.

1. Lookup the contact Sarah Baker.

2. On the **SECONDARY CONTACTS** tab shown in Figure 10-11, click the **NEW SECONDARY CONTACT** button.

	Contact	Title	Phone	Extension	E-mail

New Secondary Contact   Promote

Secondary Contacts

Figure 10-11 Secondary Contacts tab

3. Enter the information in Table 10-1 in the appropriate fields on the Secondary Contacts dialog box.

   If you have access to the Internet, you could click on the link in the Web site field and the web site would open in your browser.

Field	Type This
Contact	Terry London
Title	Purchasing Agent
E-mail	tlondon@xcapri.com
Web site	www.xcapri.com

Table 10-1 Secondary contact information

4. The dialog box should look like the one shown in Figure 10-12.

   Click OK.

   You should see the contact on the Secondary Contacts tab of the contact record.

Figure 10-12 Secondary contact information

Exercise 10.5: Promoting A Secondary Contact

There may be a time when a secondary contact needs to become a primary contact. Instead of creating a new primary contact record for the secondary contact (which would also leave the secondary contact record in place if you did not delete it) you can promote the secondary contact to a primary contact by following the steps below. When a secondary contact is promoted, it is automatically deleted from the primary contact record.

1. Add a secondary contact record to the contact John Doe, by clicking the **NEW SECONDARY CONTACT** button on the Secondary Contacts tab.

   Add the secondary contact information shown in Figure 10-13.

Figure 10-13 Secondary contact to be promoted

2. Click on the secondary contact that you want to promote. In this exercise select the secondary contact record that you just created, then click the **PROMOTE** button shown earlier in Figure 10-11. You will see the dialog box shown in Figure 10-14.

   The **DUPLICATE DATA** option will copy data from the primary contacts record (like the company name and address fields) to the record that you are promoting.

Figure 10-14 Promote Secondary Contact dialog box

3. For this exercise select the Duplicate data option, then click OK. You will see that the record is no longer on the Secondary Contacts tab and has become a contact.

Deleting A Secondary Contact

If a secondary contact should no longer be associated to the primary contact and you currently do not have a replacement contact, you should delete the secondary contact by following the steps below. For now you can just read the steps to become familiar with the process.

1. Right-click on the secondary contact that you want to delete, then select **DELETE SECONDARY CONTACT**.

2. Click Yes to permanently delete the secondary contact.

Notes And History Tabs

You have learned a little about these tabs and what types of data they have. You will see that they have a lot in common.

Notes Tab

The Notes tab contains details including business and personal information about contacts, companies and groups. The goal of entering notes is to build a profile of your relationship with the contact, company or group. Notes can be edited unless the **ALLOW NOTES EDITING** option is not enabled. [See Lesson 2, General Tab Preferences]

The Notes tab may be under utilized because many people are use to writing messages on a note pad or on a loose piece of paper or worse, think that they will remember details of a phone call or meeting. Days later when they need this information they cannot find the piece of paper that it was written on or they mentally draw a blank. I fall into the category of not being able to find the envelope that I wrote the information on. If you start off using the Notes tab when you first start using ACT!, the easier it will be to continue the good habit.

Whether you think that you are going to use ACT! daily or not, it may help if you open ACT! when you first turn your computer on. What I do is open the Contact List view and sort it by last name, then when I need to add a note, I do not have to wait to open ACT! and find the contact record. By the time I waited for ACT! to open, I would forget what I wanted to put in the note <smile>.

Attaching A Document To An Existing Note

In Lesson 3 you learned how to add an attachment to contact records and how to attach a document on the Documents tab. In Lesson 6 you learned how to attach a document to a group record. Now you will learn how to attach a document to an existing note. The process is the same when you are first creating a note. You can read the steps below to become familiar with the process.

1. Double-click on the note on the Notes tab that you want to attach a document to.

2. Click the **ATTACH** button, then select File on the Edit Note dialog box.

3. Double-click on the file that you want to attach, then click OK to close the Edit Note dialog box.

How To Copy A Note From One Contact Record To Another

If you attach a note to a contact record and want to attach the note to a different contact record, you can, by following the steps below. Both records need to be displayed before you start step 1.

1. On the Notes tab, click on the note that you want to copy, then press **CTRL + C**.

2. Click on the Notes tab of the contact record that you want to copy the note to, then press **CTRL + V**.

Editing A Shared Note

If you edit a note that is shared, you will see the dialog box shown in Figure 10-15, when you click OK after editing the note.

The options on this dialog box are to save the changes for all contacts that are associated with the note or to create a new note for the contact record that you opened the note from, to edit. You can try this by editing the note with green text, that you created in Lesson 3 for George, Mary and Peter Bailey.

Figure 10-15 Edit Shared Note dialog box

Filtering Notes

Over time, contact, company or group records can accumulate a lot of notes. While they can be sorted, it may be more effective to filter the notes.

If you right-click in the detail section of the Notes tab on the Contact or Company Detail view and select **FILTER NOTES**, you will see the dialog box shown in Figure 10-16 on the Contact Detail view and Figure 10-17 on the Company Detail view.

Figure 10-16 Contact Filter Notes dialog box

While filters narrow and reduce the number of records displayed (in this case notes), filters can be tricky and give the appearance that records are lost.

If you cannot find records, check the filter options on the tabs and change them to display all of the records.

Figure 10-17 Company Filter Notes dialog box

History Tab

You have already viewed the records on the History tab for the My Record. History records display changes that you have made to records in the database. The History tab picks up where the Notes tab leaves off. The entries on the History tab are a chronological recap of the communication and events for contacts, companies and groups. The majority of entries on this tab come from other tabs, but you can manually create a History record.

Some entries on the History tab are created automatically when you delete a contact, when the Last Results field is updated, create a mail merge, change the value in the ID/Status field or complete an activity. The date and time are automatically added to each entry that is added to the History tab.

You can add an entry to the History tab from any detail view by right-clicking in the detail section of the History tab and selecting **RECORD HISTORY** on the shortcut menu shown in Figure 10-18.

You will see the dialog box shown in Figure 10-19. It looks similar to the Schedule Activity dialog box. You can also create a history record from the list views. The **FOLLOW-UP** button opens the Schedule Activity dialog box.

Figure 10-18 History tab shortcut menu

Figure 10-19 Record History dialog box

Automatic Additions To The History Tab

As you just learned, you can manually add records to the History tab. By default, ACT! has designated the ID/Status and Last Results fields as history fields when you create a new database. When the data in a history field is changed, a record is automatically created and added to the History tab. In the next lesson you will learn how to designate a field as a history field.

Finding Records On The History Tab

At the top of the History tab shown in Figure 10-20, there are options that you can use to find specific records as discussed below.

Figure 10-20 Companies History tab

The Dates Field

The options in this drop-down list are used to select the date range for the records that you want to view on the History tab.

As time goes on, you will have more and more entries on the History tab, but you may not want to see all of them all the time.

You can reduce the number of records displayed by selecting a date range. You can also create a **CUSTOM** date range to select history records, as shown in Figure 10-21.

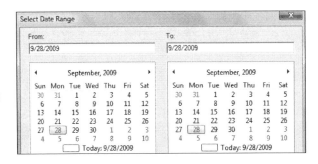

Figure 10-21 Select Date Range dialog box

History Record Types

There are three types of history records that you can view, as discussed below.

Figure 10-22 shows the history type options.

Figure 10-22 History record options

① **Histories** This type of record is created when you change the value in a field that has been designated to automatically have a history record created.

② **Attached Files** This type of history record is created when a document is attached to a contact, company or group record.

③ **E-mails** This type of history record can be created when you send an email message.

Select Users Button

This option is useful if more than one person is using the database.

The dialog box shown in Figure 10-23 is used to you select which users entries you want to view on the History tab.

To select multiple users calendars to view, select the first user then press and hold down the Shift key and click on the other users names. The maximum number of users that you can select is 10.

Figure 10-23 Select Users dialog box

Using The Record History Tool

This tool is used to create a history record for tasks that you complete that do not have a scheduled activity. This is helpful when you need to remember something like an email or phone conversation that you had with a contact that was not scheduled. History records can also be created from the company and group views.

How To Open The Record History Tool

Earlier in Figure 10-19 you saw the Record History dialog box. You can open this dialog box by doing any of the following:

① Pressing the Ctrl + H keys.

② On the History tab of a detail view, right-click and select Record History.

③ Click the History button on the Global toolbar.

How To Create A History Record For Multiple Contacts

Just like you can schedule one activity with multiple contacts, you can create a history record for multiple contacts at the same time. There are two ways to accomplish this, as discussed below.

① Open the Record History dialog box, click the Contact button, then select the contacts that you want to create the history record for.

② Tag the records that you want to create the history record for, then open the Record History dialog box. Earlier in this lesson you learned how to tag records.

How To Edit History Records

After viewing the history records that ACT! creates, you may decide that they need more information or that the information needs to be changed.

If this is the case, double-click on the history record that you want to change. You will see the dialog box shown in Figure 10-24. Make the changes that are needed, then click OK.

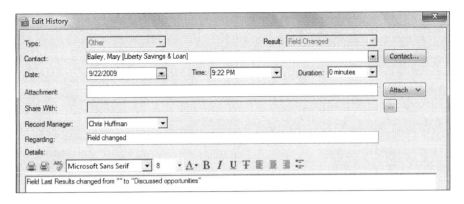

Figure 10-24 Edit History dialog box

How To Edit A History Record Associated With Multiple Contacts

After you create a history record that is associated with multiple contacts you may have the need to change it.

After you make the change, you will see the dialog box shown in Figure 10-25.

These options are used to select whether to save the change for the current contact or for all contacts associated with the history record.

Figure 10-25 Edit Shared History dialog box

Select the option that fits your need, then click OK. These options are similar to the options on the Edit Shared Note dialog box shown earlier in Figure 10-15.

Preventing History Records From Being Deleted

You can delete history records. If you are the only person that is using the database, it may not be necessary to prevent history records from being deleted. If other people will be using the database, you may want to consider preventing history records from being deleted by clearing the **ALLOW HISTORY EDITING** option on the General tab of the Preferences dialog box.

The Documents Tab

If you will attach a lot of documents to contact, company and group records, this section will give you a better understanding of the features that the Documents tab offers. The Documents tab is the repository for attachments in the database. Unless an attachment is marked as private, all users of the database will have access it. The attachments are usually stored in the Attachments folder for the database.

Figure 10-26 shows the Documents tab with several types of attached documents. The first column displays the icon for the file type. Sometimes the icons are not correct. An example is the last document listed in Figure 10-26. It has the icon for ACT!. The file was created in a software package called Crystal Reports, which it seems ACT! partially recognizes.

The **FILE TYPE** column will automatically be filled in as long as the file type is one that ACT! recognizes. Now that ACT! has functionality to have its databases attached to, in Crystal Reports, I was expecting to see "Crystal Reports" in the File Type column. Ironically, in ACT! 2009 and earlier versions, Crystal Reports was listed in the File Type column. Table 10-2 explains the buttons on the Documents tab.

	Documents			
Add Document ▾	Remove Document	Edit Document	Map To Excel	E-mail Document
Name	**Size**	**File Type**	**Date Modified**	
WorkshopInvoice.xls	20 KB	Microsoft Excel Worksheet	7/3/2007	
Scottsdale Area Prospects4.QRY	3 KB	QRY File	8/3/2005	
Scottsdale Area Prospects3.QRY	3 KB	QRY File	8/3/2005	
Scottsdale Area Prospects2.QRY	3 KB	QRY File	8/3/2005	
L2.1 My First Report.rpt	32 KB	RPT File	2/7/2008	

Figure 10-26 Documents tab

Button	Description
Add Document	Attach a document. If the **FILE** option is selected, remote database users can access the document.
Remove Document	Delete the selected attachment. This action deletes the document from the Documents folder. (1)
Edit Document	Opens the attached document so that you can view or edit it. To view or edit the document, you have to have the software that the document was created in installed on your computer. For example, in Figure 10-26 above the fourth document was created in Crystal Reports. If you do not have this software installed, you will not be able to open this document.
Map To Excel	Map fields in the database to fields in an Excel spreadsheet. You will learn how to do this later in this lesson.
E-mail Document	Used to send the selected file via email.

Table 10-2 Documents tab buttons explained

(1) If you do not have another copy of the document on your hard drive, the file cannot be retrieved after it is deleted. Unlike many Windows applications, deleting files from ACT! does not send the deleted files to the Recycle Bin.

You can also right-click on the document (on the Documents tab) that you want to delete and select **REMOVE DOCUMENT**, as shown in Figure 10-27.

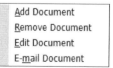

Add Document
Remove Document
Edit Document
E-mail Document

When you select this option you will see the message shown in Figure 10-28. Click Yes to delete the document. You can also delete an attachment from the History tab by right-clicking on the file and selecting **DELETE SELECTED**, as shown earlier in Figure 10-18.

Figure 10-27 Documents tab shortcut menu options

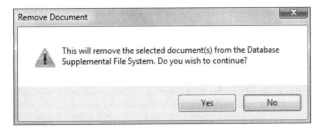

Figure 10-28 Remove Document message

Record Creation Options

The options shown in Figure 10-29 are used to make contact, company, groups and opportunity records public or private by default.

If you know that one of these types of records needs to be private, most or all of the time, select the **PRIVATE** option on this dialog box.

Tools ⇒ Preferences ⇒ Startup Tab ⇒ Record Creation Options button, opens this dialog box.

Figure 10-29 Record Creation Options dialog box

Exercise 10.6: Using The Attach Web Pages To ACT! Contact Option

This option is added to the Tools menu in Internet Explorer when ACT! is installed. Attaching a web page to a contact in ACT! is different then book marking or saving a link in your web browsers Favorites folder. When you save a link to a web page in your Favorites folder and go back to it later, you will see the current version of the web page, which could be different if it was changed (or worst, deleted) since the last time that you viewed it.

Attaching a web page in ACT! saves the actual web page as it is right now, which means that three years from now you are still able to see the exact page that you saved today. You do not have to be connected to the Internet to view web pages that are attached to a contact in ACT!. The steps below will show you how to use this feature to attach a web page to all contacts in a group.

 If you have pop-up blocker software turned on, you may have to disable it to complete this exercise.

1. Open the web page in Internet Explorer that you want to attach to a contact record. For this exercise, you can use www.tolana.com.

2. Tools ⇒ Attach Web page to ACT! contact, as illustrated in Figure 10-30.

Figure 10-30 Tools menu options

3. Open the **SELECT FROM** drop-down list and select Groups.

4. Open the drop-down list to the right and select the Sales Reps group.

   Add all of the contacts in the left column to the **SELECTED CONTACTS** list, as shown in Figure 10-31.

Figure 10-31 Attach Web page to the Following Contacts dialog box

5. Click OK, then close the browser.

6. Select one of the contacts in the Sales Reps group shown above in Figure 10-33, then click on the History tab.

Near the top of the History tab you should see an entry with "Web Attachment" in the **REGARDING & DETAILS** column, as shown in Figure 10-32. The entry will have today's date.

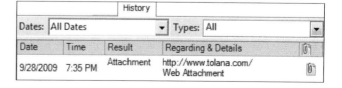

Figure 10-32 Web page attachment illustrated

7. If you click on the paper clip icon in the **ATTACHMENTS** column (to the far right of Figure 10-32 above), your browser will open the web page. Close the browser.

Exercise 10.7: Managing Links

In the previous exercise you attached a web page to contact records. If you think that you will have a need to reference the same web page more than once, you should keep the link in the Manage Internet Links dialog box.

1. View ⇒ ACT! Links ⇒ Manage Links.

2. Click the Add button, then type the link name and web site address shown in Figure 10-33.

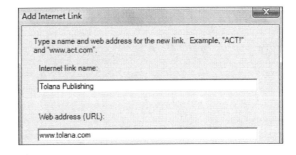

Figure 10-33 Add Internet Link dialog box

3. Click OK. You will see the link that you just created in the dialog box shown in Figure 10-34.

Figure 10-34 Manage Internet Links dialog box

4. Click the Close button when you are finished.

> **Internet Services And MapQuest**
>
> In ACT! 2010, these options have been removed.

NEW Marketing Results Tab

The options shown in Figure 10-35 are used to create and view the marketing efforts that have been made to the contact. The marketing options include email, surveys and forms and drip marketing. To utilize these features, you need a paid subscription account with Swift Page. There is a link for this company on the tab.

Figure 10-35 Marketing Results tab

NEW Web Info Tab

The options shown in Figure 10-36 are used to create and view web content information for a contact or company. This tab is an internal (to ACT!) browser that is used to display web pages. The options are used to display information from web sites like Yahoo™, Google™, Facebook™ and more, that the contact or customer is listed on or is a member of.

Clicking the **EDIT LINKS** button shown in the figure opens the dialog box shown in Figure 10-37. You can add and edit the links that will display on the Web Info tab.

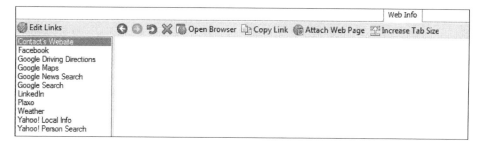

Figure 10-36 Web Info tab

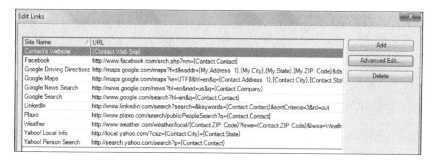

Figure 10-37 Edit Links dialog box

Exporting Data To Excel

If you need to work with contact, company or group data in a spreadsheet, you can export the data to Excel. Exporting contact data is similar to exporting opportunity data that you learned about in Lesson 8.

 The **EXPORT TO EXCEL** option is only available on the Contact, Company, Group or Opportunity List views. To view the exported records, you need to have Excel installed. The only columns that are exported are the ones that are visible. If you want to export data that is not currently visible, add the column(s) of data that you want to export to the view before exporting data, then remove the column(s) that you added if you no longer need them in the view, once the export is completed.

Exercise 10.8: Export Contact Data To Excel

In this exercise you will export all of the contacts for a specific company to Excel.

1. Create a lookup for the CH TechONE company. Nine records should be displayed.

2. Click the **EXPORT CURRENT LIST TO EXCEL** button on the toolbar. The records from the lookup will be exported to Excel, which will automatically open and display the records, as shown in Figure 10-38. When you are finished viewing the spreadsheet close Excel.

	A	B	C	D	E	F	G	H	I	J	K	L
	Contact Type	Private	Company	Contact	Phone	Extension	Title	Address 1	Address 2	City	State	ZIP Code
2	User	Public	CH TechONE	Ernst Anderson	(212) 555-2485		Vice President of US Operations	13 East 54th St.	Suite 300	New York	NY	10008
3	User	Public	CH TechONE	Betty Browser	(212) 555-2485		Sales Representative	13 East 54th St.	Suite 300	New York	NY	10008
4	Contact	Public	CH TechONE	Jane Chan	(212) 555-4447		Controller	13 East 54th St.	Suite 300	New York	NY	10008
5	User	Public	CH TechONE	Chris Huffman	212-555-2486		CEO	13 East 54th St.	Suite 300	New York	NY	10008
6	User	Public	CH TechONE	Allison Mikola	(212) 555-2485		Sales Representative	13 East 54th St.	Suite 300	New York	NY	10008
7	User	Public	CH TechONE	Melissa Pearce	(212) 555-2485		Assistant	13 East 54th St.	Suite 300	New York	NY	10008
8	User	Public	CH TechONE	Juliette Rosseux	(212) 555-2485		CFO	13 East 54th St.	Suite 300	New York	NY	10008
9	User	Public	CH TechONE	Jonathan Sommer	(212) 555-2485		Vice President AsiaPac Operations	13 East 54th St.	Suite 300	New York	NY	10008
10	User	Public	CH TechONE	Sarah Whiting	(212) 555-2485		Vice President European Operations	13 East 54th St.	Suite 300	New York	NY	10008

Figure 10-38 Exported contact records in Excel

Exercise 10.9: Mapping ACT! Fields To An Excel Spreadsheet

This tool is used to update fields in an Excel spreadsheet if they are mapped to fields in an ACT! database. Contact, company and group fields can be mapped to fields in a spreadsheet. In order for mapping to occur and for fields to be updated, the spreadsheet has to be attached on the Documents tab.

The ACT! menu in Excel is used to map fields from the database to an Excel worksheet.
[See Lesson 15, The ACT! Menu In Word And Excel]

Attach The Spreadsheet To The Documents Tab

The ACT! database and Excel have to be open to complete this exercise.

1. Lookup the contact Tim Dynamic.

2. Display the Documents tab for the contact.

3. Click the **ADD DOCUMENT** button and select File, then double-click on the Map ACT Fields To Spreadsheet file.

Map The Fields In ACT! To The Spreadsheet

The fields that are selected to be mapped in the spreadsheet are the ones that need to be updated when data is changed in the ACT! database.

1. Right-click on the spreadsheet on the Documents tab and select **EDIT DOCUMENT**.

    You should see the spreadsheet shown in Figure 10-39.

	A	B	C	D
1	Company	Contact	Title	E-mail
2		Tim Dynamic	Sales Manager	
3		Tina Dynamic	Sales Representative	
4		Tom Dynamic	Sales Representative	

Figure 10-39 Spreadsheet to map the fields to

2. Click on the Sales Manager title in the spreadsheet. Open the ACT! menu in Excel, then select **MAP TO CONTACT**.

3. Scroll down the list of fields and click on the Title field, as highlighted in Figure 10-40, then click the **ADD** button.

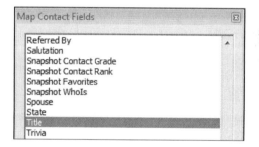

Figure 10-40 Map Contact Fields dialog box

4. Repeat the steps above for each field that you want to map.

    For now, just map the E-mail field. The spreadsheet should look like the one shown in Figure 10-41.

	A	B	C	D
1	Company	Contact	Title	E-mail
2		Tim Dynamic	<Title>	<E-mail>
3		Tina Dynamic	Sales Representative	
4		Tom Dynamic	Sales Representative	

Figure 10-41 Spreadsheet with fields mapped

5. Click the Close button. Save the changes to the spreadsheet and close it.

Test The Field Mapping

The way to test if the fields in the spreadsheet are mapped correctly is to add or change data in ACT! and see if the changes appear in the spreadsheet.

1. In ACT!, type `testmap@email.com` in the E-mail field for Tim and Tina Dynamic.

2. On the Documents tab for Tim Dynamic select the spreadsheet, then click the **MAP TO EXCEL** button.

When the spreadsheet opens you will see that the E-mail field has been updated for Tim Dynamic, but not Tina. That is because Tina's record in the spreadsheet was not mapped to a field in the ACT! database.

3.   Save the changes and close Excel.

> **Sharing A Database Tip**
>
> When designing a database, one thing that you need to consider is whether or not the database will be used by more than one person. If so, when the database is created, you should put it on a server or shared drive. Creating a database on your computers hard drive and then trying to move it, is more work then it is worth. You would have to back up and restore the database and all associated files to put them on the server.

Using The Timer

ACT! comes with a timer that you can use to record a history item, time an unscheduled activity or to time and clear a scheduled activity. You can also use it to record how long a phone call is. I am not sure that this feature is important to know, but since it exists, I decided to cover it. The steps below will show you how to use the timer to clear a scheduled activity (task).

1.   Click on the Task List view. Click on the 6/10/2010 scheduled task for David Yale.

2.   Tools ⇒ Timer.

3.   Click the Start button illustrated in Figure 10-42, then move the timer away from the middle of the screen.

Figure 10-42 ACT! Timer

4.   Click in the check box in the first column (It is called Cleared.) for the task for David Yale. You will see the dialog box shown in Figure 10-43.

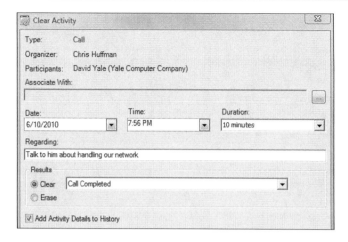

Figure 10-43 Clear Activity dialog box

5. Type Testing the timer in the Note field, then click OK. The task will be moved to the History tab.

6. Click the Stop button on the timer. You will see the message shown in Figure 10-44.

Figure 10-44 Clear activity message

7. For now, click Yes to restore the activity. The activity will reappear on the Task List.

Adding Graphics To ACT! Notes

You can add graphics or images to notes by following the steps below.

1. Open an existing note or create a new one. Leave the note open.

2. Open the graphic file that you want to add to the note in a graphics viewer or other software package that will let you see the graphic.

3. Right-click on the graphic and select Copy (or Edit ⇒ Copy), then right-click in the note in ACT! and select Paste.

   Your note field should look similar to the one shown in Figure 10-45.

Figure 10-45 Graphic file added to a note

How To Edit Attachments

The steps are the same to edit word processing documents and other types of attachments. Attachments can be on the Notes, History, Activities or Documents tab. The only difference is that you need the software that other file types were created in. There are two ways to open attachments as discussed below.

① Clicking on the attachment icon for the document that you want to edit.

② Double-clicking on the row that has the attachment that you want to edit will open the Edit dialog box. Click on the attachment.

CREATING QUERIES

Overview

In this lesson you will learn the following query techniques:

- ☑ Create queries using the Lookup By Example tool
- ☑ Query operators
- ☑ Running and saving queries
- ☑ Advanced queries
- ☑ Creating dynamic groups
- ☑ Sorting records retrieved from a query

Queries Overview

Queries and lookups for that matter, are used to get answers to questions like "Which contacts are in a particular state and were referred by Agency 1 or Agency 2?". Another question a query could answer would be "Which customers have not been contacted in the last 60 days?". You have learned how to use the Lookup command to find contacts. Depending on the types of contacts that you are trying to find, you will have to perform several lookups. If you needed to find contacts in two cities, you would have to perform two lookups and add the results of the second lookup to the results of the first lookup.

The Lookup By Example window resembles the Contact Detail view. It contains all of the fields that are on the layout. If you add a field to the top of a layout or to a tab, it will also appear on the Lookup By Example window.

Queries have several advantages over lookups. Queries are used to find contacts based on multiple values in the same field or find contacts that match criteria in more than one field at the same time. Another advantage of using queries is that you can save them and use them again. You can create contact, company and group lookups on the Lookup By Example window. If you need to lookup data in a range of values, you have to use the Advanced Query tool.

Like other features in ACT!, there is more than one way to create a query. You can use the Lookup By Example window or the Advanced Query tool. In this lesson you will learn how to create queries using both options.

> **Saved Query File Extensions**
>
> Saved queries have one of the file extensions listed below.
> **.QRY** are contact queries.
> **.CRY** are company queries.
> **.GRY** are group queries.
> **.ORY** are opportunity queries.

Exercise 11.1: Creating Queries Using The Lookup By Example Tool

The primary reason to use the Lookup By Example tool is to save a query without having to create all of the syntax that is required when using the Advanced Query tool. The other reason to use the Lookup By Example tool instead of the Lookup technique is if you need to perform the lookup on more than one field. In this exercise you will create a query to find all customers in Arizona.

1. Make sure that all of the contacts are displayed. Lookup ⇒ By Example. You should see the Lookup By Example window.

2. Select AZ in the State field.

3. Check the Customer option in the **ID/STATUS** field drop-down list. You should have the options selected that are shown in Figure 11-1.

Figure 11-1 Lookup By Example search criteria

Some of the tabs like Personal Info, Contact Access, and User Fields, display fields and some do not, like the History and Notes tabs. The tabs that have fields displayed can be used in the lookup.

Saving Lookup By Example Queries

If you create a query that you will want to run again, you should save it. If you save the query you can also edit and use it as the basis for another query. Actually, you should save the query before you run it. If you do not save the query before it is run and discover that you did not select the correct options, you will have to start over. You cannot save the query on the Lookup By Example window. You have to save it using the Advanced Query tool.

1. Click the Advanced Query button, then click the **SAVE** button (third button at the top) on the Advanced Query window. The default folder for saving queries that ACT! uses is automatically displayed.

2. Navigate to your folder and type `Customers in AZ` as the query name, then press Enter.

3. You should see the query name in the Title bar at the top of the Advanced Query window. Click the Preview button. The contact records that meet the criteria of the query will be displayed at the bottom of the window.

There should be nine customers in AZ.

If you scroll through the records in the Contact Detail view, you will see that each record has **CUSTOMER** in the ID/Status field and **AZ** in the State field, as shown in Figure 11-2.

Figure 11-2 Query results

The **ADD TO LIST** button adds the criteria from the Type, Field Name, Operator and Value fields to the grid in the middle of the dialog box.

The **EDIT** button opens the Edit dialog box so that you can modify the selected row of criteria in the grid.

The **MOVE UP** and **MOVE DOWN** buttons are used to change the order of the criteria in the grid.

The **REMOVE** button will delete the criteria on the row that is selected.

The **REMOVE ALL** button deletes all of the criteria.

The **PREVIEW** button runs the query and displays the results at the bottom of the dialog box.

4. Click OK. You will see the dialog box shown in Figure 11-3.

    Click OK.

Figure 11-3 ACT! Run Query Options dialog box

Wildcards

The Lookup By Example tool has two wildcard characters that are used to search for characters in a field. They are discussed below. The default search method will only search for the characters that you enter.

① The **%** (percent sign). This wildcard character is used to find characters any place in the field. If you wanted to find all companies that had a specific word or character, you would type the percent sign followed by the characters that you want to search for like this, %Toys. If you entered this in the Company field, all of the records with "Toys" any place in the Company field would be retrieved.

② The _ (underscore). Use this wildcard character to replace one character in the string of characters that you are searching for. If you entered t_n as the search criteria, the search would return records that have ten, tan and ton in the field, but not toon.

> If you used a version prior to ACT! 2007 and used the asterisk (*) in a lookup or query and tried it in ACT! 2009 or higher, you saw that it did not work. I do not know why, but the functionality of the asterisk has been changed to the percent sign (%).

Exercise 11.2: How To Run A Saved Query

There are two ways that you can run a saved query as discussed below.

① From the Advanced Query window (Lookup ⇒ Advanced ⇒ Advanced Query).

② Add it to the Lookup menu and run it from there. You will learn how to modify menus in Lesson 18.

How To Run A Query From The Advanced Query Window

1. Lookup ⇒ Advanced ⇒ Advanced Query.

2. Click the Open button, then double-click on the query, Customers in AZ, in your folder.

3. Click OK, then select **REPLACE LOOKUP** and click OK. You will see the same nine contacts. If more records were added to the database that met the criteria, they would appear at the bottom of the window. Lookup ⇒ All Contacts.

Advanced Queries

You will need to create an advanced query when the Lookup command and Lookup By Example query options will not retrieve the records that you need. This is usually the case when you need to search for two or more values in the same field. An example of when you would need to create an advanced query is if you need to find all customers and prospects in AZ.

Advanced queries are a little harder to create then Lookup By Example queries because syntax is required, but it is not as difficult as you may think. Some conditions must be enclosed in parentheses as shown below.

(ID/STATUS = CUSTOMER OR ID/STATUS = PROSPECT) AND STATE = AZ

The equation above will find all contacts that have "Customer" or "Prospect" in the ID/Status field and AZ in the State field. There is a syntax checker to help you fix syntax errors. You can convert a Lookup By Example query to an advanced query. This may save you some time when creating an advanced query.

Earlier you created a query to find all customers that are in AZ. You can recreate this query on the Lookup By Example window and then open the **ADVANCED QUERY** window to add the prospect criteria to the query.

Even though you can create the entire query in the Advanced Query window, some people feel more comfortable creating as much of an advanced query in the Lookup By Example window as possible and then open the Advanced Query window to finish it.

Advanced Query Options

There are four options (drop-down lists) on the Advanced Query window that are used to create the criteria for a query, as discussed below.

① **Type** Is used to select the record type (Contact, Company, Opportunity, etc) for the field that you need to create criteria for. The option selected in this field controls the fields that are displayed in the Field Name drop-down list. For example, if you select Company in the Type field, the fields in the Field Name drop-down list will be Company fields.

② **Field Name** Is used to select the field that you will create the criteria for.

③ **Operator** They are used to describe the relationship between the criteria in the query. This relationship is a comparison of the data in the database to the value selected in the query. "Starts With" is the default operator. Table 11-1 explains the query operators. You will only see operators that the selected field can use.

④ **Value** This field contains the data that you want to use in the comparison. If the field selected has a drop-down list, the options in the Value drop-down list come from the data in the field in the database. If the field does not have a drop-down list, you have to type in the value.

This Operator	Will Find Records That . . .
After Next [days]	Have a date in the future that is at least the number of days from today that you enter in the Value field. (4)
Contains	Have the criteria that you enter any place in the field.
Contains Data	Have data in the field, meaning the field is not empty. (1) (2)
Day Equals [number]	Have the day of the month that you enter. (4)
Does Not Contain	Do not have the value entered in the Value field.
Does Not Contain Data	Do not have any data in the field, meaning that the field is empty. (1) (2)
Ends With	Have data in the field that ends with the criteria that you enter. (1)
Equal To (=)	Are equal to the criteria that you enter. (1)
Greater Than	Have an amount higher than the amount that you specify in the Value field. If you want to see all orders with an order amount over $500, enter $500 in the Value field and the query will display records with an order amount of $500.01 or more. (3)

Table 11-1 Query operators explained

This Operator	Will Find Records That . . .
Greater Than or Equal To	(Works similar to "Greater than"). The difference is that this operator will also select records that have the amount that you specify. In the greater than example above, the query would not retrieve records with an order amount of exactly $500. The greater than or equal to operator will. (3)
Less Than	Have an amount less than the amount that you specify in the Value field. If you want to see products that have a reorder level of less than 10 items in stock, enter 10 in the Value field and the query will display products with a reorder level of nine or less. (3)
Less Than or Equal To	(Works similar to "Less than"). The difference is that this operator will also select records that have the amount that you specify. In the less than example above, the query would not retrieve records with a reorder level of 10 items. The less than or equal to operator will. (3)
Month Equals [number]	Have the month that you enter. (4)
Not Equal To (!=)	Do not have data that matches the criteria that you enter. (1)
Starts With	Have data in the field that starts with the criteria that you enter. (1)
Older Than [days]	Have a date that is more than the number (of days) that you enter. (4)
On or After	Have a date that is greater than or equal to the date that you enter. (4)
On or Before	Have a date that is equal to or less than the date that you enter. (4)
Within Last [days]	Have a date that is within the previous number of days that you specify. (4)
Within Next [days]	Have a date that is within the next number of days that you specify. (4)
Year Equals [number]	Have the year that you enter. (4)

Table 11-1 Query operators explained (Continued)

(1)   This operator is for text fields.
(2)   The Value field is not enabled when this operator is selected.
(3)   This operator is only for numeric fields.
(4)   This operator is only for date fields.

Exercise 11.3: How To Create An Advanced Query

1.   Lookup ⇒ Advanced ⇒ Advanced Query, then open the Customers in AZ query.

2.   Select the criteria in the Field Name, Operator and Value fields shown at the top of Figure 11-4. The criteria shown at the bottom of the figure is from the Customers in AZ query.

Type:		Field Name:		Operator:		Value:		
Contact	▼	ID/Status	▼	Starts With	▼	Prospect	▼	Add to list
								Edit...

(	Type	Field Name	Operator	Value	)	And/Or	
	Contact	State	Starts With	AZ		And	Move Up
	Contact	ID/Status	Contains	Customer		End	

Figure 11-4 Criteria options to select

If you look in the **AND/OR** column in the grid, you will see that contacts must meet the criteria of the State starting with AZ and the ID/Status field starting with Customer. Changing the value of the And/Or field in the first ID/Status criteria row to **OR** will retrieve contacts if the value in the ID/Status field is Customer or Prospect, which is what you want in this exercise.

If you previewed the contacts now, based on the criteria shown in Figure 11-5, the query would not retrieve any records. That is because the query criteria needs to enclose the two ID/Status rows of criteria in parentheses so that if a contact has the status of Customer or Prospect, the state still has to be equal to AZ.

(	Type	Field Name	Operator	Value	)	And/Or
	Contact	State	Starts With	AZ		And
	Contact	ID/Status	Contains	Customer		And
	Contact	ID/Status	Starts With	Prospect		End

Figure 11-5 And operator illustrated

Using **AND** means that you want both conditions to be met: The condition on the first row with the And condition (in the And/Or column) and the condition on the row below it.

For example, if you want to find all customer and prospect records in AZ that were edited between 1/1/2006 and 5/21/2007, you would create the criteria shown in Figure 11-6.

(	Type	Field Name	Operator	Value	)	And/Or
(	Contact	ID/Status	Starts With	Customer		Or
	Contact	ID/Status	Starts With	Prospect	)	And
	Contact	State	Starts With	AZ		And
(	Contact	Edit Date	On or After	1/1/2006		And
	Contact	Edit Date	On or Before	5/21/2007	)	End

Figure 11-6 Date range criteria

I am not sure why "Starts With" is used as the default operator on the Lookup By Example window and Lookup Opportunities dialog box when most people really want to use **EQUAL TO**. The "Starts With" operator does just that. The operator will look for all records that have the value that you enter at the beginning of the field. Using the Starts With operator can return unexpected results. The problem that I have with using the Starts With operator is that if there are other values that "Start with" the same characters as those in the Value field, those records will also be retrieved when the query is run.

I personally do not use the Starts With operator for this reason. From a programmers perspective, the query criteria shown earlier in Figure 11-5 is not what most users want. The criteria shown in Figure 11-7 is what should be used. You will find out how to correct this query later in the lesson when you learn how to edit a query.

(	Type	Field Name	Operator	Value	)	And/Or
	Contacts	State	Equal To (=)	AZ		And
((	Contacts	ID/Status	Equal To (=)	Customer		Or
	Contacts	ID/Status	Equal To (=)	Prospect	))	End

Figure 11-7 Equal to criteria

3. Click the **ADD TO LIST** button.

4. Click in the **(** column of the first ID/Status criteria row, as shown in Figure 11-8, then select ((.

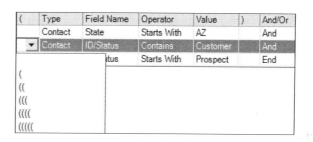

Figure 11-8 Left parenthesis criteria options

5. Open the And/Or drop-down list for the first ID/Status criteria row and select **OR**, as shown in Figure 11-9.

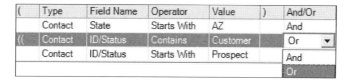

Figure 11-9 And/Or criteria options

Check The Query Syntax

If you preview a query and see a message similar to the one shown in Figure 11-10, it means that there is something wrong with the syntax (code) of the query.

In this example, the message is telling you that there is something wrong with the parentheses.

Figure 11-10 Query syntax error message

Look at the parentheses in the query. There should be an equal number of each type of parentheses that you select and the parentheses should be on different lines. (See the options in the drop-down list shown earlier in Figure 11-8).

1. If you see the message shown above in Figure 11-10, click OK and fix the query criteria based on the message.

2. Click in the) column on the last criteria row and select)), as shown in Figure 11-11.

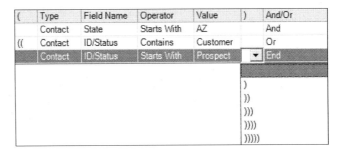

Figure 11-11 Right parenthesis criteria options

Save And Run The Query

1. File ⇒ Save As.

2. Type Customers & Prospects in AZ in the File name field, then click the Save button.

3. Click OK. Select Replace Lookup, then click OK. There should be 14 contacts displayed in the Contact List view.

Exercise 11.4: Find Records Created In The Last 30 Days Query

You may have the need to know which contacts you added to the database or modified in the past. An example would be if you wanted to review all of the contacts that you added to the database in the last 30 days. The field that stores when a contact record is added to the database is the **CREATE DATE** field.

1. Lookup ⇒ Advanced ⇒ Advanced Query.

2. Select the Create Date field.

. . . .

3. Select the **WITHIN LAST [DAYS]** operator, then type 30 in the Value field.

4. Click the Add to list button. You should have the criteria shown in Figure 11-12.

(	Type	Field Name	Operator	Value	)	And/Or
	Contact	Create Date	Within Last [days]	30		End

Figure 11-12 Last 30 days criteria

5. Save the query in your folder as New contacts in last 30 days.

6. Preview the results. You will see the contact records that you have added in the last 30 days. Close the Advanced Query window.

 If you edit the criteria shown above in Figure 11-12 and change the Field Name to **EDIT DATE**, you will see all of the contacts that you have edited in the last 30 days.

Exercise 11.5: Find Contacts In CA With Open Opportunities

In this exercise you will create a query that finds contacts in California that have opportunities with an open status.

1. Lookup ⇒ Advanced ⇒ Advanced Query.

2. Select the State field.

3. Select the Equal To operator, then select CA from the Value drop-down list.

4. Click the Add to List button.

5. Open the Type drop-down list and select Opportunity.

6. Select the Status field.

7. Select the Equal To operator, then type 1 in the Value field.

8. Click the Add to List button. You should have the options shown in Figure 11-13. Click the Preview button.

Type:		Field Name:		Operator:		Value:		
Contact	▼		▼		▼		▼	

(	Type	Field Name	Operator	Value	)	And/Or
	Contact	State	Equal To (=)	CA		And
	Opportunity	Status	Equal To (=)		1	End

Figure 11-13 Contacts in CA with open opportunities criteria

9. Save the query as Open Opportunities in CA.

10. Run the query. You will see the contacts in CA that have open opportunities. If you double-click on a contact, on the Opportunities tab, you will see at least one open opportunity for the contact.

 Opening Existing Queries From The Advanced Query Window

Before you open an existing query, you have to select the type of query that you want to open in the Search for drop-down list at the top of the window.

How To Edit A Query

If you need to edit a query you can follow the steps below. For now you can just read this section. If you want to practice editing a query you can change the operator on each criteria row to Equal To (=) in the Customers & Prospects in AZ query.

1. Open the query that you want to edit in the Advanced Query window.

2. Click on the criteria row that needs to be changed, then click the Edit button. You will see the dialog box shown in Figure 11-14.

Figure 11-14 Edit dialog box

3. Make the criteria changes that you need, then click OK. Save the changes.

Exercise 11.6: Sorting Records Retrieved From A Query

You can sort the records that the query retrieves. This will be useful if you will do a bulk mailing and need the records sorted in order by zip code when you print the mailing labels. You can sort the records from the query in the detail or list view by following the steps below.

1. Lookup all contacts. Edit ⇒ Sort.

2. Open the **SORT BY** drop-down list and select Zip Code.

3. Change the **AND THEN BY** option to <None>.

You should have the options selected that are shown in Figure 11-15.

Click OK. The records in the Contact List view will now be sorted by zip code.

Figure 11-15 Sort dialog box options

Dynamically Linking Contacts To Companies

In Lesson 5 you learned how to manually link contacts to companies. If you want to be able to have contacts automatically linked to a company, you have to create a query.

An example of when this would be useful is when you want to have certain fields filled in for the contact. This is one way to make sure that the data is being maintained. If you needed to make sure that every contact record has a company name, you could create a query that looks for records that do not have data in the Company field.

This works for the Company field, but not for other types of linked fields. For example, if you wanted to put all contact records that do not have a zip code into a company. If the Zip Code field is a linked field, this would not work. You would have to put the records in a group instead of a company.

Exercise 11.7: Find Prospects Query

In this exercise you will create a query to find prospect contacts in the US that do not have an email address. You can use the Lookup By Example and Advanced Query windows to get the contacts that meet the criteria. Using the Lookup By Example window to create as much of the query as possible and then use the Advanced Query window to complete the query is a good idea. This will keep you from having to create the entire query manually.

1. Create a query to display all customers with a prospect status in the United States that do not have an email address.

2. Save the query in your folder as US Prospects with no email address. Your query should retrieve 15 records. Figure 11-16 shows the query syntax.

(	Type	Field Name	Operator	Value	)	And/Or
	Contacts	Country	Starts With	United States		And
	Contacts	ID/Status	Contains	Prospect		And
	Contacts	E-mail	Does Not Contain Data	Nothing		End

Figure 11-16 Prospects without an email address query

Exercise 11.8: How To Create A Dynamic Group

In Exercise 6.6 you created a Sales Reps group and added contacts to it. As time goes on, more contacts will be added to the database and some of them will be sales reps. You could create a lookup to find the new contacts that are sales reps, but you would have to do that on a regular basis so that all of the contacts with this title will be in the group. ACT! has a dynamic option that can be used to create criteria to automatically add records to a group. This is done by creating a query. You can also use the dynamic option to automatically remove records from a group. In this exercise you will modify the Sales Reps group so that it is dynamic. You can add as much criteria as needed to create a dynamic group.

1. On the Group Detail view, click on the Sales Reps group in the tree, then click the Add/Remove Contacts button on the Contacts tab.

2. Click the Edit Criteria button on the Add/Remove Contacts dialog box.

3. Open the Field Name drop-down list and select **TITLE**.
   Open the Operator drop-down list and select **EQUAL TO (=)**.
   Open the Value drop-down list and select **SALES REPRESENTATIVE**.

4. Click the **ADD TO LIST** button. You should have the criteria shown in Figure 11-17.

(	Type	Field Name	Operator	Value	)	And/Or
	Contacts	Title	Equal To (=)	Sales Representative		End

Figure 11-17 Sales rep group criteria

 If you made a mistake, click on the criteria under the drop-down lists that needs to be changed, then click the **EDIT** button to correct the mistake.

5. Click the **PREVIEW** button. You should see five contacts at the bottom of the dialog box.

6. Click OK to close the Group Criteria dialog box.

   This is the Advanced Query dialog box with a different name, as shown in Figure 11-18.

Figure 11-18 Group criteria dialog box

7. You should see the criteria in the **DYNAMIC MEMBERS** section of the Add/Remove Contacts dialog box, as shown in Figure 11-19. Click OK.

Figure 11-19 Dynamic criteria

Contacts that are added to the group via a query will stay in the group as long as they meet the criteria. In the exercise that you just completed, if any of the contacts that were added dynamically has a change in title, they will automatically be removed from the Sales Reps group. If you add a contact to this group manually, they will stay in the group whether or not they meet the criteria.

It is probably best to link contacts to a company on more than the Company name field. It is possible that there is more than one company with the same name in the database, meaning one company could end with "Inc" and the other one doesn't. If you also linked on the street address, the chances of linking to the wrong company is greatly reduced.

Test The Dynamic Group Criteria

1. Create new records for the contacts in Table 11-2.

   The last two records in the table should automatically be added to the Sales Reps group.

Contact	Title
Tim Dynamic	Sales Manager
Tina Dynamic	Sales Representative
Tom Dynamic	Sales Representative

Table 11-2 Test records for the dynamic group criteria

2. Click the Groups button, then click on the Sales Reps group.

   You should see the records for Tina and Tom Dynamic, as illustrated in Figure 11-20.

Figure 11-20 Result of the dynamic group criteria

The Groups/Companies tab on the Contact Detail view does not automatically show dynamic groups that the contact is a member of. You have to click the **SHOW DYNAMIC MEMBERSHIP** button, illustrated in Figure 11-21, to see if the contact is a member of a dynamic group. When you click this button you will see the dialog box shown in Figure 11-22. This dialog box lets you know which dynamic groups the contact is a member of.

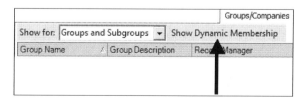

Figure 11-21 Groups/Companies tab options

Figure 11-22 Dynamic Groups Membership dialog box

The query for the dynamic group that you just created will automatically run each time either of the following actions occur:

① The Group Detail view is opened.

② The Groups/Companies tab is displayed.

How To Create A Dynamic Company

You can create a dynamic company if the need arises by following the steps below.

1. On the Company Detail view, click on the company in the tree that you want to create a dynamic company for.

2. On the Contacts tab, click the Add/Remove Contacts button below the tabs on the right.

3. Click the Edit Criteria button on the Add/Remove Contacts dialog box.

4. Create the criteria for the company, then click the Add To List button.

5. Once you have the criteria correct, click OK to close the Company Criteria and Add/Remove Contacts dialog boxes.

DASHBOARDS

Overview

In this lesson you will learn how to use Dashboards and how to modify them by exploring the following topics:

☑ What is a dashboard?
☑ Dashboard toolbar
☑ Dashboard views
☑ Components
☑ Adding data from the dashboard
☑ Filtering data in a dashboard
☑ Modifying dashboard layouts
☑ Modifying dashboard components
☑ Data Chart component

LESSON 12

What Is A Dashboard?

A dashboard displays a snapshot of data in a graphical format. So far in this book you have created, viewed and edited different types of data, including contacts, activities and opportunities. While it is easy to switch between views to see all of these types of data, you cannot view more than one of these types of data at the same time. You also cannot get a feel for the big picture of your data, as they say.

This is where dashboards come into play. Like other features in ACT!, the data that is displayed in a dashboard can be filtered. You can create, view and edit data from a dashboard. You can edit the default dashboard layouts by adding, modifying and removing components in a dashboard. To create a dashboard from scratch involves selecting the components that are needed, adding them to the layout, then select the options on the Component Configuration Wizard.

NEW Dashboard Layouts

ACT! comes with five layouts as shown in Figures 12-1 to 12-5. The Administrative and Contact layouts are new. Each layout can be customized. The layouts contain components which have preset filters. Later you will learn how to customize the layouts and how to change the preset defaults and filters.

The **ACTIVITIES DASHBOARD** displays the contacts schedule and activities.

The **ADMINISTRATIVE DASHBOARD** displays user status and remote database information.

The **CONTACT DASHBOARD** displays contact records that you have created or edited and a count of history records.

The **DEFAULT DASHBOARD** displays your schedule, activities, history and opportunity information.

The **OPPORTUNITY DASHBOARD** displays opportunity sales information in several formats.

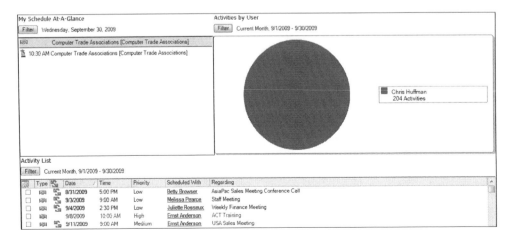

Figure 12-1 ACT! Activities Dashboard

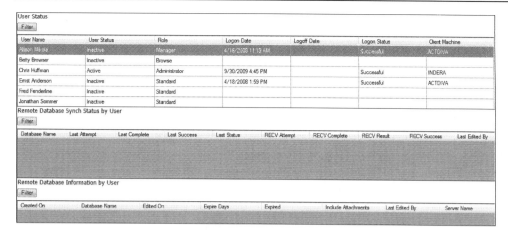

Figure 12-2 ACT! Administrative Dashboard

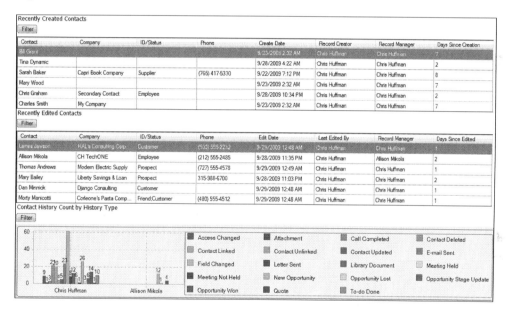

Figure 12-3 ACT! Contact Dashboard

Figure 12-4 ACT! Default Dashboard

Figure 12-5 ACT! Opportunities Dashboard

Dashboard Toolbar

Figure 12-6 shows the Dashboard toolbar. Table 12-1 explains the buttons on the toolbar.

Figure 12-6 Dashboard toolbar

Button	Description
1	Is used to edit the dashboard that is displayed.
2	Prints the dashboard that is displayed.
3	Copies the dashboard that is displayed to the clipboard.
4	Refreshes the data in the dashboard.
5	Is used to select a different dashboard layout.

Table 12-1 Dashboard toolbar buttons explained

Exercise 12.1: Selecting A Dashboard Layout

The steps below show you how to select a dashboard.

1. Click the **DASHBOARD** icon on the Navigation Pane.

2. To select a different dashboard, open the Dashboard drop-down list and select one of the options shown in Figure 12-7.

Figure 12-7 Default dashboard layouts

Dashboard Components

Components display different types of data from the database. The majority of components display opportunity data. As shown earlier in Figures 12-1 to 12-5, each dashboard can have different components in different locations on the dashboard.

There are six components in two categories that can be added to a layout as discussed below. The options shown are the defaults for the component, which can be modified. For example, the Closed sales to date component displays opportunities in the CHT1 Sales process. If you created a process, you can modify this component to display your process by default, instead of the CHT1 Sales process.

Activity Components

There are two activity components that come with ACT!, as discussed below.

① **MY ACTIVITIES** Displays a chart with your activities for the current month. (This component displays as Activities by User.)
② **MY SCHEDULE AT-A-GLANCE** Displays your scheduled activities for today.

Opportunity Components

There are four opportunity components that come with ACT!, as discussed below. The opportunity data that each component displays is from the CHT1 Sales process.

① **CLOSED SALES TO DATE** Displays opportunities that have the Closed - Won status for the current month.

② **MY OPPORTUNITIES** Displays a bar chart that has open opportunities for the current month. (This component displays as Opportunities by User.)

③ **OPPORTUNITY PIPELINE BY STAGE** Displays a pie chart with open opportunities for the current month.

④ **TOP OPPORTUNITIES** Displays a list of your top 10 opportunities for the current month that have the Closed - Won status.

Getting Things Done From A Dashboard

Yes, the dashboard provides a great way to view a lot of data in a graphical format, but you still need to be able to get work done. Many of the components have a shortcut menu. This is in addition to the menu and toolbar options on the dashboard.

Exercise 12.2: Activity Component Shortcut Menu Options

The activity shortcut menu options discussed in this section are available, regardless of the dashboard that they are on.

1. Open the ACT! Activities Dashboard.

2. Right-click in the My Schedule At-A-Glance section.

   You should see the shortcut menu shown in Figure 12-8.

   These are the activity options that you can use.

Figure 12-8 My Schedule At-A-Glance shortcut menu

3. If you right-click in the Activities by User section, you will see the options, shown in Figure 12-9, is the only one available.

Figure 12-9 Activities by User shortcut menu

The **COPY TO CLIPBOARD** option creates an image of the component. This image can be pasted into a document.

4. If you right-click in the Activity List section, you will see the shortcut menu shown earlier in Figure 12-8. The Activity List shortcut menu also has the **CUSTOMIZE COLUMNS** option available on the menu.

Exercise 12.3: Opportunity Component Shortcut Menu Options

The opportunity shortcut menu options discussed in this section are available in dashboards that have an opportunity component.

1. Open the ACT! Default Dashboard.

2. Right-click in the grid in the Top 10 Opportunities section. You should see the shortcut menu shown in Figure 12-10.

   These are the opportunity options that you can use.

   Other opportunity sections only have the Copy To Clipboard option shown above in Figure 12-9.

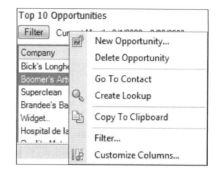

Figure 12-10 Opportunity shortcut menu

Filtering Data In A Dashboard

As you have seen, each activity component has a filter button. The filter button is used to change the data that is displayed in the component. The options that you will see on the Filter dialog boxes are the default options that were set for the component.

If you select different options on a filter dialog box, the next time that you open a dashboard, those options will still be selected. The exception to this is if you or another administrator or manager of the database modifies the default filter options for the component.

Exercise 12.4: Filtering Activity Component Data

In this exercise you will learn how to filter the activity component data.

My Schedule At-A-Glance Filter Component Options

1. Open the ACT! Activities Dashboard.

2. Click the **FILTER** button for the My Schedule At-A-Glance component. You will see the dialog box shown in Figure 12-11.

   The filter options on this dialog box are a subset of the filter options that are on the Activities tab.

   If the My Schedule At-A-Glance component displays a lot of activities, you can clear some of the options on this dialog box to reduce the number of activities that appear in the component.

Figure 12-11 My Schedule At-A-Glance component filter options

Activities By User Filter Component Options

1. Click the **FILTER** button in the Activities By User component.

   You will see the dialog box shown in Figure 12-12.

   The filter options on this dialog box are the same filter options that are on the Activities tab of the Contact Detail view.

   The **SHOW OUTLOOK TASKS** option is helpful if you are using Microsoft Outlook as your email reader in ACT!. Selecting this option means that you want to display tasks that were created, based on an email in Outlook.

Figure 12-12 Activities By User component filter options

2. Open the Dates drop-down list and select Custom, then select the date range for all of 2009.

3. Clear the **SHOW PRIVATE** option, then click OK. The Activities by User component should look like the one shown in Figure 12-13.

   This display of activities may be more helpful if they were displayed in a bar chart because that would allow you to better see how many of each type of activity was listed. Later in this lesson you will learn how to modify this component.

Figure 12-13 Activities by User component with different filter options

In ACT 2009! and earlier, by default, the Activities by User component displayed totals of the activities for the user by category, at the bottom of the component. In Exercise 12.8, you will learn how to add these totals to this component.

Activity List Filter Options

The Activity List filter is the List view display type of the My Activities component.

1. Click the **FILTER** button in the Activity List section. As you see, the Filter dialog box has the same options as the one shown earlier in Figure 12-12.

2. Clear the Call and To-Do **TYPES**, then click OK. You will see less activities in this section of the dashboard.

Exercise 12.5: Filtering Opportunity Component Data

In this exercise you will learn how to filter the opportunity component data.

1. Open the ACT! Default Dashboard.

2. Click any **FILTER** button in either Opportunity component.

    You will see the dialog box shown in Figure 12-14.

    The options on this dialog box are the same filter options that are on all of the Opportunity components.

    They are the same options that are on the Opportunity List view. [See Lesson 8, Using The Opportunity List Filters section]

Figure 12-14 Opportunity component filter options

3. Select the options that you want to filter the opportunity records by, then click OK.

Administrative Dashboard

The components on this dashboard display users of the database. The filter buttons in both remote database sections open the dialog box shown in Figure 12-15.

This dialog box is used to enter the name of the remote database that you want to view the status of, as shown in Figure 12-16. In Lesson 20 you will learn how to create a remote database.

Figure 12-15 Filter Criteria dialog box

Figure 12-16 Remote database dashboard information

Dashboard Designer

The Dashboard Designer is used to create new dashboards and modify the dashboards that come with ACT!. The Dashboard Designer has two functions, as discussed below.

① **CREATE OR MODIFY THE LAYOUT** Select this option when you want to create a new dashboard layout or modify an existing layout.

② **MODIFY A DASHBOARD COMPONENT** Select this option when you want to modify a component, like changing the default filter options.

Dashboard Designer Window

When you open the Dashboard Designer in Edit mode, you will see the window shown in Figure 12-17.

Figure 12-17 Dashboard Designer window

Dashboard Designer Toolbar

Not to be out done, the Dashboard Designer has its own toolbar, as shown in Figure 12-18. Table 12-2 explains the buttons on the toolbar.

Figure 12-18 Dashboard Designer toolbar

Button	Description
1	Creates a new dashboard.
2	Opens an existing dashboard.
3	Saves the changes.
4	Deletes the selected component.
5	Copies the selected component.
6	Pastes the selected component.
7	Undoes the last action.
8	Redoes the previous action.

Table 12-2 Dashboard Designer toolbar buttons explained

Dashboard Designer Menu Options

The Dashboard Designer has some menu options that are unique. They are explained in Table 12-3.

Menu	Option	Description
File	Layout Settings	Opens the dialog box shown in Figure 12-19. These options are used to change the size of the dashboard.
Format	Insert/Delete	Both options have the submenu shown in Figure 12-20. The options are explained below.
Tools	Add Component	Opens the submenu shown in Figure 12-21. This is one way to add a component to the dashboard. The components are divided into the activity, opportunity and custom categories that you learned about earlier in this lesson.
Tools	Component Configuration	Opens the **COMPONENT CONFIGURATION WIZARD**, which is covered later in this lesson.

Table 12-3 Dashboard Designer menu options explained

The dimensions shown in the **TARGET SIZE** drop-down list are the same size as computer screen resolutions.

This means that if you are creating or modifying a dashboard and all of the people that will use it have the same screen size resolution, you can select that size instead of using the smaller default size.

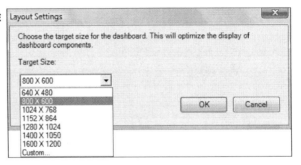

Figure 12-19 Layout Settings dialog box

The **COLUMN ON THE FAR RIGHT** option will add/delete a column on the right side of the dashboard.

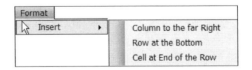

Figure 12-20 Insert and Delete layout options

The **ROW AT THE BOTTOM** option will add/delete a row at the bottom of the dashboard.

The **CELL AT END OF THE ROW** option will add/delete a cell at the end of the row that is selected.

Figure 12-21 Add Component options

Dashboard Designer Toolbox

The Dashboard Designer toolbox options are shown in Figures 12-22 to 12-24. Each component was explained earlier in the Dashboard Components section. These are the components that you can add to the dashboard.

Figure 12-22 Activity toolbox components

Figure 12-23 Opportunity toolbox components

Figure 12-24 Custom toolbox component

Dashboard Layout Overview

By default, a new layout has six sections that you can add a component to. It is not a requirement that all six sections be used in a layout. Each section can be resized. I think the Dashboard Designer is a good first step in being able to modify dashboards. It has some quirks that I hope will be worked out in the next release. It is not as user friendly as the other designers in ACT!. For example, in the exercise below, the goal is to move the component that is at the bottom of the dashboard to the top of the dashboard. Sounds easy right? As you will see, it requires several steps.

Exercise 12.6: Modify The ACT! Activities Dashboard Layout

In this exercise you will modify the Activities dashboard layout to put the Activity List component at the top of the layout.

1. Open the ACT! Activities Dashboard, then click the **EDIT CURRENT DASHBOARD** button on the Dashboard toolbar. You will see the Dashboard Designer window, shown earlier in Figure 12-17.

2. File ⇒ Save As.

    You will see the dialog box shown in Figure 12-25.

Figure 12-25 Dashboards folder

This is where the dashboard layouts are stored that appear in the drop-down list at the top of the dashboard. If you want the dashboard layouts that you create to appear in the drop-down list, you have to save them in this folder.

3. Type My Activities Dashboard in the File name field, then press Enter.

4. The My Schedule component should be selected.

   Format ⇒ Insert ⇒ Row at the bottom.

   You should see a new row at the bottom of the window, as illustrated in Figure 12-26.

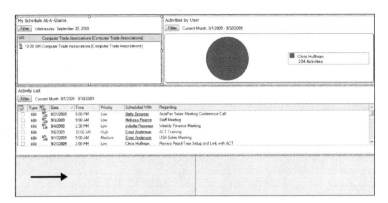

Figure 12-26 New row added to the dashboard layout

5. Move the Activity List component in the layout to the bottom row.

6. Right-click in the middle row and select Insert ⇒ Cell at end of the row.

7. Place the mouse pointer on the line between the two cells in the middle row, as shown in Figure 12-27, then drag the line to the left so that it lines up with the one at the end of the My Schedule component.

Figure 12-27 Mouse pointer in position to resize a cell

8. One by one, move the two components in the first row to the cells in the middle row.

9. Right-click in the first row and select Delete ⇒ Cell at end of the row.

10. Move the Activity List component in the third row to the first row.

11. Format ⇒ Delete ⇒ Row at the bottom.

12. File ⇒ Exit. Click Yes, when prompted to save the changes to the dashboard. Wasn't that a lot of steps to rearrange the components on the layout? <smile>

View The Changes

1. On the Dashboard view, open the Dashboard drop-down list.

   You should see your dashboard in the list, as shown in Figure 12-28.

Figure 12-28 Dashboard added to the list

2. Select your dashboard.

   It should look like the one shown in Figure 12-29.

   Compare it to the one shown earlier in Figure 12-1.

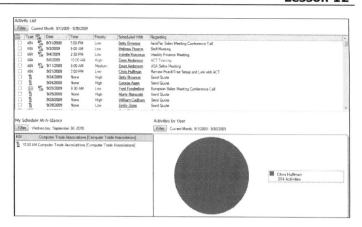

Figure 12-29 Modified Activities dashboard

Exercise 12.7: Modify The ACT! Default Dashboard Layout

In this exercise you will modify the Default Dashboard by removing some of the components and rearranging the remaining components.

1. Open the ACT! Default Dashboard, then click the **EDIT CURRENT DASHBOARD** button on the Dashboard toolbar.

2. File ⇒ Save As. Type My Default Dashboard as the file name, then press Enter.

3. Delete the following components by clicking on them and then pressing the Delete key: My Schedule At-A-Glance, Contact History Count by History Type and Top 10 Opportunities.

4. Move the Activities by User component to the cell on the left of the same row.

5. Move the Closed Sales to Date component up to the first row.

6. Move the Opportunity Pipeline by Stage component to the first cell in the same row.

7. Click in the middle row, then delete the cell on the right in the middle row.

8. Delete the bottom row.

9. Make the first row longer so that it takes up more than 50% of the space in the dashboard.

10. File ⇒ Exit. Save the changes.

11. Select the My Default Dashboard from the drop-down list.

    It should look like the one shown in Figure 12-30.

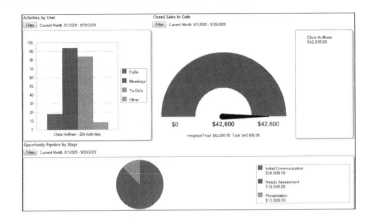

Figure 12-30 My Default Dashboard

Component Configuration Wizard

This wizard is used to add components to a dashboard. Once you select an option on a component wizard screen, you can preview the change by clicking the **PREVIEW** button. The following seven steps are available on the Component Configuration Wizard for components once they have been added to a dashboard. All steps are not available for each component. The options available for some steps vary depending on the component that is being added to the dashboard.

Step 1: Select Display Type

This step is used to select the chart type, as shown in Figure 12-31.

All chart types are not available for all components.

You can also select where to place the filter bar, as illustrated at the bottom of Figure 12-31.

Figure 12-31 Display type options for the Closed Sales to Date component

Step 2: Edit Default Filters

This step displays the current default filter options for the component and is used to select new default filter options.

The filter options change, depending on the display type (chart) that is selected.
Figure 12-32 shows the filter options for the My Activities component.
Figure 12-33 shows the filter options for the Opportunity Pipeline by Stage component.

Figure 12-33 Filter options for the Opportunity Pipeline by Stage component

Figure 12-32 Filter options for the My Activities component

Step 3: Edit Header/Footer

This step is used to add or edit the header and footer information for the component, as shown in Figure 12-34.

Figure 12-34 Header and footer options

Step 4: Change Legend

This step is used to select whether or not the component displays a legend and where the legend should be placed, as shown in Figure 12-35.

Figure 12-35 Legend options

Step 5: Change Totals

This step is used to select whether or not the component displays totals. The totals for each component type are pre-determined, which means that you can only select whether or not to display totals. Figure 12-36 shows the totals for the Closed Sales to Date component. Figure 12-37 shows the totals for the My Activities component.

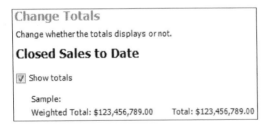

Figure 12-36 Change totals options for the Closed Sales to Date component

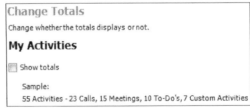

Figure 12-37 Change totals options for the My Activities component

Step 6: Specify Targets

This step is used to select whether or not the component displays the minimum acceptable amount or value that will reach the expected goal. Figure 12-38 shows the target options. Figure 12-39 illustrates the target option applied to a chart. The line illustrated in Figure 12-39 across the chart, represents the target. This allows the user to see which items meet the goal and which ones do not.

As illustrated in Figure 12-40, the target is $30,000. The target is indicated by a triangle pointer on the chart. In this example, the target has not been met. In Figure 12-41, the target is $17,500, which means that the target has been exceeded.

Figure 12-38 Target options

Figure 12-39 Target option on the chart

Figure 12-40 Target has not been met

Figure 12-41 Target has been met

Step 7: Scale/Limits

This step is used to select the range that numeric data should be displayed on the chart.
The scale and limits change depending on the display type that is selected.
Figures 12-42 to 12-44 show different types of scale/limits. The **BREAKPOINT** options are used to measure progress.

Figure 12-42 Top Opportunities component Scale/Limits options

Figure 12-43 My Activities Scale/Limits component options

Figure 12-44 Closed Sales to Date Scale/Limits component options

Top Opportunities Component

This component has an additional step, as shown in Figure 12-45. The options shown are used to change the columns that are displayed in the grid and how the opportunity records are sorted.

Figure 12-45 Change Columns options for the Top Opportunities component

Exercise 12.8: Modify The Components Of The My Default Dashboard

In this exercise you will modify the default filter options for the My Default Dashboard. Currently, all of the filters are using the current month as the date range.

1. Open the My Default Dashboard, if it is not already open, then click the **EDIT CURRENT DASHBOARD** button on the Dashboard toolbar.

2. File ⇒ Save As. Type My New Filter Dashboard as the file name, then press Enter.

Modify The Activities By User Component Filter Options

1. Right-click on the Activities by User component and select **COMPONENT CONFIGURATION**.

2. Click on the Select Display Type link, then select the **HORIZONTAL BAR CHART** display type.

3. Open the **FILTER BAR PLACEMENT** drop-down list and select Below Display.

4. On the Edit Default Filters screen, open the Dates drop-down list and select Today and Future.

5. On the Change Legend screen, select Top.

6. On the Change Totals screen, select the Show totals option, then click Finish.

7. Click Yes, when prompted that the changes will affect all users.

As shown in Figure 12-46, the Details section of the Configuration Wizard screen shows the options that have been selected for the component.

Figure 12-46 Details section

8. Click Close to close the Component Configuration dialog box.

Modify The Closed Sales To Date Component Filter Options

1. Right-click on the Closed Sales to Date component and select Component Configuration.

2. On the Edit Default Filters screen, open the Dates drop-down list and select Today and Future.

3. On the Edit Header/Footer screen, type `Pending Sales` in the Header field, then change the font size to 14. Change the color to red.

4. On the Specify Targets screen, change the Target value to $100,000.00.

5. On the Scale/Limits screen, make the following changes.

   Breakpoint 1 25000
   Breakpoint 2 75000
   Maximum 250000

   You should have the options shown in Figure 12-47.

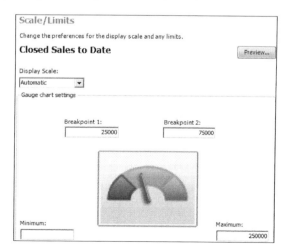

Figure 12-47 Scale/Limit options

6. Click Finish. Click Yes to continue with changes, then click Close.

7. File ⇒ Exit, then click Yes. The dashboard should look similar to the one shown in Figure 12-48. Compare this to the dashboard shown earlier in Figure 12-30.

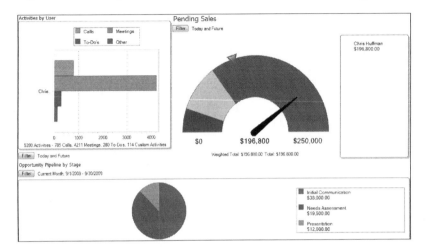

Figure 12-48 Modified dashboard components

Create A New Dashboard

If you need to create a dashboard from scratch, you can follow the steps below.

1. Click the **NEW DASHBOARD** link in the Related Tasks section on the Navigation Pane. You will see an empty layout in the Dashboard Designer.

2. Drag the component from the Toolbox to the layout.

3. The Component Configuration Wizard will automatically open. Select the default options that you need, for the component.

4. Repeat steps 2 and 3 for each component that you want to add to the dashboard layout.

5. Remove any sections from the layout that are not needed.

6. Save the dashboard and give it a descriptive name.

NEW Data Chart Component

This component is used to create a custom component. The steps below explain the process of creating a component.

1. Add the Data Chart component to a section of the layout. You will see the dialog box shown in Figure 12-49. The options on this dialog box are used to configure the component. The options are explained below.

Figure 12-49 Data Chart Designer dialog box

CHOOSE A TEMPLATE The options shown in Figure 12-50 are the layouts that you can select from to create your custom component. You have seen many of these layouts earlier in this lesson.

Some of these templates will disable other options on the dialog box.

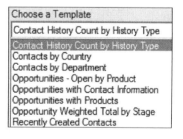

Figure 12-50 Choose a Template drop-down list options

SHOW DATA AS CHART If checked, the data will be displayed as a chart in the component instead of in grid format, as shown in Figure 12-51.

Count	History Type	Record Creator
9	Access Changed	Chris Huffman
6	Attachment	Chris Huffman
3	Call Completed	Chris Huffman
23	Contact Deleted	Chris Huffman
56	Contact Linked	Chris Huffman

Figure 12-51 Data displayed in grid format

CHART TYPE The options shown in Figure 12-52 are the chart types that can be created.

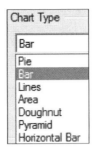

Figure 12-52 Chart Type options

SHOW LEGEND If checked, a legend for the charts data will be displayed on the component.

SHOW POINT LABELS If checked, the value that each part of the chart represents will be displayed on the component, as shown in Figure 12-53.

Depending on the size of the chart, the lines may not be displayed. The lines are displayed when the chart size is small.

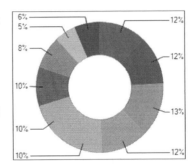

Figure 12-53 Show Point Labels option

CHART 3D If checked, the chart will be displayed in 3D format, as shown in Figure 12-54.

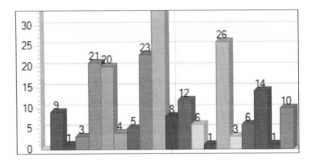

Figure 12-54 Chart in 3D format

HEADER Is used to type in information that you want to appear at the top of the component. By default, the template name is added to this field.

FOOTER Is used to type in information that you want to appear at the bottom of the component.

PREVIEW DATA BUTTON Depending on the template type that is selected, a different dialog box will appear. The options are used to set up the default filter criteria and to view the data.

Figure 12-55 shows the filter criteria options for the Contact History Count By History component.

Figure 12-56 shows the filter criteria options for the Contacts By Department component. Figure 12-57 shows the filter criteria options for the Opportunities with Products component.

Figure 12-55 Contact History Count By History component Filter Criteria dialog box

Figure 12-56 Contacts By Department component Filter Criteria dialog box

Figure 12-57 Opportunities with Products component Filter Criteria dialog box

NEW Dashboard Related Tasks

NEW DASHBOARD Opens the Dashboard Designer to create a new dashboard.

EDIT LAYOUT OF DASHBOARD Opens the current dashboard layout in the Dashboard Designer so that it can be modified.

COPY DASHBOARD Is used to make an image of the entire dashboard that can be pasted in a document.

For example, if you click on this link, then open Microsoft Word, right-click and select Paste, you will see an image of the dashboard in the document, as shown in Figure 12-58.

Figure 12-58 Image of dashboard pasted in a document

PRINT CURRENT SCREEN Opens the Quick Print Options dialog box so that you can select options for how the screen, in this case the dashboard, will be printed.

USING THE TASK LIST & CALENDAR

Overview

In this lesson you will learn the following Task List and calendar features:

- ☑ How to use the Task List view to work with activities
- ☑ How to use the calendar views
- ☑ How to filter activities in a calendar view
- ☑ Granting calendar access

Task List View

You have learned how to create activities and view them. You have also learned how to view several contacts at the same time using the Contact List view. If you need to view activities for several contacts at the same time, you can use the Task List view. The entries displayed in the Task List are linked to the current My Record. This means that by default, each person that uses the database has their own Task List and calendar that only displays activities that they scheduled or activities that are assigned to them.

In the Task List view you can add and delete columns, sort by column headings and change the order of the column headings, just like you can with the Contact List view. In addition to being able to view activities for several contacts in the Task List view, you can also modify, sort, filter, clear, schedule and delete activities on the Task List view, the same way that you can on the Activities tab.

Task List Toolbar

Figure 13-1 shows the Task List toolbar. Table 13-1 explains the buttons on the toolbar.

Figure 13-1 Task List toolbar

Button	Description
1	Prints the current view.
2	Create a lookup.
3	Opens the Customize Columns dialog box, which is used the change the order of the columns on the Task List.
4	Exports the Task List to Excel.

Table 13-1 Task List toolbar buttons explained

Status Bar

At the bottom of the Task List window is the status bar shown in Figure 13-2. It displays the date range and totals for each type of activity that is displayed on the Task List view.

All Dates: 374 Activities - 39 Calls, 152 Meetings, 109 To-do's, 74 Custom Activities

Figure 13-2 Task List status bar

When you click the Task List button on the Navigation Pane. You will see the view shown in Figure 13-3.

 If you double-click on an activity in the Task List, you can edit it or see more information about the activity.

Figure 13-3 Task List view

Filter Options

The filter options for the Task List are explained in Table 13-2.

Filter	Description
Dates	Select the date or date range that you want to see activities for, as shown in Figure 13-4. If none of the options shown fit your needs, select the **CUSTOM** option at the bottom of the drop-down list.
Types	Check the activity types that you want to see and clear the check mark of the option(s) that you do not want to see, as shown in Figure 13-5.
Priorities	Check the priority of the activity types that you want to see. Clear the check mark of the option(s) that you do not want to see, as shown in Figure 13-6.
Select Users	View the public activities of others users in the database. If you select other users, keep in mind that their activities will continue to be displayed in your Task List until you remove the user from your view.

Table 13-2 Task List filter options explained

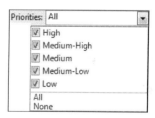

Figure 13-6 Priorities options

Figure 13-4 Date filter options

Figure 13-5 Activity Types options

Options Button

The options shown in Figure 13-7 are other options that can be selected to filter activities on the Task List view. They are explained below.

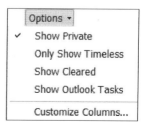

① **Show Private** Displays or hides private activities.

② **Only Show Timeless** Hides tasks that have a time.

③ **Show Cleared** Displays tasks that have been cleared, but not deleted. Cleared tasks have a line through them, as illustrated in Figure 13-8.

Figure 13-7 Task List Options button options

④ **Show Outlook Tasks** Displays tasks that were imported from Microsoft Outlook.

⑤ **Customize Columns** Opens the Customize Columns dialog box.

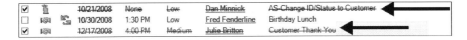

Figure 13-8 Cleared tasks illustrated

Exercise 13.1: Create A Task List Lookup Using Filters

By default, the activities are in ascending order by date. If you have hundreds of activities, you will probably not want to see all of them. You can create a lookup to only display certain activities.

1. Open the Dates drop-down list, then select the **CUSTOM** option at the bottom of the list. You will see the Select Date Range dialog box.

2. Select the range 9/1/2009 to 9/8/2009, as shown in Figure 13-9.

   Click OK.

   You should only see activities that have a date in the range that you selected.

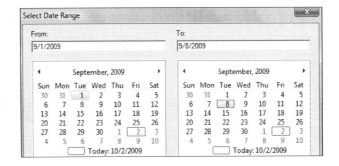

Figure 13-9 Select Date Range dialog box

3. Display all of the activities, then clear the Activity Type options that you do not want to see. In this exercise clear all of the options except Call and To-Do.

4. Select the priority of the activities that you want to see. For this exercise clear all of the options except Medium-High.

5. If you want to see activities for other users, click the **SELECT USERS** button. Select the first two users, then click OK.

6. View all of the activities.

 If you prefer to see all of the Task List filter options in one place, use the dialog box shown in Figure 13-10. Right-click in the Task List view and select **FILTER TASK LIST**.

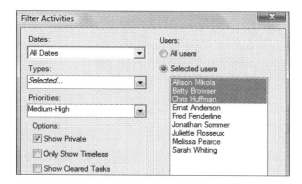

Figure 13-10 Filter Activities (Task List) dialog box

Exercise 13.2: Clearing Tasks From The Task List View

Once you have completed a task or no longer need it, you can clear the activity. You can also create a follow up task. Use the activity dated 9/19/2008 to complete this exercise.

1. Click in the **CLEARED** column (the column with the ✓) next to the activity that you want to clear. You will see the Clear Activity dialog box.

2. In the Details field type
    Clearing this task,
    as illustrated in Figure 13-11.

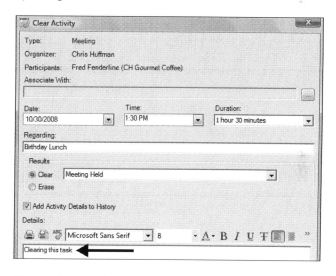

Figure 13-11 Clear Activity dialog box

3. Click OK. You will not see the task in the list unless the **SHOW CLEARED** option is selected on the Options button.

How To Print The Task List

The Task List can be printed by following the steps below.

1. From the Task List view, File ⇒ Quick Print Current Window.

2. Select any options that are needed on the Print dialog box, then click OK.

Looking Up Records On The Task List

If you like working from the Task List, you can accomplish the same tasks that you can from other views by using the options on the shortcut menu shown in Figure 13-12.

Like other views, you can look up contacts from the Task List. If you do, the contacts will open in the Contact List view.

There are two ways to create a lookup from the Task List view as discussed below.

Schedule	▶
Reschedule Activity...	
View Details...	
Send Activity E-mail...	
Clear Activity...	
Clear Multiple Activities...	
Erase Activity	
Go to Contact	
Create Lookup	
Filter Task List...	
Customize Columns...	
Print Task List	

① Click the **CREATE LOOKUP** button on the Global toolbar.
② Right-click in the Task List view and select Create Lookup, as shown in Figure 13-12.

Figure 13-12 Task List view shortcut menu

Exercise 13.3: Customizing The Task List View

The columns on the Task List view can be customized by following the steps below.

1. Open the Task List view.

2. Right-click in the view and select **CUSTOMIZE COLUMNS**. You will see the Customize Columns dialog box.

Adding the **SCHEDULED BY** field to the Task List will show who created the activity.
Adding the **SCHEDULED FOR** field will show who the activity has been assigned to.

These two fields are useful to see on the Task List view if you view other users activities on a regular basis. Figure 13-13 shows these two fields.

Regarding	Scheduled By	Scheduled For
Prospect Call	Chris Huffman	Allison Mikola
Demonstration	Chris Huffman	Juliette Rosseux
Network Breakfast	Chris Huffman	Chris Huffman

Figure 13-13 Modified Task List view

𝕹𝔼𝖂 Task List Related Tasks

SCHEDULE SERIES OF ACTIVITIES [See Lesson 7, Activity Series]

EXPORT TO EXCEL Exports the tasks that are displayed to Excel, as shown in Figure 13-14.

	A	B	C	D	E	F	G	H	I	J	K	L	
	Cleared	Type	Recurring	Date	Time	Priority	Scheduled With	Regarding	Details	Duration	Attachment	Private	Associate With
1													
2	FALSE			6/26/2006 12:30	12:30 PM	Low	Jonathan Sommer	Birthday Lunch		1 hour 30 minutes			
3	FALSE			9/1/2006 9:00	9:00 AM	Low	Melissa Pearce	Staff Meeting		1 hour 30 minutes			CH TechONE[CMP]
4	FALSE			9/1/2006 14:30	2:30 PM	Low	Juliette Rosseux	Weekly Finance Meeting		1 hour			
5	FALSE			9/4/2006 11:00	11:00 AM	Low	Chris Huffman	Write Article for E-Newsletter		1 hour 30 minutes			CH TechONE[CMP]
6	FALSE			9/5/2006 20:30	8:30 PM	Medium-Low	Chris Huffman	Soccer Practice-Taylor		1 hour			CH TechONE[CMP]
7	FALSE			10/9/2006 10:00	10:00 AM	Low	+Ernst Anderson	ACT Training		7 hours 30 minutes			CH TechONE[CMP]
8	FALSE			10/24/2006 17:00	5:00 PM	Low	+Chris Huffman	Presentation		1 hour 30 minutes			CH TechONE[CMP]

Figure 13-14 Tasks exported to Excel

VIEW ALL RELATED CONTACTS Displays the contacts (in the contacts list view) that are related to at least one task that is displayed.

PRINT CURRENT SCREEN Opens the Quick Print Options dialog box so that you can select options for how the screen will be printed.

CHANGE COLUMNS Opens the Customize Columns dialog box.

Calendar Preferences

In Lesson 2 you learned that there are preferences that you can set for the calendar views. ACT! has calendar options that you can customize as needed.

Calendar Views

The default date when you open any calendar is today's date. Each calendar view has a daily check list and date selector. **TIMELESS** activities are not displayed on calendars. They are displayed under the calendar on the right side of the window with the rest of the activities. There is also a mini calendar that you can use. The calendar views can also be used to schedule and modify activities. The calendar views (Daily, Work Week, Weekly and Monthly), are used to see and schedule activities.

Calendar Toolbar

Figure 13-15 shows the Calendar toolbar. Table 13-3 explains the buttons on the toolbar.

Figure 13-15 Calendar toolbar

Button	Description
1	Highlights today in any calendar view except the daily calendar.
2	Displays the daily calendar.
3	Displays the work week calendar.
4	Displays the weekly calendar.
5	Displays the monthly calendar.
6	Displays the previous day, week or month, depending on which calendar view is open.
7	Displays the next day, week or month, depending on which calendar view is open.
8	Prints the calendar.
9	Look up contacts.

Table 13-3 Calendar toolbar buttons explained

Mini-Calendar

This calendar is used to view calendars for the previous month, current month and next month. This is a quick way to display activities from previous or future months. The single arrows will move to the previous and next month. The double arrows will move to the previous and next year. You can use this calendar to navigate to a day, week or month, by clicking on it.

1. Click the Calendar button on the Navigator Pane.

2. View ⇒ Mini-Calendar, or press F4. You will see the calendar shown in Figure 13-16.

If you click on a date and the weekly calendar view is open, you will see the weekly calendar for the date that you click on.

If necessary, close the mini calendar by clicking on the red X in the upper right corner of the calendar.

Figure 13-16 Mini-calendar

Calendar Tips

Mini-Calendar and **Recap List Calendar** If you right-click on the month name in the mini calendar shown above in Figure 13-16, you will see the Recap List calendar shown in Figure 13-17. You can view one of the months in the list. The dates in bold on the mini-calendar have activities. If you right-click on a date that is bold, you will see all of the activities for that day. If you right-click on a date that is bold in either calendar, you will see the dialog box shown in Figure 13-18.

Shortcut Menu If you right-click on an activity in the calendar, you will see the shortcut menu shown in Figure 13-19. Many of the options that you will use the most are on this shortcut menu.

The **Filter Calendar** view option on the Calendar shortcut menu opens the dialog box shown in Figure 13-20. This dialog box contains all of the filter options that are at the top of a calendar view.

Drop And Drag An Activity You can move an activity from one day or time to another day or time by dragging the activity to a new location. If you select an activity to move that is part of a recurring activity, you will be prompted to change all occurrences of the activity or only the current occurrence. If you click OK to move the activity, it will no longer be part of the recurring activities, as shown by the message in Figure 13-21.

Figure 13-17 Recap List calendar

Figure 13-18 Activities list

Figure 13-19 Calendar shortcut menu

Figure 13-20 Filter Calendar dialog box

Figure 13-21 Remove Instance message

Daily Calendar

The daily calendar displays activities and tasks for one day. By default, the day is divided into 30 minute intervals. You can change the time interval on the Preferences dialog box.

1.   Display the My Record, then click on the Calendar button on the Navigation Pane.

2. View the daily calendar for January 18, 2010, by clicking the **DAILY** button and then selecting the day in the mini calendar. The calendar should look similar to the one shown in Figure 13-22.

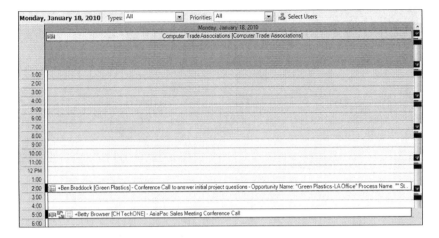

Figure 13-22 Daily calendar view

Notice that all of the activities in the **RECAP LIST** (which is under the calendar on the right) are for one day, as shown in Figure 13-23.

The items in this section are from the Task List. This list is helpful when there are activities that you can't see without scrolling.

When you click on a different day on the Recap calendar, the activities in the Recap list will change.

When you need to view a different date in the daily calendar, click on the date in the Recap calendar.

Figure 13-23 Recap list

Banner Option

The banner option will display a single line entry at the top of the daily calendar. This lets you see more information about the activity. The banner option can be disabled on the Schedule Activity dialog box. Double-clicking on a banner, like the one shown earlier at the top of Figure 13-22, will open the Schedule Activity dialog box for the activity.

Calendar Pop-Ups

If you hold the mouse pointer over an activity on a calendar you will see a pop-up like the one shown in Figure 13-24. This allows you to see some of the information about the activity.

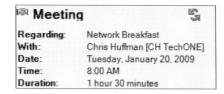

Figure 13-24 Calendar pop-up illustrated

Today (Calendar) Button

When clicked, this button will display today's date in the calendar view that you are in, except for the daily calendar view. For example, if today is September 19, 2009 and you are viewing the monthly calendar for June 2010, if you click the **TODAY** button, the calendar will go back to the September 2009 monthly calendar and highlight September 19th.

Work Week Calendar

The work week calendar view shown in Figure 13-25 displays all activities and tasks that have a start time between Monday and Friday or the work days that are selected in the calendar preferences. If you double-click on the day of the week at the top of the calendar, that day will open in the Daily calendar. Double-clicking on an activity will open the Schedule Activity dialog box.

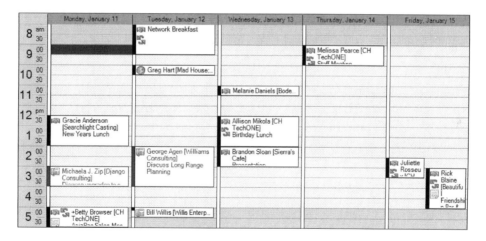

Figure 13-25 Work Week calendar view

Weekly Calendar

The weekly calendar view shown in Figure 13-26 displays all activities for the week.
The activities under the Recap calendar on the right are for the day that is selected in the calendar.

Figure 13-26 Weekly calendar view

 If you double-click on a date header on the weekly calendar you will open the daily calendar for the day that you double-click on.

Monthly Calendar

The monthly calendar displays all activities and tasks that have a start time in the month selected, as shown in Figure 13-27. If you click on the button illustrated in the figure, the daily calendar will be displayed.

Figure 13-27 Monthly calendar view

Cool Calendar Tip

I stumbled across this by accident, with the slip of the mouse. By default, the Recap calendar on the right side of the calendar view only displays one month. The border to the left of this calendar moves. Who knew? Place the mouse pointer in the position illustrated in Figure 13-28, then drag the mouse to the left until you see as many months as you need, as shown in Figure 13-29. You can also display more calendars below, by dragging the bottom of the calendar down.

Figure 13-28 Mouse pointer in position to display more calendars

Figure 13-29 Multiple calendars displayed

 The numbers to the left of the calendar, references the week of the year.

Status Bar

At the bottom of each calendar view is a status bar, as shown in Figure 13-30.

70 Activities - 7 Calls, 37 Meetings, 8 To-do's, 18 Custom Activities

Figure 13-30 Status bar for the weekly calendar

The status bar displays a count of the activities that are scheduled, based on the view that is displayed.

Filtering Activities In A Calendar View

Some calendar views are better able to handle a lot of activities then others. You may only want to view a certain type of activity on a calendar. If either of these options is what you want to do, you can filter the activities that appear on calendars. You can filter activities in a calendar the same way that you filter activities on the Activities tab. The filter that you select will be applied to each calendar view until you remove or change the filter. You can select which activity types and priorities to display.

Calendar Filter Options

Figure 13-31 shows the calendar filter options. They are explained below. They are similar to the Task List view filters that you learned about earlier in this lesson.

Figure 13-31 Calendar filter options

① **TYPES** The options in this drop-down list are used to select the activity type(s) that you want to display. The default is to display all activity types. Clear the check box of the activities that you do not want to display.

② **PRIORITIES** This option is used to select the priority of the activity types that you want to display, as shown earlier in Figure 13-6.

③ **SELECT USERS** This button opens the Select Users dialog box.

④ The **OPTIONS** drop-down list options are used to display private and cleared activities.

How To Filter Activities On The Calendar

1. Select a month that has a lot of activities, like January 2010.

2. Only display the scheduled meetings that do not have a low priority. You will see fewer activities.

Using The Calendar To Schedule Activities

In addition to being able to schedule activities from a contact view, activities can also be scheduled from any calendar view. A benefit of scheduling activities from a calendar view is that you are able to see if the start date and time are already booked. I find the daily calendar the easiest to use to schedule activities because you can select the start and end times before opening the Schedule Activity dialog box.

1. Display the start date of the activity that you want to create on a calendar.

2. If you are using the daily or work week calendar, double-click on the time that you want the activity to start. If you are using the weekly or monthly calendar, right-click on the day that you want to schedule the activity on, then select the schedule option and the type of activity that you want to create.

 If you highlight the start and end time for the activity that you want to create in the daily calendar, as illustrated in Figure 13-32, before you double-click on a time, you will not have to type this information in on the Schedule Activity dialog box.

Figure 13-32 Activity time range selected

3. Enter the remaining information for the activity, then click OK.

Exercise 13.4: Granting Calendar Access

This tool is used to give another user access to your calendar. Granting access is helpful when you need to allow someone to schedule or manage your appointments or activities.

 All users of the database can view everyone's calendar. By default, only administrators and managers have the security level to schedule activities for other users.

1. Schedule ⇒ Grant Calendar Access.

   The names that you see in Figure 13-33 are the people that currently have rights to use the database.

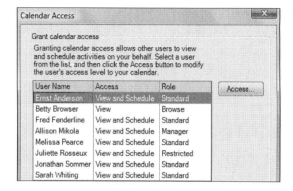

Figure 13-33 Calendar Access dialog box

2. Select the people that you want to have access to your calendar. For this exercise select the five Standard users.

3. Click the **ACCESS** button, then click OK to grant access to **VIEW AND SCHEDULE** activities for other users, as shown in Figure 13-34.

Figure 13-34 Edit Access dialog box

4. Click OK again to close the Calendar Access dialog box.

Viewing Other Users Calendars

When you have the access to view other users calendars, one day in the weekly calendar will look similar to the one shown in Figure 13-35.

Activities for other users will have their name in brackets after the time.

Figure 13-35 Calendar with multiple users

If you look under the calendar on the right side of the window you will see a button for each users activities that you have access to, as shown in Figure 13-36. If you click on one of these buttons, you will see the activities for the user below the button.

Figure 13-36 Buttons to select a user

Exercise 13.5: Printing Calendars

ACT! provides several options to print calendars. If you already use Day Runner or Day-Timer products, you can print calendars in these formats in addition to printing calendars on plain paper. ACT! has three types of calendars that you can print: Daily, Weekly and Monthly.

1. Open the daily calendar.

2. File ⇒ Print. The Day Calendar option should be selected in the **PRINTOUT TYPE** section of the Print dialog box.

3. Select the **PLAIN LETTER FULL PAGE (P) (2 COL)** option in the Paper Type section, as shown at the bottom of Figure 13-37.

Figure 13-37 Calendar print options

4. Click the Options button. The options shown in Figure 13-38 are used to customize how the calendar will print.

If you want to print the Activity Details or Column for Priorities for each calendar entry, check the option.

The **START HOUR** field is the hour of the day that you want the calendar to start printing from.

The **FILTER** button opens the Filter Calendar Printout dialog box shown below in Figure 13-39. These options are used to filter the activities that will print on the calendar. You can select which users activities, the date range and activity options, including the type and priority that you want to print on the calendar.

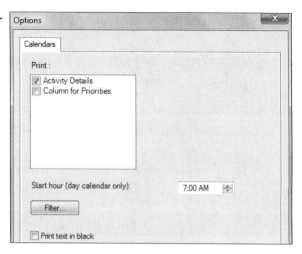

Figure 13-38 Calendar options

By default, the users calendars that you have access to are selected when this dialog box is opened.

 PRINT TEXT IN BLACK I did not get an answer for what this options does. My guess is that this option is for color text items on the calendar that you want to print in black.

5. Check the Activity Details **PRINT** option, then clear the Column for Priorities option, if it is checked.

6. Select 7 AM in the **START HOUR** field. You should have the options selected that are shown above in Figure 13-38.

7. Click the **FILTER** button and change the Date Range to 1/18/2010 to 1/22/2010.

8. Clear the **SHOW CLEARED** option.

    You should have the options selected that are shown in Figure 13-39.

    Click OK.

Figure 13-39 Filter Calendar Printout dialog box

9. Click OK to close the Options dialog box.

    If you want to print the calendar, click the Print button on the Print dialog box.

    The calendar will look like the one shown in Figure 13-40.

Figure 13-40 ACT! daily calendar

NEW Calendar View Related Tasks

PRINT CALENDAR VIEW [See Lesson 9, Exercise 9.10]

GRANT CALENDAR ACCESS [See Exercise 13.4, earlier in this lesson]

SCHEDULE SERIES OF ACTIVITIES [See Lesson 7, Activity Series]

MODIFY TYPES OF ACTIVITIES [See Lesson 16, Exercise 16.11]

FILTER VIEW [See Calendar Tips - Filter Calendar, earlier in this lesson]

PRINT CALENDAR USING TEMPLATE [See Exercise 13.5 earlier in this lesson]

MODIFY PREFERENCES AND SETTINGS Opens the Calendar & Scheduling tab on the Preferences dialog box. [See Lesson 2, Calendar & Scheduling Preferences]

USING THE ACT! WORD PROCESSOR

Overview

In this lesson you will learn the following word processing features:

- ☑ Creating, editing and formatting a document
- ☑ Creating bulleted lists
- ☑ Creating and changing tab stops
- ☑ Creating tables
- ☑ Header and Footer options
- ☑ Using Spell Check, Find and Replace
- ☑ How to add graphics to a document

If you do not plan to use the word processor that comes with ACT!, you can skip this lesson and the next one.

ACT! Word Processor Overview

There is a word processing program included with ACT!. It should handle the majority of your needs. You can create letters, use existing templates and create new templates. You can also use the word processor to perform mail merges. This lesson does not go into detail on every word processing feature. The focus of this lesson is to demonstrate some of the word processors capabilities and options that you may use to complete tasks in ACT!.

Opening The Word Processor

If you have used another Windows based word processor, you will be very comfortable using this one.

1. Write ⇒ New Document. You will see the window shown in Figure 14-1.

Figure 14-1 ACT! Word Processor window

Word Processor Toolbar

Figure 14-2 shows the word processor toolbar. Table 14-1 explains the buttons on the toolbar.

Figure 14-2 Word processor toolbar

Button	Description
1	Opens a new document or template.
2	Opens an existing document.
3	Saves the active document.
4	Deletes the selected text.
5	Copies the selected text to the clipboard.
6	Copies the selected text in the clipboard to a document.
7	Prints the active document.
8	Select a font.

Table 14-1 Word processor toolbar options explained

Button	Description
9	Select a font size.
10	Makes the selected text bold.
11	Makes the selected text italic.
12	Underlines the selected text.
13	Aligns the text on the left side of the paragraph. This is the default alignment.
14	Aligns the text on the right side of the paragraph.
15	Centers the text between the margins.
16	Stretches the text between the left and right margins.
17	Creates a bulleted list.
18	Creates a numbered list.

Table 14-1 Word processor toolbar options explained (Continued)

Word Processor Status Bar

The Status Bar provides the information shown in Figure 14-3. Table 14-2 explains the options.

Figure 14-3 Word processor status bar

Button	Description
1	Shows which page in the document the insertion point is on.
2	Shows which line on the page the insertion point is on.
3	Shows how many spaces from the first character in the line, the insertion point is.
4	Shows the current zoom percent. View ⇒ Zoom, as shown in Figure 14-4, displays the zoom percent options that you can select. The larger the percent, the larger the document text is displayed in the word processing window.
5	Informs you that the Num Lock key on your keyboard is on if you see the letters **NUM**, as shown above in Figure 14-3.

Table 14-2 Word processor status bar options explained

Figure 14-4 Zoom options

The Ruler

The ruler can be used to change the paragraph margins. You can also modify the Tab stops on the ruler. Figure 14-5 shows the left margin, ruler and tab stops.

Figure 14-5 Ruler with margin marker and tab stops illustrated

Using The Ruler To Change Paragraph Margins

If you need to change the margins of a paragraph you can change them on the ruler. To change a margin, click in the paragraph that you want to change the margin of, then drag the left or right margin marker on the ruler to where you want the new margin.

Using The Ruler To Change Tab Stops

If you need to change the Tab Stops you can change them on the ruler.

To change a tab stop, click on the tab stop that you want to change, then drag the tab stop on the ruler to the new location.

Figure 14-6 First tab stop moved to the one inch mark on the ruler

In the left corner of the ruler you will see the actual number in inches of where the tab stop is. If you want to delete a tab stop, drag it off of the ruler. Figure 14-6 above shows that the first tab stop has been moved to the one inch mark.

Exercise 14.1: Document Editing Techniques

In this exercise you will learn several techniques that are commonly used to edit documents. You may have the need to edit a document to enhance it or to use it for a different task, then it was originally created for.

1. Click the Open an existing document button. Navigate to your folder.

2. Open the Files of type drop-down list and select the **RICH TEXT FORMAT (*.RTF)** option, highlighted in Figure 14-7.

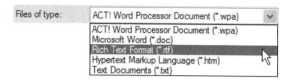

Figure 14-7 Files of type drop-down list options

3. Double-click on the New Classes Letter file. Save the document as Word Processing Practice.

4. Click on the line above the word Dear. Insert ⇒ Date. You should see the dialog box shown in Figure 14-8.

   If you want the date to change every time that you open the document, select the **ALWAYS UPDATE IN DOCUMENT** option.

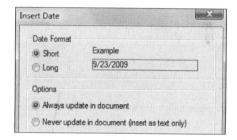

Figure 14-8 Insert Date dialog box

   If you do not want the date to change every time that you open the document, select the **NEVER UPDATE IN DOCUMENT** option.

5. Select the Never update in document option and click OK, then press Enter.

Copying Text

If you need the same text in more than one place in the document, you can copy it, by following the steps below.

1. Select the first sentence in the third paragraph, as shown in Figure 14-9.

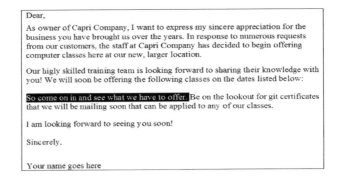

Dear,

As owner of Capri Company, I want to express my sincere appreciation for the business you have brought us over the years. In response to numerous requests from our customers, the staff at Capri Company has decided to begin offering computer classes here at our new, larger location.

Our higly skilled training team is looking forward to sharing their knowledge with you! We will soon be offering the following classes on the dates listed below:

So come on in and see what we have to offer. Be on the lookout for git certificates that we will be mailing soon that can be applied to any of our classes.

I am looking forward to seeing you soon!

Sincerely,

Your name goes here

Figure 14-9 Text highlighted to be copied

2. Click the Copy button on the toolbar or press the **CTRL + C** keys.

3. Place the cursor on a blank line after the word **SINCERELY**, then click the Paste button or press the **CTRL + V** keys. You should see a copy of the text.

Moving Text

If you need to move text from one part of the document to another, follow the steps below.

1. Select the second paragraph, then right-click on the highlighted text. You should see the shortcut menu shown in Figure 14-10.

   Select Cut.

   The options on the shortcut menu work the same way as the corresponding buttons on the toolbar.

	Cut	Ctrl+X
	Copy	Ctrl+C
	Paste	Ctrl+V
Ab	Font	
	Paragraph...	
	Tab...	

Figure 14-10 Shortcut menu

2. Right-click on the line below the words "Your name goes here", in the letter shown earlier in Figure 14-9, then select Paste.

Using The Replace Command

This command is used to search for text in a document and replace it with different text. You should place the insertion point at the beginning of the document before you use this command so that the entire document will be searched. The default search process is to start the search where the insertion point is in the document.

1. Click in front of the date at the top of the letter. Edit ⇒ Replace. You should see the Replace dialog box.

2. Type Capri Company in the **FIND WHAT** field, then press the Tab key and type Capri Book Company in the **REPLACE WITH** field, as shown in Figure 14-11.

Figure 14-11 Replace dialog box

3. Click the Replace All button, then click OK.

4. Click the Cancel button to close the Replace dialog box. Every place that the phrase "Capri Company" is in the document, it will now have "Capri Book Company".

5. Save the changes.

Exercise 14.2: Formatting A Document

There are three types of formatting that you can apply to a document as discussed below. Character and paragraph formatting work in a similar way.

① **Character** formats the selected text.
② **Paragraph** formats the entire paragraph.
③ **Page** formats the entire document.

 You can right-click in a paragraph to add font, paragraph and tab formatting as shown earlier in Figure 14-10.

Character Formatting

You can change the default font and font size options, as well as, add color to the text.

1. Select the first line in the first paragraph.

2. Open the **FONT LIST** drop-down list and select Arial.

3. Change the font size to 16, then click the Italic button.

Paragraph Formatting

1. Select the second paragraph. Format ⇒ Font.

2. Open the Text drop-down list at the bottom of the dialog box and select the color Red, then click OK. Click the Bold button.

3. Select the first paragraph. Click the Align Center button on the toolbar. Each line in the paragraph should now be centered.

4. With the text still selected, right-click and select Paragraph.

Paragraph Dialog Box

In addition to the paragraph formatting options that you just learned about, paragraph formatting also includes alignment, indenting and line spacing. Figure 14-12 shows these paragraph formatting options. Figure 14-13 shows the Frame and Page Break paragraph formatting options.

Figure 14-12 Paragraph dialog box

Figure 14-13 Frame and Page Breaks options

5. On the Formatting and Indents tab, open the **LINE SPACING** drop-down list and select Double, then click OK. The first paragraph should be double spaced.

Indenting Text

This option is used to change the left and right margins of a paragraph. The options in the **INDENTS** section of the Paragraph dialog box are used to change the indentation. To change the margins for a paragraph, click in the paragraph that you want to change, then select the left and right options.

1. Click in the second paragraph, then open the Paragraph dialog box.

2. Change the Left indent option to 4.000, then click OK.

   The second paragraph should look like the one shown near the bottom of Figure 14-14.

   Notice that no other paragraph has changed.

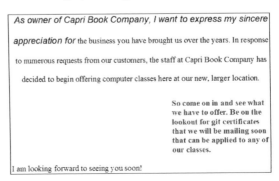

Figure 14-14 Text indented

Using Bullets

Bullets are often used to make lines of text stand out in a document. They are also used to create lists.

Two Ways To Create A Bulleted List

① Position the cursor in the document at the place where you want the first bullet. Click the **BULLETED LIST** button on the toolbar. Start typing the items for the list. Press the Enter key after typing each item. When you type the next item a bullet will appear. After you type the last item in the list do not press the Enter key, press the down arrow key instead.

② Type the list of items first, then select all of the items and click the Bulleted List button.

 To remove the bullets, select the bulleted list in the document, then click the Bulleted List button on the toolbar.

Exercise 14.3: How To Create A Bulleted List

1. Move the cursor to the line above **I AM LOOKING FORWARD TO SEEING YOU SOON**, then press Enter. Type Introduction To Multimedia, then press Enter.

2. Type Introduction To Web Page Creation, then press Enter. Type Introduction To Networking, then press Enter.

3. Select the three lines that you just typed, then click the Bulleted List button.

Your bulleted list should look like the one shown in Figure 14-15.

> - Introduction To Multimedia
> - Introduction To Web Page Creation
> - Introduction To Networking
>
> I am looking forward to seeing you soon!

Figure 14-15 Bulleted list in the document

Exercise 14.4: Changing Tab Stops With The Tabs Dialog Box

Earlier in this lesson you learned how to change tab stops on the ruler. If you need more tab stop functionality, you can use the Tabs dialog box. By default, the tab stops are at every half an inch. In this exercise you will learn how to use the Tabs dialog box to modify the tab stops so that they are only at every inch. You will also learn how to create a new tab stop.

1. Format ⇒ Tab.

2. The 0.50 tab stop should be selected, as shown in Figure 14-16.

   Click the Clear button.

Figure 14-16 Tabs dialog box

3. Click on the 1.50 tab stop and clear it. Leave the dialog box open.

How To Create A Tab Stop

1. Type the location of the tab stop that you want to create in the **TAB STOP POSITION** field. In this exercise type 1.25 in the field.

2. Select the **RIGHT** alignment option.

3. Click the **SET** button.

   You should have the tab stops shown in Figure 14-17.

Figure 14-17 Modified tab stops

4. Click OK. If you press the Tab key you will see that the cursor only stops at the places shown above in Figure 14-17.

5. Save the changes and close the document.

Exercise 14.5: Creating Tables

Tables are used to add rows and columns like a spreadsheet to a word processing document. In this exercise you will create a table that contains data for upcoming classes.

1. Open the New Classes Letter and save it as New Classes Letter (with table).

2. Place the cursor on the blank line after the second paragraph, then press Enter.

3. Table ⇒ Insert ⇒ Table.

4. Change the **NUMBER OF COLUMNS** field to 3,
   by clicking on the up arrow at the end of the field.

   Change the **NUMBER OF ROWS** field to 4.

   You should have the options shown in Figure 14-18.

   Click OK.

Figure 14-18 Table options

5. Add all of the data in Table 14-3 to
   the table in your document.

Class	Price	Next Class Starts
Works	$295	February 10
Word	$495	February 12
Access	$1,295	February 10

Table 14-3 Data to add to the table

 To move from one column to the next, press the Tab key or press the arrow key that points in the direction that you want to move.

Modify The Table Properties

1. Select all of the text in the table. Table ⇒ Table Properties.

2. Click on the **GRID** option illustrated
   in Figure 14-19, then click OK.

Figure 14-19 Frame and Color tab options

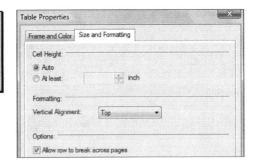

If you want to force the entire table to display and print on the same page, clear the **ALLOW ROW TO BREAK ACROSS PAGES** option shown in Figure 14-20, then click OK.

Figure 14-20 Size and formatting tab options

3. Select the first row in the table, then click the Bold button.

4. With the first row still selected, open the Table Properties dialog box and change the **BACKGROUND COLOR** to yellow, then click OK.

5. Make each column smaller so that your table looks like the one shown in Figure 14-21.

Save the changes and leave the document open.

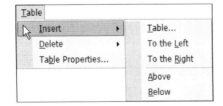

Class	Price	Next Class Starts
Works	$295	February 10
Word	$495	February 12
Access	$1,295	February 10

Figure 14-21 Modified table

 I find changing the column size some what difficult. If you start adjusting the columns from left to right, meaning change the size of the first column first, the table does not stay aligned on the left.

Adding Rows And Columns To A Table

In addition to right-clicking in a cell in the table and then selecting one of the **INSERT** options on the shortcut menu shown in Figure 14-22, the last four options shown on the submenu in Figure 14-23 are used to add rows and columns. Table ⇒ Insert, will also open the menu shown in Figure 14-23.

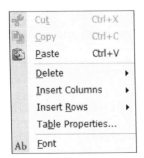

Figure 14-22 Table cell shortcut menu

Figure 14-23 Table Insert (Row & Column) menu options

Header And Footer Settings

The header and footer sections of a document have their own margins. You can select how far from the page border they will start.

Format ⇒ Header/Footer Settings.

You should see the dialog box shown in Figure 14-24.

These options are used to change the margins for the header and footer sections of a document.

Figure 14-24 Header and Footer Settings dialog box

If checked, the **FIRST PAGE DIFFERENT** option allows different information to be added to the header and footer section on the first page of the document. An example of how this option works is the first page of every lesson in this book. The first page does not have any text in the header.

Exercise 14.6: Using Headers And Footers

Headers and footers are used to print information that you want to appear on every page, or almost every page of the document. Headers print at the top of the page and footers print at the bottom of the page. Items commonly placed in headers and footers include page numbers or the document name. Anything that you can put in the main portion of a document you can put in the header or footer, including clip art.

1. Open the New Classes Letter document. View ⇒ Header/Footer. Scroll to the bottom of the first page. You should see a dotted box. That is the footer section. If you do not see the footer section, click near the bottom of the page.

2. Tab over to the three inch mark in the footer section. Type `Page`, then press the space bar.

3. Insert ⇒ Page Number. The footer should look like the one shown in Figure 14-25. Save the changes.

Figure 14-25 Page number added to the footer

Exercise 14.7: Page Formatting

You can change the page margins to fit the needs of the document. Unlike using the Indent option to set the margins for a single paragraph or a few paragraphs, the page margins that you set are for the entire document. There are two ways to set page margins, as discussed below:

① Use the ruler which you learned about earlier in this lesson.
② Use the Page Setup dialog box.

1. Open the New Classes Letter document, if it is not already open. File ⇒ Page Setup.

2. Change the left and right margins to 1.5 inches, as shown in Figure 14-26, then click OK.

Figure 14-26 Page Setup dialog box

Exercise 14.8: Using The Spell Checker

You can check the spelling for an entire document or a portion of the document. To spell check a portion of the document, highlight the portion that you want to check before starting the spell checker.

1. Place the cursor above the word Dear at the top of the letter.

2. Spelling ⇒ Check Document.

   You will see the dialog box shown in Figure 14-27.

Figure 14-27 Spell Check dialog box

3. The word **HIGHLY** in the Suggestions list is the word that you want. Click on it now, then click the Replace button.

If the word that you need to use is not in the Suggestions list, you can type the word in the **REPLACE WITH** field. If the word is spelled correctly, you may want to add it to a custom dictionary. If you do not want to change the word, click the **SKIP** button.

You should now see the message shown in Figure 14-28.

This message lets you know how many words were checked and how many questionable (misspelled) words were found.

Figure 14-28 Spell Check Status message

4. Click OK and save the changes.

Saving Documents

When you create a new document and are ready to save it, click the Save button. You will then be prompted to type in a file name. To save an existing document with the same name, click the Save button.

If you want to save an existing document with a new name, File ⇒ Save As. Type in the new name for the document. Saving an existing document with a new name will leave the original document unchanged.

Printing Documents

Once you have created, edited and spell checked a document, you may want to print it. If you only need to print a portion of a document or need to print more than one copy, select the appropriate options on the Print dialog box.

1. File ⇒ Print. You will see the Print dialog box.

2. Click the Cancel button. File ⇒ Exit. Do not save the changes.

To print more than one copy of the document, change the value in the **NUMBER OF COPIES** field shown in Figure 14-29 to the number of copies that you want to print.

If you need to print more than one copy of a document that has more than one page, check the **COLLATE** option after selecting the number of copies.

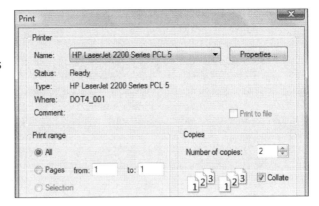

Figure 14-29 Print dialog box

Printing Specific Pages Of A Document

To print a specific page or a range of pages, select the **PAGES** option.

If you only want to print one page of a document that has more than one page, type the page number that you want to print in the **FROM** and **TO** fields.

If you want to print a range of pages, like pages 2, 3, 4 and 5, you would type 2 in the **FROM** field and 5 in the **TO** field.

Adding Graphics To Documents

If you need to add graphics to a word processing document, follow the steps below.

1. Open the document that you want to add the graphic to, then click on the location in the document where you want to add the graphic.

2. Insert ⇒ Image, as shown in Figure 14-30, then select one of the options explained below.

    The **FIXED POSITION** option causes the text to be wrapped around the image.

    The **CHARACTER POSITION** option causes the image to move when the text around it moves.

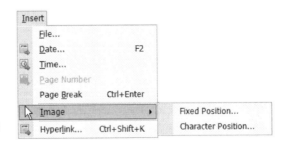

Figure 14-30 Insert image options

3. Select the image that you want to add to the document.

WORD PROCESSING TEMPLATES

In this lesson you will learn about the following word processing template features:

- ☑ Modifying existing templates
- ☑ Mail merge
- ☑ Creating a template
- ☑ Using the Setup Assistant Wizard to set up Microsoft Word

LESSON 15

Templates Overview

Templates are a special type of document that can contain text and fields that you want to merge together to create a new document. Examples of templates are a fax cover page or a form letter. More than likely you have received several of these form letters. Some refer to this type of letter as "junk mail". You can also have fields in a template that will retrieve data from an ACT! database and merge the data into a template.

The difference between a template and a document is that you can use the template over and over. Templates do not save the data in the fields. The document saves the content from the template and the data from fields.

You can customize a template as much or as little as you need. The majority of a letter template is the same for each person that it is sent to. The customizations could include the customers name, address and amount of their last order. If you know that you will have the need to create form letters, make sure that the fields that you need in the database are being filled in. You may find that you need to collect additional information. If so, you can use the fields on the User Fields tab or create your own fields.

ACT! comes with templates that you can use as they are, or you can modify them. It is best to save the templates that come with ACT! with another file name, if you need to modify them. That way, you will still have the original template should something not work as expected. You can also create your own templates. You can add a template that you create to the Write menu, just like you added a look up that you created to the Lookup menu.

Exercise 15.1: How To Modify An Existing Template

If there is an existing template that meets most of your needs, it is easier to use that one and modify it as needed. In this exercise you will modify the Fax Cover Page template to include the senders email address.

1. Write ⇒ Edit Template.

2. Double-click on the file
   FAX COVER PAGE.TPL,
   illustrated in Figure 15-1.

   You will see the Fax
   Cover Page template,
   as shown in Figure 15-2.

Figure 15-1 ACT! templates

The options on the right side of the window are used to add fields from the database to the template.

You can add fields from the Contact record and the My Record.

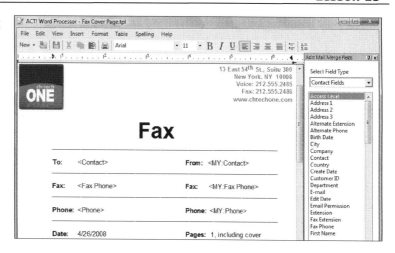

Figure 15-2 Fax cover page template

Notice that the fields in the second column of the template have the word **MY** in the field name, as shown in Figure 15-2. This lets you know that these fields are from the My Record.

Adding A Field To The Template

1. Click after the word **SUBJECT,** then press the Enter key twice.

2. Type E-mail:, then press the space bar once.

3. Click the Bold button. This will turn the bold option off for the field that you will add next.

4. Open the **SELECT FIELD TYPE** drop-down list and select the My Record Fields option.

5. Double-click on the E-mail field.

   The template should look like the one shown in Figure 15-3.

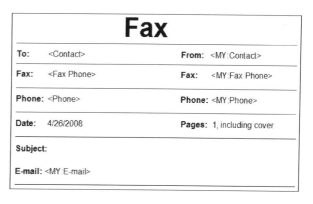

Figure 15-3 Fax Cover Page with a new field added

Saving Templates

Templates are saved the same way that you save any other word processing document. The only difference is that you have to change the Save As Type field to **ACT! WORD PROCESSOR TEMPLATE (*.TPL)**. The default location to save templates in, is the Templates folder.

1. File ⇒ Save As. Type New Fax Cover Page in the File name field.

2. Select ACT! Word Processor Template (*.tpl) as the **SAVE AS TYPE**, if it is not already selected.

If you know that you will not use the Fax Cover Page template that comes with ACT!, you can save a fax cover page template that you create or modify with the same name as the one that comes with ACT!, as illustrated earlier in Figure 15-1. The one you save will open when you select the Fax Cover Page option on the Write menu. If you want to do this, it may be a good idea to save the original one with a different file name in case you need it in the future.

3. Click Save. File ⇒ Exit.

Exercise 15.2: Mail Merge

Mail merge is used to take data from fields like names and addresses and put the data into a document to make it personalized. During the merge process, a copy of the template is created for each contact in the database that meets the criteria. This tool is often used to customize a form letter. Creating a mail merge is a two step process as discussed below.

① Look up the contacts that you want to use in the mail merge.
② Merge the contact fields with a template.

What may not be obvious is that you can use the same mail merge template for letter and email mail merge tasks.

Create The Merge

Before creating the merge you should look up the contacts that you want to use in the merge.

1. Create a lookup to find the contacts in the company CH TechONE. There should be nine contacts.

2. Write ⇒ Mail Merge. You will see the first screen of the Mail Merge Wizard. Usually, the first screen of a wizard does not provide any useful information, so it is ok to check the option to hide the first screen in the future.

3. Click Next. Select the Word processor option if it is not already selected, as shown in Figure 15-4, then click Next.

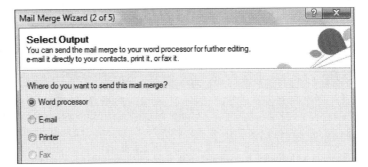

Figure 15-4 Select Output wizard screen

4. Click the Browse button and double-click on the 01 Initial Communication file in the Templates folder. The Templates folder is under your database folder. You should see the template name in the field shown in Figure 15-5.

By default, the last template used in the Mail Merge wizard will be displayed in the field the next time the Mail Merge wizard is run.

Figure 15-5 Select Template wizard screen

5. Click Next.

The options on the screen shown in Figure 15-6 are used to select the contacts that will be used in the mail merge.

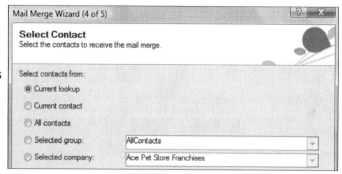

Figure 15-6 Select Contact wizard screen

The **CURRENT LOOKUP** option will use the contacts from the lookup as the data source for the mail merge.

The **CURRENT CONTACT** option will only create the mail merge for the contact that is visible or the contact that is selected (highlighted) if the current view is a list view.

The **ALL CONTACTS** option will create a mail merge letter for every contact in the database.

The **SELECTED GROUP** option is used to select a group to send the mail merge document to, as shown in Figure 15-7.

A mail merge document will be created for all of the contacts that are associated with the group.

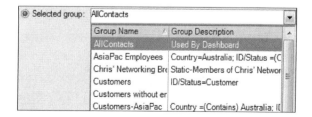

Figure 15-7 Selected group options

The **SELECTED COMPANY** option is used to select a company to send the mail merge document to. A mail merge document will be created for all of the contacts that are associated with the company.

6. Select the Current Lookup option, then click Next.

   The last screen in the wizard displays the options that you selected for the mail merge, as shown in Figure 15-8.

Figure 15-8 Last mail merge wizard screen

7. Click Finish. You will see the letter shown in Figure 15-9.

   If you count the number of letters in the document, you will see eight letters.

   You may be asking why there are only eight letters instead of nine, which is the number of contacts in the lookup.

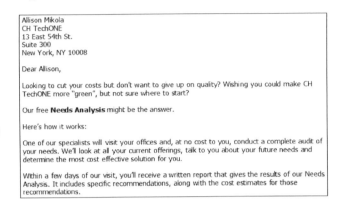

Figure 15-9 Mail merge letter

The reason is because one of the contacts in the lookup is the My Record. ACT! figures that you do not want to send a letter to yourself.

8. File ⇒ Exit. Click Yes to save the changes. Navigate to your folder, if necessary. Type Mail Merge as the file name, then press Enter.

Email Mail Merge Options

Figures 15-10 and 15-11 show the additional email mail merge options.

The email options are for external email software, like Internet email and records with missing email addresses.

Figure 15-10 E-mail mail merge options

Figure 15-11 Options for missing email addresses

Printer Mail Merge Options

Figure 15-12 shows the record history options for a printer mail merge.

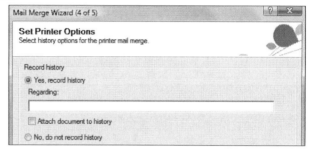

Figure 15-12 Printer mail merge options

Exercise 15.3: How To Create A New Template

When creating a mail merge the template must have all of the information, including the body of the letter, before you start the merge process. Some of the templates that come with ACT! are empty (ie. EmailBody, Letter and Memo). They are a good starting point for you to create your own template when none of the templates that come with ACT! are close to what you need. In this exercise you will learn how to create a template from scratch.

Add The Merge Fields

1. Write ⇒ New Letter/E-mail Template.

2. Click in the body of the document, then Insert ⇒ Date.

    Select the options shown in Figure 15-13, then click OK.

Figure 15-13 Insert Date dialog box

3. Press the Enter key five times. Make sure that the Field type **CONTACT FIELDS** is selected, then double-click on the Contact field in the list box.

4. Press Enter, then add the fields shown in Figure 15-14.

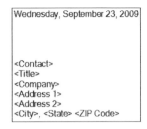

Wednesday, September 23, 2009

\<Contact\>
\<Title\>
\<Company\>
\<Address 1\>
\<Address 2\>
\<City\>, \<State\> \<ZIP Code\>

Figure 15-14 Fields for the template

5. Place the cursor between the City and State fields (between the > < brackets). The easiest way to do this is to use the arrow keys to move the cursor. Type a comma, then press the space bar.

6. Add a space between the State and Zip Code fields. Put the cursor after the Zip Code field, then press the Enter key three times.

7. Type Dear, then press the space bar.

8. Insert the Salutation field, then type a comma.

Add The Body Of The Letter

1. Press the Enter key three times, then type You were referred to us by.

2. Press the space bar, then add the Referred By field.

3. Type a comma, then press the space bar.

 Before you would run this merge, you should create a lookup for the contacts that you want to use in the merge to make sure that the Referred By field is not empty. If the field is empty in some records, you need to fill it in, otherwise there will be a blank space in the letter where the field is. The other option is to remove the record from the merge.

4. Type as the person that is in charge of buying computer equipment.

5. Press the Enter key twice, then type Enclosed please find our latest catalog.

6. Press the Enter key four times, then type Sincerely,. Press the Enter key four times.

7. Open the Select Field Type drop-down list and select the My Record Fields option.

8. Add the Contact field.

. . . .

9. Highlight the entire letter and change the font to Arial and the font size to 10.

The letter should look like the one shown in Figure 15-15.

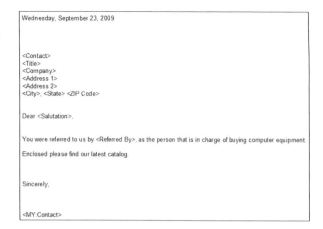

Figure 15-15 Mail merge template

10. Save the template in your folder. Type `My Sales Letter Template` as the file name.

11. File ⇒ Exit. The nine contacts should still be on the screen.

Run The Mail Merge

Now that the mail merge template has been created, you can run the merge.

1. Write ⇒ Mail Merge.

2. Select the My Sales Letter Template file on the second wizard screen (Select Template), then click Next.

3. Select the Current Lookup option. Click Next, then click Finish.

You will see the letter shown in Figure 15-16 for each of the contacts except the My Record.

Notice that there is no name after the word "By" on the first line of the letter. This is because the Referred By field on the contact record is empty.

```
Wednesday, September 23, 2009




Allison Mikola
Sales Representative
CH TechONE
13 East 54th St.
Suite 300
New York, NY 10008


Dear Allison,


You were referred to us by , as the person that is in charge of buying computer equipment.

Enclosed please find our latest catalog.



Sincerely,


Chris Huffman
```

Figure 15-16 Mail merge letter

4. Save the mail merge document in your folder. Type `Sales Letter Mail Merge` as the file name.

5. Close the word processor. Lookup ⇒ All Contacts.

Create History Dialog Box

After you print the letters you will see the dialog box shown in Figure 15-17.

The **REGARDING** field will be filled in automatically for some tasks. If not, you can type something descriptive in the field.

If checked, the **ATTACH DOCUMENT TO HISTORY** option will save a copy of the document with the history record.

A history record like the one shown in Figure 15-18 will be created for each contact that a mail merge letter was printed for.

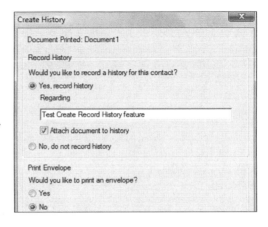

Figure 15-17 Create History dialog box

Figure 15-18 History record

Using The Setup Assistant Wizard To Set Up Microsoft Word

In the previous exercise you created a mail merge using the word processor that comes with ACT!. If you normally use Microsoft Word or want to start using it with ACT!, for mail merges and other types of word processing documents, you can. One of the options on the Setup Assistant wizard is to set up Microsoft Word to work with ACT!. You do not have to complete these steps now.

1. Help ⇒ Setup Assistant. Click Next on the first screen.

2. Click Next until you get to screen 10.

3. Select Microsoft Word, as illustrated in Figure 15-19.

   Click Next, then click Finish.

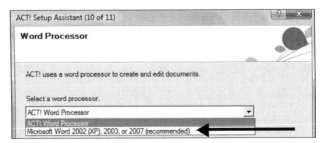

Figure 15-19 Word processor options

ACT! Menu In Word And Excel

A menu for ACT! is installed in Word and Excel even if you will not use these software packages with ACT!.

Figure 15-20 shows the ACT! menu in Word. Table 15-1 explains the menu options.
Figure 15-21 shows the ACT! menu in Excel. Table 15-2 explains the menu options.

Figure 15-20 ACT! menu in Word

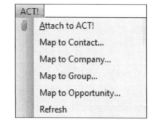

Figure 15-21 ACT! menu in Excel

ACT! Menu Options In Word

Option	Description
Attach to ACT!	Saves a copy of the document in the Attachments folder. If the document has already been saved in a folder other then the Attachments folder before selecting this option, you will see a message asking if you want to use the copy of the document that is in the Supplemental Attachments folder. (1)
Send Email	Places the current document in the body of the email message or as an attachment, so that it will be included in the email.
Send Fax	Faxes the current document to the contact(s) that you select. You have to have the fax software installed to use this option.
Show Field List	Displays the **SHOW MAIL MERGE FIELDS** dialog box so that you can select fields from the ACT! database to use in your mail merge document.

Table 15-1 ACT! menu options in Word explained

ACT! Menu Options In Excel

Option	Description
Attach to ACT!	Saves a copy of the document in the Attachments folder. If the document has already been saved in a folder other then the Attachments folder before selecting this option, you will see a message asking if you want to use the copy of the document that is in the Supplemental Attachments folder. (1)
Map to Contact	Opens the Map Contact Fields dialog box shown in Figure 15-22, which is used to select the contact field(s) that you want to map to.

Table 15-2 ACT! menu options in Excel explained

Option	Description
Map to Company	Opens the Map Company Fields dialog box, which is used to select the company field(s) that you want to map to.
Map to Group	Opens the Map Group Fields dialog box, which is used to select the group field(s) that you want to map to.
Map to Opportunity	Opens the Map Opportunities Fields dialog box shown in Figure 15-23, which is used to select the opportunity field(s) that you want to map to.
Refresh	I posted a question in the forum to find out the purpose of this option, but did not get a response.

Table 15-2 ACT! menu options in Excel explained (Continued)

(1) This menu option opens the Select Contacts dialog box in ACT!, which is used to select the contact(s) for the task that you are working on.

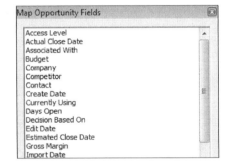

Figure 15-22 Map Contact Fields dialog Box

Figure 15-23 Map Opportunity Fields dialog box

Normal.dot Potential Problem In Microsoft Word 2003

If you see a message when you close Word that says "Changes have been made that effect the global template, Normal.dot. Do you want to save these changes?", there are three options in Microsoft Word that you can use to try and fix the problem, if you are sure that the hard drive does not have a virus.

① Turn off the option in Word that prompts to save changes to Normal.dot.
Tools ⇒ Options ⇒ Save tab.
② Remove the ACT! menu from the menu bar in Word.
③ Run the **DETECT AND REPAIR** option on the Help menu in Word.

CUSTOMIZING ACT!

Overview

In this lesson you will learn several ways to customize ACT!, including how to:

- ☑ Modify preferences
- ☑ Create and edit drop-down list fields
- ☑ Modify fields
- ☑ Customize columns
- ☑ Create an annual event

Why Waiting To Customize ACT! Is A Good Idea

I suspect that this may be the lesson that many readers are very interested in. There was a time when I wanted to customize (aka tweak) software as soon as I installed it, even if I did not know how to use the software. When you think about it, how could one customize software that they really do not know? I call it "Click Fever". We really like clicking on options to see what will happen. Depending on how well you already know the software, that may not be a problem.

If you are not very familiar with the software, waiting until you have used it for a while before customizing it is probably a good idea. If you have a question or something does not work as expected, you will not know if it is a problem with the software or if the cause is from a change that you made and were not aware of all of the ways that a certain customization effects the software.

Modifying Preferences

There are several options in ACT! that you can modify. In Lesson 2 you learned how to modify the General preferences. In this lesson you will learn how to modify other options on the Preferences dialog box.

Name And Salutation Preferences

In Lesson 3 you learned how ACT! displays the contact names that you enter. [See Lesson 3, Exercise 3.1] If the default prefix and suffix options do not meet your needs, the options shown in Figures 16-1 to 16-4 should help. The options that are selected in the figures are the defaults.

Tools ⇒ Preferences ⇒ General tab. Click the Name Preferences or Salutation Preferences button.

The options shown in the list on the right of Figure 16-2 are the prefixes that ACT! will ignore as being the contacts first name. You can add or delete items in these lists.

Figure 16-1 Salutation Preferences

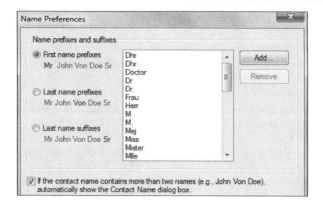

Figure 16-2 Name Preferences

The **LAST NAME PREFIX** options shown in Figure 16-3 are the first part of a two word last name. An example would be Dr. Van Ost. "Van" is the type of prefix that you would add to this list if it was not already there.

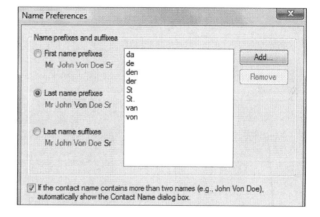

Figure 16-3 Last name prefix options

The **LAST NAME SUFFIX** options shown in Figure 16-4 are a list of abbreviations that people use after their last name. If they are the last word entered in the Contact field, they are ignored with the default options that ACT! uses.

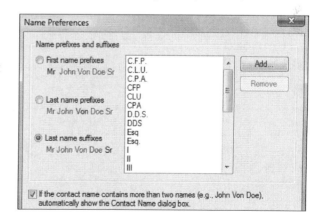

Figure 16-4 Last name suffix options

Exercise 16.1: Calendar Preferences

You can change some of the default calendar settings. The ones that you can change are the day the calendar week starts on, the time slot increments on the daily and weekly calendars and whether or not you want to only show the current month in the mini-calendar.

1. Tools ⇒ Preferences. On the Calendar & Scheduling tab, click the **CALENDAR PREFERENCES** button.

2. Change the options in Table 16-1. The Calendar Preferences dialog box should have the options shown in Figure 16-5.

Option	Change To
Start Time	9 AM
Daily Calendar	60 minutes

Table 16-1 Calendar options to change

Changing these options will cause the daily calendar to display the time slots in one hour increments.

The default starting time of the calendar will now be 9 AM.

Figure 16-5 Calendar Preferences options

Pop-Up Options

This option is on the Calendar Preferences dialog box shown above in Figure 16-5. ACT! has pop-ups that you may find useful. They will not slow down your computer like the pop-ups that you may see when surfing the Internet. Figure 16-6 shows the parts of ACT! that you can enable pop-ups for. By default, the calendar pop-ups are enabled. Check the options that you want and clear the check mark for the option(s) that you do not want pop-ups for.

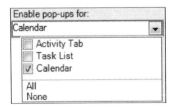

Figure 16-6 Pop-up options

3. Click OK to close the Calendar Preferences dialog box.

Exercise 16.2: Scheduling Preferences

You can modify the following scheduling preferences:

① Activity type (Call, Meeting, To-Do).
② Priority levels.

③ Alarm options.

④ Have certain types of activities automatically roll over to the next day if they are not completed.

⑤ Designate how cleared activities should appear.

1. Click the Scheduling Preferences button on the Calendar & Scheduling tab.

To change the settings, click on the activity type that you want to change (call, meeting etc.), then select the options that you want to change. If modified, the options in the **DEFAULT ACTIVITY SETTINGS TO** section will change the default values that you see when you create an activity.

2. Change the options in Table 16-2 for the To-Do activity type. Your dialog box should have the options selected that are shown in Figure 16-7.

Option	Change To
Ring alarm	15 minutes
Duration	1 Hour

Table 16-2 To-do activity options to change

If set, the alarm will start warning you 15 minutes prior to the start time of the activity.

If checked, the **AUTOMATICALLY ROLL OVER TO TODAY** option will cause all uncompleted activities of the activity type selected to be moved to the next day.

Figure 16-7 To-Do activity preference options

Depending on how many activities you schedule, you may want to check this option. I find this option most useful for phone calls that I did not complete. Take caution when using the roll over option because it is cumulative, meaning that all past activities that were not completed will be rolled over.

If there were 500 activities that were not completed, all of them will be rolled over. The roll over is not automatic though.

When you open the database, you will be asked if you want to roll over the activities. You will see how many activities would be rolled over, as shown in Figure 16-8.

Figure 16-8 Roll Over Activities dialog box

3. Click OK twice to close both dialog boxes.

Exercise 16.3: How To Customize The Contact List View

The Contact List view, as well as the Task List view, which you will learn about later, can be customized to sort records according to your needs. You can rearrange the order of the columns. You can make a column smaller or wider. You can also add or remove columns.

Rearrange The Order Of Columns

1. In the Contact List view, click on the Title column heading and drag it to the left, so that it is before the Contact column. The Contact List view should look like the one shown in Figure 16-9.

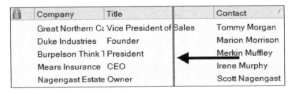

Figure 16-9 Title column moved

Resize A Column

1. Place the mouse pointer on the line between the Company and Title column headings. The mouse pointer is in the right place when you see a double-headed arrow, as shown in Figure 16-10.

Figure 16-10 Mouse pointer in position to resize a column

2. Hold down the left mouse button and drag the line to the right, as shown in Figure 16-11.

   Release the mouse button. The Company column should be wider.

Figure 16-11 Company column made wider

Add A Column

1. Right-click in the list and select **CUSTOMIZE COLUMNS**.

   You should see the dialog box shown in Figure 16-12.

   The **AVAILABLE FIELDS** list contains all of the fields that have not already been added to the view.

Figure 16-12 Customize Columns dialog box

The fields in the **SHOW AS COLUMNS IN THIS ORDER** list are the order that the columns will be displayed in, on the tab, from left to right.

The **MOVE UP** and **MOVE DOWN** buttons are used to rearrange the order of the columns in the view. Click on the field that you want to move, then click on the appropriate button.

The **RESET** button will restore the columns back to the order they were when ACT! was first installed.

 Tools ⇒ Customize ⇒ Columns, will also open the Customize Columns dialog box.

2. Click on the Department field in the **AVAILABLE FIELDS** list. Press and hold down the CTRL key. Scroll down the list and select the Last Meeting and Last Results fields.

3. Click the Add button (the top arrow button), then click OK.

4. Scroll to the right in the list view so that you can see the three fields that you just added to the view.

 Another Way To Add Or Remove Columns

If you double-click on a field in the Available Fields section on the Customize Columns dialog box you will add the field to the view. If you double-click on a field in the Show as columns in this order section, you will remove the field from the view. When you remove a column from a view, the data is still in the database. If you need to view the data from a field that you removed, you can add it back.

Delete A Column

1. Open the Customize Columns dialog box.

2. Click on the Last Meeting field in the list on the right, then click the Remove button (the second arrow button from the top) and click OK. The column will be removed from the Contact List view. Click OK.

Customizing The Columns On The Notes Tab

There are two ways to customize the columns on the Notes tab, as discussed below.

① **Resize the columns** by placing the mouse pointer on the line to the right of the column as shown earlier in Figure 16-11 that you want to resize. Drag the mouse pointer to the right to make the column wider or to the left to make the column smaller.

② **Add or remove columns** You can change which columns are displayed on the tab by using the Customize Columns dialog box shown above in Figure 16-12.

Exercise 16.4: How To Customize Columns On A Tab

Customizing columns on a tab is very similar to adding a column to a view.

1. Click the arrow on the Options button and select **CUSTOMIZE COLUMNS**, as shown in Figure 16-13.

   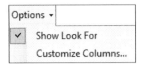

   You will see the Customize Columns dialog box that you saw earlier in Figure 16-12.

   Figure 16-13 Options drop-down list

 All tabs do not have the Options button. Some tabs only have the Customize Columns option on the drop-down list and other tabs have additional options.

2. Add the fields that you want to see on the tab, then remove the fields from the list on the right that you do not want to see on the tab.

3. Rearrange the order of the fields if necessary, then click OK.

Creating New Fields

If you have the need to customize a layout, fields are probably the item that you will customize the most. Depending on your needs, the fields that come with ACT! may not be sufficient. You may have to create additional fields to store data. You have to have administrator or manager rights to create fields. Users cannot be logged into the database while you are creating new fields or editing existing fields. If anyone else is logged in, you will see a message that contains a list of who is logged in.

While the process of creating fields is easy, you should have a plan for the fields that you need to create. If the database has been in use for a while or has a lot of contacts, you can still add fields. You may have to go through all of the records that were in the database before the field was added and fill in the data for the new field. This could be very time consuming. At a minimum, you should have the following items in your plan for each field that you want to add:

① What type of field (drop-down, date, free form, etc.) is best suited for the data that the field needs to store.
② Which view(s) should the field be placed on.
③ Will the field be used as a lookup field or in a report? If so, determine if the field would be more useful if it was a drop-down list.

Field Data Type Options

If you are creating a new field you can use the data types that are explained in Table 16-3. When editing a field, not all of the data types in the table are available. Each field that is created can only have one data type.

Data Type	Description
Address	When you select this field type, seven fields are automatically created: Address 1, 2 and 3, City, State, Zip Code and Country. (1)
Annual Event	Creates a date field for events that only happen once a year. (2) (3)
Character	Creates a free form data type, which means that any combination of data (text and numbers) can be entered in the field. While it is tempting to use this data type for all fields, it should really only be used when none of the other data types discussed in this table are a better option.
Currency	Only accepts monetary values. By default, a dollar sign, commas and decimal point (for cents) are automatically filled in. If the user entered 123456 in a currency field, the number would be displayed as $1,234.56. (2)
Date	Allows a date to be entered in the field. (2) (3)
Date/Time	Allows a date and time to be entered in the same field. (2) (3)
Decimal	Only allows numbers and decimal points to be entered. (2)
Email	Used to enter an email address. (1)
Initial-Caps	This data type forces the first character of each word entered in the field to be a capital letter and the remaining letters in each word to be lower case.
Lower Case	Converts all upper case characters to lower case.
Memo	Similar to the Character data type because it is free form. The difference is that a memo field allows a lot more data to be entered in the field.
Number	Only accepts numeric values.
Phone	Used to enter telephone numbers. By default, a dash is automatically filled in after the area code and after the first three digits of the phone number. (1)
Picture	Used to store graphic files, images or photos. (1)
Time	Allows a time to be entered in the field. The drop-down list shown in Figure 16-15 is added to this field type. A time can be selected from the drop-down list or the time can be typed in. (2)
Upper Case	Converts all lower case characters to capital letters.
URL Address	Enter a web site address.
Yes/No	Creates a check box field. ACT! queries do not use Yes and No values, instead they use True and False. If this field is used in a query, keep in mind that Yes equals True and No equals False. (1)

Table 16-3 Field data types explained

(1) This field type is only available if you are creating a new field.
(2) The format for this field comes from the Regional and Language Options dialog box shown in Figure 16-14. The currency field formats on the Opportunities view also come from this dialog box, which is part of the Windows operating system.
(3) A calendar object is automatically added to this field type so that all dates will be entered in the same format.

 To view the dialog box shown in Figure 16-14, open the Control Panel in Windows, then double-click on the **REGIONAL AND LANGUAGE OPTIONS** icon.

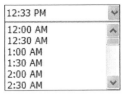

Figure 16-15 Time data type drop-down list

Figure 16-14 Regional and Language Options dialog box

Field Behavior Options

The field behavior options discussed below are used to customize the fields that you create or modify. All of the attributes are not available for each data type.

① **ALLOW BLANK** If checked, this option will not require data to be entered into in the field.

② **GENERATE HISTORY** Automatically creates a history record each time the value in the field is changed. By default, several fields have this option enabled.

③ **PRIMARY FIELD** Designates the field as a primary field. Fields that have this option checked will be duplicated. This is useful when you duplicate a contact record.

④ **USE DROP-DOWN LIST** Is used to select an existing drop-down list or create a new drop-down list.

Customize Field Behavior

The options discussed below are some of the options on the Customize Field Behavior screen.

They allow for more functionality to be added to fields.

The options on the Customize Field Behavior screen shown in Figure 16-16 change depending on the data type that is selected.

Figure 16-16 Customize field behavior options

① **DEFAULT VALUE** The value that you enter in this field will automatically be filled in the field for each new record added to the database. This is useful if the majority of records need to have the same value in the field.

② **FIELD FORMAT** Is used to enter symbols that will automatically appear in the field. This formatting is used to help the user enter the correct type of numeric data.

③ **FIELD LENGTH** The number entered in this field is the maximum number of characters that can be entered in the field. Try not to make the field length too long because that will waste space in the database and make the database larger than it needs to be. This will cause the database to run slower then it should.

④ **LINK TO COMPANY FIELD** This option is used to link a contact field to a field in the company record. When the company field is updated, the linked field in the contact record is automatically updated. [See Lesson 5, Linking and Unlinking Contact And Company Fields]

Triggers

Triggers allow an action to take place on a field in one of three ways, as shown in Figure 16-17.

Figure 16-17 Set field triggers screen

Types Of Triggers

There are three types of triggers that can be set, as discussed below.

① **NONE** This is the default trigger type. It means that the trigger will not have an event occur.

② **PROGRAMS** Is used to select a program (software package), file or web site to open.

③ **ACTIVITY SERIES** Is used to select a list of activities that you want to schedule. [See Lesson 7, Activity Series]

Trigger Options

There are three triggers that can be set for a field, as discussed below.

① **WHEN CHANGING A FIELD,** an event will happen when the value in the field changes.

② **WHEN ENTERING A FIELD,** an event will happen when the cursor first enters the field.

③ **WHEN LEAVING A FIELD,** an event will happen when the cursor leaves the field.

An example of when to use the **WHEN CHANGING A FIELD** trigger would be when the data in a field changes, you want a document to automatically open. You would select the programs option from the drop-down list and add the file name in the field to the right. You could also use this trigger to open a file that provides helpful information about what type of data should be entered in the field.

An example of when to use the **WHEN ENTERING A FIELD** trigger would be when the cursor leaves a field, a web site will open to display information about the value being entered in the field.

An example of when to use the **WHEN LEAVING A FIELD** trigger would be to set up an activity series automatically when the cursor leaves the field, like the activity series that you created in Lesson 7.

Exercise 16.5: Create A Trigger

In this exercise you will create the **WHEN LEAVING THE FIELD** trigger shown above in Figure 16-17. You will add the trigger to the User 7 field.

1. Tools ⇒ Define Fields. Scroll down and click on the User 7 field.

2. Click the **EDIT FIELD** link, then click the Next button twice. You will see the Set field triggers window.

3. Open the **WHEN LEAVING A FIELD** drop-down list and select Activity Series.

4. Click the button at the end of the section and select the Activity Series that you created, as illustrated in Figure 16-18.

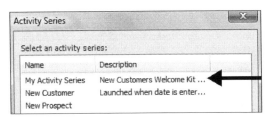

Figure 16-18 Activity Series dialog box

5. Click OK. You will see the Activity Series name shown earlier in Figure 16-17. Click Finish, then close the Define Fields dialog box.

Test The Trigger And Submit An Activity Series

1. Display the record for Tom Dynamic.

2. On the User Fields tab, type Test trigger in the User 7 field, then press the Tab key. You should see the Schedule Activity Series dialog box shown in Figure 16-19. If you need to add more contacts for the activities you can.

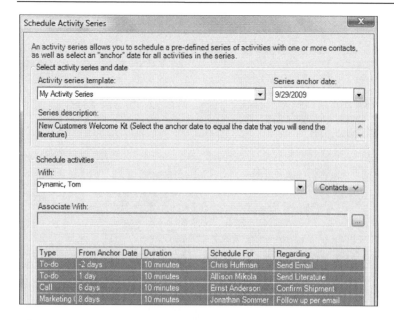

Figure 16-19 Schedule Activity Series dialog box

3. Click the Cancel button to close the Schedule Activity Series dialog box.

Creating And Editing Drop-Down List Fields

You have already seen and used many of the default drop-down lists that come with ACT!. You can create drop-down lists for a field that you need. You may have a database that has all types of doctors and may want to list their specialty. You could modify a user defined field and add a drop-down list to it that contains specialties. A list can be used by more than one field.

Exercise 16.6: How To Create A Drop-Down List Field

In this exercise you will create a drop-down list field for doctor specialties.

1. Tools ⇒ Define Fields. If the **DEFINE FIELD** option is not enabled, you are not logged in as an administrator or manager and cannot complete this exercise until you are.

2. Click the **MANAGE DROP-DOWN LISTS** option, then click the **CREATE DROP-DOWN LIST** option.

3. Type Specializes In in the **DROP-DOWN LIST NAME** field.
   Type What the doctor specializes in in the Description field.
   The options in the **TYPE** drop-down list were explained earlier in Table 16-3.

 You should avoid using special characters in field names because they can create problems in reports and queries.

4. Clear the **AUTOMATICALLY ADD NEW ITEMS USERS ENTER TO THE LIST** option.

5. You should have the options shown in Figure 16-20.

   Click Next.

   The **ALLOW USERS TO EDIT ITEMS IN THIS LIST** option has to be checked for each field that you want to let users add, delete or edit the values in the drop-down list.

Figure 16-20 Drop-down list name and type options

If checked, the Automatically add new items users enter to the list option is used to allow users type in a value that is not already in the list. When this happens, the value will automatically be added to the list. This could be a problem because typos will not be caught and the lists can get out of hand to manage.

 The following options cannot be accessed when the **ALLOW USERS TO EDIT ITEMS IN THIS LIST** option is selected: **ALLOW MULTI-SELECT**, **SHOW DESCRIPTIONS** and **TYPE-AHEAD**. These options can only be enabled from the Define Fields dialog box.

6. Click the Add button, then type `Brain Surgery` in the Value column.
   Click the Add button, then type `OB-GYN` in the Value column.

   You should have the options shown in Figure 16-21.

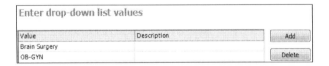

Figure 16-21 Drop-down list values

7. Click Finish.
   You should see the drop-down list that you just created on the window shown in Figure 16-22.

   If you look in the **DETAILS** section illustrated on the left, you will see information about the drop-down list that is selected.

Figure 16-22 Details for the drop-down list

8. Click the Back button in the upper left corner of the dialog box. Leave the Define Fields dialog box open to complete the next exercise.

Managing Drop-Down List Options

If the field has a drop-down list you can decide whether users can add or delete entries in the list. If you need to change the contents of a field like the address field, click in the field and back space out what you do not want and type in the new information. ACT! is in **INSERT** mode by default. In the next exercise you will learn several drop-down list editing techniques.

You can modify drop-down lists on the Define Fields dialog box or as you learned earlier, you can select the Edit List Values option at the bottom of a drop-down list. System fields can be modified on the Define Fields dialog box. Other fields are modified in a view. To use the Define Fields dialog box, other users cannot have the database open.

Exercise 16.7: How To Add Items To A Drop-Down List

In this exercise you will add a value to the Contact ID/Status field.

1. Open the Define Fields dialog box if it is not already open, then click the Manage drop-down lists option in the List Tasks section.

2. Select the Contact ID/Status list name, then click the **EDIT DROP-DOWN LIST** option.

3. Click Next on the Enter drop-down list name and type screen.

4. Click the Add button, then type Purchased Book in the Value field.

   Press the Tab key, then type Purchased the ACT! Book in the Description field.

   The entry should look like the one shown at the bottom of Figure 16-23.

Enter drop-down list values	
Value	Description
Distributor	
Employee	
Family	
Friend	
Gate Keeper	
Influencer	
Investor	
Lead	
Manufacturer	
Prospect	
Reseller	
Resource	
Retailer	
Supplier	
Vendor	
Wholesaler	
Purchased Book	Purchased the ACT! Book

Figure 16-23 Drop-down list values

5. Click Finish. The item will be added to the drop-down list. Close the Define Fields dialog box.

View The New Entry

1. Switch to the Contact Detail view, then open the ID/Status drop-down list on any contact record.

2. Scroll down the list. You will see the item that you created, as illustrated in Figure 16-24.

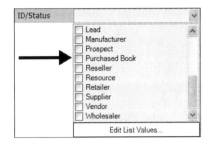

Figure 16-24 ID/Status drop-down list options

Exercise 16.8: How To Edit The Values In A Drop-Down List (From A View)

Many of the fields in the contact and company detail views have drop-down lists. You can add, modify or delete the entries in these lists.

How To Add An Item To A Drop-Down List

In this part of the exercise you will learn how to add an item to a drop-down list.

1. Select the 1024x768 contact layout, if it is not already selected.

2. Click on the arrow at the end of the Department field on the Contact Detail view, then click the **EDIT LIST VALUES** option. You should see the Edit List dialog box. This is a list of all of the items that can currently be selected for the Department field. The list looks similar to the one that you saw earlier in Figure 16-23.

3. Click the Add button. Type Computer in the Value field. If you wanted, you could type in a description to help clarify the item that you are adding.

4. Click OK to close the Edit List dialog box. The item that you just added will be available in the Department drop-down list.

How To Modify Or Delete An Item In A Drop-Down List

The steps below explain how to modify or delete an item in a drop-down list. Read through the steps now, but do not modify or delete anything.

How To Modify An Item In The List

1. Open the Edit List dialog box for the drop-down list that you want to modify.

2. Select the value that you want to modify, then change the item to what you want it to be, as illustrated in Figure 16-25. Click OK.

Notice in Figure 16-23 shown earlier, that the value below the Manufacturer option was Prospect. In Figure 16-25, the value was changed to Brand Marketing.

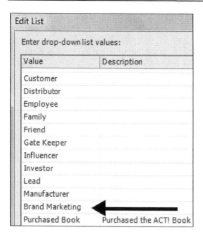

Figure 16-25 Prospect value changed to Brand Marketing

How To Delete An Item In The List

I do not advise deleting items from a drop-down list unless you know that the value is not being used for any contact. If you delete a value and it is being used, the records that are using it will retain the value, but the value will not be available for any other records. If the value that you want to delete for example, is "Computer", I would change it to "Not in use - Computer" or something similar. That way, it is still available and if at some point in the future you need to reclassify contacts that have the value, you will be able to easily find the records.

1. To delete an item in a drop-down list, open the Edit List dialog box shown above in Figure 16-25.

2. Select the value that you want to delete, then click the **DELETE** button. Click Yes, when prompted to delete the list value, then click OK.

 You can also delete an item using the Define Fields dialog box.

Exercise 16.9: How To Modify A User Field

There are 10 contact user fields that you can customize to store data that does not exist in the fields that come with ACT!. If you customize these fields, the name changes on the Define Fields dialog box, but not on the User Fields tab. This is because the "User 1" label on the layout has to be modified. You will not see the label change on the User Fields tab until you edit the layout, which you will learn how to do in Lesson 19. In this exercise you will modify the User 1 field.

1. Tools ⇒ Define Fields.

2. Select the **CONTACTS** field from the drop-down list, if it is not already selected.

3. Scroll down the list and click on the User 1 field, then click the **EDIT FIELD** link.

4. In the Field Name field, type `Specializes In`.

5. Open the Select a field drop-down list and select **INITIAL-CAPS**. This will cause the first letter of each word that you type in this field to automatically be capitalized. Click Yes when prompted that data may be lost.

6. Check all of the options in the **CUSTOMIZE FIELD BEHAVIOR** section, as illustrated in Figure 16-26, then click Next.

Figure 16-26 Customize field behavior options illustrated

7. In the **DEFAULT VALUE** field type General Practitioner, as shown in Figure 16-27.

Figure 16-27 Default value for the user field

8. None of the triggers need to be set. Click Finish. The field will be created.

Exercise 16.10: How To Create A Field

So far in this lesson you have learned how to create and manage drop-down list fields and modify user fields. These are probably the types of fields that you will need to create and modify the most. It is possible though that you may need to create a field that is not a drop-down list. You can create fields and link them to an existing drop-down list. The steps below will show you how to create a field that will be linked to an existing drop-down list.

1. Open the Define Fields dialog box if it is not already open, then click the **CREATE NEW FIELD** link.

2. Type Specialty in the Field name field.

. . . .

3. Check the **USE DROP-DOWN LIST** option shown in Figure 16-28, then select Specializes In from the drop-down list.

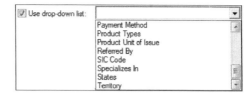

Figure 16-28 Fields with drop-down lists

 The options shown above in Figure 16-28 are the default fields in ACT! that have data for a drop-down list. If one of them is appropriate for the field that you are creating, you can use it.

4. Click Next, then select the **LIMIT TO LIST** option shown in Figure 16-29.

   This will prevent a value from being entered that is not already in the list.

Figure 16-29 Customize field and list behavior options

5. Click Finish. The field will be created. In Lesson 19 you will add this field to the Basic Contact layout.

6. Close the Define Fields dialog box. When prompted to modify the layout, click No.

As shown above in Figure 16-29, the **SHOW DESCRIPTIONS** option is not enabled by default. This description refers to the one that you created in Exercise 16.7.

If the Show Descriptions option is checked, the drop-down list will also display the description, as shown in Figure 16-30. Notice that some options do not have a description.

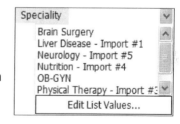

Figure 16-30 Show Descriptions option illustrated

Deleting Fields

As a programmer, I do not delete fields that have data from a database when I first come to the conclusion that the data is no longer needed. Instead, I will modify the layouts that display the field, so that the field is not visible on the layout. I will also remove the field from the queries and reports, but not from the database. If you want to delete a field right away, make a backup copy of the database, then delete the field. While deleting the field from the database is easy to do, you should also remove it from the layouts, queries and reports that it is used in. The steps below show you how to delete a field.

1. Tools ⇒ Define Fields.

2. Open the **VIEW FIELDS FOR** drop-down list and select the record type of the field that you want to delete.

3. Click on the field that you want to delete in the list, then click the Delete Field link on the left.

4. Click Yes, when prompted if you are sure that you want to delete the field. Once the field is deleted, close the Define Fields dialog box.

Managing Priority Types

Schedule ⇒ Manage ⇒ Priorities, will open the dialog box shown in Figure 16-31.

In Lesson 7 you learned how to schedule activities and set the priority for the activity. Renaming or disabling a priority does not effect activities that already have a priority.

They will still display with the priority they had when the activity was created.
The changes that you make on this dialog box only effect new activities. There are five priority options that come with ACT!.

Figure 16-31 Manage Priorities dialog box

You cannot create new entries, but you can modify the names of the existing entries to better meet your needs or to be more descriptive.

If you need to rename a priority, click on it, then click the **EDIT** button and type in the new name.

If you do not need a priority, clear the check mark for it in the **ACTIVE** column. This prevents users from selecting the priority on the Schedule Activities dialog box.

The **RESTORE DEFAULTS** button will reset the priorities back to what they were when ACT! was first installed.

Exercise 16.11: Creating Activity Types

In Lesson 7 you learned about the six activity types that come with ACT!. Only users with administrator or manager level security rights can create new activity types. In this exercise you will learn how to create activity types.

1. Schedule ⇒ Manage ⇒ Activity Types, then click the Add button.

2. Type Post Card Mailing in the **NAME** field.

3. If you want the activity type to have an icon, click the **BROWSE** button. Navigate to and double-click on the icon file that you want to use.

4. Click the Add button on the Add Activity Type dialog box. Type Post Card Mailing Completed in the **RESULT NAME** field on the Add Result Type dialog box, then click OK.

5. Check the option that you just created on the Add Activity Type dialog box to make it the default. You should have the options shown in Figure 16-32.

   The options on the bottom half of this dialog box are the values that will appear in the Results drop-down list field on the Schedule Activities dialog box. These options are also used to clear an activity on the Clear Activity dialog box. You can enter as many options as you need.

Figure 16-32 Add Activity Type dialog box

When a new activity type is created, the **COMPLETED** and **NOT COMPLETED** result types shown in Figure 16-32 are automatically added.

6. Click OK. The dialog box should have the Post Card Mailing activity shown in Figure 16-33.

   The activity types that come with ACT! cannot be deleted.

   Click the Close button.

Figure 16-33 Manage Activity Types dialog box

Annual Events

Annual Events are activities that can be displayed on your calendar, but not on the Task List. Events can be recurring like birthdays or one-time events like a business trip. A good use of the events option is to set up holidays on your calendar. Events do not cause scheduling conflicts and do not appear on reports. Administrator or manager level accounts are needed to create events.

Exercise 16.12: Create An Annual Event Activity

In this exercise you will create an event for July 4th.

1. Schedule ⇒ Manage ⇒ Events.

2. Click the **ADD** button, then type 4th of July in the **EVENT NAME** field.

3. Select July 4th of next year in the Date field.

4. Change the **DURATION** to 1 day.

5. Change the **OCCURS** option to yearly.

   You should have the options shown in Figure 16-34.

Figure 16-34 Add Event dialog box

6. Click OK. You will see the event on the dialog box shown in Figure 16-35.

   Click the Close button.

Figure 16-35 Manage Events dialog box

Add The Event To Your Calendar

In this part of the exercise you will add the event that you just created to your calendar.

1. Tools ⇒ Preferences.

2. On the Calendar and Scheduling tab, click the Calendar Preferences button.

3. Check the **DISPLAY EVENTS** option, illustrated in Figure 16-36, if it is not already checked, then click OK twice to close both dialog boxes.

4. Open a calendar view and display July 4th of next year. You will see the entry illustrated in Figure 16-37. If you do not see the entry, make sure that all of the filter options are set to show all.

Figure 16-36 Calendar Preferences dialog box

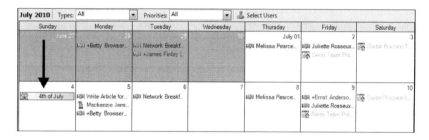

Figure 16-37 Event added to the calendar

CUSTOMIZING REPORT TEMPLATES

In this lesson you will learn the following report template customization techniques:

- ☑ Sizing fields
- ☑ Adding fields to a report
- ☑ Saving templates
- ☑ Hiding report sections
- ☑ Creating subreports

LESSON 17

Report Design Overview

As you have seen, ACT! comes with over 50 reports. Many of the reports may be exactly what you need and others you may wish were slightly different. For example, you may need an existing report to have totals. ACT! has a tool called the **REPORT DESIGNER**. It is used for the following:

    ① To modify existing reports.
    ② Creating a new report based off of an existing report.
    ③ If you need a report that is not similar to any of the reports that come with ACT!, you can create a report from scratch.

Many of the report design techniques that you will learn about are similar to the techniques that the Layout Designer has to modify the layouts (data entry screens and tabs). You will learn how to use the Layout Designer in Lesson 19.

Having modified and designed reports for close to two decades, I can tell you that it is much easier to modify and create reports when you are familiar with the data that the report needs and the structure of the database. By structure, I mean knowing which table each field is in that you need for the report. The other thing that will be helpful is to have a draft of what the new or modified report should look like.

Report Creation Options

There are two ways that you can create a report; From an existing report and from scratch. Each option has pros and cons. Once you understand all of the options, you can select the report creation option that best meets the need for each report that you need to create.

Create A Report Based Off Of An Existing Report

If a report exists that is similar to the report that you need to create, select this report creation option. Save the existing report with a new file name and make the necessary changes to the new report. An example of when to create a report based off of an existing report would be when two groups of people need to see the majority of the same fields, but one of the groups needs additional information that the other group does not need. Another example is when one group needs the same fields but in a different layout then the other group. You can use one of the templates that come with ACT! and format the report as needed.

Reports ⇒ Edit Template ⇒ Select report, are the menu options to select when you want to modify an existing report.

Create A Report From Scratch

This option gives you the most flexibility to create a report. You start with a blank canvas so to speak and add the fields and other objects to the layout. For many, this can be intimidating, especially in the beginning. But being the fearless person that you are, I am sure that when you get to the exercise that has you create a report from scratch, that you will do just fine.

Reports ⇒ New Template, will open the dialog box shown in Figure 17-1.

The **REPORT TYPES** list shown in Figure 17-1 is how you select the type of report that you want to create.

The report types are based on the type of data. Select the type for the new report, then select the **EMPTY REPORT** option in the Templates list on the right.

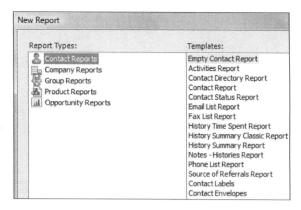

Figure 17-1 Options to create a report from scratch

Report Designer

The Report Designer window shown in Figure 17-2 is used to create new reports and modify existing reports.

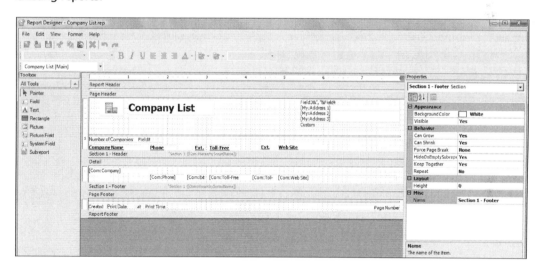

Figure 17-2 Report Designer window

Report Designer Toolbars

The Report Designer has two toolbars that you can use to create and modify reports. Many of the options are the same as options in most word processors. Figure 17-3 shows the Editing toolbar. Table 17-1 explains the buttons on the Editing toolbar. The first eight buttons on the Formatting toolbar shown in Figure 17-4 are the same buttons that are on the Formatting toolbar in most word processors. The remaining buttons on the Formatting toolbar are explained in Table 17-2. The buttons on this toolbar are used to change the look of objects, like fields or labels on the report.

Figure 17-3 Report Designer Editing toolbar

Button	Description
1	Creates a new report.
2	Opens an existing report.
3	Saves the changes.
4	Cuts the selected object(s). (1)
5	Copies the selected object(s).
6	Pastes the selected object(s).
7	Deletes the selected object(s). (1)
8	Undoes the last change.
9	Redoes the last change.

Table 17-1 Report Designer Editing toolbar buttons explained

(1)   The difference between these options is that the Delete option does not allow the selected object(s) to be pasted back into the report.

Figure 17-4 Report Designer Formatting toolbar

Button	Description
1	Changes the color of the font.
2	Changes the background color of the object.
3	Changes the border color.
4	Changes the border style.

Table 17-2 Report Designer Formatting toolbar buttons explained

Sections Of A Report

There are five sections of a report that you can modify and place fields and other objects in, as shown in Figure 17-5.

The sections are the Report Header, Page Header, Detail, Page Footer and Report Footer.

You cannot change the order of or delete these sections. If you place the same calculated field in different sections of the report, it could produce different results.

It is important that you understand how each section of the report functions, because they function independently of each other.

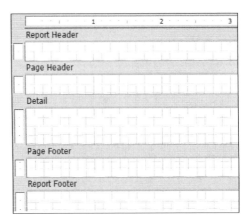

Figure 17-5 Report layout

Keep the following in mind when deciding where to place fields and objects on the report.

① Not all sections are needed for every report.
② If a report does not need a section, the section can be suppressed so that it does not display blank space on the report.
③ Sections can be resized as needed.

Section 1: Report Header

By default, data fields and other objects placed in this section will only print at the top of the first page of the report. It is quite possible that many of the reports that you create will not have anything in this section. Something that you may want to include in this section of the report is the criteria and parameters of the report. If the report needs a cover page, the report header section can be used for the cover page. If this is what you need to do, add a page break after this section so that the actual report data from the other sections of the report starts on a new page.

Section 2: Page Header

Data fields and other objects placed in this section will appear at the top of every page in the report. This is where the report title and headings for the fields in the detail section of the report are usually placed. Other objects that are commonly placed in this section include the date and page number.

Section 3: Detail

Data fields and other objects placed in this section will print for each record in the database that meets the criteria. This section is automatically repeated once for each record that will be printed on the report. The data fields in this section usually have field headings in the page header section.

Section 4: Page Footer

Data fields and other objects placed in this section will print at the bottom of each page of the report. The page footer section is similar to the page header section. Items like page numbers and footnotes can be placed in this section.

Section 5: Report Footer

Data fields and other objects placed in this section will print once at the end of the report. This is usually where grand totals and other types of report summary information is placed.

Customizing Report Templates

In Lesson 9 you learned how to run several reports. Now you will learn how to customize report templates. By customizing report templates, you can add fields to a template and delete fields that you do not need. ACT! also allows you to create your own envelope and label templates from scratch.

Exercise 17.1: Customizing The Report Templates

In this exercise you will learn how to add fields to a report. You will also learn about the tools in the Report Designer window.

Saving Templates

If you modify a template that comes with ACT!, it is a good idea to save it with a different name before making any changes. That way, the existing template is not changed. The **UNDO** option does not work in the Report Designer as you may expect.

Unless instructed otherwise, save the reports that you create or modify in your folder.

1. Lookup all contacts.

2. Reports ⇒ Edit Template.

    You will see the dialog box shown in Figure 17-6.

Figure 17-6 Report templates that come with ACT!

This is also the dialog box that opens when you select the "Other Reports" option on the Reports menu.

3. Double-click on the file **CONTACT STATUS.REP**.

4. File ⇒ Save As. Type My Missing Email Address as the file name, then press Enter or click the Save button.

Field vs Label

Figure 17-7 shows the fields and labels. The **LABEL** for a field is on the left by default. It is not a requirement to keep the label on the report, nor does the label have to have the same name as the field name. If you do not need the label you can delete it by right-clicking on it and selecting **CUT**, as shown in Figure 17-8.

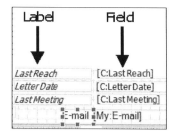

Figure 17-7 Label and field illustrated

Figure 17-8 Label and field shortcut menu

The **FIELD**, which is in brackets, will display data (from the database) on the report. You can modify the field by right-clicking on it and selecting an option on the shortcut menu shown above in Figure 17-8. Table 17-3 contains the field codes. The field codes are the letter(s) before the colon in the field name. The Table column indicates the table that the field is stored in. The abbreviations in the middle of Table 17-3 are the codes.

For example, the code GA is a group activity. This is how you know if the field is a contact, company, group or opportunity field. System fields do not have an abbreviation in front of them.

Table	Contact	Notes	History	Activity	Secondary Contact	Opportunity
Contact	C	CN	CH	CA	SC	CO
Company		COMN	COMH	COMA		COMO
Group		GN	GH	GA		GO
Opportunity						O

Table 17-3 Field codes

How To Manually Resize A Field

Often when you add a field to a report, you will probably have to resize it. Just be careful not to make the field so small that all of the data in the field does not print.

1. Click on the field, **C:LAST RESULTS** in the Status section of the report. You should now see squares around the field.

2. Place the mouse pointer on the middle square on the right side of the field. You may have to scroll to the right to see the end of the field.

3. When the pointer changes to a double headed arrow, press and hold down the left mouse button, then drag the mouse to the left until the pointer is near the end of the field, as illustrated in Figure 17-9.

Last Results	[C:Last Results] ←
Last Attempt	[C:Last Attempt]
Last Reach	[C:Last Reach]
Letter Date	[C:Letter Date]
Last Meeting	[C:Last Meeting]

Figure 17-9 Last Results field made smaller

> To **MOVE A FIELD OR LABEL,** click on it. Press and hold down the left mouse button. The mouse pointer will change to a hand when you start to move the field, as shown in Figure 17-10.

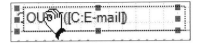

Figure 17-10 Mouse pointer in position to move the field or label

Report Designer Toolbox

A report can have different types of objects. Earlier you learned about fields.

The options in the toolbox shown in Figure 17-11 are used to add fields and other types of objects to the report.

Table 17-4 explains the options in the toolbox.

Figure 17-11 Report Designer Toolbox

Option	Description
Pointer	You have to click this button before clicking on an object on the report to select it.
Field	Adds a field from the database to the report.
Text	Free form field for adding text to the report.
Rectangle	Adds a rectangle or box to the report. This object is often used to visually group fields together.
Picture	Adds a graphic or image to the report. In the upper left corner of the Contact Status report you will see the logo, which is a graphic.
Picture Field	Adds an image to the report. A different image will be displayed for each record on the report. This field is often used for photos.
System Field	Adds a field shown in Figure 17-12 to the report.
Subreport	Adds a report to an existing report. This feature is often used when you want to add multiple rows of the same type of data to a report. Subreports allow a field or fields to be repeated an unlimited number of times on the report. A popular use for a subreport is to add data stored on any of the System tabs. [See Lesson 19, Tabs Overview]

Table 17-4 Report Designer Toolbox options explained

Figure 17-12 System fields

How To Add A Field To A Report

In this part of the exercise you will learn how to add different types of fields to a report template. You will also learn basic report editing techniques.

1. Click the **FIELD** button in the Toolbox. The mouse pointer will change to a cross hair (+) when it is on the report.

2. Place the mouse pointer under the C:Last Meeting field. Press the left mouse button and draw a rectangle the same size as the C:Last Meeting field. You will see the dialog box shown in Figure 17-13.

   The options in the **SELECT A RECORD TYPE** drop-down list are tables in the database. Each table contains different fields.

   Some of the tables correspond to a tab on a detail view.

Figure 17-13 Select Field dialog box

3. Open the drop-down list and select MyRecord, then click on the E-mail field.

4. Check the **INCLUDE A LABEL** option at the bottom of the Select Field dialog box, if it is not already checked, then click the Add button.

5. Click the Close button.

How To Align Fields On A Report

As you can see, the field that you just added to the template is not lined up with the field above it. The steps below show you how to align and resize fields using menu options.

 When aligning fields, select the fields that need to be aligned first, then select the field that you want those fields to line up with. Figure 17-14 shows several fields selected. The one that has the dark handles (the Com:Address 3 field) is the one that the other selected objects will be aligned to.

Figure 17-14 Fields selected to be aligned

1. Click on the E-mail label, then press and hold down the Shift key.

2. Click on the Last Meeting label. Format ⇒ Align ⇒ Left. The E-mail label should now be lined up with the Last Meeting label.

3. Click on a blank space in the report, then click on the E-mail label. Change the font and size to match the Last Meeting label. (For me that is the Tahoma font, size 8, italic.)

4. Click on a blank space in the report, then click on the E-mail field. Change the font and size to match the Last Meeting field. (For me that is the Tahoma font, size 8, no italic.)

5. Click on the My:Email field. Press and hold down the Shift key, then click on the C:Last Meeting field. Format ⇒ Make Same Size ⇒ Height.

6. With the two fields still selected, Format ⇒ Align ⇒ Left. Click on a blank space on the report, then save the changes.

How To Add Text To A Template

You may have the need to add text to a report to help explain something about the report. For example, the report may need a sub title.

1. Click the **TEXT** button in the Toolbox. Place the mouse pointer below the Contact Status report title in the Page Header section and draw a box.

2. If you do not see the Properties window on the right, View ⇒ Properties Window.

3. Type Missing E-mail Addresses in the **TEXT** field on the Properties window, as illustrated in Figure 17-15. Make the field smaller on the report so that the frame is closer to the text on the right.

The Properties Window

Earlier you learned that the options on the toolbox are used to add a variety of fields and objects to a report. You also learned that each field or object on the report can be modified.

The Properties window shown in Figure 17-15 is used to customize the fields and objects, which are sometimes called **ELEMENTS**.

Figure 17-15 Properties window

 The **F4** key opens and closes the Properties window. The options on this window will change depending on the type of object that is selected. If you want to apply the same change to several objects on the report at the same time, select the objects first, then make the changes in the Properties window.

 How To Resize A Section Of The Report

If you are creating a new report or making a lot of changes to an existing report, you may find it easier to work if a section of the report was larger. To make a section larger, place the mouse pointer on the top edge of the section bar of the section below the one that you want to resize. Drag the section down. When you are finished making the changes, drag the section bar back up so that a lot of blank space does not appear at the bottom of the section when you preview or print the report.

 If you need to have more than one text field have the same formatting, create the first field and format it as needed. To duplicate the field, right-click on it and select **COPY**, then right-click on the report and select **PASTE**.

How To Add A Summary Field

Summary fields are used for calculations. You can use summary fields to get totals and averages, as well as, minimums, maximums and counts. Summary fields are usually placed in the report and page header or footer sections.

The purpose of the report in this exercise is to provide a list of contacts to call, to either verify the email address that you have or get an email address from contacts that do not have one. The report already prints the total number of contacts. You will add a summary field to count the number of contacts that have an e-mail address.

1. Click the **FIELD** button in the Toolbox, then draw a rectangle to the right of the **NUMBER OF CONTACTS** field in the Page Header section.

2. Select the E-mail field on the Select Field dialog box. Click Add, then click Close.

3. Right-click on the C:Email field and select Properties.

4. On the Data tab, select the **SUMMARY** Field Type option. The **COUNT** option should be selected, as shown in Figure 17-16.

    Options that are not enabled cannot be used on the field that is currently selected.

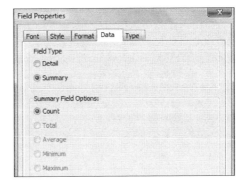

Figure 17-16 Data tab options

5. Click Apply, then click OK.

6. Change the label of the field to `Contacts with E-mail Addresses:`.

7. Move and resize the field and label as needed. Left align the field, then save the changes.

Test The Report

You should test the report template that you create before you close the Report Designer window.

1. File ⇒ Print Preview.

    The top of the report should look like the one shown in Figure 17-17.

    The arrows indicate the items that you added. You may have different totals then the ones shown in the figure.

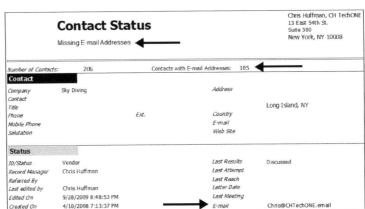

Figure 17-17 Revised Contact Status report

2. Close the Print Preview window. Make any changes that are needed, then save the changes.

How To Align Text In A Label And Field

If you are having trouble aligning the text in the label and field, follow the steps below.

1. Select the label and field.
2. On the Properties window, open the **ALIGNMENT** drop-down list shown in
Figure 17-18 and select the option that will best line up the text in both fields.

Figure 17-18 Alignment options

Custom Fields

Custom fields are not stored in the database. Many of the reports that come with ACT! have custom fields. The custom field in the upper right corner of the Contact Status report is an example. This field contains the City, State and Zip Code fields.

One of the more popular custom fields that is created is to combine two or more fields into one. Combining the city, state and zip code fields is probably the most popular custom field. If you added these three fields to a report individually, they would be printed as shown in Figure 17-19.

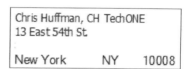

Figure 17-19 City, state and zip code fields added to the report

This is probably not the way that you want the fields to print. You probably want these fields to look the way that they do at the top of the Contact Status report shown earlier in Figure 17-17. You can create custom fields in one of two ways, as discussed below:

   ①   Use fields that are already on the report.
   ②   Add fields to the report and then hide them.

The benefit of using option 1 is that it is less work. To get the name of the field(s) that you want to use, click on the field in the report.

Figure 17-20 shows that the Email count field is selected. If you look at the top of the Properties window on the right of the figure, you will see the field name E-mail2. If you wanted to use this field in a custom field, you would reference it as E-mail2.

Figure 17-20 Properties for the E-mail count field

Select the second option listed above when the fields that you need are not already on the report. If you look closely below the custom field in the Contact Status report, in the design view, you will see light gray lines.

If you click on the first gray line and then look at the top of the Properties window, you should see Field6, as illustrated in Figure 17-21.

If you see Field7 or 8, you are in the right place. Field6 is the City field. Field7 is the State field and Field8 is the Zip Code field.

Figure 17-21 Hidden field selected

Exercise 17.2: How To Create A Custom Field

In this exercise you will create a custom field for fields that are not on the report. You will create a custom field that combines the city, state and zip code fields into one field.

1. Save the Birthday List report as My Custom Field Report.

2. Delete the three fields below the custom field shown above in Figure 17-21. If you cannot see them, click in the area below the custom field.

3. Delete the Custom field shown above in Figure 17-21.

Hiding Fields On A Report

When you have to use fields that are not already on the report to create a custom field, you have to add them to the report and then hide them. The reason that you hide the fields is because they should not be printed in their current format. When you draw the box for a field that you have to hide, you should make it as small as possible and place it in a location that is not in the way of the other fields on the report. In step 2 above, you deleted three fields. You do not have to make the fields as small as the ones that you deleted, if you do not want to.

 Once you double-click on the first field that you need to add to the report, you do not have to close the Select Field dialog box. Double-click on the next field in the dialog box that you need to add.

4. Add the My Record type City, State and Zip Code fields, but not the labels, to the Page Header section.

5. Select the three fields that you just added, then change the **VISIBLE** option on the Properties window to False.

Figure 17-22 shows the hidden fields. I don't know about you, but I find these fields easier to work with and know what they are, then the three fields that you deleted under the custom field earlier in this exercise, that you can't see.

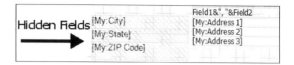

Figure 17-22 Hidden fields

6. Click the System Field button in the Toolbox, then draw a box under the My:Address 3 field in the Page Header section.

7. Select the Custom field option, then clear the **INCLUDE A LABEL** option. Click Add, then click Close.

8. Select the custom field. Type the following in the **EXPRESSION** field on the Properties window, as shown in Figure 17-23. City1&", "&State1&" "&ZipCode1. The only place that there should be a space is between each set of quotes and after the comma.

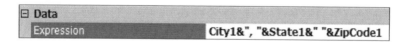

Figure 17-23 Expression for the custom city, state and zip code field

 If you look at the fields above the Custom field that you created, you will see that there is no space between them. This is done to make the report look better. It is not mandatory though.

9. Align the custom field on the left with the Address 3 field.

10. Make the font and size of the custom field the same as the My:Address 3 field if it is not already.

11. Save the changes and preview the report.

    The name and address section should look like the one shown in Figure 17-24.

Chris Huffman, CH TechONE
13 East 54th St
Suite 300
New York, NY 10008

Figure 17-24 Custom city, state and zip code field

Modifying Report Sections

There will be times when an existing report has the layout and many of the fields that you need for a new report. Instead of creating a report from scratch, you can save an existing report with a different name and modify it. You can hide or delete the fields in sections of a report that are not needed. You can also force a section to start on a new page.

Exercise 17.3: Hiding A Report Section

As you learned earlier, sections of the report cannot be removed. If a report does not need a section, you can hide it by following the steps below.

1. Lookup all contacts.

2. Save the Contact Status report as My Contact Report - Hidden Section.

3. Click on the Page Footer section bar, then press the F4 key if the Properties window is not open.

 If the Properties window is already open, you can open the drop-down list at the top and select the section of the report that you want to change the properties of.

4. Click in the **VISIBLE** property to open the drop-down list, then select No.

5. Save the changes. If you preview the report you will not see the fields in the Page Footer section.

Exercise 17.4: Adding A Section To A Report

Sections are added to a report to group and sort the detail records. Once you add a section to the report, you can add fields and other objects to it. You will group the report by company name, sorted in ascending order.

1. Save the My Contact Report - Hidden Section report as My Contact Report - Added Section.

2. Edit ⇒ Define Sections. Click the Add button.

3. Select Company in the Fields list on the dialog box shown in Figure 17-25, then click OK.

Figure 17-25 Select a Field to Group By dialog box

4. Click on the **SECTION 2** option on the left. At the bottom of Figure 17-26 you will see that the section will be sorted in ascending order, which is what you want. Leave the dialog box open to complete the next part of the exercise.

Figure 17-26 Define Sections dialog box

> Double-clicking on any section header in the Report Designer window will open the Define Sections dialog box.

Define Sections Dialog Box Options

The options shown in Figure 17-27 are used to customize the sections of the report.

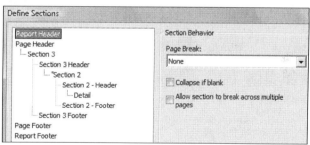

Figure 17-27 Section Behavior options

① The **PAGE BREAK** options shown in Figure 17-28 are used to determine whether or not a section will start on a new page. I often use the **AFTER** option on the Report Header section as the way to make that section print on a page by itself, so that it can be used as a cover page for the report.

② If checked, the **COLLAPSE IF BLANK** option shown on the right of Figure 17-27 above, will hide the section when the report is printed if it does not have any fields or objects in it.

③ If checked, the **ALLOW SECTION TO BREAK ACROSS MULTIPLE PAGES** option allows a report section to print on more than one page.

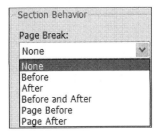

Figure 17-28 Page Break options

How To Remove A Section Of The Report

If you slide the dialog box out of the way, you will see that the report is also grouped on the Contact field. (See Section 3 Header.) This group is not needed. The steps below show you how to remove a section.

1. Click on the section that you want to remove on the Define Sections dialog box. In this exercise click on the Section 3 Header option, then click the **REMOVE** button.

2. Click Yes when prompted to delete the report section, then click OK to close the Define Sections dialog box.

3. Save the changes and preview the report.

You should see that the contacts on the first few pages do not have a company name, which is why the records are at the beginning of the report. When you get past the contacts without a company name, you should see that the report is now in order by company name.

Resize A Section Of The Report

You can manually resize a section to make it smaller or you can hide a section by dragging the section bar above or below the section that you want to resize. In Exercise 17.3 you used the **VISIBLE** option on the Properties window to hide a section of the report.

> **Report Margins**
>
> File ⇒ Page Setup, is used to change the margins for the report. The options on this dialog box work the same way that they do in word processing software.

Exercise 17.5: How To Create A Section Break

In this exercise you will create a section break. You will use the Report Header section to create a cover page for the report. You will also add a system field to the Report Header section.

Create The Cover Page

The Contact Status report already has the Print Date, Print Time and Page Number system fields in the Page Footer section. In this part of the exercise you will add the Print Date system field to the Report Header section of the report. Yes, I know that the report already has this field, but I did not want to select a field that would not make sense on a cover page.

. . . .

1. Save the Contact Status report as My Cover Page Report.

2. Make the Report Header section longer, then add a Text field to the section and type Report Cover Page in the Text field in the Properties window.

3. Change the Border Style to **DASH DOT DOT**.

4. Change the font to Comic Sans MS, bold, size 18.

5. Center the text across the top of the Report Header section.

Add A System Field

1. Click the System Field button in the Toolbox and draw a box below the text that you just added. Select the Print Date field. Click Add, then click Close.

2. Change the label of the field to This report was printed on. Resize the label so that you can see all of the text.

Add A Page Break

In this part of the exercise you will add a page break after the Report Header section so that it is the only content that prints on the first page of the report.

1. Double-click on the Report Header bar.

2. Open the Page Break drop-down list and select **AFTER**, then click OK.

 Selecting the Page Header section and the **BEFORE** Page option will produce the same result as the two steps above.

3. Save the changes, then preview the report.

   The first page should look like the one shown in Figure 17-29.

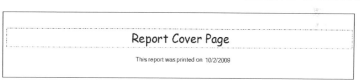

   Report Cover Page

   This report was printed on 10/2/2009

Figure 17-29 Report cover page

At the bottom of the page you should see the Page Footer information. I could not find a way to keep this from printing on the first page. The second page of the report contains the data.

Exercise 17.6: Using The Picture Field

The Picture field will display a different image or photo for each detail record on the report. In this exercise you will modify the Birthday List report to print the contacts photo on the report.

1. Save the Birthday List report as My Photo Birthday List Report.

2. Make the Detail section a little longer. Click the Picture Field button on the Toolbox, then draw a box to the right of the Birth Date field.

3. Select the Photo field, then clear the Include a label option. Click Add, then click Close.

4. Save the changes, then preview the report. It should look like the one shown in Figure 17-30.

Ernst Anderson	CH TechONE	6/22/1964
Gracie Anderson	Searchlight Casting	1/4/1968 2:00:00 AM
Thomas Andrews	Modern Electric Supply	

Figure 17-30 Report with photo added

If you scroll through the report, you will see some photos that are a lot larger than the one shown in Figure 17-30. The best way to handle this is to make all of the photos the same size before adding them to the database.

Exercise 17.7: Create A New Report

So far you have modified existing reports. At some point you may need a report that is completely different then the ones that come with ACT!. If so, you will have to create a report from scratch. What many people do is create their own template to use as the basis for new reports. The template that you will create in this exercise will include fields and objects that you want to include on every new report. That way, you do not have to spend time adding page numbers, print dates and logos to every report that you create from scratch.

Create A Custom Report Template

In this part of the exercise you will use an existing report as the basis for the template for new reports that you will create.

1. Save the Contact Status report as `My Report Template`.

2. Change the Contact Status title to `Report Title goes here`.

3. Leave the logo and blue line in the Page Header section. Delete all of the other fields in this section including the three hidden fields below the Custom field.

4. Delete everything in the Detail section.

5. Save the changes. Minimize the Report Designer window.

Look Up The Records

In this part of the exercise, you will use an existing query as the basis for the records that will appear on the report. In Lesson 4, you created a lookup to find all records that were created in the last 30 days. If you recall, you typed in a specific date. If that lookup was saved as a query, 60 days from now you would still see the same records, which is not what you want. The query tool has an operator that is used to select how many days you want to go back, instead of typing in a specific date. To complete this report, I created a query that you will use to find the records.

1. Lookup ⇒ Advanced ⇒ Advanced Query.

. . . .

2. File ⇒ Open. Double-click on the Last 30 Days query file in your folder.

3. Click the Preview button. You should see the query and results shown in Figure 17-31. The records at the bottom of the dialog box are the ones that you created in the last 30 days.

Figure 17-31 Last 30 Days query

4. Click OK. Click OK again to replace the current lookup.

5. Restore the Report Designer window.

Create A Report From Scratch

Before creating a new report, it is a good idea to look up all of the contacts so that you will have some data to test the report with. In this part of the exercise you will create a new report. You will use the template that you created earlier in this exercise.

1. Save the My Report Template report that you created as My Custom Contact Report.

2. Change the report title to the file name.

3. Click the Field button in the Toolbox and draw a box in the Detail section. Add the following fields with labels: Contact, Company, Create Date and Record Creator.

To select the field and label, hold down the left mouse button and draw a box around the label and field. This allows you to move both objects at the same time. This is sometimes referred to as the **LASSO** technique.

4. Rearrange the fields and labels so that your report looks like the one shown in Figure 17-32.

   Drag the labels to the bottom of the Page Header section.

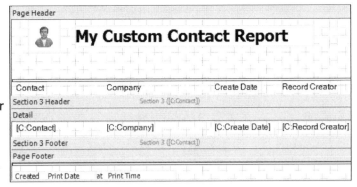

Figure 17-32 Layout for a new report

5. Save the changes, then preview the report. You should see the same records that were in the Contact List view.

Subreports

A subreport is a report inside of another report. Subreports have many uses. Often a subreport contains data from a tab on a detail view, but you are not limited to only using data from a tab on a subreport. For example, if you are a realtor, you could add three image fields to the top of the Contact Detail view to display three photos for each house. Subreports can be used to display an unlimited amount of the same type of information, like all of the opportunities for a contact.

Another example is you may have the need to display all of the notes for each contact.

The Notes field would be added to the subreport.

If you look at the bottom of the Detail section of the layout shown in Figure 17-33, you will see five subreports.

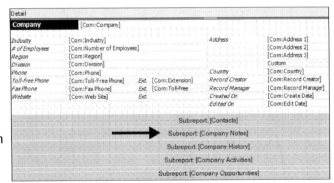

Figure 17-33 Subreports illustrated

Exercise 17.8: Create A Subreport

In this exercise you will create a subreport and add it to the report that you created in the previous exercise. The subreport will contain data from each contacts History tab.

1. Open the My Custom Contact report, if it is not already open and make the Detail section a little longer.

2. Click the Subreport button in the Toolbox and draw a box below the fields in the Detail section. The box should start at the one inch mark go to the 7.5 inch mark on the ruler.

3. Type `My History Subreport` in the Subreport name field, as shown in Figure 17-34.

Figure 17-34 Subreports dialog box

4. Double-click on the Contact1 field on the Subreports dialog box.

5. Save the changes, then double-click on the Subreport field in the Detail section.

6. Make the Header and Detail sections longer, then change the Visible option to Yes for both sections.

7. Add a text field to the Header section. Type `History Records`. Make the field bold.

8. Add a field to the Detail section. Open the Record Type drop-down list and select Contact History.

9. Add the following fields with labels to the Detail section of the subreport: Date, Result, Regarding & Details, Record Manager.

Add The Subreport To The Main Report

In this part of the exercise you will add the subreport that you just created to the Detail section of the My Custom Contact report. Adding the Subreport is not sufficient. The subreport must also be linked to the Custom Contact report by a field that is unique and in both tables. This is usually an **ID** field. ID fields hold unique values like a social security number. The ID field that both tables have that is unique is the Contact ID field. This is how the correct records are retrieved for the subreport.

1. Add the Contact ID field without a label to the right of the Record Manager field. Change the Visible option to False.

2. When you move the labels to the Header section below the History Records text field, make them bold and underlined.

3. Add a rectangle above the labels in the Header section. Make it narrow so that it looks like two lines.

4. Rearrange and align the fields and labels to match the layout shown in Figure 17-35. You can make the Date field smaller and the Regarding & Details field wider.

Figure 17-35 Subreport layout

5. Change the **RICH TEXT** property of the Regarding & Details field to Yes.

6. Save the changes. Open the drop-down list above the Toolbox shown in Figure 17-36, then select My Custom Contact Report [Main].

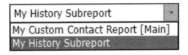

Figure 17-36 Subreports drop-down list

7. File ⇒ Run. Clear the Exclude My Record option because this report retrieves the records that you created in the last month.

The History tab was automatically added to the Define Filters dialog box when you created the subreport for history records.

8. On the History tab, check all three history type options, then change the Date Range to All.

   Click OK.

   The report should look like the one shown in Figure 17-37.

Figure 17-37 My Custom Contact report

9. Close the Report Designer.

Modifying Labels And Envelopes

In previous exercises in this lesson you learned how to modify reports. Modifying labels and envelopes is very similar. The main difference is that there are less options. The steps to modify labels are the same as envelopes. In the next exercise you will learn how to modify an envelope. If you want to modify a label, in step 2 below, select "Labels" instead of "Envelopes" on the Print dialog box. Like reports, the first thing that you should do when you open a label or envelope template is to save it with a new name if you are going to modify it.

Exercise 17.9: Modify An Envelope (Or Label) Template

In this exercise you will add text to an envelope. If you were sending out letters to invite people to an event, you could add a line of text to the envelope that lets the recipient know that they have been invited.

1. Look up the records in the Potential Book Customer group.

2. File ⇒ Print. Select **ENVELOPES**, then select the size. In this exercise select the US Letter Paper Type.

3. Click the **EDIT TEMPLATE** button.

4. File ⇒ Save As. Save the file as `My Custom Envelope`.

5. Add a Text field above the first custom field in the center of the envelope. Type `You are invited to our Spring Gala` in the Text field.

6. Change the Font size to 10 and make the text italic. Save the changes.

7. File ⇒ Run. Select the Current Lookup option, then click OK. When you preview the envelope it should look like the one shown in Figure 17-38.

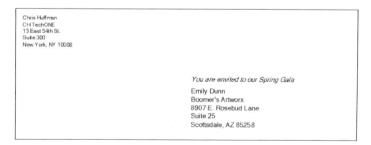

Figure 17-38 Custom Envelope

Creating Label And Envelope Templates

If the label or envelope size that you need is not in ACT! you can create your own. The majority of the steps are the same as creating a report. The steps below are for envelopes. If you need to create labels, in step 2 select a label template.

1. File ⇒ New, from the Report Designer window or Reports ⇒ New Template, from an ACT! view. You will see the New Report dialog box.

2. Select the Contact Reports type, then double-click on the Contact Envelopes option.

3. Open the Select an envelope size drop-down list and select Custom. Accept the default height and width options, then click OK. The rest of the process is the same as creating a report.

CUSTOMIZING THE MENU & TOOLBARS

Overview

In this lesson you will learn several ways to customize the menu and toolbars, including how to:

- ☑ Modify menus
- ☑ Create custom menus
- ☑ Create custom commands
- ☑ Modify toolbars
- ☑ Create keyboard shortcuts
- ☑ Modify the Navigation Pane

LESSON 18

Modifying Menus

You can modify menus by adding more commands to them. You can also create custom submenus. If you created several of your own reports, you could create a submenu off of the Reports menu and add your reports there. The commands that are on the menus that come with ACT! can also be modified. If you run the same queries all the time you can add them to a menu or a toolbar.

Modifications to menus and toolbars are not saved in the database. If you make changes to the menus and toolbars and want other users to have the same changes, the changes have to be added to each computer.

Toolbars May Become Corrupt

As you go through the toolbar exercises, you may notice that when you open the Customize Menus and Toolbars dialog box, that the workspace automatically changes to a different view and that the corresponding toolbar is checked on the dialog box. This did not happen in ACT! 2009. This appears to be a bug. Sometimes, closing ACT! and reopening it works.

If you get one of the following error messages, your toolbars may be corrupt and need to be deleted so that they can automatically be recreated.

① "Exception has been thrown by the target of an" (then nothing).
② "ACT has encountered an error, please shut down the application."

If you see either of these errors, the solution posted in the forum is to delete the ACT for Windows 12 folder. Below is the path to this folder.

Windows XP C:\Documents and Settings\YourUserName\Application Data\ACT
Vista C:\Users\YourUserName\App Data\Roaming\ACT

Exercise 18.1: Using The Customize Dialog Box To Modify Menus

In this exercise you will learn how to perform the following tasks to modify menus.

① Add a command to a menu.
② Create a custom menu.
③ Create a custom submenu.
④ Rearrange commands on menus.
⑤ Delete commands on a menu.

How To Add A Command To A Menu

In ACT!, a command is a series of instructions that perform a task like open a dialog box. Usually, commands are created for repetitive tasks. In this part of the exercise you will add a command to the Contacts menu.

1. Open the Contact Detail view.

   Tools ⇒ Customize ⇒
   Menus and Toolbars.

   You will see the dialog box
   shown in Figure 18-1.

   These are the toolbars that
   come with ACT!.

Figure 18-1 Customize Menus and Toolbars dialog box

2. On the Commands tab, click on the Opportunities option in the **CATEGORIES** list.

3. Click on the **CREATE QUOTE** command in
   the Commands list, as shown in
   Figure 18-2.

Figure 18-2 Commands tab options

4. Drag the Create Quote command to the Contacts menu, as illustrated below in Figure 18-3.
   The Contacts menu will open.

5. Drag the mouse down past the **NEW SECONDARY CONTACT** option, as illustrated below in
   Figure 18-4, then release the mouse button.

6. Close the Customize Menus and Toolbars dialog box. The Contacts menu should look like
   the one shown in Figure 18-5.

Figure 18-3 Command dragged to the Contacts menu

Figure 18-4 Command moved on the menu

Figure 18-5 Modified Contacts menu

How To Create A Custom Menu

If you have the need to add several commands to menus, it may be easier to find the commands by creating your own menu and placing all of your commands there. The steps below show you how to create a custom menu. You can add commands to menus that you create, just like you did in the previous part of this exercise.

1. Tools ⇒ Customize ⇒ Menus and Toolbars.

2. Click the **NEW** button on the Custom Commands tab.

3. Type MyMenu in the Command name field, then click the **ADD COMMAND** button.

   Your dialog box should look like the one shown in Figure 18-6.

Figure 18-6 Command name added

4. On the Commands tab, click on the Custom Commands category.

    You should see the menu that you created on the Custom Commands tab, as shown in Figure 18-7.

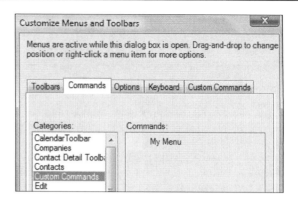

Figure 18-7 Customized menu created

5. Drag the MyMenu command shown above in Figure 18-7 to the menu bar in ACT!. Place it to the right of the Help menu, as shown in Figure 18-8. Leave the dialog box open.

Figure 18-8 Custom menu added to the menu bar

 You can add menus that you create between existing menu options, meaning you could add your menu after the Reports menu for example.

How To Create A Custom Submenu

Submenus are menus that open from an option on a menu. You can add as many commands to a submenu as you need. Commands that have a triangle, as shown earlier in Figure 18-5, have submenus.

In this part of the exercise you will add a submenu to the custom menu that you just created. Adding submenus is the same process as adding other commands.

1. On the Commands tab, select the Reports category.

2. Drag the Company Reports command to the menu that you just created and added to the workspace. You will see a white box below the menu that you created, as shown in Figure 18-9.

Figure 18-9 Menu command in position

3. Drag the submenu to the white box and release the mouse button.

4. Close the Customize Menus and Toolbars dialog box. Your menu should look like the one shown in Figure 18-10.

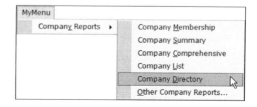

Figure 18-10 Submenu added to the menu

Rearrange Commands On A Menu

If you decide that you do not like the order of the commands on a menu, you can change the order by following the steps below. In this part of the exercise you will move the Create Quote option on the Contacts menu.

1. Open the Customize Menus and Toolbars dialog box.

2. Open the Contacts menu on the workspace and drag the Create Quote command up and place it below the **EDIT CONTACT ACCESS** command, as illustrated in Figure 18-11.

   In addition to being able to add commands to a menu from the dialog box, you can drag items from one menu to another.

Figure 18-11 Command moved on the menu

How To Delete Commands From A Menu

You can delete a command from a menu by following the steps below. In this part of the exercise you will delete the Create Quote command from the Contacts menu.

1. Open the Customize Menus and Toolbars dialog box.

2. Open the Contacts menu, then right-click on the **CREATE QUOTE** command and select Delete, as shown in Figure 18-12.

Figure 18-12 Option to delete a menu command

Exercise 18.2: Creating Custom Commands

If you use documents like a template or another software application on a regular basis in conjunction with ACT! and do not want to keep opening the file from outside of ACT!, you can create a custom command to open the template or software package from inside of ACT!.

In this exercise you will create two custom commands. One to open a document and one to open an application. You will then add the commands to the custom menu that you created earlier in this lesson.

Create A Custom Command For A Document

1. Tools ⇒ Customize ⇒ Menus and Toolbars.

2. On the Custom Commands tab, click **NEW**.

3. In the Command name field type My Document Command.

4. In the **TOOLTIP TEXT** field type Opens the Specialties document.

5. Click the Browse button at the end of the **COMMAND LINE** field, then double-click on the Specialties.txt file in your folder.

    You should have the options shown in Figure 18-13.

Figure 18-13 Options to open a document

 If you know the full path to the file or application that you are creating the command for, you can type it in the **COMMAND LINE** field instead of clicking the Browse button. If you wanted to use a different icon then the one in the **CHOOSE ICON** section, click the **ICON** button to select the icon file that you want to use.

6. Click the Add Command button. Leave the dialog box open to complete the next part of the exercise.

Create A Custom Command For An Application

1. On the Custom Commands tab, click New.

2. In the Command name field, type My Application Command.

3. In the Tooltip text field, type Opens Notepad.

4. Click the Browse button at the end of the Command line field, then double-click on the **NOTEPAD.EXE** file in the C:\WINNT folder if your file system is NTFS or C:\Windows if your file system is Vista or FAT32.

   You should have the options shown in Figure 18-14.

Figure 18-14 Options to open an application

5. Click the Add Command button.

Add The Commands To The Menu

Earlier you added a command to the custom menu that you created. Follow the same steps to add the two commands that you just created to your custom menu.

Place the commands below the Company Reports option. Your custom menu should look like the one shown in Figure 18-16.

Figure 18-15 Custom menu with commands added

Close the Customize Menus and Toolbars dialog box. Notice that the icons that are at the bottom of the dialog boxes shown earlier in Figures 18-13 and 18-14 are displayed on the menu.

Test The Commands

1. My Menu ⇒ My Document Command. The Specialties document will open.

2. My Menu ⇒ My Application Command. The Notepad application will open.

Deleting Custom Menus

If you have created a custom menu that you no longer need, you can delete it by following the steps below.

1. Open the Customize Menus and Toolbars dialog box, then click on the Custom Commands tab. You should see the menu that you created, as shown earlier in Figure 18-14.

2. Select the command that you want to delete, then click the Delete button. Click OK when you see the Delete Custom Command message.

3. Close the dialog box. The custom menu that you created should no longer be on the menu bar.

Modifying Toolbars

As you learned, each of the views has a toolbar. You can modify the toolbars by adding or removing commands. You can also rearrange the order of the buttons on the toolbar. Each of the views have their own toolbar. That means that if you add a button to the Groups toolbar you will not see it on the Contacts toolbar. You can also add custom commands to a toolbar like you can to a menu. The difference between customizing a menu and a toolbar is that the changes to menus are visible throughout ACT! regardless of the view that is open. Changes to toolbars are only visible on the views that have the toolbar that you change.

One reason people customize toolbars is to place the commands, files and applications that they use the most out in the open where they can be seen. This allows you to be more efficient because you do not have to remember which menu has the option that you are looking for.

Exercise 18.3: Customizing Toolbars

In this exercise you will learn how to perform the following tasks to customize toolbars.

① Add a command to a toolbar.
② Add a custom command to a toolbar.
③ Rearrange commands on a toolbar.
④ Customize toolbar buttons.
⑤ Distribute and install custom menus and toolbars.
⑥ Delete commands from a toolbar.

How To Add A Command To A Toolbar

In this part of the exercise you will add a command to the Contacts toolbar.

1. Open the Contact List view.

2. Right-click on the Contact List toolbar (not a button) and select Customize, as shown in Figure 18-16.

Figure 18-16 Toolbar shortcut menu

3. Move the dialog box off of the toolbar if necessary.

4. On the Commands tab, click on the **REPORTS** category.

5. Drag the Contact Report command to the Contact List toolbar and place it after the **EXPORT TO EXCEL** button.

6. Close the dialog box.
    The Contact List toolbar should
    look like the one shown in
    Figure 18-17.

Figure 18-17 Command added to the Contacts toolbar

How To Add A Custom Command To A Toolbar

Just like you added a custom command to a menu, you can add a custom command to a toolbar. In this part of the exercise you will add the custom command that opens an application that you created earlier in this lesson to the Groups toolbar.

1. Open the Group Detail view.

2. Right-click on the Group Detail toolbar and select Customize.

3. On the Commands tab, click on the Custom Commands category.

4. Drag the **MY APPLICATION COMMAND** to the toolbar and place it after the Save Changes button.

5. Close the dialog box. The Group Detail toolbar should look like the one shown in Figure 18-18.

    If you click on the button that you just added, the Notepad application will open.

Figure 18-18 Custom command added to the Group Detail toolbar

How To Rearrange Commands On A Toolbar

If you do not like the order that the commands (buttons) are in on the toolbar, you can change the order, just like you rearranged the order of the commands on a menu in Exercise 18.1. In this exercise you will move the report command to the left of the Export to Excel command on the Contact List view toolbar.

1. Open the Contact List view, then open the Customize Menus and Toolbars dialog box.

2. Drag the Contact Report command to the left of the Export to Excel command and release the mouse button.

How To Customize Toolbar Buttons

You can customize each button on a toolbar. Figure 18-19 shows the toolbar button customization options. Table 18-1 explains the customization options that are available when the Customize Menus and Toolbars dialog box is open.

To open this shortcut menu right-click on a button on the toolbar.

Figure 18-19 Toolbar button shortcut menu

Option	Description
Reset All	Resets all toolbars and menus to the way they were when ACT! was first installed. I don't know why the menus are reset with this option when all of the other options on this shortcut menu are only for toolbar buttons. The only thing that I can think of is because the Reset All command shares code with the Reset Menus and Toolbars command.
Delete	Deletes the command that you right-click on.
Name	Is used to change the name of the button.
Default Style	Only displays the icon for the command without any text. This is how many of the toolbar buttons are, by default.
Text Only (Always)	Only displays text with no icon as shown earlier in Figure 18-17.
Image and Text (Always)	Displays the icon and name of the button, as illustrated in Figure 18-20.
Begin Group	Creates a group of buttons by inserting a vertical line on the toolbar, as illustrated in Figure 18-21. The buttons in the group do not have to have anything in common. One use for this may be if you need to add a few buttons to the toolbar that open the applications that you use often. You could add vertical lines to group them together.

Table 18-1 Toolbar button shortcut menu options explained

Figure 18-20 Image and Name button illustrated

Figure 18-21 Vertical line added to the toolbar

 If you right-click on a blank space at the end of the toolbar and select **CUSTOM COMMANDS** on the shortcut menu shown earlier in Figure 18-16, you will see all of the commands that you have created on their own row of the toolbar, as illustrated in Figure 18-22.

Figure 18-22 Custom commands on the toolbar

How To Distribute Custom Menus And Toolbars To Other Users

Earlier in this lesson you learned how to customize menus and toolbars. If you want other people that use the database to have the same customized menus and toolbars that you created, follow the steps below. For now you can just read the steps.

1. File ⇒ Back Up ⇒ Personal Files.

2. Click the **BROWSE** button. Select a folder on a server or external device like an external hard drive that you want to store the files on that will be copied to other computers.

3. You can rename the zip file or accept the default zip file name that is shown in Figure 18-23.

    Clear all of the options except the Menus and Toolbars option, then click OK. The files will be backed up.

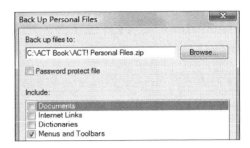

Figure 18-23 Back Up Personal Files dialog box

How To Install The Custom Menu And Toolbar On Another Computer

Before installing the customized menus on another computer, you should confirm that the computer does not already have a custom ACT! menu or toolbar. If it does, you will overwrite it when you copy your custom menu or toolbar to the hard drive.

1. Go to the computer that you want to install the custom menu and toolbar on, then open ACT!.

2. File ⇒ Restore ⇒ Personal Files.

3. Click the Browse button shown in Figure 18-24, then navigate to the folder that has the zip file with the customizations that you created and double-click on the zip file.

Figure 18-24 Restore Personal Files dialog box

4. Click OK on the Restore Personal Files dialog box. The custom menus and toolbars will be installed on the computer. Repeat this process on each computer that you want to have the custom menus and toolbars.

How To Delete A Command From A Toolbar

Deleting a command from a toolbar is the same as deleting a command from a menu. In this part of the exercise you will delete the Open NotePad command shown earlier in Figure 18-18 from the toolbar.

1. Open the view that has the toolbar that you want to delete a command from. In this exercise open the Group Detail view.

2. Open the Customize Menus and Toolbars dialog box.

3. Right-click on the command on the toolbar that you want to delete and select Delete.

4. Close the Customize Menus and Toolbars dialog box.

Exercise 18.4: How To Reset Menus And Toolbars

If you have made changes to a menu or toolbar and no longer want or need the changes, you can manually remove the changes one by one or you can reset the menus and toolbars back to the way that they were when ACT! was first installed. Any keyboard shortcuts that you created will also be reset. If you need to reset these tools, follow the steps below. The commands that you create are not deleted, just removed from the menus and toolbars.

1. Tools ⇒ Customize ⇒ Reset Menus and Toolbars.

   You will see the message shown in Figure 18-25.

Figure 18-25 Reset Menus and Toolbars message

2. Click OK and the menus and toolbars will be reset.

Creating Keyboard Shortcuts

In addition to being able to customize menus and toolbars, you can create keyboard shortcuts. Keyboard shortcuts are the keystrokes shown at the end of some options on a menu, as shown earlier in Figure 18-11. The steps below show you how to create a keyboard shortcut.

1. Tools ⇒ Customize ⇒ Menus and Toolbars.

2. On the Keyboard tab, click on the Custom command category at the bottom of the list.

3. Click on the My Document command, as shown in Figure 18-26.

Figure 18-26 Command selected

4. Click the **ASSIGN SHORTCUT** button.

5. Press and hold down the Alt key, then press the letter D.

    You should see OK in the bottom field on the dialog box shown in Figure 18-27.

Figure 18-27 Assign Shortcut dialog box

6. Click OK, then click Close. If you open the menu that you created, you will see the keyboard shortcut next to the My Document command, as shown in Figure 18-28.

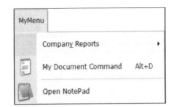

Figure 18-28 Keyboard shortcut added to a command

Keyboard Shortcuts

ACT!, like other software has keyboard shortcuts. Many of them use the Control (CTRL) key. Table 18-2 contains some of the keyboard shortcuts. If you want to know whether or not a specific command has a shortcut, open the menu that the command is on to find out. If you want to print a copy of the keyboard shortcuts in the table, the file ACT_Keyboard_Shortcuts.pdf is in the zip file that you downloaded for this book.

Shortcut	What It Does
CTRL + C	Copies the selected text.
CTRL + D	Clears an activity.
CTRL + H	Creates a history record.
CTRL + I	Attaches a file.
CTRL + L	Schedules a telephone call activity.
CTRL + M	Schedules a meeting activity.
CTRL + P	Prints an address book, calendar, envelope, label and reports.
CTRL + T	Schedules a To-Do activity.
CTRL + V	Pastes the contents of the clipboard into a field in ACT!.
CTRL + X	Cuts (deletes) the selected text.
CTRL + Z	Undoes the last action.
CTRL + F5	Refreshes the window.
CTRL + F11	Opens a new sales opportunity.

Table 18-2 ACT! keyboard shortcuts explained

Shortcut	What It Does
F1	Opens the Help system.
F3	Opens the weekly calendar.
F5	Opens the monthly calendar.
F7	Opens the Task List view.
F8	Opens the Contact List view.
F9	Inserts a note.
F10	Opens the Group List view.
F11	Opens the Contact Detail view.

Table 18-2 ACT! keyboard shortcuts explained (Continued)

Navigation Pane Customization Options

The default buttons on the Navigation Pane provides links to the screens in ACT!. This section explains the customization options.

 If you used ACT! 2009 or earlier, you will see that ACT! 2010 has fewer customization options for the Navigation Pane.

1. Click on the arrow on the last button on the Navigation Pane. You will see the menu shown in Figure 18-29. The options are explained below.

Figure 18-29 Navigation Pane shortcut menu

The **SHOW MORE BUTTONS** option restores the first option on the empty button to the Navigation Pane.

The **SHOW FEWER BUTTONS** option removes the last visible button on the Navigation Pane and places it on the empty button at the bottom of the Navigation Pane.

The **NAVBAR OPTIONS** option opens the dialog box shown in Figure 18-30.

This dialog box is used to display or hide buttons and change the order of the buttons on the Navigation Pane.

Figure 18-30 Navigation Pane Options dialog box

The **ADD OR REMOVE BUTTONS** option displays the options shown in Figure 18-31.

The options without a square frame like the Welcome and Groups options, shown in Figure 18-31 means that they will not appear on the Navigation Pane.

To restore a button to the Navigation Pane, open the Navigation Pane Options dialog box shown above in Figure 18-30 and select the corresponding option.

Figure 18-31 Add or Remove Buttons menu options

USING THE LAYOUT DESIGNER

Overview

In this lesson you will learn how to use the Layout Designer to modify the views. To modify the views, you will learn about the following:

- ☑ Layout Designer options
- ☑ Formatting toolbar
- ☑ Layout Designer toolbox
- ☑ Customizing tabs on a view
- ☑ Adding fields to a tab
- ☑ Adding graphics to a layout
- ☑ Changing the background color of a tab
- ☑ Using the Properties window
- ☑ Changing the label for a field on a layout
- ☑ Aligning fields on a layout
- ☑ Changing the tab stop order

LESSON 19

What Is A Layout?

A layout is how the fields and tabs are arranged on the view.

ACT! Layouts

ACT! comes with the layouts shown in Figure 19-1. Each layout can have different fields. An example of this is the Photo field shown in Figure 19-2. This is on the ACTDemo layout. The Basic Contact Layout - 800x600 layout does not have this field on the Personal Info tab.

Figure 19-2 Photo field on the Personal Info tab of the ACTDemo layout

Figure 19-1 ACT! Layouts

Layout File Extensions

As shown above in Figure 19-1, layout files have one of the file extensions explained below.

The **.CLY** extension is for contact layouts.
The **.GLY** extension is for group layouts.
The **.ALY** extension is for company layouts.
The **.OLY** extension is for opportunity layouts.

 The numbers after the Basic Layouts shown above in Figure 19-1, refer to the screen resolution. If your monitor or LCD has a resolution of 1024x768, that is the layout that would look best on your computer screen. What I noticed between these two layout resolutions is that some fields are in different places. This was probably done to accommodate the different screen resolutions. Figure 19-3 shows the 800x600 basic contact layout. Figure 19-4 shows the 1024x768 basic contact layout.

Figure 19-3 800x600 resolution basic contact layout

Figure 19-4 1024x768 resolution basic contact layout

Layout Designer

The Layout Designer shown in Figure 19-5 is used to change what the views, including the tabs, look like. You can change the background color, add fields, remove fields, rearrange the order of fields and much more.

In Lesson 16 you learned how to create new fields. Fields can only be used when they are on a layout. If an existing layout meets most of your needs, you can add the new fields to it or you can save an existing layout with a new file name and add the fields to the layout with the new file name. You can also create a new layout from scratch. Creating and modifying layouts require administrator or manager rights. While the layout modification exercises in this lesson are for the contact view and tabs, you can modify the company and group layouts also.

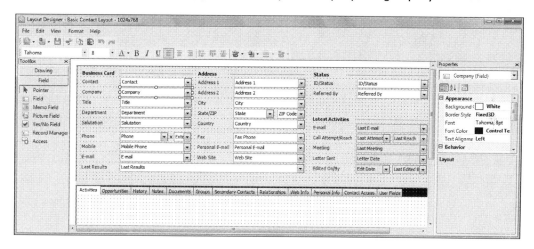

Figure 19-5 Layout Designer window

Layout Design Tips

There are some things to take into consideration when creating or modifying a layout, as discussed below.

① Many new layout designers are often more concerned with how a layout looks, rather then how functional it is. A primary goal of a layout is to make the data entry as easy as possible.

② If you find that you are constantly going from tab to tab to enter basic information, the layout may need to be modified. If there are fields on a layout that are not being used, consider deleting them from the layout.

③ Layouts that you modify or create can be used by other databases. If you plan to use a layout created or modified in one database in a different database, make sure that the second database has the same fields.

Layout Designer Options

There are a lot of options that you can use to design or modify the layout for a view. Many of them are similar to the options used to modify a report.

Edit Menu The options on this menu are the same as the editing options in word processing software. The exception to this is the **TABS** option. The tabs option opens the Edit Tabs dialog box. You can create new tabs, delete tabs and rearrange the order of tabs on a view.

View Menu The first option on this menu opens the Properties window shown in Figure 19-6.

Different options are available on the Properties window depending on the object that is selected in the layout before the Properties window is opened.

If the Properties window is too small, you can resize it by putting the mouse pointer on the edge of the window and dragging the edge to the size that you want.

As shown at the bottom of Figure 19-6, the tabs can be placed at the top or bottom of the tab section.

Figure 19-6 Properties window

The default is to display the tabs at the top. Figure 19-7 shows the tabs displayed at the bottom of the layout.

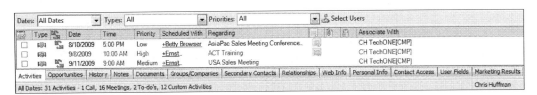

Figure 19-7 Tabs displayed at the bottom of the layout

The **Toolbox** option opens and closes the Toolbox that is on the left side of the Designer window.

The **View ⇒ Tab Stops ⇒ Show Tab Stops** option displays the order (in red numbers) that the Tab key will move, through the fields on the layout, as shown in Figure 19-8.

The **View ⇒ Enter Stops ⇒ Show Enter Stops** option will display the order (in green numbers) that the Enter key will move, through the fields on the layout. It looks like the one for Tab stops.

. . . .

Format Menu The options on this menu are used to align, size and space the fields on the layout.

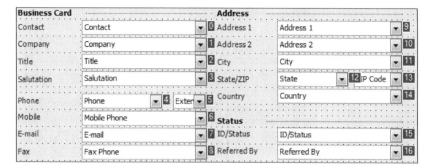

Figure 19-8 Tab key order for a layout

Layout Designer Formatting Toolbar

The first nine buttons on the toolbar shown in Figure 19-9 are the same buttons that are on the formatting toolbar in most word processors. The remaining buttons are explained in Table 19-1. The buttons on this toolbar are used to change the look of objects like fields or labels on the layout.

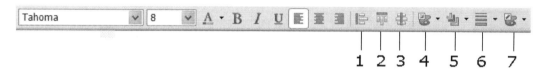

Figure 19-9 Layout Designer Formatting toolbar

Button	Description
1	Aligns the selected object(s) on the left side of the object. (1)
2	Aligns the selected object(s) on the top of the object. (1)
3	Aligns the selected object(s) on the center of the object. (1)
4	Select the background color of the object. (2)
5	The options shown in Figure 19-10 are used to add a border around the object.
6	Change the size (height) of a line. (3)
7	Change the color of a line. (3)

Table 19-1 Layout Designer Formatting toolbar buttons explained

(1) This option is only available if two or more objects are selected. The align options are also available on the shortcut menu shown in Figure 19-11.

(2) If you want to match the color of an existing background on the layout, view the **BACKGROUND COLOR** option on the Properties window in the top portion of the view or the tab that has the color that you want to match.

(3) The border is created by using a Drawing Object. This option is not used for fields.

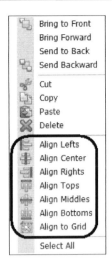

Figure 19-10 Border Style options

Figure 19-11 Object shortcut menu

Layout Designer Toolbox

Figures 19-12 and 19-13 show the tabs on the Toolbox.

The **FIELD** tab has all of the field types that can be added to a layout.

The **DRAWING** tab contains other objects that can be added to a layout.

Figure 19-12 Field tab options

Figure 19-13 Drawing tab options

The **MEMO FIELD** is a free form field that is used as a comments field. It is similar to the fields on the User Fields tab. The difference is that you can allow more text to be entered into a memo field.

The **YES/NO FIELD** is a check box field. The Yes/No fields that you have seen on the layout are some of the fields used to filter records.

Tabs Overview

In previous lessons you have entered data in fields on the tabs. The tabs in ACT! have features that you need to be aware of before you modify them. The following tabs are **SYSTEM TABS**: Notes, History, Activities, Opportunities, Groups/Companies, Secondary Contacts and Documents. If you do not need these tabs you can hide them. Each of these tabs has its own table in the database and because of this, you cannot customize these tabs like you can the other tabs that come with ACT! or tabs that you create. This is the reason that you can enter an unlimited number of records on each of these tabs for the same contact. This is known as **RELATIONAL** data.

The detail views in ACT! come with tabs. If you need to add more fields to an existing tab or if you want to put certain fields on a tab by themselves, you can. The only limitation is that you cannot add a field to a tab that is already on a tab.

Customizing Tabs

Tabs are used to organize fields. If there are fields that are only used for a season or promotion, it may be a good idea to put them on their own tab or create a layout for them. If the order of the tabs on a layout does not meet your needs or your users needs, you can change the order that the tabs are in. An example would be if you rarely use the History tab. Moving it to the last position in the row of tabs may be a good idea.

Exercise 19.1: Create A Tab On A Layout

In this exercise you will create a new tab on the Basic Contact Layout and add the Specialized In field that you created in Exercise 16.6 to the layout.

1. Tools ⇒ Define Layouts ⇒ Contact. You should see the words **BASIC CONTACT LAYOUT - 800x600** in the Title bar of the Layout Designer window.

2. Edit ⇒ Tabs, then click the **ADD TAB** button on the Edit Tabs dialog box.

3. Type My Tab in the Tab name field, as shown in Figure 19-14, then click OK.

Figure 19-14 Add Tab dialog box

4. On the Edit Tabs dialog box, click on the tab that you just created, then click the Move Up button once.

Hiding A Tab

To keep a tab from being displayed on the layout, click on the Tab name in the **SHOW TABS IN THIS ORDER** list, shown in Figure 19-15, then click the **<** button.

The tab will now be in the **HIDDEN TABS** list.

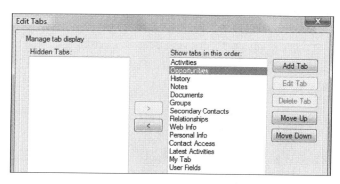

Figure 19-15 Edit Tabs dialog box

5. Your tab should be the second one from the bottom in the list, as shown above in Figure 19-15. Click the Close button.

Changing The Order Of The Tabs

The **MOVE UP** and **MOVE DOWN** buttons shown above in Figure 19-15 are used to change the order that the tabs are displayed in, from left to right on the layout.

Edit Tab Options

In addition to being able to add and hide tabs on the Edit Tabs dialog box you can also rename and delete tabs as discussed below.

① The **EDIT TAB** button is used to rename any tab except the System tabs.
② The **DELETE TAB** button is used to delete any tab except the System tabs. When deleting a tab, the fields on the tab are not deleted from the database. If you are not comfortable deleting a tab or are not 100% sure that the tab should be deleted, you should hide it instead.

Fields On A Layout

Like fields on a report, fields on a layout have two parts and work the same way that they do on a report. [See Lesson 17, Field vs Label]

Exercise 19.2: Adding Fields To A Tab

1. Click on the tab that you created at the bottom of the layout.

2. Click the **FIELD** button in the Toolbox.

3. Place the mouse pointer in the position where you want the upper left corner of the field to be placed on the layout. Draw a rectangle in the grid below the tabs. When you release the mouse button you should see the dialog box shown in Figure 19-16.

    The fields on this dialog box are fields that have not already been added to the layout. You may be wondering why you do not see the Specializes In field that you created. The reason that you do not see the field in the list is because it was created as a drop-down list, not a field.

    The **NEW FIELD** button is used to create a new field.

Figure 19-16 Select Field dialog box

4. Click on the Specialty field at the bottom of the list, then click the Add button.

5. Click on a blank space on the layout so that the field is not selected. If necessary, click on the label and drag it to the left so that it is not touching the field. It should look like the one shown in Figure 19-17.

Figure 19-17 Field added to a tab

 You can add more than one field to the layout at the same time. Click on the first field that you want to add in the Select Field dialog box. Press and hold down the **CTRL** key, then click on the other field(s) that you want to add, as shown in Figure 19-18. Once you have selected all of the fields, click the Add button.

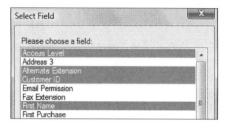

Figure 19-18 Multiple fields selected to be added to the layout

Text Boxes

Text boxes serve the same purpose that text fields serve in reports. They are used to add free form text to the layout. The one thing that text boxes are useful for in a layout is to provide helpful information or a reminder for the type of information that should be entered in a field. The other reason that I have added a text box to a layout is to add a name to a group or section of fields.

For example, there is no requirement that the fields have to be in a two column layout like you see on the Contact Detail view. I have had the need to create a custom layout. The majority of contacts did not have street addresses (don't ask), so I put the address fields all the way on the right side of the layout to make room for new fields that were needed.

To save space, I used a text box to indicate that the fields on the right side of the layout were address fields. Another use for a text box is to indicate that a field is required. If you need to add a text box to a layout, follow the steps below. For now you can just read the steps to become familiar with the process.

1. Click on the **DRAWING** button on the Toolbox, then click the Text button.

2. Draw a box on the layout where you need it. To add the text, double-click on the text box, then type in the text.

3. If you need to change an attribute of the text box like the font, you can change it on the Properties window.

Resizing Fields On A Layout

When you select a field or object, you will see **HANDLES** around the object, as shown in Figure 19-19.

Address
Address 1
Address 2
Address 3

Figure 19-19 Handles illustrated

If you need to resize several objects, select all of them first and then resize the objects. When you place the mouse pointer on a handle, you can drag the border of the object(s) to change the size.

When you add fields to a layout, it is very possible that the fields are not the exact size that you need them to be. There are two ways to resize fields as discussed below.

① **Use the anchor** This option is used to resize fields to match the size of an existing field in the layout. To use this method, select the field(s) that need to be resized. Press and hold down the **CTRL** key, then click on the field that has the dimensions that you want the other field(s) to be the size of. The handles on the field that you want to use to resize the other fields to should be white, as shown above in Figure 19-19. Format ⇒ Make Same Size ⇒ Select the option that you need (width, height or both).

② **Resize a field manually** Use this option when none of the fields on the layout is the size that you want. Select the field(s) that you want to resize. Place the mouse pointer on the side of the field that you want to resize and drag the handle to the size that you want all of the selected fields to be.

 If you want to move a field and label, you have to select both of them because they are separate objects.

Exercise 19.3: Adding Graphics To A Layout

If your company has a logo, you may want to add it to a layout. The steps below show you how to add a graphic file to a layout. You will add the ACT! icon to the tab that you created.

1. If there are fields where you want to put the graphic in the layout, move the fields out of the way.

2. Click the Drawing button in the Toolbox, then click the Image button. Draw a small box to the left of the drop-down field that you added to the tab.

3. Right-click on the image field and select Edit Properties. Navigate to the location of the graphic file that you want to add, then double-click on the image file name. To complete this exercise, use the ACT! icon, which is in this location: C:\Program Files\ACT\Act for Windows\act.ico.

4. Make the frame of the image smaller, then click on a blank space on the tab.

Exercise 19.4: Changing The Background Color Of A Tab

While this exercise will change the background color of a tab, the steps are the same to change the background color of the top portion of a layout.

1. Click on the tab that you created, then click on the arrow on the **BACKGROUND COLOR** button on the toolbar, as shown at the top of Figure 19-20.

Figure 19-20 Background color options

2. Click on the first yellow square in the second row. The background color of the tab that you created should now be yellow.

How To Use An Image For The Background

If you wanted to use an image for the background instead of a color, follow the steps below.

1. Click the button at the end of the Background Image option, in the **APPEARANCE** section of the Properties window illustrated in Figure 19-21.
2. Select the image file for the background.

Figure 19-21 Background options

Saving The Layout Changes

You have two options for saving changes to a layout. You can save the changes to the existing layout or save the changes as a new layout. In this exercise you will save the changes to a new layout.

1. File ⇒ Save As. You should see the Layouts folder. Type My Basic Contact Layout as the file name, then press Enter or click the Save button.

2.	Close the Layout Designer window. (File ⇒ Exit.)

View The Layout

1.	Open the Select Layout drop-down list, then select the layout that you just created, from the list shown in Figure 19-22.

Figure 19-22 Layout options

2.	Click on the tab that you created, then open the Specialty drop-down list, as shown in Figure 19-23.

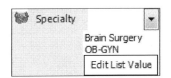

Figure 19-23 Drop-down list field added to a tab

3.	Switch back to the Basic Contact 800x600 layout.

Using The Properties Window To Change The Appearance Of A Field Or Label

Earlier in this lesson you used the Properties window to change the behavior of a tab. You can also use the options on this window to modify the appearance of a field. When you click on the field(s) that you want to modify, you can change the border style and font.

If you click on the label(s) that you want to modify, you can change the label text. The differences between the Properties window and the Edit Properties dialog box is that the Properties window has more options and you can modify more than one field or label at the same time.

Using The Edit Properties Dialog Box

The options shown in Figure 19-24 are used to modify the font properties. The tab shown in Figure 19-25 has options to modify the borders. To change any of these properties, right-click on the field or label that you want to modify and select **EDIT PROPERTIES**.

Figure 19-25 Borders tab options

Figure 19-24 Font tab options

Exercise 19.5: How To Change The Label For A Field On A Layout

In Lesson 16 you modified the User 1 field. When you viewed the field on the User Fields tab, the label was still User 1. In this exercise you will change the text that is displayed on the label for the User 1 field.

1. Open the Basic Contact Layout 800x600 in the Layout Designer.

2. On the User Fields tab, double-click on the User 1 label. The background color should have changed to white.

3. Highlight the text and type MD Type. Press Enter, then click on a blank space on the layout. The label for the field should look like the one shown in Figure 19-26.

Figure 19-26 Label changed

4. Save the changes to the layout and close the Layout Designer.

5. Click on the User Fields tab. The label for the first user field should have "MD Type", as shown above in Figure 19-26.

Annual Event Fields

This type of field is used to track dates of events that happen once a year. To create an annual event field you need administrator or manager level rights. You can create a reminder of the annual event by creating a recurring To-do activity.

Exercise 19.6: Create An Annual Event Field

In this exercise you will create a renewal date annual field.

1. Display the My Basic Contact Layout that you created earlier in this lesson.

2. Tools ⇒ Define Fields. Click the Create new field link.

3. Type Renewal Date in the Field name field.

4. Open the Field data type drop-down list and select Annual Event.

5. Check the **GENERATE HISTORY** option, then click Finish.

6. Close the Define Fields window. When prompted to modify the layout, click Yes.

7. Add the Renewal Date (Annual Event) field below the Specialty field on the tab that you created.

8. Add a 3D border to the Renewal Date field and save the changes.

When you view the layout, it should look like the one shown in Figure 19-27.

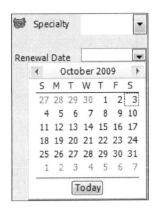

Figure 19-27 Annual Event field added to the layout

Annual Event Field Tips

These tips are for the options on the Define Fields dialog box.

① A text (character) field cannot be converted to an Annual Date field.
② A date field can be converted to an Annual Event field by changing the **SELECT A FIELD DATA TYPE TO CONVERT TO** option to Annual Event, as shown in Figure 19-28.

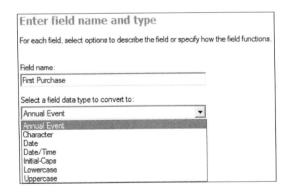

Figure 19-28 Data Type options

Exercise 19.7: Aligning Fields

In Lesson 17 you learned how to align fields on a report. Aligning fields on a layout is similar. I don't know for sure, but I get the feeling that aligning fields is not something that most people like to do, even though it makes the layout or report look more professional. Table 19-2 explains the align options. If you have to align fields, follow the steps below.

Option	How It Aligns
Lefts	On the left side of the object.
Center	On the center of the object.
Rights	On the right side of the object.
Tops	On the top of the object.
Middles	On the middle of the object.
Bottoms	On the bottom of the object.
To Grid	To the closest grid point (the dots on the layout) of the object that you right-click on. You need to have the **GRID** option turned on to see how this works.

Table 19-2 Alignment options explained

1. Open the layout that you created. Currently, there are no fields that need to be aligned on the layout.

2. On the User Fields tab, drag the User 2 field to the right, as shown in Figure 19-29.

Figure 19-29 User 2 field moved

3. Click on the field that needs to be aligned. In this exercise click on the User 2 field, then press and hold down the Shift key.

4. Click on the field that you want to align the field with. In this exercise click on the Specializes In field.

 The boxes around the field that you just selected should be white. The second field is known as the **ANCHOR** field because it is the field that the other fields will be aligned to.

5. Right-click on the Specializes In field, then select the align option that corresponds to how you need to align the field. In this exercise select **ALIGN LEFTS**. The User 2 field should now be aligned with the Specializes In field.

6. Close the layout, but do not save the changes.

7. Switch back to the Basic Contact 800x600 layout.

Exercise 19.8: How To Change The Tab Stop Order

In Lesson 3 you learned the purpose of the Tab key. Earlier in this lesson you learned that the tab order can be changed. In this exercise you will learn how to change the tab stop order on the Basic Contact layout.

1. In the Design Layout window save the Basic Contact Layout - 1024x768 as My Revised Tab Order Layout in the Layouts folder.

2. View ⇒ Tab Stops ⇒ Show Tab Stops.

3.   View ⇒ Tab Stops ⇒ Clear.

I find it easier to remove all of the existing tab stops and start from scratch, but you can change the order without clearing all of the tab stops. The way to include a field in the tab stop order is to click in the fields in the order that you want the Tab key to follow. When you click in a field without a tab stop number, the next available tab stop number is assigned.

4.   Click in the following fields in this order: Company, Contact, Address 1, Address 2, Title and Department. The fields should have the order shown in Figure 19-30.

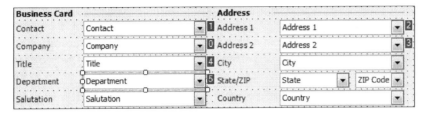

Figure 19-30 Tab stop order

5.   Right-click in the City field and type a 3 in the **ENTER THE NEW INDEX** field shown in Figure 19-31, then click OK.

You should see the tab order shown in Figure 19-32. If you do not see a number by the City field, click in the field.

Figure 19-31 Set Index dialog box

Figure 19-32 Modified tab stop order

Notice that the City field is the third field that the Tab key will go to instead of the Address 2 field shown earlier in Figure 19-30.

The **SET INDEX** dialog box is used to insert a field into the existing tab order, but there is no way to remove a field from the tab order without clearing all of the tab stops in the index and starting over.

6.   View ⇒ Tab Stops ⇒ Show Tab Stops.

7.   Save the changes and close the layout. You can test the new tab order. When you finish, switch back to the Basic Contact 800x600 layout.

UPGRADING, IMPORTING, EXPORTING & SYNCHRONIZING DATABASES

Overview

In this lesson you will learn the following importing, exporting and synchronizing database techniques:

- ☑ Upgrading older ACT! databases
- ☑ Importing data from another ACT! database
- ☑ Mapping fields to import
- ☑ Importing data from a text delimited file
- ☑ Exporting data from one ACT! database to another ACT! database
- ☑ Exporting data to a text delimited file
- ☑ Synchronizing data
- ☑ Creating Sync Sets
- ☑ Create remote databases
- ☑ Unpack and restore remote databases
- ☑ Creating and using subscription lists

Importing Data

Importing data is used to copy records from one data source (often a database) to another data source. This process can consolidate records from several data sources into one. You can also import data and add it to a drop-down list. You have already learned to manually add items to a drop-down list using the Define Fields dialog box. Later in this lesson you will learn another way to add data to a drop-down list.

The **DESTINATION** data source is the file that records will be copied to. This data source must be open before the import process begins. The **SOURCE** data source is the file that has the records that you want to copy.

You can import all of the records in the data source or you can select specific records to import. Suppose you are planning to do a mailing to all contacts in NY and a co-worker has a database of contacts in NJ, NY and PA. You can select to only import the contacts in NY from the co-workers database.

If you think that you will have the need to use the Help system while using the Import or Export Wizard, you should open the Help system and minimize it before starting the wizard because you cannot open the Help system after either of these wizards open.

While not required, it is best to close ACT! and reopen it after importing or exporting data.

Upgrading Older ACT! Databases

If you want to import data from a database from a previous version of ACT!, you have to upgrade the database by opening it in ACT! 2010 first. If you try to import records from a database from a previous version of ACT! without opening the database in the current version of ACT! first, you will see the message shown in Figure 20-1. This does not apply to ACT! Premium databases. Premium databases have to be downgraded to a non premium database to be imported.

Figure 20-1 Unable to connect message

Exercise 20.1: How To Upgrade A Database To The Current Version

In this exercise you will upgrade a database that was created in ACT! 2009. This will let you use the database in the current version of ACT! or import records from it into the database that you use with ACT! 2010.

1. File ⇒ Open Database.

2. Navigate to your folder if necessary, then double-click on the RecordsToImport.pad file.

3. When you see the dialog box shown in Figure 20-2, type in the user name Chris Huffman.

   Do not enter a password, then click OK.

Figure 20-2 Log On dialog box

4. Click No when you see the message shown in Figure 20-3.

Figure 20-3 Backup database message

This message is asking if you want to back up this database. You can select No because this is not live data. Make sure that you have another copy. Making a copy of the database outside of ACT! is quicker then letting ACT! make a backup copy.

This message is also letting you know that the database that you are trying to open must be updated to the version of ACT! that you are currently running.

5. Click Yes when prompted to update to the database, as shown in Figure 20-4.

Figure 20-4 Update database message

 If you get an error message during the update process, start the process again.

6. When you see the message shown in Figure 20-5, click OK. In a few seconds, the RecordsToImport database will open.

Figure 20-5 Updated database message

Exercise 20.2: How To Import Data From Another ACT! Database

Importing data is not as complicated as it may sound. The primary reason that many people import data is so that they can work with fewer databases.

In this exercise you will import data from the database that you updated in Exercise 20.1. In this exercise, the **MY_ACTDEMO** database is the destination data source and the **RECORDSTOIMPORT** database is the source database. The **IMPORT WIZARD** will walk you through the import process.

Step 1: Select The Import File Type And File

1. Open the My_ACTDemo database. This is the database that the records will be imported into.

2. File ⇒ Import. You should see the Import Wizard dialog box. Click Next.

3. Select the ACT! Database (12x) file type if it is not already selected. The options in the File Type drop-down list shown in Figure 20-6 are the types of files (data sources) that you can import into ACT!.

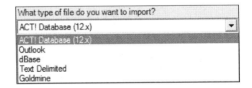

Figure 20-6 Import file types

Step 2: Specify Source

1. Click the **BROWSE** button, then double-click on the file RecordsToImport.pad in your folder. This file name should now be in the **FILE NAME AND LOCATION** field, as shown in Figure 20-7.

    If the ACT! database that you are importing is password protected, you will have to enter a user name and password before you can import it.

Figure 20-7 Specify Source screen

2. Click Next.

Step 3: Specify Record Type(s)

As shown in Figure 20-8, you can import Contact, Group, Company and Opportunity records.

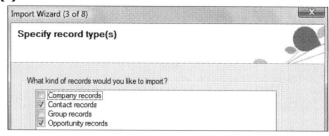

Figure 20-8 Specify record type(s) screen

1. Check the **CONTACT RECORDS** and **OPPORTUNITY RECORDS** options, then click Next.

Step 4: Mapping Fields

Mapping fields as shown in Figure 20-9 matches fields in the source database (the column on the left) to fields in the target database (the column on the right).

Mapping ensures that the data that you are importing is placed in the correct fields in the destination database.

When importing data, you should pay close attention to the field mappings.

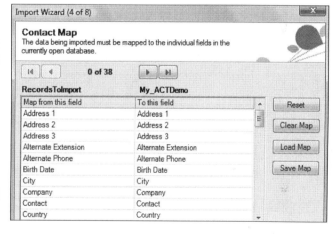

Figure 20-9 Contact Map screen

If you need to make changes or plan to import data from the same data source on a frequent basis, you should create a map. A map will save how the fields are matched between the two data sources.

The mapping tool is useful because the next time that you import the same fields from the same source database, you can load the map and not have to worry about mapping the fields. Even though you may load a map of the settings, it is a good idea to scan the list in case a field in the destination or source database has been modified. There are five import maps that you can use: Company, Contact, Group, Opportunity and Secondary.

Field names that are the same in both databases will automatically be mapped to each other, as shown above in Figure 20-9. If you have to create the data source that will be imported, it will make setting up the import easier if you use field names that are in the destination database. You can also rename the fields in the source database to match the names in the destination database before starting the import process.

How To Map A Field

The steps below show you how to map a field. The process is the same for all of the data that can be mapped. The goal of mapping fields is to make sure that each of the fields that you need to import has a field in the database that it will be added to, otherwise, all of the data that should be imported will not be.

To map a field, open the drop-down list in the second column and select the field that best matches the field in the first column, as shown in Figure 20-10.

If you do not see a field that is appropriate, you can select an available **USER** field, then modify the layout once the data has been imported. You can also create a new field.

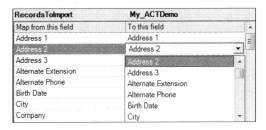

Figure 20-10 Field mapping illustrated

1. Scroll to the end of the list of fields. Open the drop-down list for the Web Site field and select **USER 4**. This will place the data that is in the Web Site field in the User 4 field.

2. Click Next.

Loading Maps

The steps below demonstrate how to load an existing map and how to save a map. You will learn how to create a map later in this lesson. For now you can just read this section, then go to Step 5: Opportunity Map, because you do not have a map to load.

1. Click the **LOAD MAP** button.

2. Navigate to the folder that has the map that you want to use, then double-click on the map file.

3. If any fields need to be remapped change them now, then click Next.

Saving Maps

If you create a map, you can save it so that you can use it later. In this part of the exercise you will save the map that you are currently using.

1. Click the **SAVE MAP** button.

2. Save the map in your folder. Type in the file name, then press Enter. If you click the Load Map button you should see the map that you just created. Click Next.

Step 5: Opportunity Map

The options on the screen shown in Figure 20-11 are used to map the opportunity fields, as well as, load and save maps for opportunities.

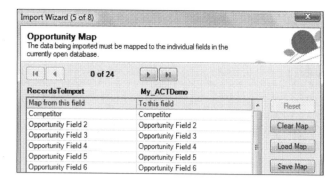

Figure 20-11 Opportunity Map screen

1. Click Next because there are no opportunity fields that need to be mapped.

Step 6: Product Map Options

The options shown in Figure 20-12 are used to map the products.

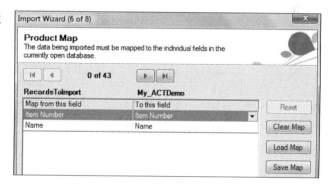

Figure 20-12 Product Map screen

1. Click Next because there are no product fields that need to be mapped.

Step 7: Specify Merge Options

The options shown in Figure 20-13 are used to select the merge options for contacts, groups, companies and opportunities.

The options available at the top of this screen depend on the types of records that were selected to be imported, as shown earlier on the third wizard screen shown in Figure 20-8.

Figure 20-13 Specify Merge Options screen

The **INCLUDE ATTACHMENTS** option allows attachments to be imported.

The **CONFIRM EACH MATCH** option is used to view each duplicate record to make sure that it really is a duplicate.

The **INCLUDE OTHER USERS PUBLIC ACTIVITIES** option is used to import the activities that other people have created for the contacts that will be imported.

The options shown in Figures 20-14 to 20-17 are used to select what you want to happen if the source records match or do not match the destination records. By default, ACT! considers contact records a "match" if two records have the same Contact name, Company and Phone number.

You can specify that the most recent record, whether it is the destination or source record, be imported. You can also specify how you want to handle data on the Notes, History, Activities, Opportunities and Secondary Contacts tabs. These options are useful when you only want to import certain information from the source records.

Figure 20-14 Contact record merge options

Figure 20-15 Group record merge options

Figure 20-16 Company record merge options

Figure 20-17 Opportunity record merge options

 If you change any of the default options on Figures 20-14 to 20-17 for an import or export and then run another import or export, the options that you selected the first time will still be selected. Therefore, it is a good idea to check every screen in the Import or Export Wizard if you previously imported or exported data without closing and reopening ACT!.

Contact Merge Options

1. Click the Contact button.

2. In the second column on the Contact Merge Options dialog box shown earlier in Figure 20-14, change the History and Secondary contacts options to **DO NOT ADD**.

3. Click OK, then click Next.

Step 8: Completing The Import Wizard

You should see the last wizard screen shown in Figure 20-18. In this exercise, the last step is step 8. If group or company records will be merged, there would be more steps.

Above the Details button is a message indicating that the import can be completed. If there was a problem, clicking the Details button will let you see more information about the problem as shown below.

Figure 20-18 Import options that you selected

Figure 20-19 shows a potential problem with the import that you are creating now.

In this example the reason that you cannot import data for the Last Yrs Purchases field is because the field has been mapped to a field with a different data type. If you needed to import data into the field, you would have to select a field with a compatible data type.

Figure 20-19 Import/Export Details information

Run The Import

If you are satisfied with all of the options that you have selected, you can click the Finish button. If you want to review the options that you have selected or want to change something, click the Back button until you see the screen that has the option(s) that you want to review or change.

1. If you made changes, click Next until you get to the screen shown earlier in Figure 20-18. You should see that the message states that all fields are compatible.

2. Click Finish on the last wizard screen. The records will be imported.

    You will see the dialog box shown in Figure 20-20. It lets you know that the records are being imported.

Figure 20-20 Importing Data dialog box

Exercise 20.3: How to Import Data From A Text Delimited File

The is probably the most used import file type other than an ACT! database. This is because most word processing and spreadsheet software packages can save files in the text delimited format. A text delimited file means that the text (fields) are delimited (separated) by a specific character like a tab or comma.

 You should open the text delimited file before you start the import and look at the data so that you will be able to select the correct options for the import.

1. File ⇒ Import, then click Next on the first wizard window.

2. Select **TEXT DELIMITED** as the file type to import.

3. Click the Browse button. Change the Files of type to Text files (*.txt) if necessary, then double-click on the Contacts table.txt file.

4. Click Next. Select the Contact Records option, then click Next.

5. Select the **TAB** option shown in Figure 20-21, then click Next.

These are the options for text-delimited files.

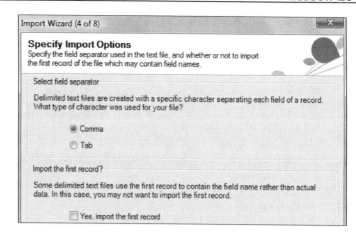

Figure 20-21 Specify Import Options screen

The **SELECT FIELD SEPARATOR** options are used to select how the fields in the text-delimited file are separated.

Before you can import a delimited file, you need to know how the fields are separated. If the first record in the text file has field names or column headings, clear the **YES, IMPORT THE FIRST RECORD** option.

Selecting A Predefined Map

The dialog box shown in Figure 20-22 is used to select an existing map.

This option is helpful if you will be importing data frequently.

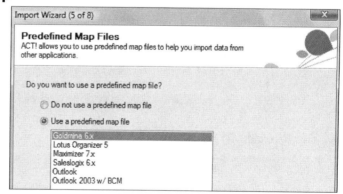

Figure 20-22 Predefined Map Files screen

6. Select the option, **DO NOT USE A PREDEFINED MAP FILE**, then click Next.

How To Map Fields

The dialog box shown in Figure 20-23 shows the fields that are in the text delimited file.

The fields shown in the **TO THIS FIELD** column are the fields that ACT! could map on its own. The blank fields in this column may or may not have a corresponding field in the file that you are importing data from.

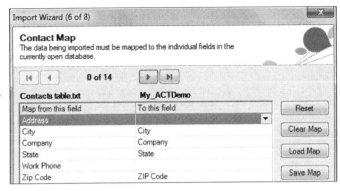

Figure 20-23 Contact Map screen

7. Open the drop-down list for the Address field, then select the Address 1 field.

8. Map the Work Phone field to the Phone field.

    You should have the options selected that are shown in Figure 20-24.

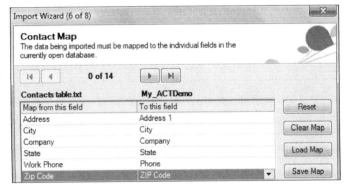

Figure 20-24 Address and Work Phone fields mapped

View The Records To Be Imported

You can view the records that will be imported before you actually import them. Fields that are empty in the Preview Data column means that there is no data in that field to be imported. After looking at a few records, you will be able to tell whether or not you have mapped the fields correctly.

9. Click the ▶ button, illustrated in Figure 20-25. You should see the preview data shown in Figure 20-25.

10. Look at a few more records to make sure that the fields are mapped correctly.

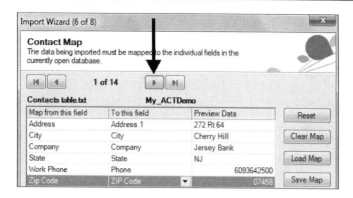

Figure 20-25 Preview data

Finish The Import

11. Click Next on the Contact Map screen. Click Next on the Specify Merge Options screen because you want to add all of the records in the text file to the database.

12. Click Finish. The records will be imported.

Exercise 20.4: How To Import A List

If you are creating a new database you will have a lot to do. One task that is time consuming is typing in the entries for drop-down lists. Importing the entries from a list is faster. The Import option can be used to add or append items that you have in a text file to a drop-down list.

1. Open the Define Fields dialog box, then select the Manage drop-down lists link.

2. Select the Specializes In list, then click the Edit drop-down list link.

3. Click Next on the Enter drop-down list name and type screen.

4. Click the Import drop-down list items link, then click the **BROWSE** button on the Import List Items dialog box.

5. Double-click on the Specialties.txt file in your folder.

   Check the **INCLUDE DESCRIPTIONS** option shown in Figure 20-26.

Figure 20-26 Import List Items dialog box

The Include descriptions option will import any descriptions that are in the file that you are importing data from.

The **APPEND IMPORTED ITEMS** option should be checked if the list that you are importing to already has records and you want to add more records to it or if you want to overwrite some of the items that currently exist in the drop-down list. If this option is not checked, all of the current records in the list will be over written.

6. Click the Import button.

   Your list should look like the one shown in Figure 20-27.

Value	Description
Brain Surgery	
OB-GYN	
Liver Disease	Import #1
Root Canal	Import #2
Physical Therapy	Import #3
Nutrition	Import #4
Neurology	Import #5

Figure 20-27 Imported drop-down list values

7. Click Finish, then close the Define Fields dialog box.

How To Create A Text Delimited File

In the previous exercises, you learned how to import text files to fill drop-down lists. The steps below show you how to create a text delimited file that can be imported. Each line of data in the text file equals one option in the drop-down list.

1. Open NotePad.

2. Type the data shown in Figure 20-28 in the text file. You have to type the quotes.

   At the end of each line, you must press Enter.

   "Product 1", "New Shoes"
   "Product 2", "Boots"

   Figure 20-28 Data for the text delimited file

3. Save the file in your folder as New Products.txt.

Exporting Data

The Exporting Data option is used to copy records from one ACT! database to another ACT! database or to a file. This is useful if you want to give someone some of the records in the database or if someone else needs to use or view the contacts in your database in another software package.

You can also use the Export option if you want to remove records that you do not use anymore. You can keep the records that you do not use in a separate database so that you will still have access to them. Once you export them, you can delete them from the current database. Many of the screens on the Export Wizard are the same as the ones on the Import Wizard.

 You cannot export records to a database that has not already been created.

Exercise 20.5: How To Export Data To Another ACT! Database

In this exercise you will select records that will be exported to another ACT! database. This is one way that you can archive records that are not needed.

Step 1: Look Up The Records To Export

Unless you are going to export the entire database, you need to look up the records that you want to export before you start the export process.

1. In the My_ACTDemo database, create a lookup to find all contacts in NY.

Step 2: Select The Export File Type And File Name

1. File ⇒ Export. You should see the Welcome Export screen. Click Next.

2. Select ACT! Database 12.x as the File type to export.

3. Click the **BROWSE** button, then double-click on the RecordsToImport.pad file. This is the database that the records will be exported to.

    You should have the options selected that are shown in Figure 20-29.

    Click Next.

Figure 20-29 Specify Destination screen

Step 3: Select The Type Of Records To Export

1. Select the **CONTACT RECORDS** option, then select the **CURRENT LOOKUP** option, as shown in Figure 20-30.

    In this exercise you only selected one record type to export. You can select as many record types as you need.

Figure 20-30 Specify Record Type(s) screen

2. Click Next. In a few seconds you will see the dialog box shown in Figure 20-31.

Step 4: Contact Map Options

Use the screen shown in Figure 20-31 to verify that the correct number of records will be exported. You should also check to make sure that the contact fields are mapped properly.

As you can see, 24 contact records will be exported. That is the same number of records that is in the lookup.

Figure 20-31 Contact Map screen

1. Change the Last Years Purchases field to blank so that the data in the field will not be exported.

2. Click Next once you have verified that all of the information is correct.

 If you had selected more record types to export, you would see a screen like the one shown above in Figure 20-31 for each record type.

Step 5: Specify Merge Options

The options on this screen work the same way that they do on the Import wizard.

1. Clear the Include other users public activities option.

2. Click the Contact button.

    Change the options in Table 20-1.

Source Records Match	Change To
Notes	Do not change
History	Do not change
Activities	Do not change
Secondary Contacts	Do not change
Source Records Do Not Match	**Change To**
History	Do not add
Activities	Do not add
Secondary Contacts	Do not add

Table 20-1 Contact options to change

3. The dialog box should have the options shown in Figure 20-32. I selected these options to reduce the time the export process will take. Click OK.

Figure 20-32 Contact Merge Options dialog box

4. Click Next.

   On the screen shown in Figure 20-33, you should see that all fields are compatible.

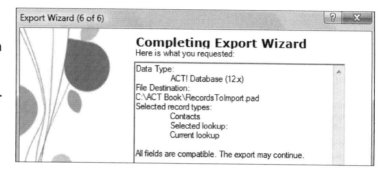

Figure 20-33 Export options that you selected

5. Click Finish. The contact records will be exported to the RecordsToImport database.

Viewing The Records That Were Exported

1. Open the RecordsToImport database and view some of the records that were added to the database. Leave the RecordsToImport database open to complete the next exercise.

Exercise 20.6: How To Export Data To A Text Delimited File

Just like you can import data from a text delimited file, you can export data to a text delimited file. You can export contact, group and company records, but not at the same time. They have to be exported separately. In this exercise you will export all of the contact records in the RecordsToImport database to a text delimited file.

1. File ⇒ Export. Click Next.

2. Select the File type, Text Delimited, then click the Browse button. Make sure that the File type is **TEXT FILES**.

3. Type MyTextExport in the File name field on the Open dialog box, then press Enter.

4. Click Next. Select the Contact Records and All records options, then click Next.

Select The Export Options

5. Select the Tab field separator option.

    Select the option, **YES, EXPORT FIELD NAMES**, as shown in Figure 20-34, then click Next.

Figure 20-34 Specify Export Options screen

How To Remove A Field From The Export

The options on the fifth screen will vary depending on the type of records that are selected to be exported.

On the dialog box shown in Figure 20-35, you can select which fields will be exported. You can also rearrange the order that the fields will be exported in and delete fields that you do not want to export. If there are fields that you do not want to export, you can follow the steps below.

Figure 20-35 Contact Map screen

6. Click on the field that you do not want to export. In this exercise click on the Create Date field.

7. Click the **REMOVE FIELD** button, then remove the following fields: Add to ACT! Note and E-mail.

If you remove fields from the **CONTACT MAP** screen and then come back to the Map screen, the fields that you removed will reappear on the screen shown above in Figure 20-35.

Exercise 20.7: How To Reorder Fields And Create A Map

Reordering fields is not the easiest task to complete on the Contact Map screen because it does not have Move up and Move down buttons. The fields that will be exported in this exercise would be more helpful if the address fields were together. Like the Contact Map screen that you saw earlier in Figure 20-31, you can select a different field from the drop-down list.

1. Change the Alternate Extension field to the City field, as shown in Figure 20-36.

    Change the Alternate Phone field to the State field.

    Change the Birth Date field to the Zip Code field.

    Change the second City field to the Country field.

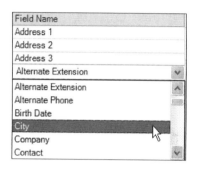

Figure 20-36 How to select a different field

2. Delete the second Country field and all of the fields below it.

    You should have the fields that are shown in Figure 20-37.

Figure 20-37 Fields that will be exported

3. Click the Save Map button. Type `MyTextExportMap` as the file name.

4. Click Next, then click Finish.

5. Open the My_ACTDemo database.

View The Exported Data

1. In Windows Explorer double-click on the file, MyTextExport.txt in your folder. The file should look like the one shown in Figure 20-38.

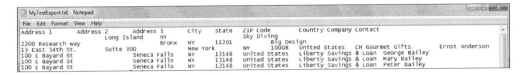

Figure 20-38 Exported data

Synchronizing Data

 In order to synchronize data, the main database has to be on a server. If your database is on your computers hard drive, you can skip the rest of this lesson.

This process allows data to be exchanged between databases so that both copies of the database have the same information. Synchronization sends and receives data changes between the databases which keeps both sets of data the same.

An example of when to use synchronization is if you are sharing a database at work with other people and you put a copy of the database on your laptop to go on a business trip. While you are on the trip, you add new contacts and modify existing ones in the copy of the database on your laptop. The people in the office make changes to the database on the server. When you return to the office, the two copies of the database do not have the same information. They need to be synchronized so that both copies of the database have the changes that were made to both databases.

Prior to synchronizing databases, you have to set up how you want to synchronize the databases. The database must be open and locked before you can synchronize it.

There are two databases involved in the synchronization process: The **MAIN** database is the one that will send and update the remote database. The **REMOTE** database receives changes from the main database. The synchronization usually takes place on a network.

 Files stored in Personal folders will not be synchronized.

 If the same field was changed for the same contact in the main and remote databases, the change with the most recent date is the change that is kept.

Sync Set

You can synchronize all of the contacts in the main database or you can synchronize a subset of contacts. A Sync Set is the tool used to specify the data and users that can access the remote database. You can use a query to create the Sync Set. Sync Sets can be created in the main or remote database. Only an administrator or manager of the main database can create a remote database using a Sync Set.

. . . .

Setting Up The Synchronization

The options needed to set up the synchronization are part of the Synchronization tool that is available in the main and remote databases. Only the tasks that can be used in each database are available.

Exercise 20.8: How To Synchronize Databases

In this exercise you will complete all of the tasks for the main database portion of the synchronization process. The three steps to setting up synchronization on the main database are discussed below.

① **Enable synchronization** Turns on synchronization so that data can be transmitted.
② **Create the Sync Set** This file stores the instructions for what data should be synchronized.
③ **Create the remote database** The remote database has to be created so that records can be synchronized.

Enable Synchronization

1. Tools ⇒ Synchronization Panel.

2. Click on either of the **ENABLE SYNCHRONIZATION** options illustrated in Figure 20-39, then click Yes to enable synchronization.

   Once synchronization has been turned on, more options on this screen will be available. The order that the administrative tasks are listed in, is the order that the tasks have to be completed in.

Figure 20-39 Synchronization screen

Create A Sync Set

In this part of the exercise you will create a sync set that uses an existing query to determine which records will be sent to the remote database.

1. Click the **MANAGE SYNC SET** link, then click the **CREATE NEW SYNC SET** link.

2. Type MyCustomers in the Sync Set name field.

   Type Customers & Prospects in AZ in the Description field, as shown in Figure 20-40, then click Next.

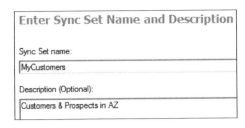

Figure 20-40 Sync Set Name and Description screen

Select The Users

On this screen, select the people that you want to have access to the remote database.

3. Select Chris Hoffman and Betty Browser. You should see the two names in the list on the right. Click Next.

Select The Contacts

The options shown in Figure 20-41 are used to select the contacts that will be copied to the remote database. The number of contacts in the main database is displayed on this screen.

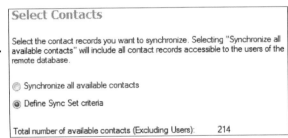

The **DEFINE SYNC SET CRITERIA** option is used to select specific contacts to send to the remote database.

Figure 20-41 Select contacts screen

4. Select the Define Sync Set criteria option, then click Next.

Create Or Edit The Sync Set Criteria

In this part of the exercise you will create the criteria that will be used to select the records that will be sent to the remote database.

1. Click the **CREATE CRITERIA** link. You will see the Sync Set Criteria dialog box shown in Figure 20-42. It looks like the Advanced Query dialog box that you used in Lesson 11.

Figure 20-42 Sync Set Criteria dialog box

You can create the criteria from scratch on this dialog box or you can use a query that has already been created.

2. Click the Open button, then double-click on the My Customers & Prospects in AZ query in your folder. You will see the query criteria. You can use the query as is or you can edit it, then save it with a new name and use the new query as the sync set criteria.

3. Click OK to close the Sync Set Criteria dialog box.

4. You will see the query criteria on the screen shown in Figure 20-43.

   Click Next.

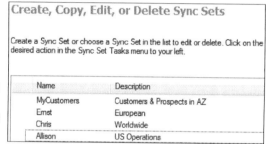

Figure 20-43 Create or Edit Sync Set Criteria screen

5. Click Finish. You will see the screen shown in Figure 20-44.

   The options on the Sync Sets screen are the sync sets that have been created for the synchronization process that is currently open. There can be more than one sync set associated with a database.

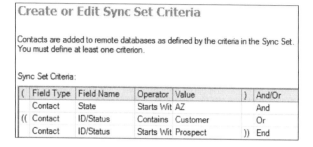

Figure 20-44 Sync Sets screen

6. Click the **HOME** button.

ℕ𝔼𝕎 Remote Database Creation

The option on the screen shown in Figure 20-45 is used to select the number of remote databases that you need to create.

Figure 20-45 Remote Database Creation screen

Create The Remote Database

1. Click either of the **CREATE REMOTE DATABASE** links on the Synchronization Task screen.

2. Select 4 on the Remote Database Creation screen shown above in Figure 20-45. If your computer is running slow, select 2 instead of 4, then click Next.

3. Type MyRemoteDB in the Remote Database Name field.

4. If your folder is not in the Location field, as shown in Figure 20-46, click the Browse button and select your folder, then click Next.

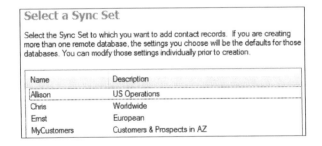

Enter Remote Database Name and Location

If you are creating more than one remote database, the name you select will be used as the basis for naming all the databases created in this session.

Remote Database Name:

MyRemoteDB

Location:

C:\ACT Book   Browse...

Figure 20-46 Remote Database Name and Location screen

5. Select the MyCustomers sync set on the screen shown in Figure 20-47, then click Next.

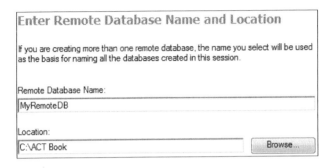

Select a Sync Set

Select the Sync Set to which you want to add contact records. If you are creating more than one remote database, the settings you choose will be the defaults for those databases. You can modify those settings individually prior to creation.

Name	Description
Allison	US Operations
Chris	Worldwide
Ernst	European
MyCustomers	Customers & Prospects in AZ

Figure 20-47 Select A Sync Set screen

Database Synchronization Options

The options on this screen are used to set synchronization options for the database.

The **ALLOW DATABASE SUPPLEMENTAL FILES TO SYNCHRONIZE** option is used when you want the reports, documents, layouts and templates in the main database to be sent to the remote database.

The two attachment options determine whether or not attachments will be sent to the remote database or synchronized.

The **NUMBER OF DAYS THAT CAN PASS WITHOUT SYNCHRONIZATION** option determines when the remote database has to be synchronized.

If attachments are not needed in the remote copy of the database, it is best not to select them because they increase the synchronization time.

1. Clear the Allow database supplemental files to synchronize option.

2. Select the **DO NOT ALLOW THIS DATABASE TO SYNCHRONIZE ATTACHMENTS** option.

3. Open the drop-down list and select the option, **DO NOT INCLUDE ATTACHMENTS IN REMOTE DATABASE CREATION**.

   You should have the options selected that are shown in Figure 20-48.

   Click Next.

Figure 20-48 Database Synchronization Options screen

Sync Server Connection Options

The options shown on the screen in Figure 20-49 are used to select the Server Connection option.

Your machine name will automatically be filled in. I removed mine from the figure for security reasons.

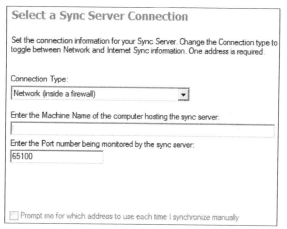

Figure 20-49 Sync Server Connection options

1. If necessary, select a different **CONNECTION TYPE**.

2. Enter the machine name if the correct one is not already filled in, then click Next.

Preview And Edit Remote Database Settings

The screen shown in Figure 20-50 displays all of the remote databases that will be created for the Sync Set. The data in each column can be changed individually for each database. Databases on this screen can be deleted. Clicking the **ADD A DATABASE** link creates another remote database.

Figure 20-50 Preview and Edit Remote Database Settings screen

3.   For this exercise, no changes need to be made. Click Next.

Build Remote Database Options

The options shown in Figure 20-51 only have to be filled in if the database has a password.

All remote databases that will be created will have the same password.

The databases in this exercise do not have a password, so you can skip the first step below.

Figure 20-51 Remote database password options

1.   Check the **PASSWORD PROTECT FILES** option, then enter the password in both fields shown above in Figure 20-51.

2.   Click Finish. You will see the screen shown in Figure 20-52. The remote database(s) will be created.

Figure 20-52 Building Remote Databases screen

When the process is finished, you will see the screen shown in Figure 20-53.

Clicking the link at the bottom of the screen will display the databases that have been created.

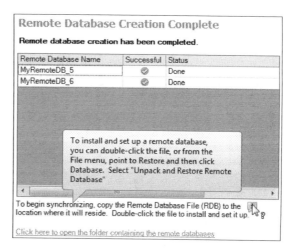

Figure 20-53 Remote Database Creation Complete screen

3. Close the Synchronization window.

Turning Synchronization On

Now that you have selected the sync options and created the remote database, the sync option needs to be turned on. When synchronization is turned on, the main database is set to listen for messages from the remote database. The synchronization will stay on until it is turned off. This is known as a communication.

1. Tools ⇒ Synchronize ⇒ Accept Incoming Syncs.

2. Accept the default port number.

    You may have a different port number then the one shown in Figure 20-54.

    Click OK twice to close both dialog boxes.

Figure 20-54 Port number dialog box

Using The Remote Database

The remote database must be unpacked and restored before it can be used and synchronized.

Exercise 20.9: How To Unpack And Restore The Remote Database

1. File ⇒ Restore ⇒ Database.

2. Select the **UNPACK AND RESTORE REMOTE DATABASE** option shown in Figure 20-55, then click OK.

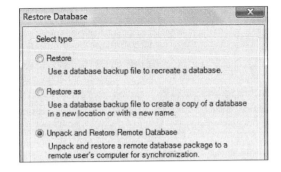

Figure 20-55 Restore Database dialog box

3. Click the first Browse button, then double-click on the MyRemoteDB.RDB_1 file. The **RDB** file is not the actual database.

The folder in the **DATABASE LOCATION** field is where you want to place the restored database. The default folder that you set up on the General tab on the Preferences dialog box is what appears in this field by default. You can change the folder for the database by typing in a different location or by clicking the Browse button and selecting the folder.

4. Type \Remote at the end of the Restore remote database location field.

5. Check the **SHARE THIS DATABASE WITH OTHER USERS** option.

    You should have the options shown in Figure 20-56.

Figure 20-56 Unpack and Restore Remote Database dialog box

6. Click OK. The Remote folder will be created. You will see the Restore Database progress window.

7. Click OK when the restore is complete.

Open And Use The Remote Database

The MyRemoteDB database that you restored will open automatically.

1.   Click No when you see the Synchronize with main database message.

The remote database will open. At this point you can add and modify records in the remote database, just like you can any other database.

2.   Go to the first record (Emily Dunn).

3.   On the Notes tab, click the Select Users button, then select Chris Huffman and click OK.

4.   Add a note. Type `This note was created in the remote database` in the Regarding field, then click OK. Leave the database open to complete the next exercise.

Using Subscription Lists To Add Contact Records To The Remote Database

If you are using a remote database and realize that you need records that are in the main database, you can create a subscription list to get the contact records that you need from the main database. The contact records that are added to the remote database from a subscription list are always synchronized unless they are deleted from the subscription list or deleted from the database.

Exercise 20.10: Create A Subscription List

In this exercise you will create a subscription list that retrieves information for several contacts. You should have the remote database open. For this exercise, that is the **MYREMOTEDB** database.

1.   Tools ⇒ Synchronization Panel.

2.   Click the **MANAGE SUBSCRIPTION LIST** link in the User Tasks section. The contact records that you see on the Manage Subscription list screen are the records that you have access to.

3.   Sort the records on the Sync Set column.

The records that have a check mark in the **SYNC SET** column shown in Figure 20-57 are the contact records that are currently part of the sync set.

The **VIEW SYNC SET QUERY** link will display the query shown earlier in Figure 20-43.

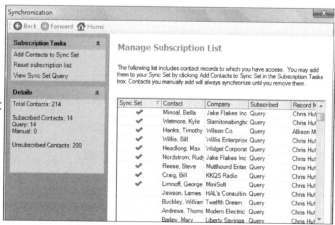

Figure 20-57 Manage Subscription List screen

4. Click the **ADD CONTACTS TO SYNC SET** link.

5. On the Contacts dialog box, add the first 10 companies shown in Figure 20-58, then click OK.

   Depending on the order that records are sorted in, you may have different companies displayed in the list. That's OK because this is practice. You will see the records in the Subscription list.

Figure 20-58 Contacts dialog box

I have the contacts sorted in ascending order (arrow pointing up on the first contact column).

6. Click Finish on the Synchronization window.

Manage Connection Information

There are two ways to move data between the main and remote databases as discussed below.

① **NETWORK (INSIDE A FIREWALL)** This option is used to synchronize through a virtual private network or remote application server.

② **APPLICATION SYNCHRONIZATION** This option requires ACT! and the main database to be open.

If you do not know if the sync will take place from behind a firewall, both connection types can be enabled.

1. Click the Home button if necessary, then click the **MANAGE CONNECTION INFORMATION** link in the User Tasks section.

2. Check the **PROMPT ME FOR WHICH ADDRESS TO USE** option at the bottom of the screen, then click Finish.

3. Close the Synchronization window.

Exercise 20.11: Synchronize The Database

So far in this lesson you have selected and designated a main database, turned the synchronization on, created a sync set, created a remote database and made changes to the remote database. The last step in the process is to sync the changes made in the remote database to the main database. There are two ways to sync a database as discussed below.

① **Manually** Synchronizes the database at any time.

② **Automatic** Synchronizes the database at pre-determined times.

In this exercise you will sync the remote database manually.

1. Tools ⇒ Synchronize ⇒ Synchronize Now.

2. For this exercise, select the Network option shown in Figure 20-59 unless you are working remotely, then click OK.

   Once the sync is completed, the 10 contacts that you just selected will be added to the remote database. There should be 10 more records in the MyRemoteDB_1 database.

Figure 20-59 Sync Connection dialog box

If you see a message saying the main database needs to accept incoming syncs, open the main database, in this exercise that would be the My_ACTDemo database, then Tools ⇒ Synchronize ⇒ Accept incoming syncs.

DATABASE MAINTENANCE & SECURITY

In this lesson you will learn how to use the following database maintenance tools and techniques:

- ☑ Delete database tool
- ☑ Backup tool
- ☑ Check and Repair tool
- ☑ Restoring databases
- ☑ Removing old data
- ☑ Using the Copy/Move Contact Data dialog box
- ☑ ACT! Scheduler
- ☑ ACT! Diagnostics

You will also learn the following security features:

- ☑ Creating, editing and deleting user accounts
- ☑ Password protecting a database
- ☑ Security roles and permissions
- ☑ Record access data security
- ☑ Password security and policies

LESSON 21

Database Maintenance

There are several things that you should do to keep a database working properly. If you are constantly adding and editing records in a database, you should back up the database frequently. Databases can become corrupt, which means that the database will not function properly and eventually may not open. It may run very slow or will not let you login. If you have a backup copy of the database you can restore it. You will have to re-enter any additions or changes that were made after the database was last backed up, but that is better than having to try to recreate the entire database. If you do not have a very recent backup, or worse, no backup at all, you will no longer have a database.

Many people say that they do not have time for maintenance. My thought is that it takes less time for maintenance then it does to type in all of the data again. More than likely, all of the notes and history records at the very least, cannot be recreated because you and anyone else that uses the database, probably cannot remember every note and activity that they created.

Most companies create a backup of all files that are on servers every night. If your database is on a server, you may not have to do the database maintenance tasks discussed in this lesson because they will be handled by the computer department in your company. The majority of the ACT! maintenance tasks require administrator rights and that no other user has the database open when you are performing these tasks. The easy way to tell if you have administrator rights is if the options on the Database Maintenance submenu are enabled.

ACT! has several database maintenance tools that you can use to keep the database running smoothly. These tools are listed below.

① Backup
② Check and repair
③ Removing old data

Tools ⇒ Database Maintenance, will display the options shown in Figure 21-1.

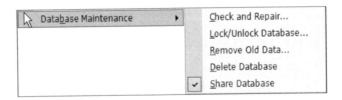

Figure 21-1 Database Maintenance tools

I do not consider all of the options on this menu a maintenance tool, but all of the options on the menu are covered in this lesson.

Locking A Database

If you need to perform any type of maintenance like deleting, restoring, repairing or updating a database other than creating a back up, you must lock the database first. Locking a database means that you are the only person that can have the database open.

How To Lock A Database

1. Tools ⇒ Database Maintenance ⇒ Lock/Unlock Database.

If no users are in the database, it is locked automatically. When locked, you will see the word **(LOCKED)** in the Title bar after the database name.

If users have the database open, you will see the Lock Database dialog box which will list all of the users that have the database open. On this dialog box you can specify how long they can keep the database open before they are locked out. A warning message will then be sent to each user telling them to close the database.

Exercise 21.1: Using The Delete Database Tool

This tool is used to delete a database and all of the files associated with the database. The steps below will show you how to delete a database. You can just read these steps now, because you do not have a database to delete.

1. Open the database that you want to delete.

2. Tools ⇒ Database Maintenance ⇒ Delete Database. You will see the message shown in Figure 21-2.

Figure 21-2 Delete Database message

3. Click Yes. You will see the message shown in Figure 21-3. Click Yes to delete the database. The database will now be deleted.

Figure 21-3 Proceed With Delete message

 Once you delete a database, you cannot restore or retrieve it.

The Backup Tool

There are three ways that you can create a back up copy of a database:

    ① Use Windows Explorer.
    ② Use the Save Copy As command.
    ③ Use the Back Up command.

Windows Explorer allows you to create a copy of the database. The **Save Copy As** command in ACT! also allows you to create a copy of the database, which you learned about in Lesson 1. Each database has additional files that the database needs and uses. Unless you select these files when using Windows Explorer, you will not make a complete back up of the database using this option. The Save Copy As command will automatically make a back up copy of the additional files.

The **Back Up** command has the same features as the Save Copy As command, plus it allows you to back up a database to disk, even if the database needs more than one disk. The back up files are saved in .zip format. The zip file format compacts files by removing the empty space in the file. The default file folder location for saving backups is:

Windows XP
C:\Documents and Settings\YourUserName\My Documents\ACT\ACT for Windows 12\Backup

Vista C:\Users\YourUserName\Documents\ACT\ACT for Windows 12\Backup

In addition to being able to back up databases, **PERSONAL FILES** can also be backed up. [See Lesson 10, What Are Supplemental Files?]

> When ACT! is installed, a backup folder is created on the same hard drive as the database. Please do not store your backups in this folder. There is nothing wrong with the folder, just hear me out. The goal of creating a backup is to have a copy of the database should something go wrong with the original one. If the "thing" that goes wrong is that the hard drive that the original database is on, dies or gets a virus, not only is the original database destroyed, so is the backup copy of the database if you store it on the same hard drive as the original database.
>
> This is why I do not understand the purpose of the Backup folder that is automatically created. The backup file should not be stored on the same hard drive as the original database. It should be stored on a different hard drive. This is also true for databases that are stored on a server.
>
> If your database is being backed up to the same server as the original database, do yourself a favor and start pricing an external hard drive if you do not already have one. Look for one that has the most space for $99 or less. You should be able to find a 500 or 750 GB drive for this price. There is an article on the web site for creating an image of the entire hard drive. www.tolana.com/tips/image.html

Exercise 21.2: How To Back Up A Database Using The Back Up Command

> Users with administrator or manager rights can back up a database, but only someone with administrator rights can restore a database.

In this exercise you will back up a database. You will save the backup file in the folder that you created. The reason that I am doing this is because I cannot guarantee that everyone that reads this book has an external device like an external hard drive, CD or DVD burner. The problem with CD's and DVD's in my opinion, is that for a reason that I do not understand, files that are copied to them are sometimes automatically set to **READ-ONLY**, which makes it difficult, if not impossible to use the file. CD-RW and DVD-RW formats work much better for me.

1. Open the RecordsToImport database.

2. File ⇒ Back Up ⇒ Database, then click the Browse button.

3. Navigate to and select your folder, then click the Save button.

    You should see the folder that you selected in the field on the dialog box, as shown in Figure 21-4.

    Selecting the **INCLUDE ATTACHMENTS** option will back up the files in the Attachments folder.

Figure 21-4 Back Up Database dialog box

4. Click OK. You will see the dialog box shown in Figure 21-5.

Figure 21-5 Back Up in progress dialog box

5. Click OK when you see the message that the backup completed successfully.

6. Open the My_ACTDemo database.

Password Protecting The Backup File

If checked, the password option shown earlier in Figure 21-4 is used to create a password for the backup file that will be created. Figure 21-6 shows the Backup Password dialog box.

Figure 21-6 Enter Backup Password dialog box

Exercise 21.3: How To Back Up Personal Files

Unlike backing up databases which requires administrator rights, anyone can back up personal files. You should give the personal backup file a different name then the file that it is being created from. This will prevent the original file from being overwritten if you have to restore it.

Tools ⇒ Preferences ⇒ General tab, will let you know where your personal files are stored. Look in the **PERSONAL FILE LOCATIONS** section and select the file type that you want to back up. The location of the files will be displayed. To complete the exercises in this book, the location for personal files is the folder that you created in Lesson 1. The steps below show you how to back up personal files.

1. File ⇒ Back Up ⇒ Personal Files.

2. If your folder is not at the beginning of the **BACK UP FILES TO** field, click the Browse button, then select your folder.

3. Change the file name to
    `ACT Dictionary Backup.zip`,
    as shown in Figure 21-7, then click the
    Save button.

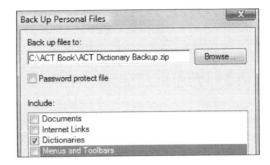

Figure 21-7 Back Up Personal Files dialog box

The reason that I had you change the file name is because you already created a backup of the custom menus and toolbars in Lesson 18 and used the default filename. Using the default file name now would overwrite that backup file.

If you have to restore a file, it will be easier to find the right backup file if your backup files have meaningful names. If you want to password protect the back up file, check the **PASSWORD PROTECT FILE** option. The Backup personal zip file is stored in the folder that you selected in Step 2 above.

4. At the bottom of the dialog box shown above in Figure 21-7, select the types of files that you want to back up and clear the options for the file types that you do not want to back up. For this exercise check the **DICTIONARIES** option and clear the other options, then click OK to back up your personal files.

Check And Repair

This maintenance tool is used to improve database performance. Checking and repairing a database is a two step process as discussed below.

① **Integrity Check** Looks for errors in the database and repairs them when possible.
② **Re-Index** Reorganizes the records in the database. This allows the database to perform better. This step removes spaces from the database and defrags the database. This can take a long time to complete, especially the first time that it is run on the database. During the defrag process, the database is rewritten to the hard drive. Doing this makes the size of the database smaller, which allows it to perform tasks faster.

One way that performance is improved is by removing fragmentation. Fragmentation is caused when records are added or deleted in the database. It also occurs when other types of records like notes, history and opportunity records are deleted.

Reindexing Databases

Reindexing databases is another feature that the Check and Repair tool handles. Reindexing databases will make the database run more efficiently. Only deleting records does not give back disk space. Compressing a database will give back the disk space that deleted records and references to them take up in the index.

Reindexing a database will make queries and lookups run faster. Reindexing and compressing a database will take more time if the database is large. You should reindex and compress databases on a regular basis.

Figure 21-8 shows the current size of the My_ACTDemo database.

Figure 21-8 Size of database illustrated

Exercise 21.4: Check And Repair A Database

Before using this tool you should back up the database. You do not have to complete this exercise now because it can take 30 minutes for this process to run.

1. Back up the My_ACTDemo database.

2. Lock the database.

3. Tools ⇒ Database Maintenance ⇒ Check and Repair.

    You will see the dialog box shown in Figure 21-9.

Figure 21-9 Database check and repair options

4. Both options shown above in Figure 21-9 should be checked to have the database perform at its best.

    Click OK.

    You will see the dialog box shown in Figure 21-10.

Figure 21-10 Check and Repair status dialog box

5. When the utility is finished click OK, then unlock the database.

Exercise 21.5: Restoring Databases

The backup database files are usually restored when the current version has been corrupted or is not working properly. Only administrators can restore databases. It is best to restore databases back to their original location, especially if it is a database that is part of a synchronization process. Not restoring a synchronized database back to its original location will break the synchronization between the two databases.

Restore Options

There are three ways that a database can be restored, as discussed below.

① **Restore** This option will restore all of the files to their original location. Select this option if the original database is corrupt or was deleted.
② **Restore As** This option is used to restore the database to a location other then the original location and to rename the database if necessary.
③ **Unpack And Restore Remote Database** This option is used to restore a remote database that has been synced back to the main database.

The steps below show you how to restore a database. For now you can read through the steps unless you have a backup copy of a database that could be restored.

1. File ⇒ Restore ⇒ Database.

2. Select the Restore option, then click OK.

3. Click the Browse button, then double-click on the zip file that contains the database that you want to restore.

4. Click OK on the dialog box shown in Figure 21-11.

    If prompted, enter your username and password, then click OK.

Figure 21-11 Restore Database (zip file) dialog box

5. Click Yes when prompted that files that were modified after the backup was created will be overwritten.

6. When the restore process is complete, open the database that was restored to make sure that it is working properly.

Removing Old Data

There may be data in the database that is no longer needed. If that is the case you can remove it. The following types of data can be removed: notes, attachments and activities. This is also known as **PURGING A DATABASE**. The main benefit of removing data that is not needed is that it will make the database smaller, which will allow it to run more efficiently. Only administrators can remove data. You should back up the database before deleting records and attachments.

 If you are using a Microsoft SQL Server 2005 Express database, from time to time you should check the file size of the .ADF file (shown earlier in Figure 21-8) to make sure that it is not close to the 4 GB limit. If it is, you should remove old data. To check the size of the database follow the steps below.

How To Check The File Size Of A Database

 The instructions below only work if you have a database open.

1. Help ⇒ About ACT!.

2. Click the **DATABASE INFORMATION** button.

   You will see the dialog box shown in Figure 21-12.

   Look in the **DATABASE SIZE** section in the lower left corner of the dialog box.

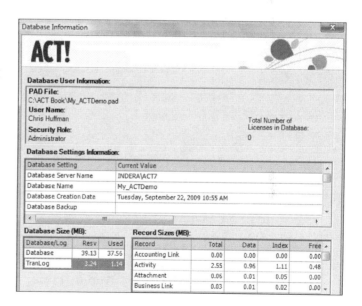

Figure 21-12 Database Information dialog box

Exercise 21.6: How To Remove Old Data

In this exercise you will create criteria that will be used to remove old data from the My_ACTDemo database.

1. Tools ⇒ Database Maintenance ⇒ Remove Old Data.

2. Check the options and number of days in Table 21-1.

   Your dialog box should have the options selected that are shown in Figure 21-13.

   The options shown in Figure 21-13 are used to select the type of data that you want to remove and select how far back to search for data that you want to remove.

Option	# Of Days
Notes older than	10
Cleared activities older than	5
Document tab entries older than	15

Table 21-1 Criteria for selecting old data

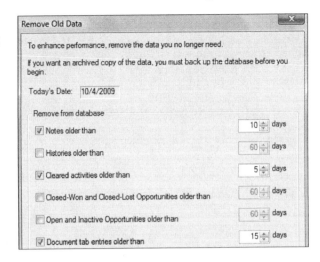

Figure 21-13 Remove Old Data dialog box

3. Click OK. You will see the message shown in Figure 21-14. You will see a different number of records to be removed because you are not running the utility on the same day that I am.

   Click Yes.

Figure 21-14 Remove Old Data message

4. When you see the purge message shown in Figure 21-15, you can click No.

   If this were a live database, you should reindex the database.

Figure 21-15 Purge message

Exercise 21.7: Finding And Deleting Duplicate Records

Deleting duplicate records will help keep the size of the database as small as possible. It will also keep the data accurate. You can delete duplicate contact and group records. By default, **Contact** records are considered duplicate if they have the same Company, Contact and Phone number. You can select other fields on the dialog box shown in Figure 21-16 to use as criteria to determine duplicate contact records. **Group** records are considered duplicate if they have the same Record Creator (the person that created the group) and group name.

1. Open the DuplicateRecords database.

2. Tools ⇒ Scan for Duplicates.

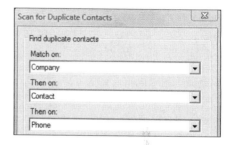

   The options on the Scan for Duplicate Contacts dialog box are used to select the fields that you want to use to determine what makes a contact record a duplicate.

   Often, duplicate contact records are caught when they are being created.

Figure 21-16 Scan for Duplicate Contacts dialog box

If you wanted to use different fields to determine if there are duplicate records, you would select them now. For this exercise you do not have to make any changes.

3. Click OK. You will see a message that says that there are duplicate contacts. Click Yes.

Using The Copy/Move Contact Data Wizard

If the scan for duplicate process finds duplicate contacts, this wizard will open automatically.

1. Click Next on the first wizard screen.

The options on the dialog box shown in Figure 21-17 are used to select what to do with the duplicate records.

The following options are available.

① Copy or move data from one record to another.
② Combine business and personal records for the same contact.
③ Merge the duplicate records for the same contact into one record.

Figure 21-17 Select the Contact Records screen

Tools ⇒ Copy/Move Contact Data, will also open the dialog box shown above in Figure 21-17.

 Take your time and be careful when merging records. Once they are merged, it cannot be undone. The good thing is that this process has to be completed for each set of duplicate records, so the worse case is that you would only have to restore a few records and not all of the duplicate records in the database.

2. Click on the first record for Paul Henderson, then press and hold down the **CTRL** key and click on the second record for Paul Henderson. Click Next.

On the screen shown in Figure 21-18, you have to decide which record you want to keep. It seems to me that this would be a great place to be able to delete a record from the main database, because enough information about each contact record is displayed.

You should scroll down and view the data in both records to determine which one you want to keep. Two contact information fields that I find helpful are the **EDIT DATE** and **IS IMPORTED** fields.

Figure 21-18 Specify Source and Target Contact Records screen

I tend to select the record that has more of the data that I want to keep as the target record.

The **SOURCE** record contains the data that will be copied.
The **TARGET** record is where the data from the source record will be copied to.
The **COPY/MOVE DATA** options are used to copy or move data on a field by field basis, as shown below in Figure 21-19.
The **KEEP/DELETE DATA** options are used to keep or delete the source record. If you copy or move data from the source record, I think that the source record should be deleted. If you have a reason to keep it, then you should.

 You can resize the columns on the wizard screens so that you can see the data better.

3. Select the **COPY CONTACT 2 TO CONTACT 1 OPTION**, then click Next. The options on the screen shown in Figure 21-19 are helpful if the source record has data in fields that the target record does not.

Figure 21-19 Copy Data from Source to Target Record screen

4. Click Next on screen 4 of 7. The options shown in Figure 21-20 are optional types of data that can be copied to the target record. Check the Notes, Histories and Activities options for this exercise, then click Next.

In a live database, you would probably select all of the items on this screen so that you would have a complete history of the contact.

Figure 21-20 Move Additional Items from Source to Target screen

The options shown in Figure 21-21 are used to select whether or not to delete the record that you designated as the source record.

Figure 21-21 Delete the Source Record screen

5. Select the option Yes, delete the source record from my database, then click Next.

6. Click Yes when you see the message that says deleting a contact cannot be undone.

7. Click Finish to close the wizard. The changes to the record that you are keeping will be made. You have to repeat this process for all of the potential duplicate records displayed in the Contact List shown earlier in Figure 21-17.

Exercise 21.8: Deleting Duplicate Records From The Contact List View

After completing the previous exercise, the database can still have duplicate records because the scan for duplicates process only checks for records that have identical information in up to three fields. If the contact name is spelled differently in two or more records, it would be skipped when the check for duplicate scan was run. Therefore, it is a good idea to visually view the records in the Contact List to see if there are other duplicate records.

When I do this, I first sort by the contact name, which is often the field that has duplicates due to typos. Then I sort the list by company to see if there are any company names that are spelled wrong. As you can imagine, as more records are added to the database the longer this can take, especially if it is not done on a regular basis.

If you do not want to merge data from one contact record to another, like you just learned how to do, you can delete the duplicate record(s) that you do not want to keep by following the steps below. Keep in mind that deleting the duplicate records from a view means that if you want to keep any data from the record that you will delete, you will have to type the information in the record that you want to keep.

1. Open the Duplicate Records database if it is not already open. In the Contact List view, right-click in the row of the record that you want to delete and select **DELETE CONTACT**.

2. Click the Delete Contact button when prompted that deleting contacts cannot be undone.

3. Click Yes. You are prompted twice to make sure that you want to delete the record.

View The Deleted Records

ACT! keeps a log of all records that are deleted on the History tab of the My Record.

1. Lookup ⇒ My Record.

2. Click on the History tab. The records that you deleted are at the top of the list, if the list is sorted in descending date order, as shown in Figure 21-22. You will see today's date and time instead of the one shown in the figure.

Figure 21-22 Deleted records on the History tab

. . . .

Exercise 21.9: How To Select Other Fields To Check For Duplicates

In a previous exercise you used the default fields to check for duplicate records. You can select other fields.

1. Lookup ⇒ All Contacts.

2. Tools ⇒ Scan for Duplicates.

3. Open the **MATCH ON** drop-down list and select Department, then click OK. You will see a message that says duplicate contacts have been found. Click No.

ACT! Scheduler

So far in this lesson you have learned about a variety of maintenance tasks. If you are thinking that you will not remember to do them on a regular basis, you can set them up in the ACT! Scheduler, because this tool will run the tasks for you at the time that you select, even if ACT! is not open.

In addition to being able to run maintenance tasks, the scheduler can also be used to automatically run a synchronization process, including the process to sync ACT! and Outlook calendars.

Exercise 21.10: Schedule A Maintenance Task

In this exercise you will schedule the database maintenance utility to check and re-index the demo database that you created, once a week.

1. Tools ⇒ ACT! Schedule.

2. Click on the **CREATE A TASK** link.

3. Click the **BROWSE** button on the Select a Database screen, then double-click on the My_ACTDemo.pad file.

4. You should see the database name, as shown in Figure 21-23.

   Click Next.

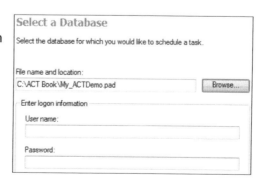

Figure 21-23 Select a Database screen

5. Open the **TASK** drop-down list and select Database Maintenance, as shown in Figure 21-24.

   Click Next.

Figure 21-24 Select a Task screen

6. Check both options shown in Figure 21-25 if they are not already selected, then click Next.

Figure 21-25 Database Maintenance Options screen

7. Select the weekly option, then select Thursday from the drop-down list on the right.

8. Change the **START TIME** to 10 PM, as shown in Figure 21-26, then click Finish.

Figure 21-26 Set a Schedule screen

9. If you click on the task that you just created, you will see the details for it in the lower left corner, as shown in Figure 21-27. Click Exit.

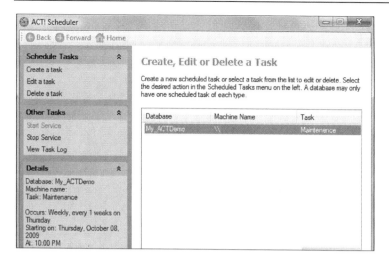

Figure 21-27 Create, Edit or Delete a Task screen

10. You should see the Scheduler icon in the Windows task bar. If not, open the ACT! Scheduler, then select the **START SERVICE** option, shown above in Figure 21-27.

Security

ACT! comes with several security options. With so many companies having their data stolen, it may be a good idea to implement as much security as possible, without going overboard.

 If you add a password to a user account or database, select one that you will remember. Using the word **PASSWORD** for a password is not a good idea, as this is the default password for some software packages. It is best to select passwords that have a combination of letters and numbers.

User Security

User security allows the administrator to create accounts so that other people can use the database. ACT! provides the following types of user level security.

① User accounts
② Security roles
③ Logon status
④ Permissions

Exercise 21.11: Creating User Accounts

In this exercise you will create a user account with your name.

1. Open the My_ACTDemo database. Tools ⇒ Manage Users. You will see a list of the users, their security role and log on status.

2. Click the **CREATE NEW USER** link.

> The Create New User option will create a new contact record. You should make sure that the person that you are creating the account for does not have a contact record in the database, so that you do not create a duplicate record.

There are two ways that you can create a new user account, as shown in Figure 21-28. If you see the message shown in the **DETAILS** section, it means that only one person at a time can use the database. This is usually the case for home users. It does not mean that additional user accounts cannot be created.

Figure 21-28 Create New User screen

> The links in the **MANAGE USER TASKS** section are used to go to the screen that you want, instead of clicking the Next and Back buttons to get to another screen.

If you select the **CREATE USER FROM CONTACT** option and click Next, you will see the screen shown in Figure 21-29.

It is used to select a name from the database to use for the user account that you want to create.

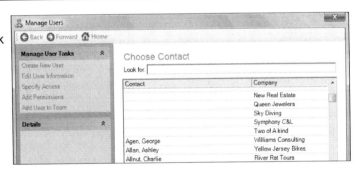

Figure 21-29 Choose Contact screen

When you click the Next button on this screen you will see the screen shown in Figure 21-30 with the Contact and User name fields filled in. From this point on, the screens are the same to finish creating the user account.

If you select the **CREATE NEW USER** option shown earlier in Figure 21-28, you will see the screen shown in Figure 21-30. It is used to enter the information for the new user. A contact record will be created for this user.

Figure 21-30 Enter User Information screen

 User Account Creation Tips

① User names and passwords are not case sensitive.
② Passwords for user accounts are optional. If you leave the password field empty, the user will not have to enter a password unless the password policy option requires one.

3. Select the **CREATE NEW USER** option for this exercise, then click Next.

4. Type your first and last name in the Contact Name field, then press the Tab key. Your name should automatically be filled in the User Name field.

5. Select the **ADMINISTRATOR** Security Role, then check the **PASSWORD NEVER EXPIRES** option. Security Roles are explained at the end of this exercise.

6. If you want to add a password, type your first name and the year in the **NEW PASSWORD** and **CONFIRM PASSWORD** fields (ie. Indera2009), then click Next.

If you do not enter the same password in the New Password and Confirm Password fields, the **NEXT** and **FINISH** buttons will not be enabled.

If any of the password options discussed below are selected, they override the password policy options that are discussed later in this lesson.

① If you check the **USER MUST CHANGE PASSWORD AT NEXT LOG ON** option, you do not have to enter a password when setting up the account. This will cause the user to be prompted to create a password the first time that they log on.
② The **USER CANNOT CHANGE PASSWORD** option if checked, will disable the File ⇒ Set Password option, which is how users change their password.
③ If checked, the **PASSWORD NEVER EXPIRES** option will not require the user to change their password.

7. Select the **INACTIVE** option, then click Next.

The options shown in Figure 21-31 are used to select the logon access options.

Figure 21-31 Specify Access screen

The options shown in Figure 21-32 are used to select the permissions for the user account.

The permissions available are based on the security role that is selected for the account.

Some security roles come with some of the permissions selected by default.

Figure 21-32 Add Permissions screen

Because you selected the Administrator security role, all of the permissions are available by default. They will appear in the **ADDED PERMISSIONS** column. These permissions are only available for Manager and Standard roles and are explained at the end of this exercise.

8. Click Finish.

The new user account and contact record will be created.

Leave the Manage Users window open to complete the next exercise.

Once the account is created you will see it on the screen shown in Figure 21-33.

Select a User

Select a user to change passwords, security roles, and other settings.

Contact Name	User Name	Security Role	Log On Status	Last Logon
Allison Mikola	Allison Mikola	Manager	Inactive	4/16/2008 11:19 AM
Betty Browser	Betty Browser	Browse	Inactive	
Chris Huffman	Chris Huffman	Administrato	Active	10/4/2009 7:33 PM
Ernst Anderson	Ernst Anderson	Standard	Inactive	4/18/2008 1:59 PM
Fred Fenderline	Fred Fenderline	Standard	Inactive	
Indera Murphy	Indera Murphy	Administrato	Inactive	
Jonathan Somm	Jonathan Somm	Standard	Inactive	
Juliette Rosseu	Juliette Rosseu	Restricted	Inactive	4/9/2008 12:33 AM
Melissa Pearce	Melissa Pearce	Standard	Inactive	8/16/2008 12:47 AM
Sarah Whiting	Sarah Whiting	Standard	Inactive	

Figure 21-33 Select A User screen

Reset Passwords

The **RESET PASSWORD** button shown earlier in Figure 21-30 will let the administrator reset the password. This is helpful when a user forgets their password. Once the password has been reset, you can tell the user to set up a new password on the dialog box shown in Figure 21-34.

File ⇒ Set Password, will open this dialog box.

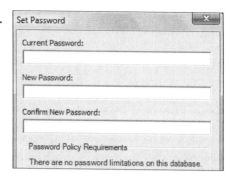

Figure 21-34 Set Password dialog box

 Earlier I stated that I believe that there should be at least two administrator accounts per database. Resetting passwords is one reason. An administrator account cannot reset its own password because the account being reset cannot be logged on. If you do not know or remember the administrator account password and the database only has one administrator account set up, the only way that I know of to retrieve the password is to send the database to Sage.

Security Roles

As you saw earlier, there are five security roles (levels) that can be given to a user. The security roles determine what data a user has access to and what they can and cannot do to the records that they have access to. The goal of setting up security is to only give enough rights so that a user can get their job done. The five security levels that you can assign a user are discussed below.

Browse This level allows the user to view records and calendars of other users that they have access to. Users at this security level cannot edit or add any data, which includes sending an email or writing a letter from inside of ACT!. This is the most limited security level.

Restricted This level can only access public areas of the database. Users at this security level can create and edit contacts and opportunities, but cannot delete any data, even data that they create. Users cannot create groups or companies.

Standard This security level allows the user to view, edit, add and delete contacts and groups, as well as, synchronize databases. This is the most common security level. Users cannot delete other users data, create backups, import and export data, schedule activities for other users without being granted access to their calendar, modify layouts or perform database maintenance.

Manager This security level has access to the entire database, except for private records, but does not have administrator rights, which means users cannot create user accounts or perform database maintenance tasks.

Administrator This security level has full rights to the database. If the database is used by several people, there should be two administrator accounts, in my opinion, in case one account becomes corrupt or one person does something wrong. If there are other users and they mark records as private, people with administrator rights cannot view the records.

Permissions

These permissions give Standard and Manager level accounts additional rights. The available permissions are discussed below.

① **Accounting Link Tasks** The user can work on accounting tasks if an accounting software package like QuickBooks has been configured to work with ACT!.

② **Handheld Device Sync** Allows the user to synchronize ACT! data with a handheld device like a PDA (Personal Digital Assistant).

③ **Remote Administration** Allows the user to repair, back up, restore and check remote databases that they have rights to. This permission is primarily useful for remote users.

④ **Manage Sync Subscription List** Allows the user to make changes to the subscription (contact) list for a remote database.

Exercise 21.12: How To Edit User Account Information

In the previous exercise you created a new user account that had administrator rights and was inactive. In this exercise you will edit the user account and set up the permissions.

1. Open the Manage Users Utility.

2. Click on the user account with your name, then click the **EDIT USER INFORMATION** link.

3. Change the Security Role to Standard, then click the **ADD PERMISSIONS** link.

4. Add the Remote Administration permission to the account, then click the Back button.

5. Change the logon access to Active, then click Finish.

   You will see that your account is active, as shown in Figure 21-35.

Select a User

Select a user to change passwords, security roles, and other settings.

Contact Name	User Name	Security Role	Log On Status	Last Logon
Allison Mikola	Allison Mikola	Manager	Inactive	4/16/2008 11:19 AM
Betty Browser	Betty Browser	Browse	Inactive	
Chris Huffman	Chris Huffman	Administrato	Active	10/4/2009 7:33 PM
Ernst Anderson	Ernst Anderson	Standard	Inactive	4/18/2008 1:59 PM
Fred Fenderline	Fred Fenderline	Standard	Inactive	
Indera Murphy	Indera Murphy	Standard	Active	
Jonathan Somm	Jonathan Somm	Standard	Inactive	

Figure 21-35 Select A User screen

How To Delete A User Account

Usually an account is deleted because the person will no longer use the database. There was a time that if you deleted a user account, all traces of the account would also be deleted. In an ACT! database, that would have meant that the attachments or notes that were added to the database by the user account, would also be deleted. The good news is that ACT! databases have evolved and now you can delete a user account and keep the work that was created under the account. You do not have to delete a user account. You can make the account inactive. The steps below show you how to delete a user account.

1. Click on the user account that you want to delete on the screen shown above in Figure 21-35. For this exercise, you can click on the account with your name.

2. Click the **DELETE USER** link.

   You will see the message shown in Figure 21-36. This message is letting you know that any private data will be deleted.

Figure 21-36 Delete User Account message

3. Click Yes, when you see the message asking if you are sure that you want to remove the user.

   You will see the dialog box shown in Figure 21-37 if the user added or modified any data.

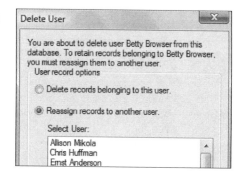

Figure 21-37 Delete User dialog box

The **DELETE RECORDS BELONGING TO THIS USER** option will do just that, delete the contact records that the user created, as well as, any notes for the contact, regardless of who created the note or activity.

The **REASSIGN RECORDS TO ANOTHER USER** option moves the records to another user. This prevents the records from being deleted. In my opinion, this is the best option to select.

4. Select the appropriate options depending on which of the dialog boxes shown above that you see. When finished, the user account will be removed from the Select a User screen.

5. Close the Manage Users dialog box.

Data Security

Some of the data security options like security roles and permissions, are handled under user security. ACT! has the following types of data security.

① Record access
② Record Manager
③ Password policy

Record Access

This option determines which users can view the record. Access to records occur on two levels as discussed below.

① Parent or Extended access
② Public or Private access

Parent Or Extended Access

Parent records are the contact, company and group records. Extended records are the notes, history, activity, opportunity and secondary contacts for the parent record. If a user does not have access to the parent record, they also do not have access to the extended records associated with the parent record. For example, if a user does not have access to the Jane Doe contact record, they will not have access to the records on the tabs for the contact Jane Doe.

Public Or Private Access

Records that are marked as public can be viewed by anyone that has access to the database. Records that are marked as private can only be viewed by the Record Manager (record owner). If you have the need for more functionality to limit access, you will have to upgrade to ACT! Premium. Like many features in ACT!, there is more than one way to mark a record as public or private, as discussed below.

① On the Contact Detail view, click on the Contact Access tab and select Public or Private, as illustrated in Figure 21-38.
② On the Contact List view, Contacts ⇒ Edit Contact Access, as shown in Figure 21-39.
③ On the Contact List view, right-click on the record(s) that you want to change the access of and select Edit Contact Access. You will see the submenu options shown in Figure 21-39.

Figure 21-38 Public and private access options

Figure 21-39 Edit Contact Access menu options

Company and group records can be marked as private. Data on some tabs can be marked as private by right-clicking on an item and selecting **MAKE <TAB NAME> PRIVATE**. On other tabs like Personal Info and User Fields, you can select the option shown above in Figure 21-39.

> There was a time when there was no option to make company records private. They were always public.

Record Manager

The Record Manager is the user that creates the record. Anyone that adds or edits data should have their own login account that has Record Manager rights. The reason is so that ACT! can fill in certain system fields with the name of the person that made a change to the record. An example of this is who created an activity for a contact. If you created an activity, but are logged into the database as me, ACT! would enter my name as the person that created the activity. Record Managers and Administrators can change who the Record Manager is.

Field Security

In addition to being able to add security to specific records, you can add security to individual fields. The security on system fields cannot be changed. The two types of field security are discussed below. The steps in the next exercise show you how to change the field security.

① **Read Only** Users can view, select and copy the data in the field, but cannot edit or delete the data.
② **Full Access** This is the default security option for all fields. Users have all of the rights that Read Only users have, plus they can edit, add and delete data in the field.

Exercise 21.13: Assigning Field Security

In this exercise you will learn how to assign security to a field.

1. Tools ⇒ Define Fields.

2. Open the **VIEW FIELDS FOR** drop-down list and select the Record type that you need to secure.

3. Select the field, then click **FIELD SECURITY** link in the Field Tasks section of the screen.

4. Select the permission that you want, as shown in Figure 21-40, then click Finish.

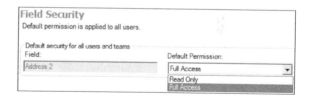

Figure 21-40 Field security options

With all of the attacks on data these days, you may be tempted to protect the database as much as possible. When applying field level security, there are some things to keep in mind when limiting access, as discussed below.

① Even with administrator or manager rights, if your rights to a field are read-only you cannot import or export data for the field.
② You cannot sync fields that you do not have full access to.
③ The data in the field with read-only access cannot be used for queries and will not appear in a report.

Password Security

User accounts have the option of having password security. Earlier in Exercise 21.11 when you created a user account, you saw the password options. These user options are managed by an administrator through a password policy for the database.

Exercise 21.14: How Users Change A Password

One of the policies that you can set is when passwords expire. If that option is enabled, users have to change their password. Later in this lesson you will learn how to set a password policy. The steps below show users how to change a password.

1. File ⇒ Set Password. You will see the dialog box shown earlier in Figure 21-34.

2. Type the existing password in the **CURRENT PASSWORD** field. If the account did not have a password, this field has to be left blank.

3. Type the new password in the **NEW PASSWORD** and **CONFIRM NEW PASSWORD** fields, then click OK.

Password Policy

Password policies are created to provide more security for a database. Whenever you change the password policy, users are prompted to enter a password the next time that they log in if their current password does not meet the new password policy. The options discussed below are the password policy options that can be set. The X in the option name represents the number that you select.

① **User cannot reuse last X passwords** This option is used to select how many of the previously used passwords cannot be reused. The maximum number that can be entered in this field is nine. For example, if this option is set to three, the last three passwords that were used, could not be used when the user creates the fourth password.

② **Password must change every X days** This option is used to select in days how often users must change their password. If this option is set to zero, users do not have to change the password. (1)

③ **Minimum duration between password changes is X days** This option is used to select the least number of days that a password has to be in use before the user can change it. (1)

④ **Password must be at least X characters in length** This option is used to select the minimum number of characters that a password must have. Setting this option to one is the same as requiring a password. A zero means that the user can enter a password up to 25 characters, which is the maximum number of characters.

⑤ **Password must contain X of 4 character groups** This option is used to select the type(s) of characters that the password has to have. The character groups are lower case, upper case, numbers and special characters. If the numbers option is selected, users must create a password that has at least one number in it.

(1) The maximum number for this field is 365 days.

Exercise 21.15: How To Create A Password Policy

In this exercise you will create a password policy.

1. Tools ⇒ Password Policy.

2. Select the options shown in Figure 21-41, then click OK.

Figure 21-41 Password Policy dialog box

3. Open the Password Policy dialog box and reset all of the options back to zero, then click OK. That way, you will not have problems the next time that you open the database that you are using for this book.

ACT! Diagnostics

This is a utility that comes with ACT!. You can use it to maintain and repair databases, as well as, manage the local ACT! SQL server. Follow the steps below to run this utility.

1. Close ACT!.

2. Windows Start button ⇒ Run.

3. Type `actdiag` in the field, then press Enter. If you see the Diagnostics Disclaimer message, click OK.

4. Click on the **DATABASES** button on the left, then select Database List. You will see the dialog box shown in Figure 21-42. The menu options shown in Figure 21-43 are the database actions that you can use.

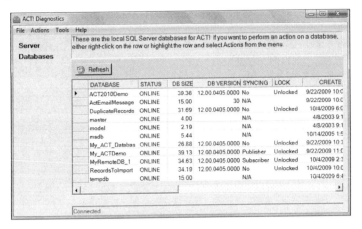

Figure 21-42 ACT! Diagnostics dialog box

Figure 21-43 Database actions menu

The End!

If you are reading this paragraph, I hope that it means that you have completed all of the exercises in this book. If so, congratulations because you have covered a lot of material. If some topics seem a little fuzzy right now, that is to be expected. Hopefully you have gained some valuable ACT! skills and techniques. As you have probably figured out, there are a lot of options and features at your disposal. I hope that you enjoyed the book.

As you read in Lesson 1, ACT! 2010 has built in functionality to make it easier for Crystal Reports to connect to ACT! databases. If you want to expand the reporting capabilities of ACT! and create your own reports, I am working on a book that will teach you how to use Crystal Reports 2008 with ACT! 2010 databases.

Because you purchased this book on ACT! 2010, you can order a copy for 50% off of the list price. This book is scheduled to be released in February 2010 (hopefully sooner). If you want to be notified when the book is available, send an email to tolanapub@yahoo.com and put Crystal - ACT! Book in the subject line. When the book is complete, I will send you an invoice.

INDEX

No Stress Tech Guides

ISBN-13: 978-1-935208-09-9
ISBN-10: 1-935208-09-8

ISBN-13: 978-1-935208-08-2
ISBN-10: 1-935208-08-X

ISBN-13: 978-1-935208-05-1
ISBN-10: 1-935208-05-5

ISBN-13: 978-0-9773912-9-5
ISBN-10: 0-977391-29-9

ISBN-13: 978-1-935208-00-6
ISBN-10: 1-935208-00-4

ISBN-13: 978-1-935208-07-5
ISBN-10: 1-935208-07-1

ISBN-13: 978-1-935208-01-3
ISBN-10: 1-935208-01-2

ISBN-13: 978-0-9773912-7-1
ISBN-10: 0-977391-27-2

ISBN-13: 978-0-9773912-8-8
ISBN-10: 0-977391-28-0

Other Titles	ISBN		ISBN
ACT! 2007	978-0-9773912-5-7	OpenOffice.org Writer 2	978-0-9773912-4-0
Microsoft Works 8	978-0-9773912-1-9	Crystal Reports/Visual Studio 2005	978-0-9773912-6-4
Windows XP	978-0-9773912-0-2	Crystal Xcelsius 4.5	978-1-935208-02-0

Visit us on the web at www.tolanapublishing.com

Made in the USA
Lexington, KY
25 November 2009